The Nicaragua Reader

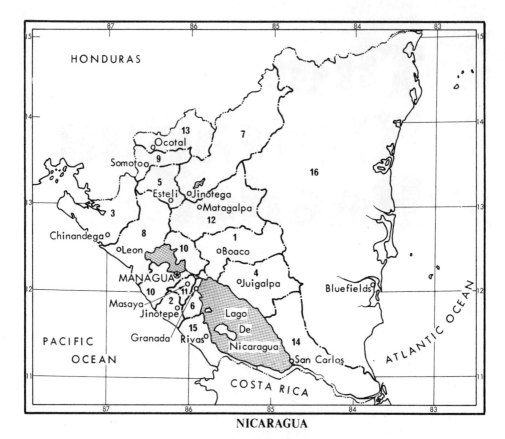

NICARAGUA

DEPARTMENTS AND RESPECTIVE CAPITALS

1. Boaco (Boaco)
2. Carazo (Jinotepe)
3. Chinandega (Chinandega)
4. Chontales (Juigalpa)
5. Esteli (Esteli)
6. Granada (Granada)
7. Jinotega (Jinotega)
8. Leon (Leon)
9. Madriz (Somoto)
10. Managua (Managua)
11. Masaya (Masaya)
12. Matagalpa (Matagalpa)
13. Nueva Segovia (Ocotal)
14. Rio San Juan (San Carlos)
15. Rivas (Rivas)
16. Zelaya (Bluefields)

·····—···—· International Boundary
·—·—·—· Department Boundary
⊗   National Capital
o   Internal Administrative Capital

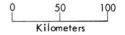

Kilometers

*From *Area Handbook for Nicaragua,* July 1970, Foreign Area Studies, American University, Washington, D.C., p. xvi.

The Nicaragua Reader

Documents of a Revolution under Fire

by Peter Rosset and
John Vandermeer

Grove Press, Inc./New York

First Hardcover Edition published in 1983
6 5 4 3 2 1

First Evergreen Edition published in 1983
6 5 4 3 2 1

Library of Congress Cataloging in Publication Data
Main entry under title:

  Bibliography: p.
  1. Nicaragua—History—1979- —Addresses,
essays, lectures. 2. Nicaragua—Foreign relations—
United States. 3. United States—Foreign relations—
Nicaragua. I. Rosset, Peter. II. Vandermeer, John.
F1528.N5175 1983   972.85'052   83-48294
ISBN 0-394-53506-5
ISBN 0-394-62498-X (Evergreen: pbk.)

Manufactured in the United States of America

GROVE PRESS, INC., 196 West Houston Street, New York, N.Y. 10014

ACKNOWLEDGMENTS

Completing a volume such as this requires collaboration with a large number of people. We wish to thank, in particular, Bob Ambrose, Pam Anderson, George Black, Doug Boucher, Betsy Cohn, Joe Collins, Tim Coone, Ismael Diaz, Antonio Dos Santos, Galio Gurdian, Charles Hale, Lillian Hall, Carsten Hellpap, Louis Head, Mike Hansen, Pam Horwith, Mike Jody, Uriel Kitron, Barbara Kritt, Ligia Lacayo, Richard Levins, Fiona Macintosh, Hugh McGuiness, Mary Minnow, Ivette Perfecto, Cruz Phillips, Sunny Power, Beverly Rathcke, Bob Rice, Donna Rich, Steve Risch, Charles Roberts, Lisa Rosset, Barney Rosset, Hannelore Rosset, Brian Schultz, and Katherine Yih. Special thanks goes to Jessica Bernstein, the Central American Historical Institute, the National Network in Solidarity with the Nicaraguan People, the North American Congress on Latin America, the Heritage Foundation, the Committee of U.S. Citizens Residing in Nicaragua, and the Latin American Solidarity Committee of Ann Arbor. The library staff at the University of Michigan, the Labadie Collection, and the Ann Arbor Public Library also deserve special thanks. Thanks also to Cathy Gander for assistance on the revised edition.

LIST OF TABLES

CONTENTS

General Introduction

> I have the most conclusive evidence that arms and munitions in large quantities . . . have been shipped to the revolutionists. . . .The United States cannot fail to view with deep concern any serious threat to stability and constitutional government . . . jeopardizing American interests, especially if such a state of affairs is contributed to or brought by outside influence or by a foreign power *

Thus spoke the president of the United States with respect to Nicaragua. The president was referring to the Sandinistas and the outside influence of foreign "communists." The year was 1927. The president was Calvin Coolidge. The "outside influence" was Mexican "Bolshevism." The alleged, though never proven, arms shipments were from the government of Mexico. And the "revolutionists" were the peasant army of Augusto César Sandino.

Today's president is Ronald Reagan. The year is 1983. But the allegations are similar: alleged arms shipments to El Salvador, outside influence by Cuba and the Soviet Union, and American interests (or national security) in jeopardy. Coolidge feared that Mexican "Bolshevism" would sweep southward through all of Central America; Reagan fears that Nicaraguan "Marxism" will start a chain of dominoes falling north to Mexico.

This recurrent motif has shaped Nicaraguan history for two centuries. One cannot fully appreciate the current crisis outside of its historical context, because it is both reminiscent of—and in important ways, different from—its predecessors.

---

*See Reading 19.

In the nineteenth century, Nicaragua offered one of the best interoceanic routes on the Central American isthmus, and as such was coveted as a potential canal site by US and British interests. In the 1850s Cornelius Vanderbilt ran a ferry and carriage service across Nicaragua that served the California gold rush. Later, aided by directors of this transit company and with the full support of the US government, the US soldier-of-fortune William Walker invaded Nicaragua and declared himself president. His death in 1861 marked the end of what Nicaraguans view as the first occupation of Nicaragua by US forces.

The United States went on to intervene militarily in Nicaragua three times in the first third of this century, occupying the country from 1912 through 1925, and again from 1926 until 1933. The Marines finally withdrew in 1933 after being fought to a standstill by the guerrilla leader Sandino, for whom today's revolutionists are named. Sandino is credited with having developed tactics that had a lasting influence on guerrilla strategists the world over. It was the intense study of Sandino, of his successes and his failures, that Carlos Fonseca Amador advocated when he helped found the Sandinista National Liberation Front (FSLN) in 1961. The FSLN's political strategy combines Sandino's military tactics with the experiences of Cuba and Vietnam, and incorporates his humanitarian philosophy and nationalism. Their strategy led to the successful overthrow of the Somoza dynasty on July 19, 1979.

Not only was Sandino a direct "grandfather" of the 1979 revolution, he was also indirectly responsible for the creation of the infamous National Guard, with its first commander, Anastasio Somoza. The Guard, trained and supplied by the United States, was formed to counter Sandino's strength in the northern mountains, and was the key part of the conflict's "Nicaragua-ization"—a response to the US public's opposition to involvement in the war. When the US Marines withdrew, Sandino's peasant army laid down its arms as part of a negotiated settlement, but within a few years Somoza had assassinated Sandino and ushered in more than four decades of rule by the Somoza family.

Since the triumph of the Sandinista Revolution in 1979, Nicaragua has been changing in many ways. The new economic, political, social, and even cultural models that are being explored in contemporary Nicaragua form a large part of this book, but they are viewed in the context of escalating tensions between the governments of Nicaragua and the United States. One cannot interpret the changes now taking place in Nicaragua without understanding the virtual state of war in which they occur. Neither can one fully understand the current relations between Nicaragua and the United States without knowing something about Nicaragua, both in terms of its historical connection with the United States and its internal situation.

Part One of this book covers what might be called the "debate" between the governments of the United States and Nicaragua. Chapter I begins with major policy statements presented to the United Nations by Daniel Ortega Saavedra, Coordinator of Nicaragua's Junta for National Reconstruction, and by Jeane Kirkpatrick, United States Ambassador to the United Nations. The next two chapters deal with the most controversial topics raised in the "debate," including alleged Nicaraguan arms shipments to the guerrillas in El Salvador, Nicaraguan "militarization," and the issue of freedom of the press and other civil liberties. The remainder of the book provides the historical and contemporary background information necessary to evaluate Nicaragua's current situation and United States policy towards Nicaragua.

Part Two elaborates the historical setting, paying particular attention to the role of the United States and to the history of the revolution itself. In Part Three we examine the evidence of US "destabilization" of post-revolutionary Nicaragua. This section is called "US Intervention," a title which at one time would have brought charges of bias. Included are *Newsweek*'s famous revelations of "America's Secret War'' (Chapter I), especially interesting in light of President Reagan's frank admission in the May 4, 1983, White House press conference that

> Now, if they want to tell us that we can give money and do the same things we've been doing—money giving, providing subsistence and so forth to these people [anti-government guerrillas] directly and making it overt instead of covert— that's all right with me.

The final section of the book, Part Four, is concerned with what Nicaragua is actually like today. It covers a broad spectrum of topics, ranging from the struggle within the Catholic Church to trade unions, women's issues, Sandinista economics, and the literacy campaign.

As the editors of this book, we cannot claim to be impartial, and indeed we feel that true impartiality on political questions does not exist. Thus we must at the outset confess our belief that as a sovereign country Nicaragua has a right to its own self-determination. This means—to quote Richard Fagen from Chapter I of this book—"the right to commit their own mistakes, to determine their own future, and ultimately to make the basic transformations so necessary in Nicaraguan society." In the spirit of open public debate, and in the hope for a critical reevaluation of US policy toward Nicaragua, we have tried to present a multifaceted book presenting different points of view.

Peter M. Rosset
John H. Vandermeer
ANN ARBOR, MICHIGAN

May, 1983

Part One

THE DEBATE

Editors' Introduction

The Carter administration's policy toward Latin America was outwardly concerned with human rights, and emphasized regional economic development to contain "communist expansionism." As administration officials explained on many occasions, poor people are easy targets for Márxist propaganda, and thus if we wish to avoid the spread of communism through Latin America, we must make the elimination of poverty a high priority. Dominant liberal ideology then, as now, assumed that poverty could be alleviated through accelerated economic development achieved through business incentives and multinational ventures. On a theoretical level, then, Carter policy had two guiding principles: human rights and the promotion of economic growth.

Jeane Kirkpatrick, the Reagan administration's ambassador to the United Nations, strongly attacked this policy in her famous essay "Dictatorships and Double Standards",[1] and further elaborated her analysis in a later essay entitled "US Security and Latin America."[2] In these articles she argues that Carter's human rights policy severely damaged various "friendly autocratic" regimes, and in the case of Somoza actually led to his downfall. She claims that the Carter Doctrine naively missed a crucial distinction between regimes that are "autocratic" and those that are "totalitarian." Most Third World countries fall into one or the other of these two categories, she argues, because they lack the sophisticated citizenry necessary to be "democratic." She further states that autocratic societies have, at least theoretically, the potential to evolve into more democratic ones through the twin processes of development of a sophisticated citizenry and gradual release of power by the autocrat. Totalitarian countries, on the other hand, are in her view incapable of ever becoming more democratic. Unfortunately, the only criterion she seems to provide for distinguishing between the two types is whether or not they are friendly toward the United States.

The next logical step in the argument, however, is that if one truly favors democracy, one must attempt to "transform" totalitarian countries into autocratic ones. This appears to be the major theoretical basis of the Reagan administration's policy toward Latin America. There is a principle—the distinction between totalitarian and autocratic—and there is a moral imperative—to transform totalitarian countries into autocratic ones.

Kirkpatrick uses the Bolivian elections of 1980 as a case study of the Carter administration's failure to recognize the difference between autocratic and totalitarian states. Through lawful electoral procedures the Bolivians had selected a president who, she claims, was friendly toward Cuba and the Soviet Union, and therefore "totalitarian." Kirkpatrick chides the Carter administration for *not* siding with the Bolivian military in their subsequent coup against the legally elected government. In her words

Even five years ago, the United States would have welcomed a coup that blocked a government with a significant Communist/Castroite component. Ten years ago the United States would have sponsored it; fifteen years ago we would have conducted it.[3]

In the case of Nicaragua the policy imperatives of this philosophy are clear: determine whether a government is totalitarian, and if it is, take whatever actions are necessary to replace it with an autocratic one.

While one may disagree with this policy on intellectual or moral grounds, one must nevertheless realize that it seems to be the theoretical justification for US policy. If we understand this, then much of the controversy over Nicaragua makes sense. We can see why US officials characterize Nicaragua as being in the Soviet or Cuban "camp," paint a picture of "totalitarianism" inside Nicaragua, and propose taking action against Nicaragua.

It is in this framework that the articles in Chapter I should be read. They are not intended to address the specific policy issues raised above, but they should be understood in the context of what might be called the Reagan/Kirkpatrick Doctrine.

Chapter II takes up the military questions raised when the United States claims that Nicaragua is "a threat to its neighbors." First is a *Washington Post* article on alleged arms shipments to El Salvador. In the following articles, Jonn T. Hughes of the Defense Intelligence Agency presents the administration's charge that Nicaragua is building up its military beyond any legitimate defensive needs, while Lt. Col. John H. Buchanan, USMC (ret.), discusses the relative military strengths of Nicaragua and Honduras. Chapter II closes with the topic of negotiations. The Reagan administration has claimed that the Nicaraguan government will not negotiate, but this assertion is difficult to support from the record.

Chapter III treats the internal issues that have been repeatedly brought to the attention of the international press as evidence that Nicaragua is "drifting toward totalitarianism," including freedom of the press, the State of Emergency, elections, and the difficult question of the Miskitu Indians on the Atlantic coast.

---

[1] Jeane J. Kirkpatrick, *Dictatorships and Double Standards: Rationalism & Reason in Politics.* (New York: American Enterprise Institute/Simon and Schuster, 1982), pp. 23-52.
[2]*ibid.* pp. 53-90.
[3]*ibid.* p.88.

Chapter I:

Overview: Setting the Terms

Editors' Introduction

The debate between the governments of the United States and Nicaragua is being played out in the international press and in forums like the United Nations. The first two articles in this chapter, excerpted from testimony given before the United Nations Security Council, present very different pictures of Nicaragua. Where Ambassador Kirkpatrick sees Nicaragua as "a conduit of war material [to] ... El Salvador," Junta Coordinator Ortega notes that this is a "never proven allegation" and further states that it is the United States who is "supplying arms, aircraft, helicopters, advisers, technical support and accelerated military training to the Salvadoran army." Kirkpatrick's Nicaragua has "declared a state of siege on its own people," while in Ortega's version, Nicaragua's government has "the moral support of our entire people."

Kirkpatrick sees Nicaragua as a threat to its neighbors because it is "seeking to augment its military forces and arsenal," while Ortega claims that the US is trying "to impose humiliating restrictions on ... [Nicaragua's] inescapable prerogatives with respect to national defense." Kirkpatrick portrays the Sandinista government as fixed in its attitude toward the US as the "enemy of mankind" and therefore opposed to normal relations, while Ortega expresses a desire for good relations to emerge from a process of negotiations.

Of course, there are charges that go unanswered. Ortega does not take up Kirkpatrick's accusation that the Nicaraguan government has displaced "some 25,000 Indians from their ancestral homes." And to Ortega's charge that the United States is sponsoring a massive destabilization program against Nicaragua, Kirkpatrick responds with ridicule.

The next two readings represent further elaborations of the Reagan/Kirkpatrick doctrine as first set forth by President Reagan and then updated in the speech by the Under Secretary of Defense for Policy Fred C. Iklé. Iklé's speech is critically evaluated in the editorial that follows by Tom Wicker. Finally, Professor Richard Fagen's essay provides a broader framework in which the Nicaragua debate can be analyzed.

1. Let There Be Peace in Central America*

By Daniel Ortega Saavedra

Comandante *Daniel Ortega Saavedra is the Coordinator of Nicaragua's three-person Junta of National Reconstruction (JGRN). As such he could be considered Nicaragua's "Head of State." He is also a member of the nine-person National Directorate of the Sandinista National Liberation Front (FSLN). After his release from Somoza's prisons in 1974 in exchange for hostages, he became a member of the* Frente's *then twelve-person National Directorate. During the FSLN's split into three factions he was a leader of the Insurrectionalist or* Tercerista *faction.**

Throughout history humanity has engaged in a constant struggle to achieve better and more just ways of life. As part of this historical process the Central American region in recent times has been in upheaval because of the constant action of its peoples, who have so long been oppressed and who are determined to free themselves, in the face of the resistance of privileged minorities which are at pains to halt the changes which, sooner or later, must come to these unjust societies.

When our revolution triumphed, notwithstanding the historical inconsistency of United States policy, we felt—and indeed proposed—that it was necessary to normalize relations with the United States within a new framework of respect and co-operation. It was in this spirit that I met in Washington in September 1980 with President Carter, and we must acknowledge that an effective dialogue then became possible. This mutual disposition to readjust and improve relations between Nicaragua and the United States underwent a sharp change when, in January 1981, the new administration assumed the presidency of the United States.

The cause of the crisis in the region is so clear and the response on the part of the United States so weak and misguided that governments such as those of Mexico, Venezuela and Canada have proposed a global and non-discriminatory programme to permit a joint response in the economic field that would help alleviate the social

---

*Excerpts from the statement of Daniel Ortega Saavedra before the United Nations Security Council on March 25, 1982. (Provisional Verbatim Record of the 2,335 Meeting.)

and political conflicts stemming from economic injustices. This initiative has not been taken up as it should have been by the United States, which has in fact pursued a unilateral, limited and exclusionary policy that has excluded Grenada, Cuba and Nicaragua, thus weakening the efforts promoted by the governments I have mentioned and making it impossible to respond to the urgent request of the Central American countries for a mimimum of $20 billion in financing and credits in order to be able to survive over the next five years.

We can affirm at this time that the policy of the present United States administration is still out of step with the realities in the region and that despite what some had predicted, the threats made against the region in the government's platform were not mere campaign rhetoric but are increasingly becoming a dreadful fact.

The waging of covert aggression against our revolution has now intensified the crisis to the point at which the imminence of intervention in Central America has compelled us to request a meeting of the Security Council of the United Nations.

I can only affirm that since my appearance before the General Assembly at its thirty-sixth session, in the course of which we transmitted concrete peace proposals from the Salvadoran revolutionaries, the crisis situation in Central America has assumed greater dimensions, and numerous efforts to bring peace and political stability to the region have been thwarted.

It is because of the dynamic of these developments that I have found myself obliged to appear before you to warn the nations of the earth that the Central American crisis has now reached the point of a tragic explosion.

I come to appeal to this United Nations body because we cannot accept our being left with no alternative but to die defending our country, as we would never allow ourselves to be subjugated by force.

I find myself obliged to appear before you because I share the legitimate concern of the responsible men and women who in the United States Congress and Senate are making great efforts to prevent the intervention, because I share the legitimate concern of the most important and high-minded mass media of the United States, and that of the United States people: those ordinary citizens, their religious leaders and those of their civic organizations, their intellectuals and their trade unions, who reject another Viet Nam in their history and share the desire of the Nicaraguan people for peace, for both are peoples whose deep-seated historical memories contain images of intervention and the agonies of war.

I want to say to you with the utmost sincerity and simplicity, and with the moral support of our entire people, that if our fervent efforts for peace should fail, neither imperial will, nor threats, nor blockades, nor invasions will be able to put an end to the historic struggle we are prepared to wage to safeguard our legitimate right to self-determination, fighting to the last man and shedding the last drop of our blood. But it is not confrontation that we desire, but peace and tranquility; that is why we have come here before you. We shall confine ourselves to a brief review of the main events that have taken place in the last few months, events which paint a picture enabling us to assert that the intervention in Central America is already under way.

Therefore, we want you to know of the existence in the state of Florida on the territory of the United States itself, of training camps for Somozist counterrevolutionaries, and of the feeble, legalistic excuses offered by the United States authorities when we have demanded the dismantling of those camps, which violate the Neutrality Act which is part of United States law.

We want you to know of the existence of Somozist counterrevolutionary camps on the territory of the Republic of Honduras in the vicinity of the border with Nicaragua, where some 2,000 counterrevolutionaries have been brought together and trained, supplied, and armed by officials of the operations section of the Division of Hemisphere Affairs of the Central Intelligence Agency. In this regard, despite the public statements made by the Honduran government concerning its position of neutrality, actions by the Central Intelligence Agency to compromise that neutrality have become increasingly forceful.

Therefore, we want you to know that in the Honduran Department of El Paraíso, on the border with Nicaragua, about 700 Somozist ex-guardsmen have been concentrated in several camps; that in the zone of Cacamuya there are another 60 counterrevolutionaries; and that in the Department of Lempira on the Honduran Atlantic coast and on the Nicaraguan border there are located several camps of Somozist counterrevolutionaries numbering more than 1,000 men. Since March 15 of this year those camps have been receiving an increasing supply of arms and war equipment, including hundreds of FAL and M-16 rifles, demolition and fragmentation grenades, grenade-launchers and explosives.

You should also know that the United States has made the decision to construct on Honduran territory both air and naval bases, the first of them on Ampala Island; and a treaty has been proposed to be signed in the next few days legalizing United States military presence on Honduran territory. This development, so unfortunate for peace and security in the Central American region, is a premeditated result of the continuous campaign which has been launched against our country about an alleged Nicaraguan military build-up.

You should also know that the United States Embassy in Tegucigalpa officially acknowledged on the 19th of this month that a minimum of 72 United States military personnel are currently stationed in Honduras. This is an unprecedented number in that country.

The United States Navy destroyer Caron, equipped with sophisticated electronic espionage technology, has been stationed off Nicaragua's Pacific coast facing the Gulf of Fonseca, carrying out surveillance tasks, as the United States government has publicly acknowledged.

We want you to know that when United States newspapers, magazines and other media publish reports that the United States National Security Council has approved a budget of $19 million to promote destabilizing and covert actions that entail, among other things, economic sabotage, attacks, training and arms shipments to Somozist counterrevolutionary groups, not a single spokesman or authority of the United States government has denied such reports. Indeed, on the contrary, those who have referred to them have wrapped them in doubt or given them an affirmative character. Furthermore, after these disclosures were made we began to feel the actual carrying out of terrorist actions: bombs aboard our passenger aircraft and in civilian airports, with a tragic toll of death and injury; destruction of bridges; and the resurgence of actions by counterrevolutionary gangs, such as the so-called Red Christmas operation along the Río Coco, which took the lives of 60 of our compatriots, who were murdered.

We want you to know that since March 14 exercises have been going on in the Southern Command in the Panama Canal Zone in which forces from United States territory and the 193rd Infantry Brigade of that same Command are taking part; and that within the framework of the Organization of American States (OAS) pressures are being exerted to obtain a resolution that would legalize intervention against El Salvador and Nicaragua.

We want you to know that, beginning in the month of June 1981 and until March 11 of this year, we were the victims of 40 violations of our air space by RC-135 aircraft of the United States Air Force. The violations of our air space which have been detected are: one on July 28, 1981; two on August 3 and 25, 1981; four on September 4, 11, 17 and 25, 1981; 10 on October 2, 9, 13, 17, 20, 22, 24, 25, 28 and 30, 1981; 10 on November 1, 3, 4, 5, 7, 10, 12, 14 and 16, 1981—on the 7th of that month two flights were detected; two on December 2 and 30, 1981; one on January 3, 1982, six on February 2, 4, 10, 16, 24 and 27, 1982; and four up to March 11, 1982, the flights occurring on the 4th, 8th, 10th and 11th of that month. All those flights were carried out over the Pacific coast of Nicaragua and along our borders with Honduras and Costa Rica, and it seems highly significant that 10 of them took place in October and 10 others in November 1981, precisely when both President Reagan and Mr. Haig were voicing the possibility of decisive and immediate military actions against Nicaragua.

Our military resources are the most modest in the region. We have no air force. Nevertheless, it is Nicaragua which is being encircled with military bases and it is against Nicaragua that a permanently hostile and bellicose attitude is being aimed, with spy aircraft and vessels and naval maneuvers. We are the only State in Central America over which hangs the constant threat of the world military might of the United States.

The only true military superiority for the defense of our homeland lies in the formidable combative and organizational readiness of our entire people, since we are the only government in Central America that can, in all confidence, distribute weapons to the people.

We want you to know that the State Department of the United States, in a puerile gesture aimed at accumulating any sort of evidence which could justify interventionist action against Nicaragua, presented to the United States press at the State Department on March 12 a Nicaraguan, Orlando José Tardencilla, who had been held prisoner by the Salvadoran Army for more than a year and who had been transferred from the dungeons of San Salvador to the offices of the State Department in an act without precedent in terms of violation of international juridical norms relating to the minimum respect due to the sovereignty and independence of the Salvadoran nation.

United States citizens should ask themselves whether these events do not contain serious violations of their own laws: participation and complicity in the kidnapping of a person; pressure and threats to force someone to lie and make statements against his own will; threats to a person's life and physical integrity; concealment and complicity in coercion and physical and mental torture.

We want you to know that, on March 14, at 22 hours 44 minutes [10:44 P.M.], two strategic bridges for the defense and communications of the country were blown up in acts of sabotage; the bridge over the Río Negro, which was totally destroyed, and the bridge over the Río Coco, which suffered considerable structural damage making the passage of vehicles impossible.

Both bridges are in Departments bordering on Honduras, and these criminal actions demonstrate once again the implementation of the covert actions of the Central Intelligence Agency, approved by the State Department. These assertions of ours were amply confirmed by the Presidential Adviser Mr. Edwin Meese who, when asked on March 16 by United States journalists if the destruction of the bridges meant that the covert plan had been put into operation, replied:

This is the kind of event which we can neither confirm nor deny under any circumstances, because in either case we cannot rule out what we could be doing in any other situation.

And the picture becomes even more serious if we recall that on February 15 President Reagan, when asked by *The Washington Post* about approval of plans for foreign covert political and paramilitary operations in Nicaragua, instead of categorically denying the existence of such actions, refused any comment on the subject.

Furthermore, a veteran of the United States Army's Green Berets who fought in the Viet Nam war told the CBS network that his old Special Forces Chief had tried to recruit him to participate in mercenary operations in Nicaragua on a $50,000, six-month contract and that many ex–Green Berets were already at their point of destination.

We want you to know that, already in the month of November 1981, the Southern Command of the United States with headquarters in the Panama Canal Zone had completed an electronic encirclement of our country to monitor and control and even distort or cut off, all communications in our national territory. In this operation without precedent in Central America, Phantom A-4C, AWACS and RC-135 aircraft were employed.

We also want you to know that since October 1981, in camps situated in the eastern sector of the Panama Canal Zone, three companies made up of Somozist ex-guardsmen began receiving training in paratroop landings and the use of explosives from Green Beret instructors of the United States Army.

Those are the fundamental elements that have compelled us, beginning on March 15, to adopt exceptional measures for the defense of the integrity and sovereignty of our homeland, decreeing a state of national emergency.

The five points announced by Mr. Haig do not constitute a global approach to a search for and the finding of realistic solutions. This proposal fails to take into account the fact that the fundamental problem of the Central American crisis does not lie in the never proven allegation that arms are reaching the Salvadoran revolutionaries via Nicaragua while in fact the United States is supplying arms, aircraft, helicopters, advisers, technical support and accelerated military training to the Salvadoran army. It is imperative, on the contrary, responsibly to accept that the causes of the phenomenon lie in the injustice that reigns in El Salvador and that therefore it is urgent to find by means of negotiation a response that deals with the possibilities of the wholesale transformation demanded by Salvadoran society.

It is, however, inconceivable that the country that is carrying out the greatest arms build-up and spending the most money on weaponry in the history of mankind should seek to demand of us that we fail to fulfill the minimum requirements for the defence of our own country. Nicaragua rejects the attempt by the United States to impose humiliating restrictions on its inescapable prerogatives with respect to national defence. We are certain that no sovereign State in the world would accept such a thing. This position is all the more unjustified since Nicaragua, as a revolutionary country, has categorically proclaimed that it will never use its arms against any brother country in Latin America or the Caribbean. We take this opportunity to reiterate this commitment as well as our willingness to sign non-aggression treaties and agreements with all the countries of the region.

We feel that we are all obliged to find a solution to the problems confronting the region through negotiated political means and never to consider the possibility of negotiations being exhausted. We believe that all efforts must be focused on finding responses that are in keeping with reality and that would allow us to begin negotiations immediately, discarding preconditions of any kind.

The peoples of the region demand a negotiated political solution. United States public opinion demands a negotiated political solution; the peoples of Latin America and good governments demand a negotiated political solution; the peoples and governments of the world are expecting a negotiated political solution.

We do not wish to see ourselves forced to resist and struggle to prevail over foreign intervention with the vigour and energy that peoples acquire when they are invaded, which is the same vigour and energy that enabled the Americans to win their independence in 1776.

We have not come here to level accusations but to demand an end, once and for all, to the policy of aggressions, threats, interventions, covert operations and invasions against our homeland and the region and to make it clear that the unfairly distributed resources of humanity on this planet do not give the powerful the right to act against weak and small peoples.

Nicaragua can in no way represent a threat to the security of the United States. We are a small country, a dignified and poor country that pursues a policy of international non-alignment. The national interests of the people and nation of the United States should not be confused with the particular policy of the present administration, which is trying to make its own points of view prevail even at the cost of the peace, security, and tranquility not only of its own citizens but of a whole complex of countries which, like our own, have a right to determine their own destiny.

We are willing to improve the climate of relations with the United States on the basis of mutual respect and unconditional recognition of our right to self-determination.

We are willing to begin immediately direct and frank conversations with the government of the United States, even in a mutually agreed upon third country, with the objective of reaching concrete results through such negotiations.

... The Salvadoran patriots of the FMLN-FDR have authorized us to transmit their willingness to begin immediate negotiations without preconditions, once more reiterating the call they made through me when I addressed the United Nations General Assembly at its thirty-sixth session.

Nicaragua is willing immediately to sign non-aggression pacts with all neigh-bouring countries of the Central American area in order to ensure peace and the internal stability of the zone.

The United States government officially and explicitly must voice its commit-ment not to attack Nicaragua, nor to initiate or promote any direct, indirect, or covert intervention in Central America.

Nicaragua calls on the United Nations Security Council to issue an explicit pronouncement in line with the Charter of the United Nations, regarding the obligation to seek peaceful means of solving the problems of the Central American and Caribbean region and calls on the Council to reject any acts of force or threats and to repudiate any direct, indirect, or covert intervention in Central America.

In memory of the millions of people killed in wars throughout history, in memory of the millions tortured and murdered in the Nazi concentration camps in the Second World War, in memory of the thousands of patriots who fell in the struggles for liberation and against colonialism, racism and all kinds of oppression, in memory of the Central American patriots who have fallen in the fight for independence, justice, and peace, for the right of peoples to be free, sovereign, and independent, for the right of humanity to desire peace and to demand peace, let there be peace in Central America.

2. A Paranoid Style of Politics*

By Jeane Kirkpatrick

Before being chosen as the Reagan administration's Permanent Representative to the United Nations, Ambassador Kirkpatrick was Leavey Professor of Political

---

*Excerpts from the statement of Jeane Kirkpatrick before the United Nations Security Council on March 25, 1982. (Provisional Verbatim Record of the 2,335 Meeting.)

Science at Georgetown University and Resident Scholar at the influential new right "think-tank," the American Enterprise Institute for Public Policy Research. She reportedly caught the eye of Reagan advisers for her famous essay, "Dictatorships and Double Standards."**

In his letter requesting this meeting, the Coordinator of the Nicaraguan government, Mr. Daniel Ortega Saavedra, made some extraordinary charges against the government of the United States. We naturally desire to respond to the grave charges that Mr. Ortega has leveled against our policies and our intentions and to comment on the state of relations between our two countries.

He spoke of the interventionist strategy of the government of the United States and of statements and concrete actions that clearly evidence an intention to attack Nicaragua and to intervene directly in El Salvador.

The attack made by Nicaragua on the United States is not haphazard, the charges made by the government of Nicaragua are not random. The government of Nicaragua has accused the United States of the kinds of political behavior of which it is itself guilty—large scale interventions in the internal affairs of its neighbors, persistent efforts to subvert and overthrow by force and violence the governments of neighboring states, aggressive actions which disrupt the normal conduct of international relations in the region—acts and intentions inconsistent with the Charter of the United Nations.

These charges—as extravagant as they are baseless—are an interesting example of projection, a psychological operation in which one's own feelings and intentions are simultaneously denied and attributed—that is, projected on—to someone else.

Hostility is the dominant emotion and projection the key mechanism of the paranoid style of politics, a style which, much to our regret, has characterized the political behavior of the Sandinista leadership since its arrival in power. The principal object of Sandinista hostility, I further regret, is the government and people of the United States.

Nicaragua's new political elite—which calls itself Sandinista—has constructed a historical myth to justify its demand for full power. According to this myth, the United States is responsible for all problems and disasters—natural and social—that Nicaragua has ever suffered. The Sandinista anthem describes us as the enemy of mankind and Sandinista ideology defines us as implacably opposed to the national independence and economic development of everyone and to peace in the world. Since the moment of their arrival in power, the Sandinistas have predicted that the United States was about to overrun them. The Yankees are coming, they have reiterated; the counterrevolutionaries will get us if we do not silence criticism, mobilize the population into armies, destroy freedom.

We are confronted in Nicaragua with the familiar patterns of doublespeak with which totalitarian and would-be totalitarian rulers of our times assault reality in the

---

**See Editors' Introduction to Part One.

attempt to persuade us, and doubtless themselves as well, that making war is seeking
peace, that repression is liberation, that a free press is a very carefully controlled
one. Thus, on February 19, 1982, Commander Ortega, whom we have just heard,
solemnly assured the opening session of an international conference—COPPAL—
that the forced, violent transfer of Miskitu Indians was naturally carried out only to
protect their human rights.

Given this pattern of repression, obfuscation and charges, it should, I suppose,
have come as no surprise when, last week, Commander Ortega leveled new charges
against the United States government at precisely the same time that Nicaragua
suspended its Constitution and promulgated a new Law of National Emergency
that threatens to eliminate the limited liberty and pluralism that remain in that
country. That new Law of National Emergency provides that all discussions in the
Sandinista-controlled Council of State of the proposed media and political parties
laws be suspended. It provides that the Minister of the Interior may make an
unspecified number of preventative arrests of people who are suspected of having
ties with counterrevolutionaries. Under that decree, *Radio Católico* has been closed
down indefinitely and all radio news programs, except official news statements, are
prohibited. The one remaining independent newspaper in Nicaragua—*La Prensa*—
and all other media have been required to submit their news stories for prior
censorship. Yesterday, it proved impossible for *La Prensa* to publish, since more
than 50 percent of the paper was found objectionable. Under the new Law of
Emergency, opposition political leaders have been informed that they may not leave
the country. The passport of one was seized when he attempted to make a routine
trip abroad. Under the new law, a "patriotic tax" is to be imposed on business to
help finance its latest mobilization campaign.

Nicaragua's new government could have satisfied the longings of its people for
peace instead of making war on them; it could also have accepted the United States
offer of friendship. It did not need to be thus. The United States government did
not, in fact, oppose the Sandinista rise to power and it has not attempted to prevent
their consolidation of power.

Like others in this century who have seized power by force, the Sandinista
leaders are haunted by the expectation that they will fall victim to the violent
intrigues by which they won power and exercise it. They are haunted by the fear that
their neighbors will in fact treat them in the manner in which they systematically
treat their neighbors.

It is, of course, they, the government of Nicaragua, who systematically seek to
subvert and overthrow neighboring governments. El Salvador has had the misfor-
tune to be the principal target.

A clandestine support system established in 1978 at the time of the Nicaraguan
civil war continued to operate after the fall of Somoza in July 1979, with a new final
destination: El Salvador. The existence of this support system has been repeatedly
and vigorously denied by Nicaraguan and Cuban spokesmen. Yet it is perfectly
clear that those denials are false.

Nicaragua offers a support system with three major components: external arms supplies, training, and command and control. Within weeks after the fall of the Somoza government in July 1979, the Sandinistas began to cooperate in the support of the Salvadoran insurgents by establishing training camps and the beginning of an arms supply network. This clandestine assistance initially involved local black markets and relatively limited resources. In 1980, after meetings in Havana had unified Salvadoran Marxists into a single military command structure, the Sandinista leadership agreed to serve as a conduit for an arms trafficking system of unprecedented proportions, originating outside of this hemisphere. That structure remains in place today.

Arms and ammunition for the Salvadoran insurgents reach Nicaragua by ship, and occasionally by direct flights from Havana to Nicaragua. Three Nicaraguan ships, the *Monimbo*, the *Aracely* and the *Nicarao*, frequently transport arms and ammunition to Nicaragua from Cuba in their cargo. Salvadoran guerrilla headquarters near Managua arranges for their shipment into El Salvador. The timing of the resupply operations is coordinated with the planned level of fighting, since before each surge in the fighting it is possible to detect new large arms deliveries.

When a clandestine shipment of arms is captured or a safe house is found containing arms and terrorist supplies, it is often impossible to know with certainty whether the ultimate recipients are destined to be Guatemalan, Honduran, Costa Rican or Salvadoran, since the arms supply networks established by Cuba and Nicaragua are funneling lethal military supplies to guerrillas and terrorists in all four countries.

Nicaraguan Social Welfare Minister Antonio Befred, by the way, told reporters in Lima last week that some Nicaraguan "volunteers" had gone to El Salvador to fight with the guerrillas. Perhaps they would like us to believe that the presence of the Salvadoran guerrillas' military command headquarters near Managua is also a "volunteer" effort. In fact, planning and operations in El Salvador are guided from that headquarters where Nicaraguan officers are involved actively in the command and control. The headquarters coordinates logistical support for the insurgents, including food, medicines, clothing, money and, most importantly of course, weapons and ammunition. The headquarters in Nicaragua decides on locations to be attacked and coordinates supply deliveries. The guidance flows to guerrilla units widely spread throughout El Salvador. The pattern is painfully clear; it functions until this day.

We very much wish that the government of Nicaragua would cease its efforts to repress its own people and to overthrow its neighboring governments. Frankly, we thought that some progress to that end might be in sight. We were somewhat surprised when the Nicaraguan government decided to attempt to expand and embitter regional conflict at this time. One explanation for Nicaragua's decision to expand the conflict at this time is that it fears that the United States government is about to invade. But, of course, that is a ridiculous charge. The United States government is not about to invade anyone, and we have stated as much at all levels of our government, at all times and on many occasions.

It is true that once we became aware of Nicaragua's intentions and actions, the

United States government undertook overflights to safeguard our own security and that of other states which are threatened by the Sandinista government. These overflights, conducted by unarmed, high flying planes, for the express and sole purpose of verifying reports of Nicaraguan intervention, are no threat to regional peace and stability; quite the contrary. The threat to regional and world peace lies in the activities that these photographs expose. One can well understand that the government of Nicaragua would prefer that no such photographs existed. The United States government is frankly surprised and puzzled by Nicaragua's appeal to the Security Council at this time.

As most members of this Council understand, Commander Ortega's contentious charges come at a time when we and others are actively looking for a basis on which to settle peacefully the differences of the parties involved. Only last week the government of Nicaragua stated a desire to negotiate. But then, after two high government officials visited Cuba, they called for this meeting to air baseless charges in this most public, important forum.

The Nicaraguan government has said that it wants peace; it has stated that it wishes better relations with the United States. But, unfortunately, its actions do not match its pretensions. If the Nicaraguan government was genuinely interested in alleviating tensions, would it continue to act as an active conduit for war matériel aimed at subverting the government of El Salvador? Would it have undertaken a campaign of systematic violence against its own Indian communities, displacing some 25,000 Indians from their ancestral homes on the pretext of security from a peaceful, democratic neighbor, Honduras? Would it have doubled the number of Cuban military and security advisers in the past year? Would it have continued seeking to augment its military forces and arsenal? Would it have declared a state of siege on its own people, effectively eliminating the opposition? Most importantly, would it continue incessantly to pour arms into El Salvador, even increasing that flow of arms, bullets and propaganda just when the people of El Salvador are given an unprecedented opportunity to express their views?

3. *Let Me Set the Record Straight on Nicaragua**

By Ronald Reagan

L et me set the record straight on Nicaragua, a country next to El Salvador. In 1979, when the new government took over in Nicaragua after a revolution which overthrew the authoritarian rule of Somoza, everyone hoped for the growth

*Excerpts from [Ronald Reagan's] Presidential Address to Joint Session of Congress on April 27.

of democracy. We in the United States did, too. By January of 1981, our emergency relief and recovery aid to Nicaragua totaled $118 million—more than provided by any other developed country. In fact, in the first two years of Sandinista rule, the United States directly or indirectly sent five times more aid to Nicaragua than it had in the two years prior to the revolution. Can anyone doubt the generosity and good faith of the American people?

These were hardly the actions of a nation implacably hostile to Nicaragua. Yet the government of Nicaragua has treated us as an enemy. It has rejected our repeated peace efforts. It has broken its promises to us, to the Organization of American States and most important of all, to the people of Nicaragua.

No sooner was victory achieved than a small clique ousted others who had been part of the revolution from having any voice in government. Humberto Ortega, the Minister of Defense, declared Marxism-Leninism would be their guide, and so it is.

The government of Nicaragua has imposed a new dictatorship; it has refused to hold the elections it promised; it has seized control of most media and subjects all media to heavy prior censorship; it denied the bishops and priests of the Roman Catholic Church the right to say mass on radio during Holy Week; it insulted and mocked the Pope; it has driven the Miskitu Indians from their homelands—burning their villages, destroying their crops, and forcing them into involuntary internment camps far from home; it has moved against the private sector and free labor unions; it condoned mob action against Nicaragua's independent human rights commission and drove the director of that commission to exile.

In short, after all these acts of repression by the government, is it any wonder opposition has formed? Contrary to propaganda, the opponents of the Sandinistas are not die-hard supporters of the previous Somoza regime. In fact, many are anti-Somoza heroes who fought beside the Sandinistas to bring down the Somoza government. Now they have been denied any part in the new government because they truly wanted democracy for Nicaragua and still do. Others are Miskitu Indians fighting for their homes, lands and lives.

The Sandinista revolution in Nicaragua turned out to be just an exchange of one set of autocratic rulers for another, and the people still have no freedom, no democratic rights and more poverty. Even worse than its predecessor, it is helping Cuba and the Soviets to destabilize our hemisphere.

Meanwhile, the government of El Salvador, making every effort to guarantee democracy, free labor unions, freedom of religion and a free press, is under attack by guerrillas dedicated to the same philosophy that prevails in Nicaragua, Cuba and, yes, the Soviet Union. Violence has been Nicaragua's most important export to the world. It is the ultimate in hypocrisy for the unelected Nicaraguan government to charge that we seek their overthrow when they are doing everything they can to bring down the elected government of El Salvador. The guerrilla attacks are directed from a headquarters in Managua, the capital of Nicaragua.

But let us be clear as to the American attitude toward the government of Nicaragua. We do not seek its overthrow. Our interest is to insure that is does not infect its neighbors through the export of subversion and violence. Our purpose, in conformity with American and international law, is to prevent the flow of arms to El Salvador, Honduras, Guatemala and Costa Rica. We have attempted to have a dialogue with the government of Nicaragua but it persists in its efforts to spread violence.

We should not—and we will not—protect the Nicaraguan government from the anger of its own people. But we should, through diplomacy, offer an alternative. And, as Nicaragua ponders its options, we can and will—with all the resources of diplomacy—protect each country of Central America from the danger of war.

Even Costa Rica, Central America's oldest and strongest democracy, a government so peaceful it does not even have an army, is the object of bullying and threats from Nicaragua's dictators.

Nicaragua's neighbors know the Sandinista promises of peace, nonalliance and nonintervention have not been kept. Some 36 new military bases have been built —there were only 13 during the Somoza years.

Nicaragua's new army numbers 25,000 men supported by a militia of 50,000. It is the largest army in Central America supplemented by 2,000 Cuban military and security advisers. It is equipped with the most modern weapons, dozens of Soviet-made tanks, 800 Soviet-bloc trucks, Soviet 152-millimeter howitzers, 100 anti-aircraft guns plus planes and helicopters. There are additional thousands of civilian advisers from Cuba, the Soviet Union, East Germany, Libya and the Palestine Liberation Organization. And we are attacked because we have 55 military trainers in El Salvador.

The goal of the professional guerrilla movements in Central America is as simple as it is sinister—to destabilize the entire region from the Panama Canal to Mexico. If you doubt me on this point, just consider what Caietano Carpio, the now-deceased Salvadoran guerrilla leader, said earlier this month. Carpio said that after El Salvador falls, El Salvador and Nicaragua would be "arm-in-arm and struggling for the total liberation of Central America."

Nicaragua's dictatorial junta, who themselves made war and won power operating from bases in Honduras and Costa Rica, like to pretend they are today being attacked by forces based in Honduras. The fact is, it is Nicaragua's government that threatens Honduras, not the reverse.

It is Nicaragua who has moved heavy tanks close to the border and Nicaragua who speaks of war. It was Nicaraguan radio that announced on April 8th the creation of a new, unified revolutionary coordinating board to push forward the Marxist struggle in Honduras.

Nicaragua, supported by weapons and military resources provided by the Communist bloc, represses its own people, refuses to make peace and sponsors a guerrilla war against El Salvador.

4.US Policy for Central America—Can We Succeed?*

By Hon. Fred C. Iklé

Fred C. Iklé is Under Secretary of Defense for Policy.

Central America is closer to Baltimore than is California—in terms of geographic distance, that is. But the intellectual distance between here and Central America is enormous. Most of the American people are not well informed about Central America; many are misinformed; and some are outright disdainful about the cultural and social importance of this region.

You all have an obligation to remedy this situation, so that you and your representatives in Congress can engage in constructive support—or constructive criticism—of the administration's policy.

To begin with, you should know that the President's policy for Central America has not yet been given a chance to work: the blocking votes in Congress have denied the President the means to succeed.

Indeed, members of Congress have involved themselves in the management of US policy for Central America more than for any other region in the world.

• While Congress has quickly and easily approved some $4.5 billion dollars in Security Assistance for nations in the Mediterranean region, it slashed nearly in half the much smaller allocation for nations in the Caribbean region—so much closer to home.

• While Congress has been generally supportive of the deployment of some 1200 US Marines to Lebanon, it fought fiercely to limit the number of US trainers in El Salvador to 55.

• While Congress has not objected to large military exercises in the faraway Indian Ocean region, many members have heavily criticized the recent military exercises in the nearby Caribbean region.

• While Congress has for a long time supported Radio Free Europe, the fine radio program that brings the truth to the people of Eastern Europe, members of Congress have delayed for two years President Reagan's request for Radio Martí, a new radio station that would bring the truth to the people in Cuba.

As we consult with members of Congress on these issues, we are often told that, you, their constituents, are pressing such positions on them. But as we review the public opinion polls, we discover an extraordinary lack of information. For example, in a recent *New York Times*/CBS poll, only 8 percent of the respondents knew, both for El Salvador and Nicaragua, whether the US was supporting the govern-

---

*From a speech given before the Baltimore Council on Foreign Affairs, September 12, 1983.

ment or the insurgents.

You must help us overcome not only a lack of information, but also a great deal of misinformation. This misinformation is not accidental; it is the result of a well-organized and well-orchestrated effort. A fabric of fiction has been tightly woven to conceal the essential facts. Let me review with you some of these fictions:

Fiction has it that US influence in Central and Latin America has prevented democratic development, that the spread of Leninist regimes is the tide of history, a natural process of social reform that we should not oppose. The fact is that the trend toward democratization has continued: among the 32 independent states of Latin America and the Caribbean, 17 are now democratic. Since 1978, five countries have made a peaceful transition from military regimes to elected democratic governments. It is the much criticized military regimes that are often transformed into democracies; but there has never yet been a Marxist-Leninist regime that was succeeded by democracy.

Another bit of fiction: that the Sandinista regime in Nicaragua would have developed into a pluralistic democracy, had it not been for the US intervention. The fact is that the Sandinistas, only a few weeks after they came into power, reneged on their promise for early elections, began to attack the democratic trade unions, and invited Cuban military and security personnel in steadily growing numbers. Yet, during the first 18 months of the Sandinista regime, the United States provided more than $120 million in direct aid and endorsed over $220 million in Inter-American Development Bank aid—more than the previous Somoza regime in Nicaragua had received from the United States in twenty years! Clearly, it was not US interference that drove the Sandinistas to link up with Fidel Castro—unless economic aid is regarded as "interference."

Another piece of fiction is the charge that the Reagan administration is "militarizing" the problems of Central America and is bringing the East-West conflict to the region. Well, the East is already here. The Soviets are giving ten times as much military assistance to Cuba and Nicaragua as we are providing to all of Latin America. And Soviet military advisors in Cuba and Nicaragua outnumber US military advisors in the Caribbean region 20 to 1.

Since Congress is so deeply involved in our day-to-day policy towards Central America, our key objectives need to be clear to the American people. Moreover, Congress must share with the administration an understanding of our basic strategy.

On one thing we can all agree: We do not want the United States to fail. We must succeed.

But what is it we would like to see happen, and what do we want to prevent? We have wide agreement, I believe, that the United States favors a continuation and strengthening of the trend toward open, genuine democracy. And we favor social and economic betterment for the people in Central America, a region so close to us.

Equally important is what we want to prevent. We want to prevent the expansion of totalitarian regimes—particularly Leninist ones, since they will import Stalinist police systems, bring in Soviet arms, and even invite Soviet military bases.

There are two more reasons why Leninist regimes are particularly dangerous: once entrenched, they tend to become irreversible, and they usually seek to export their totalitarianism to other nations.

Given these objectives, what should be our strategy?

First, we want to help build the road toward democracy and economic development. In the end, the people in each country will have to make their own choices. They can succeed only through their own dedicated effort. But we can help, through advice and influence, by facilitating trade, and by giving aid. The Caribbean Basin Initiative of the Reagan administration (to which Congress has now agreed) is right on target. So are our efforts in El Salvador on behalf of elections and for improvements in the judicial system.

Also, we are using diplomacy to help the government of El Salvador win over those who are willing to abandon violence and compete in elections, provided they can be assured of safe and fair participation. But we must not underestimate our adversaries. The hard core among the insurgents will never settle for a fair democratic process. We can no more negotiate an acceptable political solution with these people than the social democrats in revolutionary Russia could have talked Lenin into giving up totalitarian Bolshevism.

This leads us to the second requirement. As Secretary Shultz recently explained, the guerrillas in El Salvador have used a "rule or ruin" strategy: they seek to destroy economic assets faster than our aid can restore them. You cannot have economic development in a nation if guerrilla forces keep blowing up bridges, power lines, school buildings, buses. . . . You have to defeat these "rule or ruin" forces militarily. This is the purpose of our military assistance.

Every so often the critics of the administration proclaim—with accusatory connotation—that we seek a "military solution" in El Salvador. If a "military solution" means putting primary emphasis on military assistance and military means, then it is more factual to accuse the Reagan administration of seeking an "economic solution," since three dollars out of four in the requested assistance programs are for economic aid.

What we seek to do is to open the doors to democracy and close the doors to violence. But we have to use military means against those who insist—till they have imposed their rule—on using violence.

Let me make this clear to you:

—We do not seek a military defeat for our friends.

—We do not seek a military stalemate.

—We seek victory for the forces of democracy.

And that victory has two components:

One: Defeating militarily those organized forces of violence that refuse to accept the democratic will of the people.

Two: Establishing an adequate internal system for justice and personal security.

At this point, let us recall our first agreed principle: We do not want the United States to fail. Hence, we must allocate sufficient means so that we can succeed. As long as a group in Congress keeps crippling the President's military assistance program, we will have a policy always shy of success. We will remain locked into a protracted failure.

This the American people should not tolerate. If we are merely involved to fail, then we should not be involved at all.

The resources needed to succeed are small compared to our investment for security in other regions of the world. Once those in Congress who are now blocking adequate assistance give us the means to succeed, the capability and determination of the United States will become clear. This will make the Soviet Union more cautious, which in turn will help our success. On the other hand, if we signal that we are afraid of victory over the forces of violence, if we signal that we have opted for protracted failure, we will only encourage the Soviets to redouble their effort. We will be inviting ever-increasing difficulties.

The third requirement of US strategy for Central America is least well understood. We should seek to prevent the partition of Central America, a division of this region into two spheres, one linked to the Soviet bloc and one linked to the United States. Such a partition would inexorably lead to a hostile confrontation of large military forces, a confrontation that could last for decades.

We can see how such a confrontation works, as we look at Cuba. During the 24 years of the Castro dictatorship, while the standard of living deteriorated and human rights were widely violated, Cuba built up a large military establishment. It has the second largest army in Latin America (second only to Brazil), it has some 200 MIG fighter aircraft, submarines, 8,500 to 10,000 Soviet advisors, and several Soviet intelligence installations. In addition, Castro has sent some 30 to 40 thousand troops abroad to provide the mercenary forces to protect the Soviet imperial outposts. As a result of the militarization of Cuba, our sealines to NATO are now seriously threatened.

The Sandinista regime in Nicaragua is determined to create a "second Cuba" in Central America. Ever since they seized power, the Sandinistas embarked on a major military buildup. Today, they have a much larger army than Somoza ever had, and they have expressed the intention to build the largest force in Central America. Nicaragua is building new military airfields, and is importing Soviet tanks, helicopters, armored vehicles, and other equipment.

This "second Cuba" in Nicaragua would be more dangerous than Castro's Cuba since it shares hard-to-defend borders with Honduras and Costa Rica. The Sandinistas have already started terrorist activities in both these countries. In addition, Nicaragua provides essential support for the insurgency in El Salvador.

Even after the insurgency in El Salvador has been brought under control, Nicaragua—if it continued on its present course—would be the bridgehead and arsenal for insurgency for Central America. And once the Sandinistas have acquired the military strength that they have been planning for, they might well use that strength for direct attacks on their neighbors to help speed up the "revolution without frontiers" that they promised us.

At that time, the only way to help protect the democracies might be for the United States to place forward deployed forces in these countries, as in Korea or

West Germany. Clearly, we must prevent such a partition of Central America.

In the Democrats' response to President Reagan's April 27 address on Central America to a Joint Session of Congress, Senator Dodd said: "We will oppose the establishment of Marxist states in Central America." Yet, a majority in the House of Representatives has done exactly the opposite. It voted to oppose US assistance to those who oppose the establishment of a Marxist state in Nicaragua. That is to say, a blocking majority in the House, in effect, voted to establish a sanctuary for the Sandinistas.

Congressional legislation to deny US support to the democratic resistance forces in Nicaragua would turn Nicaragua into a sanctuary from which the nations of Central America could be safely attacked, but in which US-supported forces could not operate. This would enable the promoters of totalitarianism—while being supplied and replenished by Cuba and the Soviet bloc—to attack neighboring countries indefinitely, and always with impunity. Hence, it would deprive the Marxist groups in El Salvador of any incentive to compromise. Indeed, if such legislation were passed, the Sandinistas and Cubans might well find it safe to *increase* their assistance to the insurgents in El Salvador and to step up the destabilization of Honduras and Costa Rica. This, after all, would be fully consistent with their presently declared objectives; and the guaranteed sanctuary would render such escalation almost risk-free.

The psychological impact from cutting off US assistance to the Nicaraguan resistance forces fighting for democracy in their native land would be severe. Such a cutoff would signal throughout the region that the totalitarian Leninist forces represent the winning side. The democratic forces would have cause to despair. They would see that terrorist and insurgent attacks against them are being generously supported by Cuba and the Soviet bloc, and that these attacks could be conducted from safe havens that would be protected by the US Congress, in effect, from all counter-interference. Conversely, the totalitarian Leninist force would know that as soon as they seize control of a country, they will be secure: Cuba and the Soviet bloc will help them maintain an efficient police machinery to repress the people; and should any group arise to fight for freedom, the United States Congress would have denied it all support.

Let me recapitulate.

Our basic objectives for Central America are clear: we want to strengthen democracy; we want to prevent in this hemisphere the expansion of totalitarian regimes, especially those linked to the Soviet Union.

To this end, we extend economic support and promote democratic development. But given forces of violence that will not accept the democratic will of the people, we also have to provide military assistance—enough to succeed. In addition, we must prevent consolidation of a Sandinista regime in Nicaragua that would become an arsenal for insurgency, a safe haven for the export of violence. If we cannot prevent that, we have to anticipate the partition of Central America. Such a development would then force us to man a new military front-line of the East-West conflict, right here on our continent.

To prevent such an outcome, the administration and Congress must work together with a strategy that can succeed.

5. A Policy Revealed*

By Tom Wicker

Tom Wicker is Associate Editor of the New York Times.

Now we know. By its own declaration, the Reagan Administration seeks "military victory" rather than a negotiated settlement in El Salvador. And it aims to "prevent consolidation of a Sandinista regime in Nicaragua" rather than merely to interdict whatever arms that country supplies to the Salvadoran guerrillas.

But if arming and training insurgents to make war on the Sandinistas fails to "prevent consolidation," Washington believes the "partition" of Central America will be necessary, with U.S. troops permanently stationed there, as in Korea and West Germany.

"Let me make this clear to you," Under Secretary of Defense Fred C. Iklé told the Baltimore Council on Foreign Affairs last week. "We do not seek a military defeat for our friends. We do not seek a military stalemate. We seek victory for the forces of democracy."

Well, just three days before Mr. Iklé delivered this calculated Administration policy statement, Arthur Allen, the able young bureau chief for the Associated Press in El Salvador, was driven out of that country by those very "forces of democracy."

Mr. Allen had incurred the ire of the Treasury Police, a dangerous thing to do in El Salvador; he left after the United States Embassy told him that it did not have the influence or power to assure his safety against the "forces of democracy"—even though the story that caused the trouble was based on information supplied to Mr. Allen by U.S. officials.

And the day before Mr. Iklé spoke of military victory for "our friends" in El Salvador, Archbishop Arturo Rivera y Damas said in an emotional homily that 29 Salvadorans had been murdered by paramilitary death squads in the previous week. Whether these squads are secretly part of the "forces of democracy" or are privately supported is in dispute in El Salvador; but "our friends" there are doing little or nothing to put an end to them or their bloody work.

Last week, for instance, the so-called Secret Anti-Communist Army took credit for three bombings, one at the University of Central America, and for two men

---

*Reprinted from *The New York Times*, September 19, 1983.

found strangled and shot. The group's leaflets were inscribed "for peace and democracy" and declared that the "eyes and guns of the true patriots" were on those who called for "dialogue" with anti-Government guerrillas. That includes most Salvadoran political leaders outside the right wing, as well as the official Government Peace Commission.

Mr. Iklé's timing was bad in more ways than one. Reports from El Salvador suggest that even as he was calling for "military victory," the guerrilla war was heating up after a summer lull many mistook for Government success. The constitutional debate in the National Assembly drags on inconclusively. Troop morale is said to be low after a long summer in the field. And talk of a coup is being heard again in the capital, probably more from frustration than intent.

So if "military victory" is the goal, rather than negotiations and "dialogue," Mr. Iklé and his colleagues have a long and costly way to go in El Salvador. As for Nicaragua, to "prevent consolidation" of the Sandinista regime obviously requires that it be overthrown, a goal the Reagan Administration now seeks through arming and training an insurgent army but that eventually could involve U.S. forces and perhaps those of Honduras and Guatemala.

A Sandinista Nicaragua, according to Mr. Iklé, would become "an arsenal for insurgency." To prevent that, "we have to anticipate the partition of Central America." And that would mean, he said, that the U.S. would have to "man a new military front line of the East-West conflict, right here on our continent."

Breathtaking! Not only has this Administration formed an insurgent army to overthrow a Central American government in direct violation—as Senator Alan Cranston has pointed out—of the charter of the Organization of American States and of this nation's own proclaimed principles. If thwarted in that objective, it threatens to "partition" a region of five countries that it does not own, and to impose there its own forces to defend this new "front line of the East-West conflict."

That's a classic example of the historic U.S. attitude, that Central America is "our backyard," a region where we are entitled to assert our perceived interests and never mind those of the peoples involved. It's a typical expression, too, of the geopolitical view that Central America—or Africa or Southeast Asia—is a mere pawn in an "East-West conflict," and has no important problems or interests of its own.

It was just such attitudes, acquiesced in by Central American governments installed or supported by the U.S., that resulted in the insurgency in El Salvador, that gave the Sandinistas their opportunity in Nicaragua. And these attitudes still largely preclude sensible policies of socioeconomic development that might be far more effective than the belligerent quest for "military victory."

6. *The Nicaraguan Crisis**

By Richard Fagen

Richard R. Fagen is Gildred Professor of Latin American Studies at Stanford University, and author of numerous books and articles on Latin America and US foreign policy, including "The Nicaraguan Revolution: A Personal Report."**

In Nicaragua, 1982 is offically the "Year of Unity Against Aggression." Unofficially, it is the year of difficulties, contradictions, and—in many ways—the radicalization of the Sandinist revolution.

There is more than ample reason for the official characterization. Beginning with the electoral rhetoric of Reagan and his advisers, there has been an unremitting campaign on the part of the current US administration to make life difficult and costly, if not impossible, for the Nicaraguan revolution. Although the accusations have varied in tone and detail, more recently the claims that Nicaragua is "totalitarian"—or rapidly moving in that direction—and a "platform of terror and war in the region" have been used to justify a program of diplomatic and economic pressures and covert action against Nicaragua.

Washington's ultimate goal is not entirely clear. Undoubtedly, some US officials dream of the day when Edén Pastora, the ex-Sandinist commander, will march triumphantly into Managua at the head of a "liberating army." Others may harbor no such illusions, but nevertheless feel that with the right mix of finely tuned pressures it will be possible to tame and de-radicalize the revolution. Yet others may coldly calculate that a more radicalized and Soviet-oriented Nicaragua is a much-to-be-desired outcome. Only then, with Nicaragua as "proof" that the Soviets and Cubans are the real masterminds and beneficiaries of discontent in the region, will it be possible to mobilize the public opinion, dollars, and firepower needed to destroy other revolutionary movements in Central America.

But whatever Washington's hopes, Nicaraguan realities are both more complex and less easily manipulated from outside than its enemies would like to believe. Not surprisingly, the complexities are rooted in the extremely serious economic difficulties facing the revolution—difficulties which at first glance seem almost insurmountable. But the revolution also has significant strengths stemming from its capacity to organize and reorganize the economy and society in response to challenges and threats.

This capacity is at the heart of the revolutionary paradox. On the one hand, a fundamental social transformation of the sort underway in Nicaragua creates a range of problems over and above those encountered by other poor societies. On the

*Reprinted from *Monthly Review*, November, 1982, Vol. 34, No. 6.
**Institute for Policy Studies, Washington, D.C. (1981).

other hand, however, this process of transformation also unleashes energies and resources not available to elites in nonrevolutionary situations. The revolution is simultaneously both a problem-maker and a problem-solver. The men and women who with so much courage and tenacity defeated Somoza and his allies understand this. They will not easily abandon what was so dearly won on the battlefield—the right to commit their own mistakes, determine their own future, and ultimately to make the basic transformations so needed in Nicaraguan society.

After the Deluge

In May of 1982 the heavens opened up and western Nicaragua was hit with the heaviest rains in decades. The floods that followed swept away highways, bridges, houses, crops, and people, causing damages estimated by the United Nations at more than $350 million, equal to 70 percent of the value of all Nicaraguan exports for 1981. Little wonder that religious members of the opposition to the Sandinists claimed that the same God who sent the 1972 earthquake to punish Somoza had now sent the floods to punish the revolutionary government. . . .

If we add to this scenario some basic structural characteristics of the Nicaraguan economy, the situation appears even more complex and potentially difficult. Although about 40 percent of Gross Domestic Product is generated in the state-owned sector of the economy, about 73 percent of all productive activity is still in private hands. In agriculture, which accounts for over 70 percent of all exports, an even higher percentage of productive assets is in private hands—almost 86 percent. Nicaraguan development, and particularly export performance, is thus highly dependent on the behavior of capitalists, both large producers and small.

In this context, the Sandinist state must necessarily play a double game. On the one hand it must give sufficient incentives, opportunities, and security to these producers. It must treat them like the capitalists they are. In fact, it must actually "overincentivize" them, because to the normal uncertainties of the market are added uncertainties generated by the revolutionary process itself. On the other hand, the state must also ensure sufficient benefits and dignity to both urban and rural workers. It must honor its vow that this is a revolution of workers and peasants, a revolution for the majority.

Under the best of circumstances, it would not be easy to run a mixed economy of the sort being attempted in Nicaragua. And in a country not yet fully recovered from the war of 1978–79, still very underdeveloped technologically and managerially, under assault by its huge neighbor to the north and by counterrevolutionaries much closer to home, it seems a Herculean task.

The World to the Rescue?

The Sandinist leadership has no illusions about the possibilities of eradicating in a few years the unequal relationships and developmental weaknesses that were centuries in the making. Thus Nicaraguans do not speak of the possibility of ending dependency but rather of the necessity of "diversifying dependency." This means receiving technology (including weapons) from Western as well as Eastern countries. It means vigorous attempts to break away from the political and economic hegemony of the United States, so long the dominant factor in Nicaragua's international and often domestic relations. But perhaps most importantly, in this period of economic crisis, diversifying dependency means searching for as much foreign aid from as many different sources as possible.

In search of this aid—and international solidarity in general—representatives of the government of Nicaragua must by now have broken the small-country record for hours spent in airplanes flying from one capital to another. In April and May of 1982, for example, Sergio Ramírez of the governing Junta and other high officials visited 12 countries in Western Europe. During the same period, Commander Daniel Ortega of the Junta and Commander Henry Ruiz, the Minister of Planning, were in the Soviet Union. During these same two months, other officials traveled to the United States, Germany, Bulgaria, Brazil and Argentina.

By July 19, 1982, the date of the third anniversary of the triumph of the Revolution, the leadership would look back on this vigorous effort with substantial satisfaction. In three years, almost $1.5 billion of new loans, credits, and donations had been secured. Much of the old debt contracted during the Somoza period had been renegotiated on favorable terms, and the new debt was quite well distributed across various countries and institutions: about 39 percent had been contracted with multilateral organizations, 18 percent with the United States and Western Europe, another 18 percent with Latin America, 17 percent with the socialist countries, and 8 percent with Libya. The announced policy of "walking on four legs"—Latin America, Western Europe, the socialist bloc, and Arab oil exporters—seemed to be working.

But the big question had by then become: Would it continue to work? Much more aid was needed if Nicaragua's short- and medium-term foreign exchange crisis was to be met. The country's total public foreign debt had edged up to almost $2.5 billion, one of the highest per capita in Latin America, helping to make Nicaragua substantially less attractive as a credit risk than it had been less than a year earlier. Furthermore, the vigorous campaign being waged by enemies of the Revolution, both Nicaraguans and others, was straining relations with at least some previous supporters in Latin America and Western Europe.

Thus in the near future "walking on four legs" may well become "limping on two." Not only pessimists were suggesting that the following self-reinforcing spiral might be beginning. To the extent that support from Latin America and Western Europe becomes problematic, the necessity of turning to the socialist bloc becomes more urgent. But the closer Nicaragua's relations with the socialist bloc, the more problematic further support from Western Europe and Latin America becomes.

The more conventional response to a foreign exchange crisis of the sort that Nicaragua is now suffering is, of course, to turn to the International Monetary Fund (IMF). Removing restrictions on the operation of market forces both internationally and domestically, reduction of public expenditures, and devaluation are typical components of an IMF-imposed program of "recovery." It is difficult to imagine, however, that the government of Nicaragua would accept such conditions—with their clear implications of subordination and distortion of revolutionary priorities—in exchange for a loan. As one planner said to me, "We are not about to sell our revolutionary birthright for a mess of IMF pottage."

If an IMF-imposed solution is not probable, and if walking on four legs—much less limping on two—cannot fully address the profundity of the crisis, what then is the answer? Whether planned or unplanned, Nicaragua is headed for a period of austerity deeper and longer than anything yet experienced in more than three years of revolution. The key questions thus become: How will this austerity be distributed and experienced in Nicaraguan society, and what will be its political consequences?

The Price of Squash

A visitor to Nicaragua soon becomes aware of opposition to the revolutionary government, for among the Reagan administration's many falsehoods about Central America, none is more gratuitous than the characterization of Nicaragua as "totalitarian." A vast array of political, social, and cultural forces are at work in the country. Professional and business associations in deep disagreement with government policy meet openly and protest loudly. Opposition political parties, although not able to mobilize wide popular support, are nevertheless active and vocal. The opposition trade-union movement is small but vigorous. The Catholic Church, some of whose members are supportive of the Sandinist revolution and some of whom are in opposition, continues as a major cultural and political force. A multitude of Protestant sects flourish. Private schools, both religious and secular, remain open. Even in the state of emergency decreed in March as a result of multiple threats from the Reagan administration and the constant incursions of ex–National Guard members across the border from Honduras, the opposition newspaper *La Prensa* continues to publish—albeit under the censorship which is also applied to other publications. And certainly in the streets, markets, churches, bars, and buses of the country one hears plenty of openly voiced complaints and criticisms—hardly what one would expect in a "totalitarian" society.

In this context of debate, criticism, and economic difficulties, the first half of the revolutionary paradox mentioned earlier operates with a vengeance. Not only do people look to their government for improvements in living and working conditions—thus creating expectations that are very difficult to fulfill in a situation of scarcity—but the relatively permissive political climate presents ample opportunities to those who wish to embarrass or discredit a revolution whose accomplishments inevitably fall short of popular expectations in many areas.

Thus, in an inflationary economy, where real purchasing power is declining, every trip to the market is an opportunity to hear and perhaps to internalize messages which assault the prestige of the revolution. That things are much worse in Costa Rica is not important or even known to the Nicaraguan shopper buying vegetables. The point of comparison is much closer to home: last month a squash cost one *córdoba*, and this month it costs one-and-a-half. Who is to blame?

At this point, however, the second half of the revolutionary paradox comes into play. Just as the revolutionary process creates certain problems (unfulfilled expectations, disruptions in production and distribution), it also creates special opportunities and new resources. Ideally, at least, the FSLN should be in a position to fight back, not only ideologically, but also in the distribution of real benefits.

As a successful example of the latter, the massive literacy crusade of 1980 is outstanding. In only five months, illiteracy was reduced from almost 50 percent to about 13 percent. Additionally, during this period hundreds of thousands of Nicaraguans working as temporary literacy instructors received their first real taste of what life in the most backward sectors of their own nation was really like. Unfortunately, however, both individuals and whole segments of society tend to forget the long-term material and moral benefits of such revolutionary undertakings when confronted with expensive squash.

Over the long run, victories for the Revolution in the ideological struggle depend on the effective functioning of the Sandinist National Liberation Front. Here the Reaganite view of the iron hand with which the FSLN rules Nicaragua is totally misleading. It is true that at the level of macro-political decisions the FSLN is in command. But at the day-to-day, grass-roots, organizational level needed to educate and mobilize the population to confront problems in the revolutionary process, it is actually quite weak. This is equally true in the affiliated mass organizations of women, youth, urban and rural workers, and even in the Sandinist political party-in-the-making.

In part the organizational thinness of the FSLN and affiliated mass organizations is to be expected, given the relatively short time since the victory over Somoza and the fact that the FSLN was initially organized to do battle against the tyranny, not to govern. But the current grass-roots organizational weakness of the FSLN also reflects the legacy of 46 years of despotic rule. At the time of Somoza's defeat, Nicaragua basically had only a political culture of opposition, and a very narrow and undemocratic political culture at that. Thus, the revolution quite literally must create a citizenry with the skills, attitudes, and experiences appropriate to participatory politics. It must do battle against apathy, suspicion, the sub-culture of corruption that characterized the Somoza years, and against dogmatic tendencies and errors committed by the *Frente* itself. In this situation it should come as no surprise that the revolutionary government is not always well prepared to explain the price of squash—or for that matter to counter the criticisms and often the outright lies that emanate from certain sectors of the Catholic hierarchy, the private sector, the opposition press, and Washington, D.C.

Countryside and City

> I talked to Sandino
> And he told me
> That you don't have to be big

To fight against the enemy.

If it weren't for Sandino
And the revolution
I wouldn't be singing
My humble little song.

—Verses written by a Nicaraguan peasant

To travel in the Nicaraguan countryside is to enter a world very different from the cities, particularly from the capital city of Managua. The peasants, rural workers, and even many of the private producers are more solidly with the revolutionary process than most urban dwellers. In part this reflects an agrarian reform that is both sophisticated in design and administered with honesty and substantial efficiency. Combining direct land grants to peasants, the establishment of cooperatives, state ownership of certain large production units (primarily those confiscated from Somoza and his followers), and incentives to private producers, the reform has been one of the most successful revolutionary programs.

Rural support for the revolution also draws strength from the comparisons which most peasants and rural workers make with the wretched conditions under which they previously lived. Not to be insulted and kicked around by the overseer and not to be cheated on payday (or in the boss's store) represent a vast improvement over what prevailed just a few years earlier. A peasant may not be making much more money or living in better housing, but he or she is probably now at least marginally literate and is for the first time being treated like a human being.

Additionally, almost everywhere in the countryside the multiple irritations that perturb urban dwellers, from food prices to crowded buses, are less immediately felt. When food is grown locally, and when most simple folk have always walked or ridden horses, high prices and shortages have a different meaning. "We can get by" is a rural, not an urban, response.

Substantial rural support for the revolution is also, somewhat surprisingly, to be found among the thousands of small and medium-sized landowners who produce most of the cotton, coffee, and other agricultural commodities that constitute the bulk of Nicaragua's exports. Many such producers are, of course, deeply distrustful of the revolution. Many hold investment to a minimum, producing only what is necessary to keep their farm or ranch from deteriorating or being nationalized under the "idle lands" provision of the agrarian reform law. But others, realizing that they quite literally have no place to go, respond to the credit and marketing incentives provided by the government. If they encounter a consistent set of problems in trying to produce in the Nicaraguan mixed economy, those problems are more likely to derive from the acute shortage of foreign exchange which affects all sectors than from their political differences with the revolutionary government.

In his Worker's Day speech on May 1, 1982, Commander Tomás Borge, the only surviving member of the group that founded the FSLN in 1961, emphasized that workers were "correct to continue demanding their economic rights." He also added, however, that their first responsibility is to consolidate revolutionary power—implying that in these difficult times salaries are going to have to take a back seat to other national priorities. At this massive May Day rally in Managua, Borge was literally and figuratively speaking to the urban population, for it is in the city-based activities of manufacturing, services, and government that Nicaragua's economic difficulties are and will continue to be felt most acutely. It is also in the cities that unemployment translates most immediately into hardship and discontent.

How the balance between countryside and city, between support and opposition to the revolution, will play itself out over the next months and years is impossible to predict with any accuracy. As noted earlier, much will depend on the organizational capacity and the political skills of the FSLN. But what *can* be predicted with a high degree of certainty is that Managua will continue to provide more than its fair share of problems, as well as the lens through which most outside observers will view the Nicaraguan revolution.

It is in Managua that the major opposition leaders who are still in the country hold forth. It is there that visiting journalists make their contacts and assess "public opinion." It is in the capital that a political confrontation or a police action is immediately known and given meaning—or many meanings. Thus the city plays its many roles: stronghold of the old and often anti-revolutionary culture and values, generator of problems that are both different from, and often more intractable than, those of the countryside, amplifier and broadcaster of these problems to the rest of the nation and to other nations as well. No wonder one frustrated municipal official said, only half in jest, "What we really need around here is another earthquake to get rid of what the quake of 1972 left standing."

The Struggle Continues

In Nicaragua today, class struggle is not simply some dusty Marxist concept; it is an everyday reality. Political power has passed from the Somocistas and what allies they had among the middle and upper classes to the FSLN and other revolutionary organizations speaking in the name of *las clases populares*—the majority of Nicaraguans who never before had a voice in how or for whom their country was run. This process is neither easy nor is it complete. The interests of the wealthy and comfortable are inevitably hurt, or at least deeply threatened; social tensions not allowed expression under the old order now surface and are given voice in streets and workplaces. It cannot be pleasant for middle-class families to hear the common folk marching through their neighborhoods chanting revolutionary slogans which promise the end of the old class-based system of power and privileges.

In revolutionary Nicaragua, as would be expected, class struggle reflects very directly the way in which economic power is related to political power. This relationship is very different from what would be found in either a fully developed capitalist economy or its socialist counterpart. In either case, a high degree of congruence between economic and political power would be expected. But in Nicaragua, such is not the case. The mixed economy depends on very substantial participation by the private sector, but at the same time this sector has only minority participation in the political system. (The expression "private sector" refers to medium and large capitalists who find their most organized expression in COSEP, the Higher Council of Private Enterprise. Technically, private enterprise includes everyone from the smallest peasant producer to the owner of the largest factory. COSEP, however, represents only the upper reaches of this pyramid.)

There are two related sources of tension embedded in this state of affairs. First, the social classes represented by or affiliated with the private sector resent the fact that they neither have nor are going to get the political clout which they feel their economic role entitles them to. Second, since most of the private sector still remaining in Nicaragua was either neutral during the insurrectionary period or openly anti-Somoza, many of its members feel that in addition to their economic claims on power, they also have claims based on their opposition to the dictator. But all of this argumentation matters little, for a self-proclaimed government of the *clases populares* is not about to shape its new institutions to suit the desires of classes which are numerically in the minority and whose overall average income is perhaps 20 to 30 times higher than that of the impoverished majority.

This understandable intransigence on the part of the FSLN has important implications for the way in which the current economic crisis has been and will be handled. Every effort will be made to soften the blows that fall on the mass of the citizenry. If petroleum products have to be rationed, it is the owners of private automobiles (a small but vocal fraction of the total population) who will feel the pinch most acutely. As food becomes scarcer and more expensive, it is the supply and distribution of rice and beans that will receive first priority. As complaints and dissent mount, it is the voices of the poor that will be listened to most attentively.

There is, in this dynamic, a high probability that class tensions will rise. As tougher and tougher public-policy choices have to be made—accelerated by shortages of foreign exchange and the resultant economic slowdown—grist for the opposition mill will be produced in abundance. Those sectors of the Church hierarchy, the press, and private enterprise that are already highly critical of the government will become even more resentful. Their voices will be listened to avidly not only in Washington but in some other capitals around the world. In official circles in Managua, the temptation to shut them up, by whatever means necessary, will increase.

The economic crisis thus implies a reaffirmation and deepening of the class character of the Nicaraguan revolution. Almost by definition it also implies a radicalization of the revolution—understood as a quickening of the pace at which the economy is moved away from the market orientation which still guides most of its operations. The management of scarcity in favor of the *clases populares* cannot be left to the vagaries of the market, or to capitalists, large or small. As producers, private entrepreneurs may still retain an important role, but priorities with respect to production, prices, distribution, and much else will increasingly be determined by the state. Both as capitalists and as consumers, the private sector is going to see its opportunities diminish.

Imperialism's Many Faces

On the eve of the third anniversary of Nicaragua's liberation from Somoza and the National Guard, sporadic military confrontations flared into heavy fighting in the northeastern corner of the country. Bands of well-armed and well-coordinated "contras"—as active opponents of the revolution are called in Nicaragua—were engaged by units of the Sandinist armed forces. In the first battles, more than three dozen Nicaraguan soldiers lost their lives. Subsequently, many more were killed and wounded.

The area in which these clashes took place extends 80 miles south of the border with Honduras and forms part of the traditional homeland of the Miskitu Indians. Early in 1982, repeated raids by contras based in Honduras forced the Nicaraguan government to relocate almost 10,000 Miskitu from the Río Coco area into new settlements farther to the south. Other Miskitu moved north into Honduras. The relocation was, in essence, a military operation. Fear and hostility swept through the indigenous population, and an already difficult situation on the northern Atlantic coast became even more difficult.

For the Reagan administration, which had given aid and encouragement to the contras as well as support to dissident Miskitu spokespersons, the forced relocation was heaven-sent. An avalanche of outright falsehoods followed. Jeane Kirkpatrick accused the Nicaraguan government of "genocide." Alexander Haig waved a picture of burning bodies before the television cameras to "prove" that the Sandinistas were slaughtering Miskitus. An administration that in Guatemala supports a military establishment that systematically destroys whole villages and assassinates hundreds of indigenous persons, suddenly transformed itself into the defender of Indian rights in Nicaragua.

What emerges most clearly from events in northeastern Nicaragua is the determination of the Reagan administration to attack the Nicaraguan revolution whenever an opportunity can be found or created. We may never know with any certainty the degree of CIA involvement in the sowing of dissent among the Miskitu and the training and arming of the contras who first crossed the border to terrorize the people living along the Río Coco. But what is evident is that once the dynamic of relocation, distrust, and militarization began, the possibilities for both propaganda and covert operations multiplied rapidly. Who in Nicaragua would believe that the Reagan administration is not fishing in these troubled waters—or, for that matter, training and releasing sharks? Would a country whose marines occupied Nicaragua almost continuously from 1912 to 1933—and then left the Nicaraguans to the tender mercies of the Somoza family and the National Guard—hesitate to train and support the contras? Would an administration that from the earliest days of its presidential campaign systematically attacked the Sandinistas pass up the opportunity to agitate among the Miskitu?

As in the northeast with the Miskitu, so too in the cities and countryside of the rest of Nicaragua, as well as in Honduras, Costa Rica, Washington, New York, Florida, and elsewhere. The battle against the Sandinists is waged in Congress, in multilateral lending agencies, international organizations, the press, European and Latin capitals, and in the training camps for *contras*. In fact, wherever the many difficulties and vulnerabilities of the Nicaraguan revolution present an opportunity, some arm or mouthpiece of the US government is sure to be found on the offensive, with words, pats on the back, blows to the abdomen, dollars, or equipment designed to do as much damage to the Sandinists as possible.

When asked why this policy is being pursued, officials of the Reagan administration give a variety of answers. But when pressed, the US Embassy in Managua answers consistently that US hostiliy derives from the aid and comfort being given by the Sandinists to the guerrilla movement in El Salvador. Without doubt, some aid and comfort do flow from Nicaragua to opponents of the Salvadoran regime. How much and in what form remains an open question, since the original evidence offered by the US government in 1981 was extremely flimsy and no additional evidence has been forthcoming (the Embassy says that such evidence exists but cannot be made public, because to do so would jeopardize intelligence sources).

It is difficult to believe, however, that the El Salvador question is the driving force behind the imperialist assault on the Nicaraguan revolution. The hostility is too deep, too consistent, manifested in too many ways, and pursued too aggressively for this to be the case. At least from Nicaragua, it seems clear that this administration, no matter what Nicaragua's relationship to El Salvador, is seeking nothing less than the overthrow of the Sandinist government. If this can be accomplished "peacefully" through destabilization in the context of severe economic difficulties, so much the better. But if military measures are necessary, that is acceptable too, for the fighting and dying will be done by Nicaraguans and others from the region, not by North Americans.

Even a few days spent in Nicaragua suggest both the futility and the criminality of this policy toward the Sandinist revolution. Not only are the Nicaraguan armed forces and militia growing stronger every day, but with each Nicaraguan killed by the *contras* one can feel the determination to resist outside pressures. Of course, if the country is subjected to an extended period of severe military threat and aggression, important changes will undoubtedly take place. The space allowed to opposition voices would shrink and perhaps disappear altogether. The economy would go on a war footing. But none of this would mean the end of the Sandinist revolution, only its transformation.

If the futility of this approach to the revolution is obvious, its immorality is even more evident. With all of its faults and problems, the current government of Nicaragua is the first in the country's entire history that genuinely attempts to improve the living and working conditions of the majority of citizens. Housed in shacks, poorly fed, often without electricity, running water, health or educational facilities, most Nicaraguans have no future outside the revolution, and certainly no future under renewed American hegemony. As a peasant receiving the land title for a newly organized cooperative said, "Neither the imperalists nor the Somocistas ever gave us land, and we aren't going to give it back or let any of them return."

In sum, for most Nicaraguans what the Reagan administration promises is not "liberation" from Sandinist rule, but rather more hardship, more strife, and possibly a great deal of bloodshed. And all of this for a people who have already had more than their share of hardship, strife, and bloodshed. Little wonder that even Nicaraguans highly critical of the Sandinists fear Washington's policies. They too understand that if their country is again consumed in war they and their sons and daughters will be the ultimate losers. They too understand the bankruptcy of US policy toward Nicaragua. Nevertheless, yet again a US administration is desperately trying to make the history of another nation conform to its own interests and prejudices.

Chapter II

Nicaragua: A Threat to its Neighbors?

Editors' Introduction

Reagan administration representatives repeatedly claimed that a substantial arms traffic exists between Nicaragua and the rebels in El Salvador (see Readings 2 and 3), despite the fact that they were unable to come up with concrete evidence of such traffic. As Interior Minister Tomás Borge asked in the March 19, 1982, *New York Times*, "If the wise men of the C.I.A. know where it's happening, why don't they tell us so we can stop it?" Nevertheless, the result of the administration's insistence is that the alleged arms traffic has come to be accepted as fact. The first article in this chapter by Christopher Dickey of the *Washington Post*, reviews the evidence for and against the administration's claim that Nicaragua is a threat to El Salvador.

The Reagan administration has continued to claim that Nicaragua is undergoing a Soviet- and Cuban-aided "militarization." Nicaragua, on the other hand, claims justifiable self-defense. As the *New York Times* (March 10, 1982) quoted Junta member Sergio Ramírez, "When Mr. Haig is saying every day that they are going to bomb us and blockade us, how can they then turn around and ask us not to defend ourselves?"

The next two readings in this section examine the administration's claim that the "militarization" of Nicaragua presents a threat to neighboring Honduras. This is particularly relevant at a time when a war between the two countries is a real possibility. The centerpiece of the administration's case is a State Department press briefing by John T. Hughes of the Defense Intelligence Agency, excerpted here. This is followed by testimony before the House of Representatives by Lt. Col. John H. Buchanan, USMC (ret.), of the Center for Development Policy, in which he assesses the relative military strengths of Nicaragua and Honduras.

This chapter closes with the subject of negotiations. President Reagan claimed in his address to the Joint Session of Congress on April 27, 1983, that "we have attempted to have a dialogue with the government of Nicaragua but it persists in its efforts to spread violence." Peter Crabtree's summary of Central American peace initiatives would seem to question the Reagan administration's sincerity with regard to negotiations.

7. *Nicaraguan Aid to Rebels Called "Peanuts"**

By Christopher Dickey

San Salvador—US military officials in Central America, reassessing Nicaraguan support for El Salvador's rebels, say that foreign arms shipments to the insurgents are probably not as extensive or as vital to the outcome of the Salvadoran war as they once appeared to be.

Diplomats and other observers say the guerrillas have captured large amounts of weapons from the Salvadoran military. According to one US diplomat, the guerrillas have probably captured enough arms from the Salvadoran armed forces during the past four months "to sustain their needs" if some supplemental ammunition is brought in from the outside.

Despite the insistence of administration officials in Washington that Nicaragua is continuing to provide a significant amount of weapons to the Salvadoran rebels, diplomats and military officials in Central America say that for more than a year there has been very little solid evidence of material support for the Salvadorans originating in Nicaragua.

"It is very possible Nicaragua is not feeding anything but peanuts into El Salvador," said one US official concerned with investigating the traffic.

Another informed military officer said, "I never have thought [Nicaraguan arms supplies] are critical." He estimated that about "20 to 40 percent" of the guerrillas' arms may come from Nicaragua "at peak times."

"That doesn't make much difference," said the officer, except that "psychologically it's nice to know a sponsor's still there."

Administration officials in Washington, however, have continued to stress the importance of outside arms supplies to the Salvadoran guerrillas, Secretary of State George P. Schultz said at a hearing of the House Foreign Affairs Committee last week that arms "from the Soviet Union to Cuba, Nicaragua and these insurgents" fuel the war in El Salvador. A State Department official said the Salvadoran rebels

---

*Reprinted from *The Washington Post*, February 21, 1983.

"couldn't sustain the type of fighting they've engaged in now, without outside arms and coordination from Nicaragua."

In December, Central Intelligence Agency Director William Casey sought to calm congressional concern over reports of covert US efforts to overthrow the Sandinista rulers of Nicaragua. In closed-door briefings, he told congressional intelligence committees that interdicting the arms supply to the Salvadoran guerrillas was the administration's chief goal in supporting covert operations in the region.

A growing concern among some US officials in Central America is that placing too much emphasis on foreign arms supplies as the source of El Salvador's current problems allows the military here to sidestep the serious social, economic and political problems in which the conflict is rooted.

Col. Mario Enrique Acevedo, commander of Morazán province where some of the guerrillas' strongest units continue to operate, recently told a group of journalists that he gets frequent local reports of clandestine arms supply flights. He said he had firm intelligence of a Soviet military officer who spoke fluent Spanish landing at a guerrilla camp and giving orders to the insurgents. The story was a typical one, but also typically, his intelligence did not include a date for this vividly described scene.

Such stories circulated by and among some Salvadoran officers are related to the feeling that some of them have that they are really fighting Washington's East-West war and that Washington should be doing more of the job itself.

Perhaps if El Salvador had oil, said Acevedo, using an argument common among his peers, there would be no problem about US support. "They would send us one of those brigades that doesn't let anybody get by."

The rebels deny receiving any important amount of weapons from sympathetic governments. They say that they buy their arms on the international black market, from corrupt or sympathetic members of the government's armed forces, or capture them in combat. A recent guerrilla statement said they have seized more than 1,200 "weapons of war" from government forces since October.

US officials say this figure is probably exaggerated but acknowledge that "large" quantities of arms have been taken by the insurgents. These include everything from pistols to assault rifles to 120-mm mortars.

The issue of Nicaraguan support for the Salvadoran rebels has been a major obstacle in relations between Washington and the revolutionary Sandinista government in Managua. Efforts to interdict arms shipments from Nicaragua or to pressure the government there into cutting off all support for the Salvadoran insurgents have colored US policy throughout Central America.

Few US military officials in the region question Washington's overall policy toward Nicaragua, since they view Managua's internal arms buildup and the Sandinistas' ideology as a menace to Central American peace.

The Sandinistas say openly that they provide moral support and "office space" to the Salvadoran guerrillas. Nicaraguan Commander Bayardo Arce, in charge of relations with other revolutionary movements, said in an interview last year that the Sandinistas had shown the Salvadoran rebels the clandestine connections and networks they used to get arms for their own 1979 insurrection. Cuban officials have said they sent large quantities of arms to Salvadoran revolutionaries in late 1980.

Early in the Reagan administration, then-secretary of state Alexander M. Haig, Jr., said Nicaragua was the main channel through which Soviet and Cuban arms were sent to the Salvadoran guerrillas. During the past two years, the threat of a guerrilla victory in El Salvador has been used to justify a large increase in military aid to Honduras.

Last fall, high-level officials said most land and sea shipments of arms through Honduras and Nicaragua had been stopped but that air shipments had greatly increased.

Some US officials in Central America say that the Honduran Army, aided by US advisers, has virtually shut down the guerrillas' overland supply routes from Nicaragua to El Salvador. Some US diplomats in Honduras and El Salvador maintain that the slack has been picked up by increased air and sea deliveries of arms to the insurgents.

A State Department official said the administration believes the supply of arms from Nicaragua is continuing at a "relatively high level" and includes heavy weapons such as mortars. He said the arms supply is carried out "far more by air now than in the past."

But despite administration assertions of success in interdicting arms shipped by land, and more recent charges that shipments are continuing, primarily by air, not a single major shipment of arms has been captured in or near El Salvador since a Costa Rican pilot was caught in 1981. The one major smuggling network that was uncovered last year also had its base in Costa Rica.

One intelligence officer who has interviewed numerous residents along presumed nocturnal flight paths between Nicaragua and El Salvador cautioned that for some people, attuned to thinking in such terms, "every plane that flies is a 'gunrunner.'"

The most conspicuous example of this type of thinking, according to US officials, was the sighting of what was thought to be a Soviet-built helicopter by a group of conservative US lobbyists and politicians when they visited El Salvador last month in a delegation led by Rep. Phillip M. Crane (R-Ill.).

On a stop at the Salvadoran port of La Unián on the Gulf of Fonseca opposite Nicaragua, members of the group thought they saw a twin-rotor "Russian helicopter" leaving what appeared to be Nicaraguan airspace and heading toward guerrilla-dominated areas of northern Morazán province in El Salvador.

According to US officials who investigated the incident, the aircraft was "almost certainly" a US "Chinook" helicopter on its way from Panama to Honduras in preparation for joint military maneuvers there at the beginning of this month.

One element in Washington's appraisal of the arms-supply problem is electronic and photographic intelligence to which most US officials on the isthmus say they have had no access. Although the administration last year publicly presented air photographs of what it said were internal Nicaraguan military bases, heavily fortified and modeled along Cuban lines, a subsequently scheduled presentation of similar information on arms shipments was never held. US diplomats say that the information has not even been shown to the Salvadorans to aid them in catching alleged smugglers.

8. *The Military Buildup in Nicaragua**

By John T. Hughes

John T. Hughes, who conducted the famous 1962 press briefing about the introduction of Soviet missiles into Cuba, is currently Deputy Director for Intelligence and External Affairs of the Defense Intelligence Agency (DIA).

Ladies and gentlemen, our purpose this afternoon is to review some of the sensitive intelligence available to us on the continuing Nicaraguan military buildup. In this review, we will exhibit reconnaissance photography of Nicaraguan military installations and military equipment.

This presentation has two basic objectives, with respect to the Nicaraguan military buildup: first, to describe the nature and growth of Nicaraguan military facilities over the past two years, and the inherent Cuban design they represent, and second, to review efforts on the part of Cuba and other Communist nations to provide modern and upgraded military equipment to the Sandinistan ground—armed forces.

Prior to the overthrow of Somoza by the Sandinistas, Nicaragua maintained a National Guard with the strength of about 10,000 men. This force was widely dispersed throughout the country in an internal security role and had very little heavy military equipment.

When the Sandinistas came to power, they immediately began organizing regular military forces and a strong internal security police force.

The Sandinista police, similar in purpose to Somoza's National Guard, gradually have been built to a force of 5,000 to 6,000 men.

The regular military forces have grown even more quickly, from a small initial force of 5,000 to a large, active-duty army supplemented by even larger militia and reserve elements.

This combined military force is now the largest in Central America and totals up to 70,000 men.

Based on the pace of new airfield construction and the development of new ground-force installations, it is evident to us that the Sandinistas are achieving military force levels and capabilities that are in excess of those normally required

---

*Excerpted from remarks by John T. Hughes, at a State Department Press Conference on March 9, 1982.

purely for defensive purposes.

We believe that they have already upset the military balance in Central America. This is especially true since their neighbor to the south, Costa Rica, maintains no standing army.

Let me now share with you the evidence that is available to us.

In any discussion on the Sandinista military buildup, one has to talk about Nicaraguan military facilities. At the present time, we have confirmed from aerial photography and other sources 49 active military garrisons. The amazing thing about that figure is that 36 of them are new military garrisons since the Sandinistas have taken power. Thirteen of the garrisons to make up the total of 49 are old Somoza garrisons that have been refurbished to accommodate the Sandinista military units.

Most of these garrison areas are built along Cuban design. In fact, we have evidence of facilities in Cuba that we'll exhibit today that are seen in Nicaragua.

The installations we're going to talk about are shown, or highlighted, here. Fourteen are the ground-force installations—they are not all of them there—some of the main ones, here marked by the military symbol, a standing soldier. Fourteen of them, plus four new airfield activities we're watching very carefully at Puerto Cabezas, Bluefields, Montelimar and near Managua itself. And, by the way, this inset of Lake Managua is enlarged in the upper left, where you can see the town of Managua and the newly established ground-force garrison that we're going to be discussing in the context of today's presentation.

This is Sandino airfield, the main international field.

As I mentioned a moment ago, all of these take on a Cuban design and character. Let me show you what we are saying on the reconnaissance photography. Next graphic.

This is one of the new Sandinista garrisons at Villanueva. This garrison measures some 1,000 by 1,700 feet over all—across and down—having a standard rectangular configuration like we have seen in Cuba. This configuration, or a battalion-sized unit area, is broken into three parts. And that pattern repeats itself again and again and again.

Part one is the vehicle storage and maintenance area shown here. These are vehicle sheds here and here. These are foundations for four more—here, here, here and here. Here are the grease pits, where the vehicles are serviced, and that makes up one-third of the area.

The second third of the area, typical again of Cuban construction, is the barracks area. These are five barracks buildings, 55 meters in length.

And then the third segment of this battalion-sized area, ground-force fighting area, is the training area, where we see the Soviet-style obstacle course here; where we see the Soviet-style physical training area and their exercise field.

For this unit, this is the parade field and this is the reviewing stand, situated here. And as typical of Soviet military doctrine, they have antiaircraft defenses already in place at these new garrison areas.

This is the pattern we see time and time again in Nicaragua. It's the pattern we've already seen time and time again in Cuba.

Let me show you another one. Here's one dated February 19, 1982, just last month. It's just been recently completed and is now being occupied. Here are four double-bay garage areas. Here are the grease pits for servicing the vehicles; training and school centers here for drivers. And here are seven barracks buildings—one, two, three, four, five, six and seven—to accommodate 500 to 700 men making up its infantry battalion. Here's the parade field. Here's the reviewing stand. There's the standard Soviet military obstacle course that we've seen over the years, in the Soviet Union and in Cuba.

There's the Soviet physical training area, situated here, with chin-bars and other types of equipment to exercise the forces, and a running track. Notice the security in and around the building, with fences and guard towers to protect it at intermediate intervals.

This, so, is the pattern we're seeing. Now let me mention one thing. This is a completed military garrison about to be occupied. Let me show you the sequencing of photographic coverage we've had as the Sandinistas and the Cubans have built this up over time.

Now some Cuban-style activities are not conventional military, and their special troops are unconventional military related. This is typical of what we've seen in some Cuban installations. There's a special forces, there are special troops, ranger and commando training areas in Nicaragua, along the Lake Managua, which is in the upper portion of the graphic here.

What do we see at this very discrete-looking kind of area? We see hand-to-hand combat training facility, or a sawdust pit, like we have in United States garrisons. We see Soviet-style obstacle courses here. We see bulldozers working to prepare and finish off the new rifle-firing range, which is under construction. And you can see the bulldozers that are pushing the earth up into this area to flatten out this area to make it an acceptable firing range. And here is the headquarters building, all of which were new since 1980.

In addition, what we also see here is a portion of an airfield parking apron, out here in the no man's land. And on it are airfield mockups and derelicts. This is the kind of field where you train commandos and rangers on how to attack an airfield and destroy aircraft with satchel charges and explosive charges. That's being done here.

This is reminiscent, of course, of the Ilopango raid in El Salvador a few weeks or a month past.

These, of course, are not for the defense of Nicaragua. They are primarily projection-of-power elements in an unconventional way and the training is going on here. And we've seen installations like this in Cuba, and we've seen them elsewhere here in Nicaragua.

Now, there is one armored unit in Nicaragua today, so far. That armored unit includes 25 T-54/55 tanks, which have 100-millimeter guns and weigh 36 metric tons. This is a temporary armor storage and training area, until they complete their barracks and storage facilities.

In other words, the tanks arrived before they had a place to put them. And here is the training area—storage and driver-training area. Notice the roads all torn up here by tank treads, torn up through here and through here. Here is the T-54/55 tank here, with a 100-millimeter gun in the open. And here are covered revetments, or storage points, marked by these white tarpaulin covers—10 arrows—where the other tanks are hidden and covered out of view and just kept out of the sun. They have 25 of these in the garrison areas.

Now, I said there were 36 new garrison and training facilities that they were using, filmed in the last 24 months. There are 13 additional older Somoza-built garrisons that don't have that unique Cuban-like design and configuration, that were just built by increments and sprawled across the area, as one might see them.

Here's one such area. It extends from here, irregularly, down through here. The fence line enclosed the motor pool area, the antiaircraft areas and back through here. Notice again, barracks areas here, and barracks areas here. This is the training area and parade ground and notice, you can see, under this quality photography, formations of soldiers here, formations of soldiers here—squads and companies. They're being trained with Soviet antiaircraft guns, one here, one here. And they're being trained with Soviet antitank guns, one here and one here. This is the motor-pool area, where there are East German-provided trucks, some 500 and up to 1,000 provided to the Sandinistas, some of them are here. This area is enlarged and shown over here on the lower right. Here are the East German-built trucks and these four, in this upper line—one, two, three, four artillery—a 57-millimeter Soviet-built antitank gun.

So this is the pattern of construction that we see, the pattern of occupancy of barracks that we see when they're older Somoza garrisons, 13 old Somoza garrisons like this now occupied by the Sandinistas.

Now, what types of military equipment have we been able to confirm inside Nicaragua today? Our best counts in the community are as follows: 25 T-55 tanks with 100-millimeter guns; one battalion formed near Nicaragua—near the Nicaraguan capital Managua, 12 heavy 100.2- or 152-millimeter howitzers, truck drawn; 2 Soviet-built HIP helicopters; 12 armored personnel carriers, BTR 60's, which carry a squad of men under armored protection into battle.

And in order to move this heavy equipment through the tropical areas of Nicaragua and across the riverine streams, the Soviets have also provided amphibious ferries, military ferries, that can lift these 8 ton tanks and move them across water bodies and take these armored vehicles across as well. A very modern army being constructed, a fairly good and essentially effective military equipment.

Now, we show a MIG-17 configuration here, but there's a question mark behind it, the question mark because we believe that soon either MIG-17's or MIG-21's will be delivered to Nicaragua.

Why do we say that? For two basic reasons. There are 50 Nicaraguan pilots in Bulgaria and Cuba, training on MIG's today. We expect them to return sometime this year.

In addition, four major airfields are being configured in Nicaragua to accommodate heavy jet attack aircraft. Let me show you what we see at the airfields.

The four airfields in question are—we'll start first with the international field near Managua that's situated here on Lake Managua, enlarged here, and we'll talk about Sandino airfield here, Montelimar airfield on the Pacific here, and on the Caribbean, two fields being enlarged, Puerto Cabezas and Bluefields—whew, that's rough. Let's start with Sandino.

Here's the international field, which is some 8,000 feet in length and can accommodate any jet fighter aircraft today. It's primarily for commercial purposes. As you see here, there's a few commerical aircraft. Its the international field and Sandinistan Air Force headquarters here in these buildings situated through here.

On this photography, we see the two Soviet HIP helicopters. Two are shown here, here and here. They are enlarged, one and two. We also see the, per typical Soviet doctrine, the antiaircraft guns here, here and one other location here.

Most importantly, gentlemen, this field is being recently expanded in capacity by addition of hardened revetments at this end of the field, just off the main taxiway. One—U-shaped revetments—one, two, three, four, five, six, seven. These revetments are for fighter bombers, jet-capable kinds of aircraft. They're aircraft with revetments like we see in Cuba, like we see in East Germany, like we see elsewhere in the Communist bloc. These are to house fighting aircraft, probably the MIG's that we expect to be delivered to the Sandinistas sometime this year.

Now at the fields on the Caribbean, this is one that's been blacktopped. It was getting blacktopped at the time of photography, at Puerto Cabezas. It measures some 6,000 feet in length, and that's the older runway being improved and repaired by the Sandinistas.

But that's not long enough to take a MIG-21 off-loaded with bombs. You need 6,600 feet, it's only got 6,000. Look at this extension now under construction at the present time.

We expect this segment, which has been moved along very quickly, to be operational by the end of this month. It's a 2,100-foot extension of the runway over all. The Soviet-built antiaircraft guns are already in position to protect this field. Here is the construction equipment situated here.

On the Pacific Coast there's another older field that measures some 6,700 feet in length, long enough to take any jet aircraft the Soviets can build. Now, notice the expansion here. There's no place to park airplanes. If you build up an air force, you need a place to park them. And here's the parking apron, under construction, in the last six-month period, measuring some 1,500 feet in length. Fuel storage areas are being built and now, in the most recent photography, two POL lines are leading out to this area for service of the craft and to provide for refueling.

This is the kind of airfield expansion under way for an air force today that claims just a few old airplanes—light Convairs and airplanes and a few DC-3's. This is a major expansion that is now under way, we're convinced, to accommodate the arrival, this year sometime, of these new MIG aircraft.

The point is, when the pilots return, when the MIG's arrive, when these airfields are completed, the Sandinistas will probably have the best air force in Central

America, in terms of performance quality and airfield serviceability.

Who is helping the Sandinistas do this? The fingerprint we find, in every case—the special troop areas and in the areas involving the construction of the barracks, which we've shown you both in Cuba and Nicaragua—are the Cubans. And in terms of numbers, from a variety of sources available to us, we say that there are up to 2,000 military and security advisers working with these new troop units and these new construction segments; over 3,000 medical advisers, government advisers and teachers, and 750 construction engineers and advisers to build the airfields, to build the ground-force garrisons and to support the military buildup now under way in this Sandinistan-Nicaraguan area.

The total number of Cubans, we say, about 6,000 over all.

9. Soviet-Style Pizza

By Garry Trudeau

Reprinted with permission of Universal Press Syndicate. All rights reserved.

10. Honduras/Nicaragua: War Without Winners*

By Lt. Col. John H. Buchanan

The following is a prepared statement presented before the Subcommittee on Inter-American Affairs, Committee on Foreign Affairs, US House of Representa-

---

*Reprinted from *NACLA Report on the Americas*, Sept.-Oct. 1982, pp. 2–12.

tives on September 21, 1982. The author, Lt. Col. John H. Buchanan, USMC, retired in 1979, having among other things flown ground-support missions in Viet Nam. He is currently Director of Area Studies at the Center for Development Policy.

Thank you, Mr. Chairman and members of the Subcommittee, for asking me to testify this afternoon. I appreciate the opportunity to speak to you on a subject that I believe to be a matter of urgent national priority.

Speaking generally, I am here to criticize the present administration's policy toward Central America. It is a misguided policy, and if it is not soon reversed the people of this land and the rest of this continent will suffer for decades from its grave consequences. It is not in our interests as a nation.

More specifically, I am here to oppose the present administration's creation of a military crisis between Honduras and its neighbor, Nicaragua, and its sponsorship of a military buildup in Honduras, a move which will only encourage increased repression in that country.

At the outset, I wish to make it clear that I do not pretend to be an expert on Central America. I would categorize myself as a concerned US citizen who became so appalled by this administration's militarization of Central America's economic and social crisis that I felt compelled to examine thoroughly the military situation in the region to find out what is really happening there.

Six months ago I set out to develop the necessary ligatures needed to understand events in Central America. These months have been busy ones for me. I spent four weeks during April and May traveling alone through Mexico, Costa Rica and Nicaragua, and nearly two weeks in July and August in El Salvador and Honduras as a member of a delegation sponsored by the Commission on United States-Central American Relations. In the course of these travels I met with religious leaders including Mons. Rivera y Damas, the acting archbishop of El Salvador, Bishop Wilson of the Moravian Church in Nicaragua (the church of the Miskitu Indians of the Atlantic Coast), and evangelical Protestant ministers throughout the region. I talked with numerous past and present civilian politicians and many members of the international media. I was briefed by some of the leading academics of all these countries, especially political scientists and economists. I had dicussions with local and US businessmen in Mexico, Costa Rica, Nicaragua and El Salvador, including the National Private Enterprise Association (ANEP) and the Chamber of Commerce in El Salvador. I visited the refugee centers in San Salvador, shared the meager fare of the Miskitu Indians in their resettlement communities in Nicaragua and spent a night with Salvadoran refugees in their squalid camp at Mesa Grande, in Honduras. I have talked with numerous exiles from the troubled countries of El Salvador and Nicaragua; these include Guillermo Ungo, Héctor Dada, Col. Majano and Leonel Gámez of El Salvador and Heraldo Montealegre of Nicaragua.

In a daze, I have stumbled through the remains of the victims of Salvadoran death squads. And I walked confidently among the free, exuberant citizens of Costa Rica. (How long that happy state will obtain is problematic as this administration is pressuring Costa Rica to build an army.)

The knowledge and insights I gained through these experiences have been crucial to my understanding of the turmoil that the Central American isthmus is now enduring. I will be happy to answer any questions regarding these trips upon completion of my statement.

Most important for my understanding of the military situation in the region were my contacts with Central America's military commanders, their staffs and their troops. I have had long conversations with military representatives from all sides of the conflict: the Farabundo Martí National Liberation Front (FMLN), with Colonel Majano, the leader of the October 1979 coup in El Salvador, with General García and his chief of staff, Colonel Flores Lima, with several of the Sandinista commandantes, with Honduran officers, and with the US Military Group commander in El Salvador, Colonel Waghlestein.

I flew with the Sandinista Air Force in one of their two or three Cessna 180s to a small jungle airstrip on the Miskitu coast. On landing, the plane veered off the runway and crashed into the trees. The Sandinistas flew in a new propeller, and my young pilot used a screw driver and a hammer to straighten out the dents in the wings and tail of the aircraft. We later flew that aircraft back to Managua at night.

I accompanied a Sandinista combat patrol right along the border with Honduras in northwest Nicaragua near Somoto. A few weeks later I learned that several of the young Sandinista soldiers I was with were killed in one of the frequent ambushes that the Somocista counterrevolutionaries mount from Honduras. Before I left Nicaragua, I visited many of the "military installations" that US satellites photographed in Nicaragua and which were the subject of the briefing presented by the administration last March. I saw little significant difference between a "Soviet-style obstacle course" and the obstacle courses I ran as a young Marine.

During my visit to El Salvador in July, I visited a regional commander of the Salvadoran Army and was briefed by him and his staff on the military situation in his zone, Cuscatlán department, scene of many heated military encounters. After a fine lunch, we went to the "rifle range" and test fired some of his M-16 and M-60 weapons. They seemed little different from the M-16 and AK-47 weapons I inspected in Nicaragua. While in Honduras I again flew to the Miskitu coast. This time the aircraft was a US Air Force C-130 transport and I felt considerably more secure than in the Sandinistas' Cessna. This aircraft was participating in the relocation of a Honduras combat batallion to the sensitive border area next to Nicaragua. Fortunately, this plane did not crash on landing for we were hauling ammunition for the Honduran troops that were occupying the zone.

Again, I am not suggesting that these encounters with the Central American military make me a military expert. I do not possess the expertise, resources and intelligence gathering capabilities of General Alexander M. Haig or General Wallace H. Nutting or General Vernon A. Walters. But I do have enough military training and knowledge to see that a smoke screen is being laid and a military debacle is in the offing.

After analyzing the military capabilities of Honduras and Nicaragua, and the limitations that each of them faces, the nature of their conflict and the threat that they pose to each other, I can only conclude that it would be ludicrous for Nicaragua to assault Honduras and equally foolhardy for Honduras to attack Nicaragua. Yet these two countries seem to be headed for a war, one which this administration is encouraging. Information I have coming out of Central America is that a war between these two countries will start in December. I will discuss this date in more detail in a few moments. (Incidentally, throughout this testimony I will not identify my sources of "information"; for obvious reasons their names cannot be revealed.)

Before I address what I believe are the factual military capabilities and limitations of Nicaragua I want to direct your attention to a couple of military briefing techniques. Armchair generals and government officials who are locked in combat for Congress' heart, mind and pocketbook always brief using "uncluttered" maps in which the Soviet Union is pink, the United States is orange, Cuba is brown, etc. Maps like that avoid awkward questions about terrain features, lines of communication, weather patterns, time distance factors, etc. A good example of this is the CIA-DIA briefing on "Evidence of Miltary Buildup in Nicaragua" presented March 9, 1982.

The briefers include stimulating statistics like 25 "Soviet built T-55 tanks," or 12 to 16 "Cuban supplied MIGs" and then let people's imaginations run wild. The audience conjures up visions of a vast phalanx of Soviet T-55s rumbling across the plains of Western Europe or the deserts of the Middle East. They never interrupt these reveries with details about the capabilities and limitations of the equipment, the terrain, etc.

Today, however, with your permission I wish to violate the rules of military briefers. I brought with me a detailed map of the region. This is the sort of map that men engaged in mortal combat use—not the sort used in budget battles. Anyone can instantly see that Honduras has some of the most rugged topography in the region. This terrain is highly unsuited to the use of tanks. For example, if Nicaragua employed their "Soviet built T-55 tanks" in an invasion of Honduras, they would have to negotiate rises to over 7,000 feet in the vicinity of the capital, Tegucigalpa, and 9,000 feet in the western part of the country. The mountains are steep, the valleys narrow and deep and cut by rushing, rocky streams. There is only one route the T-55 could realistically follow: the Pan American Highway. Over this 290-mile route, the tanks would be easily detected by US intelligence-gathering satellites and Honduran reconnaissance aircraft. On one 30-mile stretch of road, the tanks would have to climb from about 500 feet to around 5,000 feet. The maximum gradient a T-55 can manage is 30 degrees. When I drove those twisting Honduran roads, some of them seemed at least that steep. Under optimal conditions, including level terrain, it would take 10 hours for the tanks to travel from Managua to Tegucigalpa. Given conditions, the mechanical difficulties of the T-55s, and the fact that they would be under heavy attack by the Honduran Air Force, it is virtually impossible to predict how long it would take; they probably would never make it to Tegucigalpa.

In addition to the logistical problems caused by the terrain, there are numerous

other characteristics of the T-55 that make it a less than imposing piece of armor:
- it has a loose "dead track" that is apt to shed during violent turns, rendering the tank immobile.
- internal fuel and oil supplies are supplemented by 4 light steel tanks (panniers) on the right running board of the tank and in two drums at the rear of the hull which are highly vulnerable to attack.
- the turret is so cramped that the gunner nearly sits in the commander's lap.
- the bulky D-107 gun takes up a large portion of the turret space and further congestion is caused by a ready rack of ammunition storage along the rear wall.
- space in the tank is so cramped that it is impracticable to crew the vehicle with troops taller than 5 foot 5 inches.
- this cramping is made worse because the T-55 is filled on the inside with small fittings and brackets that regularly inflict the crew with cuts and bruises.
- the loader's turret cavity is so small that he must remain seated or crouched. The gun ammunition weighs over 50 pounds and is difficult to handle under the best of circumstances. Not only does the T-55 loader have to maneuver these heavy rounds in a very cramped space, he must ram them home with his left hand.
- turret space is so limited that only three rounds can be carried in the turret. Once these rounds are expended, the loader must perform acrobatics in order to acquire ammunition from the racks at his feet.
- the interior of the T-55 is so small that the gun cannot be reloaded unless it is fully elevated.Once a round has been fired, the gun must be elevated, reloaded, and resighted.
- the average rate of fire is only four rounds per minute.
- the T-55 has no air conditioning system, a definite drawback in the tropics.
- T-55s have a notably shorter service life than Western tanks as they are designed to be expended on the battlefield and replaced with freshly equipped units.
- workmanship of the T-55 is sometimes so poor as to require vehicle overhaul even before the tank has been issued to the troops.
- engine overheating caused by poorly machined oil lines has sometimes limited effective engine life to only about 100 hours.
- transmissions in the T-55 have never been a strong point and the clutch accounts for 40 of the mechanical breakdowns alone.
- Western defense analysts estimate the effective range of a T-55 is less than 100-125 miles before a serious mechanical failure.
- the great force required to steer the tank without hydraulic boosting causes driver fatigue and would seriously hamper a small driver under trying combat conditions.
- T-55s are especially dangerous when the gyrostabilizer is turned on and the vehicle is in motion. While tracking a target, the gun breech and turret can unexpectedly swing about, pinioning or crushing the loader if he does not nimbly dodge it. Due to this and other technical deficiencies, the T-55 has virtually no fire-on-the-move capability.

As I remarked to the Sandinista *comandante,* "With friends who would supply you T-55s, who needs enemies?"

Doubtless the Sandinistas would accompany the T-55s with the 12 "Soviet built BTR-60 Armored Personnel Carriers," which can each carry two crewmen and eight troops. Thus, the Sandinistas would have only 96 troops to ward off Honduran ground forces. In addition, a Sandinista armored thrust would face intense attack from the Honduran Air Force. The Sandinistas' two T-33 and three T-28 aircraft are incapable of providing their tanks the essential air cover needed for a successful attack. My point is simply that the utility of the Soviet-supplied armor in a ground war in Central America is very limited. These facts were not pointed out by Inman and Hughes during the March 1982 briefing.

In fact, my assessment of Nicaraguan military power leads me to believe that the capabilities of the Sandinistas have been deliberately exaggerated by the Reagan administration during this briefing and on other occasions. As it is with the T-55, so it is with many other elements of the Sandinista arsenal. Many of the weapons are either ill-suited to the region, outmoded, or in a state of disrepair. This is particularly true of the logistical infrastructure needed to sustain a protracted war. There is only one oil refinery—highly vulnerable to attack—and two large-capacity fuel storage tanks, one of which was cracked in the 1972 earthquake. One can only conclude that the Reagan administration is distorting the facts in order to justify covert operations aimed at overthrowing the Sandinistas and an unprecedented military buildup in Honduras.

Across the border, in Honduras, the military's capability looks rosier at first blush. The Honduran Air Force has been almost completely reequipped since the war with El Salvador in 1969 and, while by US standards its equipment is modest, it has become the most formidable air power in Central America relative to its neighbors.

The Air Force now possesses:
- 20 Super Mystere B-2 jet fighter-bombers (approximate combat range: 400 miles/armament: 6,500 lbs. general capacity—unconfirmed).
- 10 F-86 Sabre Jet fighter-bombers (combat range: 460 miles/armament: four 20 mm cannons, 2,000 lbs. bombs, 2 Sidewinder missiles).
- 5 A-37B Dragonfly ground attack bombers (combat range: 400 miles/armament: 7.62 Minigun in forward fuselage and 4,100 lbs. bombs). (The Pentagon expected Honduras to purchase additional A-37B and T-37B aircraft in FY-82 but purchase/delivery not confirmed at this writing.)
- 24 T-28 Trojan trainer-bombers, a number of which are armed and available for ground attack missions (combat range: 500 miles/armament: undetermined at this writing. Typical load is two 50 caliber machine guns, two 750 lb. bombs, and two 2.75 in. rocket pods).
- 3 RT-33A reconnaissance aircraft.
- 23 UH-1H and UH-19D utility transport helicopters (combat radius: approximately 125 miles with 14 passengers).
- In addition the Air Force has a menagerie of obsolescent/modern trainers/transport/liaison aircraft.

General Álvarez is now arguing that his Air Force must receive 12 Northrup F-5

E/F fighters to meet its security obligations. Who will finance the $120-million price tag is a question that will soon be put to you Congressmen.

What will the formidable Honduran Air Force find when it attacks Nicaragua? First, it will find a few, but not many, lucrative military targets: port facilities at Corinto, Puerto Cabezas and Bluefields; a couple of oil tanks at Corinto; one oil refinery near Managua; four airfields, only one of which is really significant, a tank park and 49 military garrisons, many of which are so small that the Honduran pilots will have difficulty locating them. For example, the "military garrison" near Somoto, where I stopped for lunch, was comprised of two small buildings and a one-vehicle lean-to maintenance shed. The city of Managua doesn't offer much of a target either; after the 1972 earthquake most of Managua already resembles a bombed-out city. Theoretically, in one day the Honduran Air Force should be able to heavily damage most or all of the primary military targets. Surely you would think they could finish the job on the second day and then take on the secondary targets. But there are snags in the scenario.

The Honduran Air Force will also encounter the Nicaraguan air defense system. Since Nicaragua does not really possess an air force and Honduras has a relatively large one, it is only logical that Nicaragua would deploy anti-aircraft missiles and guns. My information is that the Soviet Union supplied SA-6 Gainful surface-to-air anti-aircraft missile systems to Nicaragua in early 1982. This system is very similar to that of the American Hawk. The Gainful's maximum range at high altitude is possibly 32 miles, at low altitude probably 16 miles. Its maximum altitude is about 53,000 feet. The quantity of SA-6s is unknown but I am told they are in widespread use. Inside the SA-6 envelope the Honduran pilots will run into anti-aircraft gunfire. The CIA-DIA briefing called the 57-mm guns anti-tank guns, but I had better remind the Hondurans that these guns have a dual capability of engaging air or ground targets. They have a maximum vertical range (High Explosive) of about 25,000 feet and an effective vertical range of approximately 12,500 feet. If the Honduran pilots elude these defenses, they must still escape the SA-7 Grail (once known as Strela) man-portable infra-red homing, light anti-aircraft missile. This system is very similar to that of the American Redeye. Its range is about five miles.

I am aware that the Israelis have provided training for Honduran pilots so they must know that suppression of SA-6 batteries proved to be among the most costly air missions of the 1973 Arab-Israeli war. The Israelis relied heavily on American Electronic Counter Measures (ECM) equipment and techniques and developed maneuvers to neutralize the SA-6. Nevertheless, about 40 percent of Israeli Air Force losses were due to the SA-6. I doubt that the Hondurans have sophisticated American ECM equipment or that they are likely to get it, and I know they do not have the combat skills of Israeli pilots. How many Honduran pilots will be able to run the gauntlet of SA-6s, 57-mm guns and SA-7s? I would suspect that they would be few in number.

As I understand, the United States is now providing $21 million* to improve

---

*Later cut to $13 million—EDS. (*Diario las Americas,* October 6, 1982.)

airfields and storage facilities at La Mesa, Palmerola and Golosán airfields in Honduras and airfields in Colombia for US use "in the event of an emergency." This brings me back to the question of why all the Honduran military that I talked to predict that the war will start in December. Optimally, General Álvarez should wait until the United States has "prepositioned" air munitions and fuel at these airfields before he orders a surprise air attack against Nicaragua. He could then assure ample "resupply" by "nationalizing" US air munitions and fuel. Doubtless, the United States would chide him for such an act, but would not intervene.

But the time when US air munitions and fuel are stored in Honduras is hopefully some time off and General Álvarez seems to be under personal pressure—from some of the Honduran military and the US government—to engage in a war with Nicaragua in the near future. So why do Honduran military officers think the war will start in December? "Because," they say, "the rainy season will be over and the Río Coco will be down. That is when Nicaragua will attack." In fact, the Río Coco does not recede until late April. But by the middle of December the skies have cleared and provide ideal weather for air operations. Perhaps that is why the Honduran military "expect" a Nicaraguan attack in December. How much of this is *macho braggadocio*? I cannot be sure right now. They seem to think that the US military expect to hear these claims.

Turning to ground forces, the CIA-DIA estimate that Nicaragua now has 20,000 regular troops and a militia of 50,000 people. They believe Nicaragua's goal is to create a standing army of 25,000 to 30,000 and a ready-reserve militia of between 100,000 and 150,000. But this goal will not be reached in the short term.

My information is that Honduras now has 15,050 regular military personnel (Army: 12,800, Navy: 850, and Air Force: 1,400) and 3,500 police. To this must be added the 3,000-5,000 Somocistas and counterrevolutionaries who are operating from Honduran territory. Additionally the Honduran Army has 17 of the finest, most reliable Armored Combat Reconnaissance Vehicles in the world: the British-made Scorpion. It can race along at 72 Km/h, has a 400 Km range and mounts a 67-mm gun and two 7.62 machine guns. A C-130 transport aircraft can carry two of them so they could be moved to the Miskitu coast in a matter of hours. By comparison the Nicaraguans' T-55s would have to travel over 300 miles of marginal/unpaved roads—half of which are mountain roads. If the T-55s could maintain maximum speed (30 MPH) on such roads—and not break down—the trip would require 10 hours. At half that speed it would take 20 hours, etc.

But the Hondurans should not be sanguine about this advantage in tracked vehicles. The Sandinistas have purchased 7,000 SS-11 (range: 3,000 meters) and SS-12 (range: 6,000 meters) anti-tank missiles from France. They also possess unknown quantities of Soviet supplied AT-1 and AT-3 anti-tank missiles.

In the final analysis of Honduran and Nicaraguan tracked vehicles one can only conclude that their capability in offensive combat is limited and is counterbalanced by defensive anti-tank weapons. Their real usefulness lies in internal crowd control in their major cities.

The analysis outlined above indicates a situation in which the armed forces of the two nations have different areas of strength and weakness but the overall effect is a balance of force in the realm of more sophisticated armaments. While the Honduran Air Force is markedly superior to Nicaragua's, the Nicaraguan air defense offsets this advantage. And while the Nicaraguans may have a slight advantage in heavy armored vehicles (tanks), this equipment is of limited effectiveness in the region and of inferior quality. The projected US-financed arms buildup to Honduras could tip this balance, and would likely elicit a countervailing reaction from Nicaragua. In both cases, poor nations are being forced to divert scarce resources from social and economic development into costly and increasingly lethal military hardware.

At present, the most volatile areas likely to erupt into full-scale combat are located along the Río Coco near the Miskitu coast and in the mountainous border area of northwest Nicaragua. Of these two areas, it is the isolated Miskitu region that seems to be the focal point of the conflict.

In August, USAF C-130's from the Southern Command in Panama flew a battalion of Honduran troops and their equipment into Puerto Lempira (ostensibly as part of an exercise). The Honduran battalion is now headquartered in Mocorán, about 15 miles north of the Nicaraguan border. Allegedly its mission is to prevent a Nicaraguan incursion into the Miskitu Indian camp located in Mocorán.

Perhaps the battalion is not meant so much to protect the Miskitus as to confine them. Information reaching me is that many of the older people want very much to reach an accord with the Sandinistas and return to Nicaragua. It is the young bucks who want to continue to fight and need to keep the Miskitus in Mocorán for cover and recruits.

It is no coincidence most of the counterrevolutionary military bands operating in the area are also entrenched in the vicinity of Mocorán. In actuality the Honduran battalion provides a protective screen for the Somocistas and counterrevolutionaries returning from terrorist incursions into the Miskitu coast of Nicaragua. The battalion's presence in Mocorán provides an excellent means of arming and equipping the counterrevolutionaries. Who, in that forsaken region, can keep an accurate account and control of weapons, ammunition, radios, etc. which are supplied to the battalion? How many of them reach the hands of the Somocistas?

And since our ambassadorial family in Honduras has taken a personal humanitarian interest in the Miskitu Indians in Mocorán it seems that ample food, medicine, clothing, etc. is being flown into the area. How much of this material reaches the counterrevolutionaries? Would that the same humanitarian interest was shown for the Salvadoran refugees at Mesa Grande.

Perhaps the biggest question in everyone's mind is how much coordination goes on between the battalion and the counterrevolutionaries. Do they orchestrate operations, share communications, etc? And just how much is the United States involved? At this point it is impossible to answer these questions definitively. Dr. Thomas P. Anderson, in testimony before this Subcommittee, asserted that highly placed sources within the State Department had confirmed the existence of direct US covert intervention against the Sandinista government. Given the history of US intervention in Chile, Guatemala and Cuba—not to mention Nicaragua itself—these reports are entirely credible and Mocorán is a likely element in this strategy.

One possible scenario for the outbreak of a conflict between Nicaragua and Honduras is the following. If Sandinista troops or militia are in hot pursuit of a counterrevolutionary group that is escaping back into Honduras, they must break off their pursuit at the border. If they do not, they will likely confront a unit of the Honduran Regular Army. That confrontation would be an act of war.

I would like to make one final comment about the internal situation in Honduras. When asked if significant leftist guerrilla organizations currently operate within their country, most of the Hondurans I talked to—military and civilian—say No. Clearly, however, many Hondurans fear that the political violence which characterizes El Salvador and Guatemala will spread to Honduras. Many are also leery of the Sandinista experiment that is transpiring across the border. Perhaps their greatest source of concern is that their nascent democracy, unfolding under the watchful eye of the military, will be snuffed out by the armed forces. US military aid strengthens the hands of those who are most likely to terminate democratic government in the country. Significant divisions exist within the Honduran military regarding the conflict in Nicaragua, involvement in El Salvador's civil war and the future of democratic rule. This is evident in the statement by Colonel Leónidas Torres Arias on August 31 in Mexico City in which he condemned the intent of Gen. Álvarez and other hardliners to lead Honduras into a war with Nicaragua.

Such a war would truly be a "war without winners." It seems a terrible price to pay for this administration's determination to seek a military solution to what are deep-seated social, economic and political problems. Such a war could easily spark off a regional conflagration involving all the nations of Central America, and perhaps the US and Mexico—on opposing sides. It would exact a terrible price from the people of Honduras and Nicaragua, and stain the name of the United States in the eyes of all Latin America and the world.

11. Peace Efforts in Central America and the US Response*

By Peter Crabtree

Over the past two years Central America has developed an increasingly explosive potential. The current worldwide recession has shaken the region's agro-export economic base, further aggravating social tensions. Popular struggles in El Salvador and Guatemala are visible evidence of social crises originating in decades

---

*Reprinted from *Nicaraguan Perspectives*, Number 5, Winter 1983.

of harsh military rule imposed by US foreign policy imperatives. There is a direct relationship between these backward political structures and a narrow concentration of economic benefits, as well as social and moral breakdown. Costa Rica's economic collapse is merely indicative of the larger economic crisis: reliable estimates indicate that the region will require as much as $20 billion in international transfer payments over the course of the present decade in order to preserve economic stability.

This complex, delicate regional situation requires tactful political solutions involving all relevant political forces. Resolution of border tensions between Nicaragua and Honduras is also of highest priority. It is important therefore to examine the record of the past two years in order to identify the openings for and the blocks impeding the peaceful resolution of regional conflict.

Chronology of Key Events, 1981-1982
February 1981

US State Department releases a "white paper" depicting Nicaragua as the epicenter for arms traffic to Salvadoran insurgents.

The US government begins a process of cutting off all economic loans and credits to Nicaragua.

Nicaragua calls for joint Honduran-Nicaraguan border patrols to curb any arms flow or suspected arms flow.

March 1981

Parade magazine discloses that ex-Somoza guardsmen are being trained in the US for paramilitary attacks on Nicaragua. (See Reading 29 in this volume.)

April 1981

In an official government communiqué Nicaragua protests US aid cuts and the threat of paramilitary aggression being prepared on US soil. Nicaragua also "reiterates its hope of having respectful and stable relations with all countries in the world, including the United States. We reaffirm our wish that the Central American area become a zone of peace and security."

Nicaraguan government urges Honduran government to halt paramilitary attacks on Nicaragua originating from Honduras. Honduran President Policarpo Paz agrees to meet with Nicaraguan government coordinator Daniel Ortega.

May 1981

General Policarpo Paz and Daniel Ortega meet in Guasaule, Nicaragua to discuss border tensions. Paz promises to restrain paramilitary supporters in the Honduran army.

Sergio Ramírez, a member of Nicaragua's governing junta, meets with Costa

Rican President Carazo Odio in San José. The two agree to strengthen peaceful relations between the two countries.

June 1981

In apparent response to widespread rejection of US charges against Nicaragua contained in February "white paper," Secretary of State Haig raises new charges that Nicaragua has received Soviet tanks, Press criticism of "white paper" allegations stops.

The Nicaraguan interior minister and the Costa Rican security minister sign a joint declaration establishing a base of peace and respect between the two countries.

August 1981

After repeated requests by Nicaragua for talks with US officials about improving US–Nicaraguan relations, President Reagan sends Assistant Secretary of State for Latin America Thomas Enders for discussions in Managua. While Enders is tight-lipped after the meetings, the Nicaraguan Foreign Minister Miguel D'Escoto expresses optimism. "It is premature to judge the American intentions," D'Escoto tells reporters. "We are committed to and continue to be committed to bettering the increasingly deteriorating relationship with the United States. We have made it a priority to make every effort to reach an understanding, a *modus vivendi,* with the United States," D'Escoto adds.

Honduras grants permission to the US to build a military base in the Gulf of Fonseca, a body of water shared by Nicaragua, Honduras and El Salvador.

September 1981

France and Mexico issue a joint declaration recognizing the FDR/FMLN as a "representative political force" in El Salvador.

FDR president Guillermo Ungo travels to the US to "test international reaction" to the French-Mexican declaration. Ungo declares that "the door is now open" for talks with the United States.

US State Department officials respond that the declaration will not cause the United States to re-evaluate its opposition to negotiations.

Joint US-Honduran military maneuvers are held.

October 1981

Nicaragua government coordinator Daniel Ortega addresses the United Nations General Assembly in support of a peace plan for El Salvador through negotiations without preconditions.

Nicaraguan Ambassador to the US Arturo Cruz reiterates his country's desire for a "positive and harmonious" relationship with the US. Cruz declares that "Nicaragua has not and will not permit its sovereign territory to be used as a staging point for any direct or indirect military intervention in the affairs of El Salvador, or of any other country." Cruz adds that Nicaragua "is completely and totally committed to a peaceful solution to the tragic internal conflict" in El Salvador. "The government of Nicaragua has fully endorsed the joint French-Mexican proposal for a peaceful and negotiated solution in El Salvador."

November 1981

Reagan administration intensifies charges and threats against Nicaragua. Secretary of State Haig tells members of Congress that Nicaragua is becoming a powerful totalitarian state which threatens US interests and refuses to rule out military action against Nicaragua.

Regular Honduran troops attack the Nicaragua border post at Guasaule on two separate occasions using machine guns and mortars.

Nicaraguan Foreign Minister D'Escoto, in communiqués with his Honduran counterpart, protests attacks on Nicaragua, noting that "provocations of this nature only tend to obstruct the efforts made by Nicaragua to lessen the tensions in Central America and avoid them between our two countries." D'Escoto urgently requests the Honduran government to honor the May 1981 agreements for continued dialogue and cooperation.

December 1981

President Reagan authorizes a $19 million CIA-directed plan for paramilitary and terrorist operations against Nicaragua. In apparent initial implementation of this plan, terrorist attacks, code-named "Red Christmas," are launched in Nicaragua's remote northeast border area. Other immediate targets of attack are Nicaragua's only oil refinery and cement plant.

January 1982

After meetings with US Under-Secretary of State James Buckley in San José, Costa Rica, the foreign ministers of Costa Rica, El Salvador, and Honduras announce the "surprise" formation of the "Central American Democratic Community." Nicaragua, Panama, and other Central American governments are conspicuously excluded from the meeting.

February 1982

At a meeting of Latin American political parties (COPPAL) in Managua, Mexican President López Portillo proposes a regional peace plan with three main points: the United States should cease its threats and military actions against Nicaragua; if the paramilitary units operating from Honduras are disbanded,

Nicaragua should reduce the size of its armed forces; the various affected countries should enter into mutual non-aggression pacts.

The Nicaraguan government welcomes López Portillo's proposals; the US response is uncertain.

March 1982

The US government launches a major public relations effort to demonstrate the threat posed by Nicaragua. The effort fails to demonstrate that Nicaraguan military dispositions are anything more than defensive.

The Mexican government announces that US-Nicaraguan negotiations will begin in April in Mexico City; the State Department immediately responds that the Mexican announcement is "premature."

Speaking before the U.N. Security Council, Nicaraguan government coordinator Daniel Ortega denounces the paramilitary attacks on his country. (See Reading 1.) Ortega tells reporters that Nicaragua would welcome immediate and unconditional negotiations with the US.

April 1982

The US and Nicaragua exchange negotiating positions. US official Stephen Bosworth denies that the State Department is footdragging on possible negotiations.

Despite Nicaraguan readiness to negotiate, the US stalls. A US official tells the *New York Times* that "we want to do some more probing to make sure that they're serious."

May 1982

Mexican officials express pessimism about the likelihood of US-Nicaraguan talks.

A US official tells the *New York Times* that "as you know, we were cool to the Mexican initiative from the beginning, but we were effectively ambushed by Congress and public opinion. We had to agree to negotiate or appear unreasonable."

July 1982

Paramilitary attacks on Nicaragua increase dramatically.

Joint US-Honduran military maneuvers are held near Nicaragua's remote northeast border. US planes move equipment and a battalion of Honduran troops to a new permanent base in the border area.

August 1982

Nicaraguan government reiterates its desire for talks with the US. Nicaragua proposes that the negotiating points of each side last spring be the basis for initiating talks.

September 1982

The Presidents of Mexico and Venezuela send an appeal to the heads of state of Honduras, Nicaragua, and the United States which calls for an "exploration of ways that remain open to halt the worrying escalation" of the crisis. 106 members of Congress endorse the proposal.

Lt. Col. John Buchanan, USMC (Ret.), briefs a House subcommittee on the critical border tension between Honduras and Nicaragua. (See Reading 10.) In a detailed analysis on Nicaragua's military capability, Buchanan describes Nicaragua's "military buildup" as defensive in nature. Buchanan also warns of a possible Honduran invasion of Nicaragua in December.

Buchanan states that his assessment of the Nicaraguan military leads him to conclude that the capabilities of the Sandinistas have been deliberately exaggerated by the Reagan administration. "One can only conclude that the Reagan administration is distorting the facts in order to justify covert operations aimed at overthrowing the Sandinistas and an unprecedented military buildup in Honduras," says Buchanan.

October 1982

In an apparent attempt to blunt the Mexican-Venezuelan peace initiative, the Reagan administration backs a "forum for peace and democracy" in San José, Costa Rica. Nicaragua is excluded from the forum, and Mexico and Venezuela decline to attend.

November 1982

Newsweek reveals extensive details of the US paramilitary war on Nicaragua. (See Reading 30.) US officials confirm that the operation is intended to "keep Managua off balance and apply pressure."

During a visit to Washington, Costa Rican President Monge warns President Reagan of the dangers of current US policies in the region. Reagan responds with a polite silence.

December 1982

US President Reagan designs his Latin American trip to include visits with the leaders of all three countries neighboring Nicaragua. Nicaraguan leader Sergio Ramírez points out that US diplomats continue to refuse to see high-level Sandinistas officials. The US has still not responded to Nicaragua's last diplomatic note of August 1982 urging peace talks. The US also continues to oppose peace talks between

Nicaragua and Honduras.

As the chronology reveals, efforts by various countries to promote negotiations and political solutions in the region have thus far been unsuccessful. One explantion for this failure was offered by Wayne S. Smith, former chief of the US Interests Section in Havana: "the [US] administration has denigrated negotiations and grossly misanalyzed the situation in Central America. Initially, it insisted that conflicts there were not internal . . . incredibly, at one point the administration even suggested that there was 'no native insurgency' in El Salvador." Such thinking has led the US administration to block negotiations and pursue "total military victory."

Chapter III:

Drifting Toward Totalitarianism?

Editors' Introduction

The National State of Emergency that was declared by the Nicaraguan Junta on September 9, 1981, was a response to a very real crisis, consisting of external attacks, internal sabotage, and economic destabilization. The Reagan administration has, however, described it as "drifting toward totalitarianism," and likened it to a "state of siege." The latter is a relatively common occurrence in Latin America, in which all civil rights are suspended, curfews are declared, and arrest or disappearance without due process is routine. As the first reading in this chapter indicates, the Nicaraguan State of Emergency falls far short of these measures, although it does impose prior censorship of the newspapers. At the time of this writing, the State of Emergency is still in effect, having been renewed every thirty days since it was imposed.

It is frequently noted in the popular media and by the Reagan administration that the Nicaraguan government has "postponed" elections. The implication is that this action is antidemocratic or "totalitarian," and that "free elections" will be delayed forever. In reality, the government agreed in 1980 to hold elections in 1985, a target date which it has steadfastly maintained. It is interesting to note that in similar situations, both the United States and Mexico waited considerably longer before holding their first national elections.

While it would be a relatively simple matter to offer the sort of cosmetic elections that are customary in nearby countries like El Salvador, the Nicaraguan government insists that it is intent on developing an electoral system that treats all of its citizens fairly, regardless of differences in economic status. Central to this process is the proposed "Law of Political Parties," which will define the grounds for participation in future elections.

The final topic taken up by this chapter is the highly sensitive issue of the Miskitu Indians of Nicaragua's Atlantic Coast.

12. The State of National Emergency: Background, Causes and Implementation

By the Instituto Histórico Centroamericano

The Instituto Histórico Centroamericano *is a Jesuit-affiliated research institute based in Managua, Nicaragua.*

Background

In September of 1981, the government of National Reconstruction enacted the Measures of Economic and Social Emergency. This was done in response to the economic crisis in the country at that time, which had deteriorated during the previous months.

At that time the external political threats and pressures were not as evident. On the other hand, the gravity of the economic problems, which could damage the reconstruction and the programmed recuperation, were viewed with great concern.

The Measures of Economic and Social Emergency decided upon by the Sandinista government attempted to resolve the deficits in production and productivity which were becoming chronic: e.g., the reluctance of the private sector to reinvest their earnings in the country, the speculative attitudes on the part of businesses, and the alarming increase in decapitalization. Another of its purposes was to prevent certain damaging factors like labor strikes or work stoppages (which during the '79–'81 period had caused the loss of 1 billion 500 million córdobas; one córdoba equals $0.10 US), absenteeism, state bureaucracy, low output, etc. from being used detrimentally.

The measures of economic and social emergency attempted to consolidate national unity and were directed at different groups and social sectors in order to strengthen the mixed economy and achieve a collective and multisector resolution of the crisis.

In retrospect, these measures were a partial answer to a situation of a limited nature. The State of National Emergency decreed this past 15th of March incorporates and goes beyond the limits of the September decisions. It was enacted in response to a different situation because the country is now facing a host of other problems.

While it is true that since January of 1981, with the victory of the Reagan administration in the US elections, the tone toward Nicaragua has become more harsh, until September of '81 this "hard-line policy" had been manifested principally in the cut-offs of credit for development projects and the purchase of basic foods.

In March of 1981, Commander Bayardo Arce publicly explained the policies of the Reagan administration and the dangerous consequences of the Santa Fe Document (which had been written by several of Reagan's advisors, and was indicative of an interventionist policy in Latin American affairs). But this strategy of interference, whose actions were still being prepared, was not yet evident in the political-military arena. In October of 1981, with the joint North American-Honduran maneuvers (Eagle's View) in territorial waters of Honduras, very close to Nicaragua, a new concern began to show itself and this acquired considerable dimensions in December of '81 and January of '82 with the first information of the plots against Nicaragua.

It is within that framework that the National government named 1982 the year of "Unity in the Face of Aggression." From that time, political and military events have begun to happen so rapidly that they demand a careful treatment in order to understand the National Emergency.

After the State of National Emergency was declared, Alfonso Robelo, president of the Democratic Nicaraguan Movement (MDN) and of the Democratic Coordinating Committee, as well as an influential member of COSEP, stated: "If I had been in the government Junta, I would have done the same thing." This statement surprised some of the local political media, who were even more surprised a short time later by the statement of the MDN which recognized the need to bolster the defense of the country.

The Causes behind the National Emergency

Without trying to mention all the events which led up to the State of National Emergency, we would like to give some specific examples which will demonstrate the existence of a plan to destabilize the Nicaraguan process.

A. Terrorist Acts within Nicaragua

1. A plot which tried to destroy the Cement Factory and the Oil Refinery (discovered: Dec. '81);

2. The "Red Christmas" conspiracy on the Atlantic Coast in November and December of '81;

3. A plot to destory bridges and other infrastructures in Chinandega (discovered by the State Security: Feb. '82);

4. The explosion in the A.C. Sandino Airport of Managua which caused the death of four workers (2/20/82);

5. The explosion of two bridges, one over the River Coco and the other over the River Negro (3/13/82).

B. Raids by Bands from the Border and the Training Camps

1. The existence of training camps of Somocistas within the US, in Florida and California, as well as in Honduras, which have been amply reported by the international press for several months now. In one camp alone, in El Paraíso, a department of Honduras, there are approximately 700 Somocistas.

2. The continuing penetration of these bands into Nicaraguan territory, destroying towns and killing both campesinos and militia (over 70 have died in the last few months). These raids were one of the chief reasons for the movement of the Miskitu communities from the River Coco on the Atlantic Coast. These penetrations from

Honduras include repeated attacks on border posts and customs installations, etc.

C. Regional Events and the Support of Latin American Governments

1. The increasing actions on the parts of the Honduran Navy in the Gulf of Fonseca, and now, the presence of the North American Navy destroyer CARON carrying out espionage activities;

2. The joint participation of the Salvadoran and North American governments in the removal of the Nicaraguan citizen, Orlando Tardencilla, from the prison in El Salvador to the US in order to force him to make accusations against his government, thus converting his declarations into a proof to justify open intervention into Nicaragua;

3. The training of three companies of ex-National Guard in the Panama Canal with the purpose of invading Nicaragua;

4. The presence of American troops in Costa Rica;

5. The open participation of officers of Latin American dictatorships, principally Argentina, in the training of ex-National Guard; the financial support for the counterrevolutionary bands and the maintenance of an air-bridge between Argentina, Panama and El Salvador in order to intervene in Central America. This support of the Somocista bands by Latin American dictators, as well as the support of the governments of Honduras and El Salvador, is one of the most important proofs that the Reagan administration wants to regionalize the conflict in Central America.

6. The explosion of the Aeronica plane, by Somocistas, in the airport in Mexico.

D. Direct US Intervention Activities in Nicaragua

1. The electronic circle planned by the Southern Command from the Canal Zone, which was completed in November of '81, and which permits the control and interference of all internal communications in Nicaragua;

2. The 40 violations of Nicaraguan air space by North American military planes between July '81 and the 11th of March '82;

3. The aerial photographs taken by American planes of strategic Nicaraguan places (which were shown publicly in Press Conferences given in the US to accuse Nicaragua); etc.

North American Press Reports

Also significant is the form in which some North American newspapers have analyzed the situation in Nicaragua.

On the 10th of March, 1982, the *Washington Post* published an article (based on one from February) confirming the approval of a $19 million CIA fund for use, among other things, for the training of 500 persons (which could be later increased to 1500) who would work for the destabilization of Nicaragua. This article mentions "... as a part of this plan the commandos would eventually attempt to *destroy essential Nicaraguan targets like electrical plants and bridges* in an effort to affect the economy and divert the attention and the resources of the government."(The emphasis is ours.)

Three days after the publication of this article, on the 13th of March, an explosion occurred which destroyed the bridges over the River Coco and the River Negro (one partially, the other totally).

The Decree of National Emergency
and Its Juridical Significance

There are two basic laws in Nicaragua: *The Fundamental Statute of the Republic,* decreed the 20th of July, 1979, which is the legal instrument by which the Political Constitution, the Constitutional Laws, and the other structures in force during the Somocista dictatorship were eradicated. It is a very basic and general statute which has only three articles of fundamental principles (human rights, freedom of conscience and freedom of religion). It also structures the State Powers (the Junta of the Government, the Council of State, etc.). The Statute on the Rights and Guarantees of Nicaraguans (decree number 52 of the government Junta) published the 15th of August, 1979, is a specific law of the rights of Nicaraguans.

The Law of National Emergency suspends the Statute on the Rights and Guarantees of Nicaraguans with the exception of article 49, clause 2. Article 49 legislates exceptional or emergency situations which might place the stability of the nation in danger. Even clause 2 does not authorize the suspension of some basic rights and guarantees expressed in articles 5, 6, and 7 (which refer to servitude), article 12 (paragraph 1), article 14, and article 17 (paragraph 1), article 19, and article 26. The articles which remain in force establish: respect for life, the physical, psychological and moral integrity of the person, the repeal of torture and cruel treatment, such as the death penalty; that crimes committed before the law was enforced cannot be judged under the new law; that one cannot be imprisoned because of being unable to pay economic debts; the recognition of personhood and the juridical capacity of each person; liberty of thought, conscience and religion, and the right of all persons to have a nationality.

The State of National Emergency suspends almost 45 articles (in its juridical application); in practice its implementation is highly flexible and these suspensions are relative. In effect, the State of National Emergency does not mean the radical suspension of these articles, but rather it gives the government the authority to regulate the rights and guarantees according to the gravity of the threat or a military intervention.

In Nicaragua there is no gradual classification of exceptional laws as for example: State of Alarm, State of Alert, State of Emergency, State of Siege, State of War. Therefore, the situation brought about by the decree of the Law of National Emergency is the only one that exists at this level and the application on the part of the government is flexible according to the circumstances.

Thus, in practice, the great majority of rights and guarantees of Nicaraguans are still in force: e.g. freedom of expression, the freedom to hold meetings, the freedom of movement, etc.

Three important elements of this law should be singled out:

—The State of National Emergency cancels the Measures of Economic and Social Emergency of September 9, 1982;

—The State of National Emergency does not establish a curfew nor Martial Law;

—The State of National Emergency is of a transitory nature. In principle it is for 30 days. According to the law: "The suspension can be put into practice for a limited time which is renewable according to the prevailing circumstances in the country."

Life in Nicaragua under the State of National Emergency during the First 15 Days

An account of some of the aspects of life in Nicaragua these last two weeks should bring about a better understanding of the practical implications of the National Emergency.

Trade Unions. The functioning of unions as well as the central offices of the unions, union freedoms and rights are still in force. In these days, an increase in union work and the participation of the unions in the productive activities has been noted. On the 17th of March, a meeting of representatives of all the unions was held to analyze the new situation.

On the 28th of March, the Minister of Justice, Ernesto Castillo, said: "Labor laws and relations between workers and employers are still in force, even though decisions which affect the State of National Emergency cannot be taken. Trade agreements, work demands, and union meetings are still in effect; nevertheless, these could be affected in the event that the Junta of the government of National Reconstruction would call for a massive integration of business workers to the national defense."

The Minister of Justice has the automony to decide which demands or requests affect the National Emergency and which do not.

Political Life. The activity of the political parties has been maintained. Party positions have appeared in the newspapers in these days, not only from the Patriotic Front of the Revolution (allied to the FSLN), but also from the opposition. On the 25th of March, *Barricada* (the official newspaper of the FSLN) published a Communiqué from the Ramiro Sacasa Coordinating Committee, which is a nucleus of political and trade union organizations of the opposition.

Religious Life. Religious practices and public religious acts have functioned normally. The activities in preparation for Holy Week, which have large repercussions in the Christian community, are going on with the same interest and level of participation as in previous years.

Cultural Life. Cultural activities (theaters, movies, etc.) are continuing as usual. On the 18th of March, a recital was presented by the Poet Carlos Martínez Rivas in the Edgard Munguía Theater. The 20th of March, an important assembly of Cultural Workers was held which decreed the "Cultural Emergency," meaning the permanent mobilization of this sector. The following day, a recital of Poetry Workshops was held in the Tiscapa Amphitheater. The Latin American Day of Artisans was celebrated and an event was organized by the Association of Sandinista Children in which they rolled 2,000 white barrels through the street to demonstrate the desires of peace of the Nicaraguan children.

Military Life. An increase of troop mobilization has been noted these days on the highways heading to the north of the country. There has also been a larger mobilization of the popular militia. In this second case, the reason, however, is the formation of a new group of militia, which had already been programmed.

There are no special controls on the highways nor are there searches of private houses. Neither has a curfew been imposed.

On the 19th of March, the Secretary of Migration and Foreigners stated that no restrictions exist for entering or leaving the country. This applies as much for Nicaraguan citizens as for foreigners. All the measures to obtain passports and visas are still in effect.

Information. In this area modifications have occurred. Some radio programs must be authorized by the Communication Media Secretary. The newspapers are subject to the same control. Their publications must be presented beforehand so that they are controlled by this same Secretary. All the newspapers and weeklies are open: *Barricada, La Prensa, Nuevo Diario, Tayacan, La Semana Cómica,* etc. Since the Law of National Emergency was decreed, the *Nuevo Diario* was sanctioned with a one day closure for its edition of the 16th of March that called the State of National Emergency a State of Siege. The opposition newspaper *La Prensa* has appeared regularly except on two occasions (the 24th and the 28th of March) when it was not published by decision of the Director who said that there had not been sufficient time to print it after it had been returned from the Communication Media Control.

Possibly, the office most affected by the Law of National Emergency is that of the Communication Media Control.

The government's objective is to avoid distortions of the media which could act against the process of reconstruction and the interests and defense of the nation.

Conclusions

The North American representative on the Security Council of the United Nations, Jeane Kirkpatrick, said in a session on the 25th of March, that the State of National Emergency in Nicaragua was part of the paranoia of the Sandinistas and an instrument to guarantee the repression of the democratic sectors of the opposition. (See Reading 2.)

The Reagan administration and some multinational news media have tried to demonstrate that the decision of the Nicaraguan government expresses a "totalitarian" tendency and is a violation of human rights.

If we analyze the actual situation of Nicaragua we can't find any manifestations of totalitarianism. The people, and even sectors clearly opposed to the government, find that the Law of National Emergency is a justified and necessary response. In other words, the opinions of the different sectors of the country ratified the decision of the government and the validity of the law. It is not, therefore, a measure taken behind the backs of the people in the country or which goes against the interests of the majority.

It is also important to differentiate the State of National Emergency decreed in

Nicaragua with the emergencies and States of Siege which have existed on the Latin American continent in many countries for years (9 years in Chile, 8 years in Argentina, more than 25 years in Paraguay, and even higher figures in Colombia) and which are, without doubt, a show of totalitarianism and terrorism imposed by those governments. While in those Latin American countries, the exceptional laws have arisen from internal causes, in order to quiet protest or popular rebellion, in Nicaragua, the State of National Emergency arose as a response to external causes expressed in the threats and interventions of the Reagan administration and their allies on the continent. In the case of Nicaragua, unlike the other countries, it is to defend the national integrity and the basic rights of the people.

This difference in causes underlies the great difference in its implementation. The Latin American dictatorial regimes have converted the "exception" into the essential elements of their governments. And to do that they have institutionalized repression, torture, curfews, martial law, death squads, etc.

The government of Nicaragua has used the Law of National Emergency as a transitory means to respond to an extremely grave situation created from outside, as well as to control the action of the counterrevolutionary bands of ex-Somocista National Guard. They are the conscious actors in the global political campaign of destabilization which has been launched by the United States.

The paranoia to which Jeane Kirkpatrick alludes is not a collective psychological phenomenon but it is the real fear which arises from the historic experience of Latin America and Nicaragua.

After living more than four centuries dependent on foreign powers and being victims of permanent interventions by these same powers, it is logical that when one of these countries moves to develop their national independence the superpower is not disposed to accept it. Nicaragua has had repeated military interventions from the US and the collective memory is incorporated in the actual national reconstruction, which will permit no vacillations. The Law of National Emergency is not the result of a "Sandinista paranoia" but rather the product of valid reasons and the collective memory of the Nicaraguan people.

It is to be hoped that this situation of National Emergency is transitory. A good sign is that it has only been decreed for 30 days. But it is necessary to understand that the transitory nature of the Emergency depends more on the evolution of the aggressive policy of the Reagan administration than on the political will of the Sandinista leaders. Is it right to ask the government of National Reconstruction not to call for a National Emergency when, in spite of the repeated requests, the Reagan administration has never publicly denied its threats of intervention against Nicaragua?

[The State of National Emergency was still in effect as this book went to press—Eds.]

13. The Nicaraguan Media: Revolution And Beyond*

By John Spicer Nichols

For more than 40 years, the Somoza family ruled Nicaragua as its private plantation by maintaining a stranglehold on virtually every facet of national life. But the Somozas' inability to effectively suppress the opposition newspaper *La Prensa* was an essential ingredient in the collapse of the family dynasty. By July 1979, as the Somoza government fell to the Sandinista guerrillas, *La Prensa* had earned a national and international reputation for its resistance to the dictatorship.

Today, as Nicaragua attempts to recover from the revolutionary war that claimed nearly 40,000 lives, left countless more wounded or homeless, and destroyed most of the nation's productive capacity, *La Prensa* continues to have symbolic importance in the highly volatile revolutionary process. The Sandinista leadership, which is dominated by Marxists, has espoused a philosophy of political pluralism and, probably more important, badly needs the cooperation of the non-Marxist private sector in rebuilding the war-torn economy. Therefore the Sandinistas' treatment of *La Prensa,* which has become closely allied with the private sector and hostile toward the government, is a key indicator of the viability of the tense political accommodation in Nicaragua.

La Prensa was closed several times by the government in late 1981 and early 1982 and now is subject to prior censorship. These actions greatly heightened the domestic political turmoil and contributed to the deterioration of Nicaragua's foreign relations, primarily with the United States. Reagan administration officials frequently have cited the issue of *La Prensa* (along with the Nicaraguan government's support for the guerrillas in El Salvador and domestic arms buildup) as a major justification for a stern US foreign policy toward Nicaragua.

If government-press relations within Nicaragua are to be used as a barometer upon which domestic and foreign relations are based, a better understanding of media dynamics of the country certainly is needed.

Function of the Nicaraguan Mass Media

Because the Nicaraguan media have the same physical appearance as the media of North America, analysts usually assume that they also serve the same function for

---

*This paper was adapted from the author's unpublished briefing paper for The Honorable Anthony C.E. Quainton, US Ambassador to Nicaragua, and the author's chapters on the Nicaraguan media in *Nicaragua in Revolution* (Praeger, 1982) and *World Press Encyclopedia* (Facts on File, 1982). The paper also was presented to the Tenth National Meeting of the Latin American Studies Association, Washington, DC, March 3-6, 1982.

Nicaraguan society. Nothing could be further from the truth. The major North American media developed into business enterprises primarily intended to make a profit. In order to attract the largest possible audience, North American news organizations tend to critically report about power bases of all political stripes and in the process maintain political discourse between diverse sectors of a complex society.

In the less complex society of Nicaragua, the mass media have always served as political tools of powerful combatants for national power. Rather than functioning as news media intended to carry balanced and dispassionate reporting of national affairs, all Nicaraguan media are close collaborators with specialized power contenders in society, primarily political factions. As a consequence, the Nicaraguan media advocate narrow political views and agitate for change in the existing political configuration in sharp contrast to the North American media, which tend to maintain the existing power structure by offering a forum for all major power contenders.

The most obvious manifestation of the advocacy function is the vituperative criticism of political opponents in the Nicaraguan media reminiscent of the revolutionary pamphleteers in the US; however, a more important manifestation is the journalists' tendency to be active participants in political affairs instead of just reporters or commentators of those affairs. In Nicaragua, the pen and the sword tend to be one and the same.

Symbolic Importance of La Prensa and the Chamorro Family

The epitome of an advocacy journalist was Pedro Joaquín Chamorro Cardenal, the long-time editor of *La Prensa,* Nicaragua's most important newspaper. Chamorro, the product of more than a century of highly-partisan Conservative party politics, was the descendant of one of the most prominent families in Nicaragua and a long line of public figures including four Conservative presidents. Long before Chamorro gained a worldwide reputation as an opposition journalist, he had established a domestic record of political militancy. On numerous occasions, beginning when he was a university student in the 1940s, Chamorro was arrested, jailed or exiled on various charges of revolutionary activity including leading violent political demonstrations, running guns, organizing an invasion force to overthrow the government and participating in the assassination of Anastasio Somoza García, the first of the Somoza family to be Nicaraguan president.

Chamorro became editor and publisher of *La Prensa* in 1952 following the death of his father, who founded the newspaper in 1930 as a voice of the Conservative platform and opposition to the Somoza-controlled Liberal Party. After the mid-1960s, most of Chamorro's political opposition was less overt and was channeled through *La Prensa* and Unión Democrática de Liberación, a coalition of opposition parties and groups that he formed. The Somoza family responded to the new form of opposition with long stretches of rigid censorship and a variety of other forms of harrassment.

Perhaps because of his family tradition, his social commitment or political ambition, Chamorro continued his opposition despite constant pressure from the

Somoza government. His dogged opposition eventually won the attention of press organizations and human rights groups, and by the 1970s, he was a regional *cause célèbre*. In 1977, he was awarded the prestigious Maria Moors Cabot award from Columbia University for "journalistic leadership of those forces opposed to tyranny in Nicaragua."

The external support gave Chamorro greater leverage to criticize the Somoza government. Each time Somoza punished Chamorro for his polemics, the editor's international reputation increased and the government's reputation declined, allowing *La Prensa* to print even more acid criticism of the government. This escalating conflict between Chamorro and Somoza was pivotal in the government's downfall in 1979.

Because it was virtually the only medium not entirely controlled by the Somozas, *La Prensa* attracted a wide and devoted domestic readership. Throughout the decades, the newspaper became the paramount symbol of opposition to the Somoza government and was often purchased by Nicaraguans more as a political statement rather than for the editorial content. Indeed, *La Prensa* probably had its greatest effect when it was not allowed to publish. Closure of the newspaper became a sure-fire sign of a national crisis. For these reasons, the assassination of Chamorro in January 1978 by gunmen under the direction of Somoza or his lieutenants was the spark that set off the revolution.

After the assassination, *La Prensa*'s opposition went far beyond journalistic opposition. Xavier Chamorro, Pedro Joaquín's brother and *La Prensa*'s new editor, coordinated an alliance of opposition forces from both the political left and right and plotted a general strike that crippled the Somoza government in the newspaper offices. Much of the editorial staff, while continuing their reporting duties, formed small cells that clandestinely fought with or worked for the Sandinistas. The staff members included two top Sandinista commanders, William Ramírez and Bayardo Arce, and Carlos Fernando Chamorro, the youngest son of the slain editor. Recognizing that *La Prensa* had become a dangerous opposition force, the Somoza government could no longer cater to international opinion and bombed it out of production in 1979.

Description of Post-War Media

Although the Chamorro family was united in what it opposed, it was not united in what it supported. Missing its patriarch, the family became deeply divided about the editorial policy of *La Prensa,* which resumed publication shortly after the Sandinista victory in July 1979. The family squabble, in many respects, is a microcosm of the national political debate. Carlos Fernando left the family enterprise and became Deputy Minister of Culture and eventually editor of *Barricada,* the official voice of the Sandinistas. Xavier, upset by the family's conservative resistance to the new government policies, led a walkout of most of the top editors and reporters of *La Prensa* and formed *Nuevo Diario,* a cooperatively owned and operated newspaper that editorially supports the government. The martyred editor's widow, Violeta, who briefly served as a member of the revolutionary junta, became chair of the board of directors of *La Prensa*. Her oldest son, Pedro Joaquín Chamorro Barrios, became co-editor of the paper.

In sum, the post-war version of *La Prensa,* while still owned and operated by some members of the distinguished Chamorro family, was markedly different from its namesake. Despite the substantive changes, *La Prensa* appears to have maintained it special domestic and international status, and because of the revolutionary change in governmental philosophy and the shift in the newspaper's editorial policy, *La Prensa* and the government are again at loggerheads. Currently, *La Prensa* strongly advocates the position of the business and political opposition groups and stridently opposes Marxist-Leninism in the government.

Barricada, which bears a resemblance to Cuba's *Granma,* is dogmatic, stilted and shrill in its criticism of business and political opposition. The newspaper is staffed by inexperienced journalism students and is of comparatively low technical quality; nonetheless, it ranks second in the battle for circulation and symbolism. *Nuevo Diario,* although more restrained in its content and professional in its methods, ranks third in circulation. An inordinate portion of all three dailies is devoted to acrimonious charges and countercharges about their respective editorial stances rather than hard news reporting.

Of the approximately 30 radio stations in Nicaragua, almost all are either state-owned, privately-owned but supportive of the government, or privately-owned but carry no editorial content. Only two radio stations are mildly critical of the government, but no station is as influential as *La Prensa*. All television has been declared "privileged media" and expropriated by the government.

Closures and Censorship of La Prensa

The Sandinista leadership clearly recognizes that *La Prensa* is a potent political force and has been worried by the opposition of its former ally. The commanders fear that *La Prensa*'s acid criticism of government policies and inflammatory reporting might destroy the fragile economy and upset the delicate balance of power within the leadership and with outside forces such as the church.*They also fear that *La Prensa* will tarnish the government's international image much as it did during the Somoza regime.

In 1979, the junta issued the General Provisional Law of the Media of Communication, which declared the principle of "freedom of information" but also detailed its limits. Violence, pornography, advertising of tobacco and liquor, portrayal of women as sexual objects, and other media content that promoted laziness, subversion, other crime and human degradation were specifically banned. In September 1981, as Nicaragua's economic problems worsened, the junta promulgated the Laws of Public Order and Security and Economic and Social Emergency, which provide for jail terms of up to three years and temporary suspension of publication for those guilty of "economic sabotage." Publishng false economic news or inciting foreign governments to damage Nicaragua's economy were among the forms of economic

---

*For a thorough discussion of C.I.A. manipulation of *La Prensa* see the article by psychologist Dr. Fred Landis, "CIA Psychological Warfare Operations," *Science for the People,* January/ February 1982, Vol. 14, No. 1.

sabotage defined by the law. Before the end of the year, *La Prensa* had been closed by the government several times for one to three days.

As Nicaragua's foreign relations rapidly deteriorated in the spring of 1982, new and more rigid domestic media controls were enforced. The *Washington Post* and other major US publications reported that President Reagan had approved a multi-million-dollar plan to destabilize the Sandinista government. According to the reports, which the US administration has not denied, the Central Intelligence Agency was training and equipping former Somoza national guardsmen and other counter-revolutionary forces primarily in base camps in Honduras, along Nicaragua's northern border.

In March, after a series of border skirmishes and sabotage acts, the Sandinista government, citing the threat of a US-backed invasion, declared a state of emergency under which many civil rights were suspended. All news media were placed under official censorship directed by the Minister of Interior, Tomás Borge, probably the most dogmatic of the Sandinista leaders.

The government actions led to numerous international protests and precipitated a visit by a delegation of regional editors under the auspices of the Inter American Press Association. The Sandinista leadership seems to be faced with the same dilemma that plagued Somoza. On the one hand, punishment of *La Prensa* seriously jeopardizes Nicaragua's international support, but on the other hand, failure to curb inaccurate or inflammatory reporting threatens the economic and political stability of the country.

"Press freedom . . . need(s) a minimum of stability in order to develop," Daniel Ortega, coordinator of the Sandinista junta, told *The New York Times*. "To the extent that the United States is closing the noose around us, we have to tighten the screws."

Method for Evaluating Media Controls

Freedom of the press is a worthy goal in the abstract, but in reality it has very little meaning. When defined as the absence of external controls, particularly government controls, freedom of the press does not exist in any country in the world, never has existed and never can exist. The process of mass communication, by its very nature, requires control. Individual members of the public simply cannot contend with the deluge of facts, opinions and ideas that are available in the world; therefore, societies delegate to certain organizations the responsibility to select, process and transmit a few of those messages to the public. The organizations exercising control over what information is presented to the public differ widely from country to country, but the controls are always present. In the United States, if a business enterprise intending to make a profit or a political party intending to advocate a partisan cause selects the information to be presented to the public, we call the process *editing*. But if a government selects the information, we call it *censorship*. The only major differences between editing and censorship are the organizations that make the selection, the motive for selection, and the effect of the selection process on the public good. Thus, although official government censorship is relatively rare in the United States, the flow of information to the public is nonetheless controlled.

In all Latin American countries, even the traditional democracies, the selection process is to some extent controlled by governments. The methods of control range from official government censorship to more subtle means such as licensing, economic pressure or quiet coercion. In countries such as Costa Rica and Colombia where official government censorship is relatively rare, business, labor organizations, church, political parties, terrorists or other combinations of powerful sectors in society determine what information reaches the public.

The academic literature on comparative foreign journalism indicates that, via this selection process, all countries tend to limit the amount of criticism of the established order and to limit the range of new information and ideas during times of national crisis. For example, all countries regardless of political ideology control (usually by act of government) the dissemination of criticism and unsettling information during times of war, other external threats, or domestic economic instability. In addition, research indicates that the level of national development and the degree of institutional complexity affects the amount of criticism and dissident information carried in a nation's media. In short, only after the difficult and volatile process of modernization and national development and only during times of tranquillity can a country tolerate a wide range of news and opinion.

Political Dialogue in the Nicaraguan Media

Considering that Nicaragua is an extremely poor country that has recently experienced a devastating revolutionary war and is currently confronted with a continuing power struggle, economic chaos, and real or perceived external threat, the fact that an opposition newspaper continues to publish and other government and non-government media discuss Nicaragua's political future and other unsettling topics is remarkable.

Despite the government's desire to control the flow of certain types of news, it has been relatively open in its treatment of reporters from all media, including *La Prensa*. Sandinista commanders and junta members frequently hold press conferences, grant interviews with domestic and foreign journalists, and recently met with a hostile delegation of editors from the Inter American Press Association. In the government-owned broadcast media, the Sandinistas also encourage a certain amount of political dialogue. Each week various leaders appear on a national radio and television program to answer questions and complaints of the Nicaraguan public, and Radio Sandino airs a popular daily program that pokes fun at the commanders. During one of the closings of *La Prensa* in July 1981, the newspaper's co-editor, Pedro Joaquín Chamorro Barrios, appeared on *government* radio to denounce the government action and repeat his criticisms about the direction of the revolution.

Comparison to Government Controls on the US Media

Although the principle of freedom of the press in the United States was established in the First Amendment of the Bill of Rights in 1791, suppression of
publications by state and local governments was permissible and commonplace for
150 years after the end of the American revolutionary war in 1781. In 1931, the US
Supreme Court ruled for the first time that states cannot suppress newspapers in
anticipation of wrongful printing. In the case *Near vs. Minnesota,* the court declared
unconstitutional a state law that permitted prior restraint of malicious and scandalous publications.

During the early development of the United States, government control of the
media predictably was most common during times of turmoil. The two political
factions that evolved after the revolutionary war—the Federalists led by Alexander
Hamilton and the Republicans led by Thomas Jefferson—were deeply divided on
political and economic issues and hotly contested control of the government. Each
faction sponsored newspapers to advocate its ideology, and none of the newspapers
was noted for balanced, dispassionate or accurate reporting of public affairs. In 1798,
the Federalists decided to crack down on newspapers critical of their government by
legislating the Alien and Sedition Acts, which made "false, scandalous and malicious
writing" about the government a crime. Shortly after the acts were passed, a
Republican editor was jailed for publishing a letter-to-the-editor that charged
President John Adams with "ridiculous pomp, foolish adulation and selfish avarice."

During the American civil war, General Ambrose Burnside, under the specific
direction or at least with the encouragement of President Abraham Lincoln, closed
down newspapers in Indiana, Illinois and Ohio that dared to question the President's
war policy. US history looks favorably on Lincoln despite those acts. He is seen as a
man who took extraordinary action during extremely difficult times in order to save
the union.

During World War I, newspapers were prohibited under the Espionage Act of
1917 from publishing criticism of the federal government or advocating radical
political or economic change. In support of the Espionage Act, Supreme Court
Justice Oliver Wendell Holmes wrote in *Schneck vs. US* that certain polemical
statements might be permissible during ordinary times, but during times of war or
other national crisis, the words may create a "clear and present danger" to the public
and may be legitimately suppressed by the government.

The general view that the government has the right and responsibility to control
the media in order to guarantee national security and public welfare continues today.
For example, the Federal Communication Commission has the authority to refuse
licenses to radio and television stations that do not broadcast "in the public interest,
convenience, or necessity." And the federal government in 1979 sought and received
prior restraint on an issue of *Progressive* magazine that contained an article on the
H-bomb. The courts ruled that publication of the article might jeopardize national
security.

Compared to the long and arduous history of state-press relations in the US, the three years since the end of the Nicaraguan revolutionary war does not seem to be adequate for Nicaragua to develop a healthy balance of media controls.

Conclusions

In the best of all possible worlds, all people should be able to disseminate and receive the widest variety of information, opinions and ideas. Unfortunately, the media of Nicaragua, the United States or any other nation do not operate in perfect conditions; consequently, media control always exists. While control of the media is understandable and expected, it should not necessarily be condoned. But to the extent that controls are necessary, society (via its government) has the right and responsibility to define the degree and nature of those controls.

It is, therefore, important to distinguish between controls exercised for the benefit of the citizens by a legitimate government and controls exercised for the repression of the citizens by an illegitimate government. In sum, control over the press can be used for good or evil. Simply because controls are different from the ones used in the United States does not make them dysfunctional for society.

La Prensa is both pen and sword in a highly unstable political system. Under these conditions, are the recent Nicaragua media controls a calculated repression of the voice of the people, or are they a predictable and transitory reaction to a subversive political force bent on the overthrow of a popular government?

14. Nicaragua's Law of Political Parties*

By the Central American Historical Institute

The Central American Historical Institute is an independent research organization based in Washington, D.C. It is affiliated with the Instituto Histórico Centroamericano *in Managua.*

On August 17, 1983, Nicaragua's Council of State approved a law of Political Parties. The law, a culmination of a twenty-one-month process of discussion and revision, regulates the establishment and functioning of political parties. With Junta approval it will become Nicaraguan law.

Representatives of various parties called the law an important step in institutionalizing Nicaragua's political process. The next step will be drafting of the electoral law, which should be completed by the end of 1983, as announced by the government on December 4, 1982. Thus, Nicaragua's political process is developing according to schedule: 1984 will be a pre-election year and national elections will take place in 1985.

The process leading to the Law of Political Parties began in November 1981, when six Sandinista National Liberation Front (FSLN) representatives in the Council of State presented a first draft of the law.

How Does the Law Function?
What Is a Political Party?

The Law of Political Parties' forty-one articles define principles, goals, rights and duties of political parties. It also outlines the functions of two bodies which will oversee the application of the law: the National Assembly of Political Parties (ANPP) and the National Council of Political Parties (CNPP).

The law also establishes the steps that parties must take to gain legal recognition, as well as reasons for sanctions such as temporary suspension or permanent disbanding of a political party. The law defines the right of all citizens to form and to belong to a political party. There will be no ideological restrictions placed on political parties, with the exception that a party must not promote a return to Somocismo.

In general, the rights of a party as defined in the law are similar to those recognized in laws of Western countries. Parties may publicize their views and engage in all types of propaganda and recruitment, although they can only take out

---

*Reprinted from the *Central American Historical Institute Update*, August 25, 1983, Vol. 2, No. 20.

paid media advertisements during electoral periods. Parties may hold private meetings and public demonstrations, criticize state administration, form alliances and participate in the Council of State. They can also participate in elections and run their own candidates. They may own property and open offices throughout the country.

Duties of parties stipulated by law are to respect the country's juridical order, to promote national unity in order to continue reconstruction, to defend due process in face of any attempt to impose a repressive regime, to strive for liberty and for national independence, and to promote human rights.

Opposition political parties had been doubtful as to whether they would be able to contend for political power, as they did not believe that the FSLN would risk losing its power through elections. Article 2, however, stipulates that "an objective of a political party is to seek power in order to implement a program which responds to needs of national development."

All parties now participating in the Council of State gained legal status with the passing of the law, having only to fulfill certain formalities. Three other parties which requested membership in the Council of State more than a year ago—Social Democratic Party, Nicaraguan Communist Party, and Popular Action Movement-will also be recognized, after fulfilling the same pro forma steps.

The National Assembly of Political Parties will be a consultative body and will be composed of a member of each party and a chairperson named by the government. The National Coalition of Political Parties will be an executive body made up of eight members—four elected by the ANPP, three by the Council of State and one by the government. All decisions of the CNPP, which will oversee the application of the law, may be appealed to the Supreme Court.

Initial Reactions

Representatives of almost all political parties have commented on the law. Dr. Julio Centeno Gómez, head of the Liberal Constitutionalist Party—a member of the Democratic Coordinating Committee (a coalition of parties opposed to the government)—stated that "It is a good law, with democratic and pluralistic foundation. Now we need an electoral law. The most important thing, however, is that there be a clear and just political will to fulfill the law as it stands." Dr. Orlando Quinonez, representing the Independent Liberal Party in the Council of State, added that "the law amply guarantees the rights of Nicaraguan political parties. It is a democratic law, and I think that it serves as an example for the rest of Latin America." Mauricio Díaz of the Popular Social Christian Party termed the law "momentous" and stated that it reflected the disparate interests and aspirations of parties.

Nevertheless, most of the representatives of the opposition parties criticized the composition of the National Council of Political Parties, which they say favors the FSLN, and stated that this law must be followed by an electoral law. They also recognized the importance of the right to appeal decisions by the National Council of Political Parties to the Supreme Court.

Conclusions and Interpretations

The Law of Political Parties was passed after almost two years of debate. Both the Fundamental Statute of the Republic and the Statute on the Rights and Guarantees of July 1979 recognized the right of all Nicaraguans to engage in political activity and to organize themselves politically, as well as the duty of the state to promote these rights.

The work of both the Special Commission and the Council of State has been an example of political pluralism and respect. The recognition of the right of political parties to seek political power is of decisive importance for the Nicaraguan revolution, and runs counter to remarks that Nicaragua is heading toward a single-party state.

The fact that the law was approved during a time of intense military attacks against Nicaragua, including the loss of 700 lives in 1983, highlights the political will which underlies this law. It would have been easy to use the climate of war to justify "tough political positions" and "rigidity" on the part of present leaders.

Internally, there is an open opposition in Nicaragua. The law is not consolidating a "tactical" or "opportunistic" pluralism, but is rather part of a political model that has been developing throughout the last four years. The Law of Political Parties which was passed in the Council of State is a product of the vast majority of political forces in Nicaragua and demonstrates the direction that political pluralism is taking in Nicaragua.

Editor's Note: Since the publication of this article the Nicaraguan Council of State has approved an electoral format that will include a 90-member constituent assembly to be elected by districts of equal population, and a directly elected President and Vice President. All will serve six-year terms. Finally, on February 21, 1984, the fiftieth anniversary of the death of Augusto Sandino, Junta Coordinator Daniel Ortega S. announced that the elections would be held on November 4, 1984, two days before the US Presidential elections and a year earlier than expected.

Eds.

Nicaraguan Political Parties
The Opposition Parties—Democratic Coordinating Committee
1) Social Christian Party (PSC)
2) Social Democrat Party (PSD)
3) Constitutionalist Liberal Movement (MLC)
The Pro-government Parties—Patriotic Revolutionary Front
1) Sandinista National Liberation Front (FSLN)
2) Popular Social Christian Party (PPSC)
3) Nicaraguan Socialist Party (PSN)
The Independent Parties
1) Popular Action Movement (MAP)
2) Nicaraguan Communist Party (PCN)
3) Conservative Party (PCD)
4) Independent Liberal Party (PLI)
5) "Authentic" Popular Social Christian Party (PPSCA)

15. *Atlantic Coast: Miskitu Crisis and Counterrevolution**

By the National Network in Solidarity with the Nicaraguan People

The Atlantic Coast: A History of Colonialism and Neglect

The "Atlantic Coast" refers to the provinces of Zelaya and Río San Juan, which occupy the entire eastern half of Nicaragua, comprising 56% of the national territory and 12% of the population. Its geography, ethnic composition, language, religion, history and culture are distinct from the Pacific side.

The northern area of the Coast is inhabited by the Miskitu (24%) and Sumu Indians (2.5%) who maintain their own language and culture. The Black English-speaking population known as Creoles comprise 10% of the Coastal population and are concentrated in Bluefields. They came to Nicaragua first in the 1600s as slaves or escapees from slavery. In the late nineteenth century Blacks also migrated to Nicaragua from Jamaica to work for foreign companies. Sixty-three percent of the Coast's population are people who migrated eastward from the Pacific side, most during the past 30 years. Other groups include the Rama Indians (.24%) and the Garifuna (.47%).

Spain colonized the Pacific side of Nicaragua in the 1500s but was unable to crush the Miskitu Indian resistance on the Atlantic. In the 1600s Britain entered the

---

*Reprinted from *Nicaragua*, May-June, 1982, pp. 4-5.

Atlantic Coast, forming trade relations with the Miskitu and using them in battles with the Spanish. In 1687 the British established a "Miskitu King," allowing a semblance of self-rule while real control remained in their hands. African people arrived, mixing with the indigenous people so that ethnic identity became based on language and culture rather than race. The alliance with the British allowed the Miskitu to dominate the other indigenous groups of the region. This situation lasted for two centuries.

Later the Atlantic Coast became a British Protectorate, but in 1860 the British withdrew, leaving the region a "reserve" under Nicaragua with the right of self-government. In practice, the natives of the Coast only changed one colonial ruler for another. In 1894 the Atlantic Coast was "reincorporated" into the Nicaraguan nation, which the people viewed as yet another conquest. The doors were opened to foreign corporations (mainly US), which exploited the region's gold, forests, bananas and sealife. Independent farmers were pushed off the richest lands and sealife was diminished. Overexploitation of the forests eroded the land and made it susceptible to frequent flooding. By the 1950s many natural resources had been exhausted and foreign corporations began withdrawing, leaving a population faced with hunger and malnutrition. While many people migrated to other areas in search of work, most continued to rely on bare subsistence farming, fishing and hunting.

Except for exploiting its natural resources, the Somoza regime ignored the Atlantic Coast. The one effort by Somoza that did succeed was a major propaganda campaign portraying communism as the greatest enemy of the Nicaraguan people and agitating that a Cuban invasion was imminent. This campaign's climax was the launching of the Bay of Pigs invasion of Cuba from Puerto Cabezas in 1961.

The Legacy of Colonialism and Somocismo

The victorious Sandinistas arrived on the Atlantic Coast to find a situation very different from that on the Pacific. On the Pacific side the interruption of agricultural activity and the destruction of industry caused by the war made the immediate task one of resuming production and rebuilding damaged plans. The confiscation of Somocista lands and factories gave the new revolutionary government a material base from which to begin to reconstruct economic activity to meet the needs of the people. The war itself had united the people and forged civil defense committees which served as the foundation of the new revolutionary mass organizations. On the local level the Catholic Church had placed itself clearly on the side of the people and many young people had joined the revolution out of a sense of Christian commitment.

On the Atlantic Coast the economy was also in a state of shambles, but it was due to decades of neglect and overexploitation by foreign companies, not the ravages of war. By the time of victory the last of the foreign companies had pulled out, leaving factories and machinery in disrepair, no spare parts and few technical or administrative people to help with reconstruction. The tropical lowlands and heavy rainfall make land on the coast generally unsuitable for extensive agriculture.

Communications and transportation systems were almost non-existent, except for small canoes along the extensive network of narrow rivers. Food supplies had to be airlifted at great expense from Managua or transported slowly and unreliably by boat. Bringing health care to a region where TB, malaria, parasites and malnutrition are prevalent was severely complicated by the lack of roads to many villages. There were no local newspapers, telephones and television were found only in Bluefields, and only two radios operated. The government therefore had no way of disseminating information or countering rumors. In contrast, the counterrevolutionary radio from Honduras and Voice of America are received all along the Coast and there is no effective way to combat this propaganda.

Added to these overwhelming economic problems was a legacy of oppression so deeply rooted in the Coastal people that they could not be easily convinced that these new "españoles" would treat them any differently than previous rulers. The anti-imperialism which was a foundation of Sandinismo was totally absent on the Coast, where many regarded the period of US presence as "the good old days." The Moravian church, whose missionaries adopted the simple life style of the Miskitu beginning in 1849, is the dominant religious force in the region and tended to reinforce the anti-communist, pro-US ideology of Somocismo. The Moravians also filled the vacuum imposed by Somoza's neglect, functioning as the political apparatus and government in many small villages.

During the Somoza years few National Guardsmen were stationed on the Atlantic Coast. The insurrection barely touched the Coast, except for the mining area where Somocista repression was severe and where there was significant support for the FSLN. Numerous Coastal people did fight with the FSLN, but usually on the Pacific side, where many had been students in Managua. Lack of cross-cultural awareness was a serious problem that would not be resolved overnight. People on the Pacific side knew little of the reality of the Coast, and the Coastal people viewed the "Spanish" with suspicion and distrust.

Revolution on the Coast

Viewing the situation from a class perspective, the Sandinistas found that the Coastal people were the poorest, most exploited and most alienated in Nicaragua. As such they believed that they should benefit most from the revolution. The Sandinistas came out of a Nicaragua in which ethnic minorities and indigenous rights were never an issue. They saw how the indigenous peoples and Creoles had been discriminated against by Somoza and exploited by foreign interests. Thus they believed that tackling the economic problems of the region and overcoming its isolation would eliminate the material basis for racism. In the euphoria of victory, they put foward solutions to the Coast's problems, not fully realizing the amount of time and resources needed to achieve these promises, nor adequately sensitized to the cultural issues that were just as important as the economic.

The Sandinistas did realize that the Coast was vulnerable to counterrevolutionary activity. Thousands of Somocista ex-Guardsmen were encamped across the

Honduran border, and the Miskitu who lived in this area were accustomed to crossing the Río Coco freely. The border went right through Miskitu communities and many families had members and land on both sides. The presence of the Somocistas on the Honduran side made it necessary for the Sandinistas to station soldiers in the area. They arrived with no cross-cultural education or sensitivity and almost none spoke English or Miskitu. This, plus their youth and inexperience, led to misunderstandings, resentments and incidents.

Despite these problems and tremendously limited resources, significant advances have been made by the government. The literacy campaign on the Coast was conducted in Spanish, English, Miskitu and Sumu and reached even the most remote areas. Health care problems are still numerous, but free medical attention is now available and each town of more than 2,000 has a resident doctor and clinic. Campaigns are being carried out against dengue, malaria and other diseases. A new hospital is under construction in Bluefields and should be completed within a year. A highway linking the two coasts is nearing completion, and potable water and electricity are reaching areas which never had them before. ENABAS (Government Distributors of Basic Foodstuffs) and the Peoples Stores bring basic foods to the most remote areas at the lowest possible cost while guarding against speculation and hoarding. By mid-1980 the region's gold mines, lumber companies, fisheries and cattle ranches were nationalized. The Ministry for the Atlantic Coast (INNICA) was established to coordinate all government economic programs in the region.

The FSLN and Indigenous Organizations

During the Somoza era an indigenous organization called Alliance for Progress of Miskutu and Sumu (ALPROMISU) was initiated by a Moravian pastor concerned about commercial opportunities for the Indians. ALPROMISU continued up until the time of the insurrection and was never considered a serious threat by the Somoza regime.

After the victory the people wanted to retain ALPROMISU but the FSLN was concerned that it would not fully cooperate with plans to finally integrate the Atlantic Coast with the rest of the country. This caused some friction, but it was finally agreed to change the organization's name to Misurasata (Miskitu, Sumu, Rama and Sandinistas Together). Steadman Fagoth, a young Miskitu from the Río Coco area who had studied at the university in Managua, was elected head of Misurasata. The organization operated freely for over a year, growing rapidly in size and influence among the people, and Fagoth became Misurasata's representative on the Council of State.

Certain tensions between the Sandinistas and Misurasata emerged, however, stemming from the FSLN's tendency to analyze problems from a class perspective and view ethnic distinctions as being possibly separatist in orientation, and Misurasata's view that certain government programs and policies were assimilationist in character. For example, the government saw education as a priority and in 1980 the

Council of State passed a law authorizing bilingual education (English-Spanish and Miskitu-Spanish) in Creole and Miskitu communities. Misurasata expressed concerns that the rural school through its methods, program and language was outside the people's cultural reality and looked to change the children into a type of Mestizo without definition or personality.

Misurasata gained in prominence during this time and Fagoth began to assert extraordinary influence over the Miskitu people. A charismatic personality, he positioned himself as guardian of Indian interests as against the Sandinistas, whose goals he often misrepresented when translating their presentations into Miskitu.

By 1981 Misurasata decided to press for extensive demands, including land rights and political autonomy over approximately 20% of the Coast. The government recognized the indigenous people's concern over land and the more general question of the exploitation of natural resources. The problem required extensive study to resolve, and the Misurasata proposal did not consider the interests of the Mestizo and Creole populations in the region. Misurasata also demanded five seats on the Council of State and one on the junta.

The plan came at a time of increased tension between Nicaragua and the United States. Reagan had just taken office, pledged to a platform which vowed to reverse the Sandinista revolution, Somocistas operating in Honduras were receiving support from both Honduras and the US, and the Atlantic Coast had been the scene of earlier US interventions.

The government had become somewhat suspicious of Fagoth, who often seemed more concerned about building his own power base among the Miskitu than in working for improvements. It appeared likely that Misurasata would call for international support and that its demands would be manipulated by forces bent on destabilizing the government by making the Sandinistas appear to be against indigenous rights.

On Feb. 18, 1981, Fagoth and the other Misurasata leadership were arrested, on the basis of intelligence that they were planning armed actions to foment a separatist uprising at the end of the month. While the other leaders were released after a short time, Fagoth was held another two and a half months. In examining records of Somoza's intelligence office, letters written by Fagoth were found which indicated he had collaborated with the dictatorship as an informer. Still, the people viewed him as their leader and vigorously protested his arrest. During his imprisonment many young Miskitu crossed into Honduras out of fear, ideological differences and/or general confusion.

On May 7 the government released Fagoth on the condition that he go abroad to study. The Sandinistas' worst fears were soon proven correct—Fagoth fled to Honduras and began collaborating actively with the Somocistas. He continues to influence the people, mostly through a clandestine radio operated by the counterrevolutionaries in Honduras. He has traveled extensively to the US and other countries looking for support for the counterrevolution. In Dec. 1981 he received minor injuries when the Honduran army plane in which he was traveling crashed. Also on board was Maj. Leonel Luque, the "godfather" of the counterrevolutionary forces within the Honduran military.

Red Christmas

While raids from counterrevolutionaries in Honduras occurred frequently during 1981, and emigrations continued periodically, there was a concerted effort by church and government leaders to improve relations and rebuild confidence on the Coast. But by November border raids became an almost daily occurrence. A brutal raid in December, in which 35 Sandinistas were tortured and killed, threw everything into chaos.

Through diplomatic notes, Nicaragua protested the Honduran government's "incapacity" to control these raids and reiterated its frequent appeal for joint border patrols. Nicaragua's Foreign Minister also protested the complicity of Maj. Leonel Luque. In early January Honduras retaliated by accusing the Nicaraguan military of crossing the Río Coco and massacring 200 Miskitu living in refugee camps, based on an admittedly unconfirmed report. A delegation from the Honduran College of Education visited the supposed site and found no evidence to support the charges.

The baseless accusation fueled the United States' propaganda war against Nicaragua. The State Dept. issued a travelers' warning, saying that the Atlantic Coast was a militarized zone and that major repression was being carried out against the Miskitu population. Jeane Kirkpatrick charged that concentration camps for Indians were being built. President Reagan, in a major address to the OAS, charged that Indians had been killed, and Alexander Haig echoed these charges, producing a photograph which he claimed showed the bodies of Miskitu Indians being burned. Two days later the newspaper which published the photo, Paris' *Le Figaro,* announced that the photo actually showed members of Nicaragua's Red Cross burning bodies of Somoza's victims during the 1978 insurrection on the Pacific side. Steadman Fagoth was brought to the US by the right-wing American Security Council and allowed to testify off-the-record before several Congressional committees and administration officials.

The full extent of the crisis in the northeast became known in early February when the Nicaraguan Ministries of Defense and Interior gave details of numerous counterrevolutionary attacks during November, December and January, which resulted in the deaths of 60 Nicaraguans, both civilians and military. 160 people were arrested for counterrevolutionary actions, among them Efrain Wilson, a former Moravian pastor, who described a plot called "Red Christmas." Its goal was to generate a general uprising of the Miskitu people and form a separate state on the Atlantic Coast. According to Wilson, many Miskitu went to Honduras for military training with the Somocistas, who received aid from those training in Florida and California and from the Honduran military. He also mentioned the presence of Argentine advisors. Wilson testified that once the northeastern section was controlled by counterrevolutionaries, they would then ask for outside help, which would justify air support from the US and a blockade of Nicaragua.

The government also made a decision to move people from Miskitu villages along the Río Coco further inland. The difficult decision was prompted by the need to protect the people, and to stop the counterrevolutionary attacks and cut off their source of supplies. The counterrevolutionaries actually represent a very small minority in the area. Most of the people in the remote villages are not politicized at all, but their very presence made them either collaborators or victims of the counterrevolutionaries.

The Resettlement

Some 8,000 Miskitu were relocated to five settlements 30–35 miles inland. Those who preferred to cross the river to Honduras were free to do so, and reportedly many did. Volunteers from the Sandinista Youth, the Militia and FSLN assisted in the move. For many it was a long walk, but elderly people, children and pregnant women were evacuated by helicopter or vehicle. The move was carried out peacefully and with the cooperation of the people, but they naturally felt anger and resentment at having to leave their homes and land. Once the people had been safely moved, the villages and crops were burned to deny the counterrevolutionaries encampment and food on the Nicaraguan side of the river.

Representatives from the OAS Inter-American Commission on Human Rights, the U.N. Human Rights Commission and Amnesty International have been invited to inspect the resettlement. Those who have already visited the camps, including former president of Costa Rica, José Figueres, members of the Nicaraguan Commission for the Protection and Promotion of Human Rights, Capuchin leaders and leaders of CEPAD, a powerful ecumenical organization in Nicaragua, have all reported peaceful and cooperative conditions.

The relocation areas are planned as model settlements. Church World Service is assisting with emergency relief and plans to send a delegation down, the U.N. Food and Agricultural Organization has been asked by the government to participate in planning agricultural development, and the government is applying tremendous human and economic resources as well.

There are five settlements, some of which are temporary. According to a delegation from the Central American Historic Institute, which visited four settlements unannounced, food is sufficient although there are shortages of dishes, cooking utensils, clothing and tools. All have clinics with at least one doctor, several nurses and a pharmacy. Vaccination programs have been completed against polio, measles, DPT, tetanus and malaria. All have at least a temporary school with Miskitu teachers. Moravian and Catholic church services are conducted each week. Health engineers are supervising the construction of wells and water purification systems. The government will spend 365 million córdobas on the project over the next couple of years and will provide prefabricated houses for each family. In one settlement housing lots have already been given to families who are constructing temporary bamboo and thatch houses. Each family will receive a 250 square meter plot for their home with sufficient space for planting fruit trees and truck crops. The area as a whole contains 53,543 hectares of arable land suitable for the planting of corn, rice, bananas, yucca and beans. Preparation of the land for the May planting has already started in the Sahsa community and the goal is food self-sufficiency within a year.

The recent events on the Atlantic Coast and the overall efforts of the Sandinistas to bring the benefits of the revolution to the region must be viewed in the context of the enormous problems presented by the country's lack of economic resources and the increasing efforts by the US to destabilize the government. The Sandinistas are the first to admit that their own lack of understanding of the cultural and ethnic differences of the region led to errors of cultural insensitivity. Their August 1981 "Declaration of Principles with Regard to the Indigenous Communities of the Atlantic Coast" represents an important step forward in formulating a policy which guarantees the rights of indigenous peoples.

In light of recent disclosures of a CIA covert action plan to destabilize Nicaragua, approved by President Reagan in early December, "Red Christmas" represents the most serious paramilitary attack against the revolution to date, and a possible prelude to more serious measures yet to come. The Sandinistas have shown their determination to defend the revolution against US attempts to destroy it. Now, more than ever, the US solidarity movement must increase its work in support of self-determination for the Nicaraguan people and against US intervention in the region.

16. *Inside a Miskitu Resettlement Camp*

By Katherine Yih

Tasba Pri, Nicaragua

The meeting was overflowing out the door of the Casa Sandinista at Sumubila, the largest of the Miskitu resettlements in northeastern Nicaragua. Residents were heatedly deciding what to do about a fellow inhabitant who had collaborated with a band of counterrevolutionaries. The outcome: overwhelming agreement to expel her from the settlement.

This meeting, held last month, was an expression of the growing political participation of the people of Tasba Pri ("free-land" in Miskitu, as the resettlement area was named) nearly one year after the first Miskitu Indians were moved there out of crossfire at the Nicaraguan-Honduran border. It was equally a manifestation of the ideological conflicts such participation often brings to light.

The relocation of some 8,500 Miskitu Indians one year ago created an international controversy. The Reagan administration was among those charging the move was an example of human rights violations by the Sandinista government.

---

*Reprinted from *The Guardian*, March 2, 1983.

The Sandinistas, on the other hand, pointed out that the move was made to protect the villagers from raids by US-supported Nicaraguan counterrevolutionaries operating out of camps in Honduras. They said the move was voluntary.

In the year since the relocation, this author found that the Miskitu people's attitude has shifted palpably from resentment to satisfaction with improving conditions, and a growing trust of the Sandinistas. Indeed, health, education and infrastructure, including access to markets, are now superior in most respects to conditions in the Coco River communities the people once called home. Yet, challenges remain, both economic and political.

The relocation was a response to "Operation Red Christmas," a counterrevolutionary plan designed to provoke a secessionist movement among the Miskitus. The operation began in late November 1981 with a series of armed attacks from Honduras along the Coco River border. By Christmas, 45 Sandinista soldiers and 15 civilians had been killed.

Meanwhile, the counterrevolutionary "September 15" radio station in Honduras broadcast to the people that Sandinista planes were coming to bomb their villages, that the Sandinistas believed all the Miskitus were in revolt and would punish them, and that they had better escape to Honduras. An estimated 10,000 Miskitus fled there. Others individually sought refuge in the interior of Nicaragua. On this basis, and because the Sandinistas could not defend the communities from the armed raids without risking firing into Honduras—which they feared could set off military intervention by an inter-American force—the government decided to evacuate the villages.

Beginning in January 1981, 39 Coco River communities were moved to five resettlement camps 50 miles to the south. By all accounts the experience has been difficult. The people left homes and livestock, which had to be destroyed to prevent use by counterrevolutionaries. Living conditions in the new makeshift camps were uncomfortable. Moreover, many people, having lived in relative isolation and recently assailed by counterrevolutionary propaganda, did not understand the reasons for the relocation.

There is a saying in the Miskitu culture: "The monkey says, only what you have in your stomach is yours," roughly equivalent in usage to "the proof is in the pudding." In Tasba Pri this means the Miskitus will trust the Sandinistas only to the extent that they deliver on their promises.

Counterrevolutionary elements have played on this skepticism, saying that the harvest would go to the Sandinistas, or that the land was bad. But this year the average rice harvest of all the settlements was fully twice what had been projected by local technicians. And the people decided what to do with the crop, whether to consume it or sell it to the state. As one of the political directors commented, "The counterrevolution's plan was smashed when the harvest was turned over to the communities."

Progress in filling material needs is obvious on other fronts as well. New generators, contributed by Cuba, are currently being installed, bringing the settlements reliable electricity for the first time. Oxfam, the British relief group, is working on potable water projects. Permanent wooden houses, prefabricated in Managua, have been built for almost all inhabitants of four of the five settlements. Health facilities have been in operation since the beginning, and schools since March 1982.

Scarcity of various commodities is still a frequent problem, partly due to difficulties in transportation and communication, partly due to financial constraints on the country as a whole. But the lack of currency, a serious focus of discontent a few months ago, is less severe now. Money is earned from the sale of crops, firewood, and products such as clothes and wooden ornaments, and as wages for construction work.

Improvement in the quality of life in Tasba Pri has not only been economic; popular participation in the administration of the communities has increased as well.

In each settlement an advisory council meets regularly, promoting broad participation in decision-making. Of the eight administrative and political directors of the settlements, four are now Miskitus; an explicit goal is that all be indigenous.

This is remarkable in view of the Miskitus' historical ties with Anglo culture and business and their lack of integration into the Nicaraguan revolutionary process. It is even more remarkable considering the pitch of the counterrevolution.

Education in political principles meets with varying degrees of acceptance. In two of the settlements, Sumubila and Wasminona, there were complaints that the adult education was only political. Children, on the other hand, join in revolutionary cheers with gusto.

Perhaps the most unequivocal indication of the growing solidarity between Miskitus and Sandinistas is that the Indians have been armed and integrated into the defense of the settlements. One young Sumubila resident, rifle in his lap, told this reporter with a certain amount of pride how none of the members of his Coco River community had been involved in counterrevolutionary activity and none had fled to Honduras.

Some advocates for the rights of indigenous peoples, such as the International Indian Treaty Council, the American Indian Movement and the World Council of Churches have sent delegations to the Coco River and Tasba Pri and, on the basis of their observations, supported the government's decision to relocate.

This month, three days before a 20-member US peace delegation arrived, 58 counterrevolutionaries and 5 Sandinistas died in an 11-hour combat in Bismuna, one of the evacuated communities just 19 miles south of the border. During the second night of the US "Peace Vigil," another battle took place less than five miles to the north, in which 14 Nicaraguan soldiers were wounded. These continuing clashes leave little doubt the relocation was justified, and in the long run beneficial to those who were moved.

Part Two

HISTORICAL SETTING

Editors' Introduction

This section gives a broad historical framework to the current crisis. Recent Nicaraguan history has been dominated by two themes: the penetration of the United States and the countervailing influence of Sandinista revolutionaries. It was as true when the Marines landed in 1926 as it is today. The tenets of the Monroe Doctrine and the Manifest Destiny summarize one side of the argument, the battle cry "*Patria Libre o Morir*" (free homeland or death) the other. When the United States regards hegemony as not only its right but its moral duty, and Nicaraguans prefer death to that hegemony, a situation of conflict will obviously arise. Part Two explores this fundamental conflict between the two nations which has existed for over a century.

Chapter I:

Nicaragua and the United States: A Pattern Develops

Editors' Introduction

From the Monroe Doctrine, Manifest Destiny, Roosevelt's "big stick" and its replacement by Taft's "dollar diplomacy," through three invasions and two major occupations by US Marines, F.D.R.'s "good neighbor" policy, and finally, to the cold war, the United States has played perhaps *the* key role in the history of Nicaragua and the Caribbean region.

The reading by Ilene O'Malley focuses on the critical period of the 1920s and 30s where the modern roots of *Sandinismo* and *Somocismo* may be found. During this period, "containing Mexican Bolshevism" was as important as "protecting American lives" in the official justifications for US intervention. The real reasons were more complicated, having to do with protecting US capital, and securing the US position of power in the world. President Reagan's admonition that

> The national security of all the Americas is at stake in Central America. If we cannot defend ourselves there, we cannot expect to prevail elsewhere*

is interesting in light of the events of the 1920s and 30s.

The final article in this chapter picks up the story with the assassination of Sandino in 1934, and covers the rise of the Somoza family dictatorship and its operations.

---

*Address to Joint Sessions of Congress, April 27, 1983.

17. *The Nicaraguan Background**

By Henri Weber

Nicaragua, like all the other provinces of Central America, was conquered by Cortés's lieutenants about the year 1523. In fact, the invaders only really subjugated the plains of the Pacific coast, the richest and most highly populated region inhabited by Chorotec Indians of the Aztec family. The jungle-covered mountains of the North West, the dense forests of the East, and the whole Atlantic region, or Miskitu Coast, inhabited by Carib Indians, resisted the Spaniards stubbornly and never fell completely under their control. In these hard-to-reach areas, Indian communities lived until the late nineteenth century in a state of semi-autonomy based on their traditional mode of social organization. On the Atlantic Coast, moreover, they enjoyed British political and military support throughout and beyond the period of Spanish occupation, for Britain was anxious to acquire an operational base for its rivalry with Spain and France, and later with the North Americans. Indeed, in the eighteenth century Moskitia became a *de facto* British protectorate, which has left its mark in a number of cultural traits, most notably the speaking of "coastal English." It was only in 1894, under the presidency of General Zelaya, that the region was truly integrated into the country.

Bartolomé de las Casas, a bishop who took up the Indian cause, left the following indignant account of the hell on earth to which the peoples of the Pacific plains were subjected: "In 1522 or 1523, this tyrant [the governor of the mainland] went off to subjugate the perfectly happy province of Nicaragua, and made a most wretched entry into the region. Who can speak too highly of the cheerfulness, good health, friendliness, and prosperity of the numerous people? It was truly wondrous to see that there were so many villages, spread over the length of three or four leagues and full of wondrous orchards owing to the great number of inhabitants. The land was flat and smooth, so that the population dared not foresake its save with great trouble and difficulty. Hence, they suffered as much as possible the tyranny and bondage which the Christians imposed upon them. For they were by nature very mild and peaceable. This tyrant and his companions, all the other tyrants who had helped him to destroy the other kingdom [Panama], subjected this people to so much evil, butchery, cruelty, bondage, and injustice that no human tongue would be able to describe it. . . . Today [1542], there must be four or five thousand persons in the whole of Nicaragua. The Spaniards kill more every day through the services they exact and the daily, personal oppression they exercise. And this, as we have said, used to be one of the most highly populated provinces in the world."

---

*Reprinted from *Nicaragua: The Sandinist Revolution* (London, Verso Editions and NLB, 1981).

The Burden of Spanish Colonization

Placed under the authority of the Viceroy of New Granada, the Nicaraguan province suffered the common fate of Spanish colonies for a period of three centuries.

It exported slaves to Panama, Santo Domingo, Peru, Ecuador, and Chile; wood, dried meat, tallow, leather, cocoa, and colouring to other colonies and to the mother country. Manufactured goods were legally imported from Spain and smuggled from Britain and France. But such trade was a surface phenomenon, and the colony of Nicaragua remained an essentially subsistence economy. Spanish aristocrats in their haciendas, Indian communities on their collective lands, mestizos and "ladinos" on their *chacras* or small family plots—these all lived in a condition of virtual autarky. Besides, war and piracy often interrupted trade with Europe for long intervals.

Spanish domination brought the introduction of Catholicism and aristocratic structure from the metropolis. At the apex of the social hierarchy, royal functionaries levied tribute and ensured that the colony respected the sovereign's decrees. At a lower level, the provincial aristocracy ruled over huge landed estates, fiercely exploiting an Indian and mestizo work-force held in bondage or subjected to forced labour. The *Señor* in his hacienda had more or less the same powers as the feudal nobleman in his feifdom.

This social system survived the coming of independence in 1821. Slavery was abolished in 1824, and forced Indian labour gradually became a thing of the past. But in one form or another, servile labour persisted until the last quarter of the nineteenth century, profoundly marking social relations in the country.

In this context of extreme social and economic backwardness, political conflicts took the form of unrelenting struggle among regionally based clans. Throughout the nineteenth century and part of the twentieth, endemic warfare pitted the Léon "liberals" against the Granada "conservatives": the former being, in principle, modernist, masonic admirers of the American and French Revolutions, the latter traditionalist bigots attached to aristocratic values. As in the rest of Central America, however, this did not involve a European-style opposition between pro-conservative landowners on the one side and an industrial bourgeoisie plus a feeble, craft-based petty-bourgeoisie on the other. The Nicaraguan "liberals" were champions of free trade more than civil rights and freedoms, and the personal dictatorships they established were not a whit less severe than those of the conservatives. In both camps, moreover, the troops were essentially peasants pressed into service under the command of landowners. The civil wars, very much like wars between clans of rival nobles, plunged the country into a chronic state of instability, all the deeper in that both sides unhesitatingly sought rescue from foreign powers.

The Walker Episode

Ever since its discovery in the sixteenth century, Nicaragua has always been of interest to the great powers. The British were ever present in the field, contending with the Spanish in the period before independence and with the North Americans until the Clayton-Bulwer Treaty of 1850. This country, at the heart of the isthmus between the two Americas, was strategically placed to inflame covetous desires. Its west-facing coastline made it a key point for control of the Caribbean, while its topography and the size of its lakes marked it out as one of the best possible sites for an Atlantic-Pacific canal.

The Central American Federation, of which Nicaragua formed part after independence, broke up into autonomous provinces in 1843. In Nicaragua itself, the struggle between "liberals" and "conservatives" for control of the new state degenerated into civil war. But when the "liberal" Francisco Castellán suffered defeat in the field, he looked for outside support against the "conservative" troops of Frutos Chamorro. William Walker, a journalist with ambitious ideas, responded to the appeal. With the financial backing of the new Accessory Transit Company directors, who were eager to strengthen their hold on the inter-ocean route, he raised an American "phalanx," which took the conservative capital of Granada in October 1855.

It was not long before Walker turned against his liberal bedfellows and seized power in his own right. A Southerner and ardent supporter of slavery, Walker dreamt of shepherding the five isthmus states into a single white republic. This was the period just before the Civil War, and Walker hoped that the construction of a model slave society in Central America would bolster the Southern side against the abolitionists of the North. On June 10, 1858, he duly had himself "elected" president of Nicaragua. His government was at once recognized by the president of the United States, Franklin Pierce. English was declared the official language, and the property of "enemies of the Republic" was handed over to "naturalized Nicaraguans." Slavery was reintroduced.

If Nicaragua's independence was saved, it was because the other Central American states grew alarmed at the ambitions of a pro-slavery privateer whose flag bore the motto: "Five or None!" Financed by the Accessory Transit Company and the British government (concerned at Walker's designs on Moskitia), Central American troops entered Nicaragua and scored a first victory in May 1857 at the port of Rivas. Walker found shelter on an American ship and made a triumphant landing in New York. Four years later, he was back in Central America to recover his presidency, managing to seize the Honduran town of Trujillo. Captured by the British Navy, however, he was delivered to the Honduran authorities and shot on September 12, 1861. This first contact with the United States did not bode well for the future of the region.

The Coffee Era

Once "the American phalanx" had been repelled, the two factions in Nicaragua made their peace. The conservatives would now rule the country for some thirty years.

In the second half of the nineteenth century, coffee rapidly became the major export commodity, far outstripping other products. Twenty years after Guatemala, El Salvador, and Costa Rica, Nicaragua in turn discovered the "green gold" and was swept into the world capitalist market. Coffee represented 50 percent of the value of Nicaraguan exports until the cotton boom of the 1950s and 1960s. The *cafeteleros* were hungry for good land and a "free" labour force with which to exploit it. The colonial legacy of a subsistence economy vaguely tied to the market could no longer satisfy them. Nor could the rudimentary state that corresponded to it.

The US-inspired liberal constitution of 1826, and even the conservative constitution of 1858, emancipated the peasants from obligatory labour. As a result, the Indians returned to their community lands, and small family plots sprang up again. As long as the landed gentry concentrated on extensive animal-rearing and subsistence agriculture, they could accommodate themselves to this development. But when the coffee boom broke, it became necessary to recover land and labor ready for exploitation.

During its thirty-year rule, the conservative aristocracy attempted to realize this goal by creating the legal basis for expropriation and forced labour.* The most reactionary law, promulgated in 1877 by the Pedro Chamorro government, unleashed an uprising of Indian communities in 1881 that was drowned in blood.

A Nicaraguan Bismarck

In 1893 the new plantation bourgeoisie brought to power the strongly nationalist head of the Liberal Party, General José Santos Zelaya. The sixteen-year-long Zelaya dictatorship embarked upon an authoritarian modernization of the country, only to be cut short by the US Marines. After a fashion, Zelaya tried to assemble and guarantee "the general external conditions of capitalist production."

A whole battery of laws considerarbly strengthened the process of expropriation-appropriation of the soil and proletarianization of the labour force. Farmers had to justify their occupation of land by reference to a newly created register of civil property; so that when, unbeknown to the small peasants and Indian communities, a chain of legislation demarcated national lands and identified irregular smallholdings, the legal basis for expropriations existed. In very many cases, moreover, illegal methods were hastily adopted (intimidation, terror), or usurious interest rates of 30-60 percent resulted in the short-term alienation of land and revival of forced labour. As part of the same process, land belonging to the Church and the Indian communities became legally alienable. The effective incorporation of the Atlantic coastal region, now given the name Zelaya, at last created a unified national territory. As a genuine labour market was coming into existence, the economic infrastructure (transport, electricity, communications) and the state infrastructure (public education, administrative apparatus) underwent considerable development.

---

*Jaime Wheelock, *Imperalismo y Dictadura*, Mexico City, 1979.

The growing of coffee was officially encouraged through a government bonus of 5 centavos per tree for those who already owned more than 5,000 square feet. In order to finance public investment and expenditure, Zelaya had recourse to international loans (not always on favourable terms) and to the printing of money.

This small country was not, however, able to contain the ambitions of a liberal dictator who dreamt of commanding a new Central American Federation. In 1906 a war that pitted Nicaragua against Guatemala, Honduras, and El Salvador led to the intervention of the United States and Mexico. The various states of Central America then signed the 1907 Washington Convention, undertaking not to interfere in one another's internal affairs and to submit their differences to an international court of arbitration.

Scorning the Monroe Doctrine, then still very much in force, Zelaya carried his craze for independence so far that he shunned the New York financiers and contracted a major loan with a British banking syndicate. Relations between Washington and Managua, which had at first been excellent, now continually deteriorated as Zelaya's nationalism collided with the growing power of North American imperialism.

The US decision to dig the Panama Canal set the tinder alight. General Zelaya had been counting on an inter-ocean water route for the country's economic development, and he opened negotiations with Germany and Japan for the construction of a rival canal. This was more than Uncle Sam could stand.

18. The Eagle Rises*

By Jenny Pearce

"Fate Has Written Our Policy . . . "

In 1823 President Monroe of the United States declared that interference by any European power in newly emerging Latin American republics would be considered an unfriendly act towards the United States itself. This became known as the Monroe Doctrine. It established the right of the United States to "protect" Latin America and it was based on the assumption that the two regions shared common interests which the northern power had the right to interpret.

During the nineteenth century an aggressive expansionism was added to the defensive paternalism of the Monroe Doctrine. It was rationalized at the time by the phrase "manifest destiny." The United States came to believe that it had been singled out for a special mission: to carry its particular brand of economic, social and political organization initially westwards within North America and later

---

*Reprinted from *Under the Eagle: US Intervention in Central America and the Caribbean* (Boston: South End Press, 1982).

throughout the Western Hemisphere. Westward expansion was completed by the end of the nineteenth century at the expense of the Indian population, which was decimated, and neighboring Mexico, which lost nearly half of its territory (Texas, New Mexico and California) in a war deliberately provoked by the United States.

In the mid-nineteenth century the United States gave a foretaste of its future role in Central America and the Caribbean when it began to challenge British power in the region. At this time British naval superiority and commercial dominance were considerable, and, in addition to its West Indian colonies, Britain controlled part of the Atlantic coast of the Central American isthmus including Belize and the eastern part of Nicaragua.

As the United States pushed westwards and became a Pacific as well as an Atlantic power, its desire for a cheap route linking the two oceans came into conflict with Britain's own wish to control such a route, for which Nicaragua was a favoured location. In 1850 the United States signed the Clayton-Bulwer Treaty with Britain. By this agreement neither power was to hold exclusive control over the Nicaraguan route, but this only temporarily resolved Anglo-American rivalry. Tensions between the two nations mounted in the 1850s and 1860s, particularly after the United States had recognized the short-lived "conquest" of Nicaragua by an American adventurer, William Walker. In 1867 the United States violated the 1850 treaty it had signed with Britain and made an agreement with Nicaragua granting it exclusive rights of transit across the country.

By 1890 United States westward expansion was almost complete and "manifest destiny" came to include wider dreams of empire. It was a period of great change in the United States. By 1870 more people were working in the cities than on farms, half a million immigrants a year came to the United States between 1880 and 1893 till its population (almost 70 million by 1890) overtook that of any single European country. In the 1890s the United States began to outpace Europe in the production of steel, coal and iron and giant monopoly firms emerged with surplus capital for export and in need of raw materials and markets. The strong links between United States big business and the country's foreign policy were forged in these years.

In 1890, following the publication of an influential book which suggested that sea power was the key to greatness, the United States built its first battleship. Expansion overseas seemed the logical next step and Senator Albert Jeremiah Beveridge reflected the mood of the times when he stated in 1898 that

> [American factories] are making more than the American people can use . . .
> Fate has written our policy . . . the trade of the world must and can be ours. And
> we shall get it, as our Mother England has told us how . . . We will cover the
> ocean with our merchant marine. We will build a navy to the measure of our
> greatness. Great colonies, governing themselves, flying our flag, and trading
> with us, will grow about our ports of trade. Our institutions will follow . . . And
> American law, American order, American civilization and the American flag
> will plant themselves on shores hitherto bloody and benighted by those agents of
> God henceforth made beautiful and bright.

The nearest shores, and those most likely to be granted the privileges offered by Senator Beveridge were in Central America and the Caribbean—the "backyard."

"The Great American Archipelago"

The first target was Cuba, which, since the 1840s, had been considered a prime objective of the United States' southward expansion. Unfortunately it was still a Spanish colony and the Spanish refused to agree to United States proposals to purchase and annex the island.

By the 1880s United States capital was heavily involved in the Cuban economy, particularly the sugar industry: "It makes the water come to my mouth when I think of the State of Cuba as one in our family" wrote an American financier in 1895.

In 1898 the Americans decided they would rescue Cuba from Spanish despotism and they went to war with Spain in support of Cuban independence. The contribution of the Cuban population to the country's war of independence, which had been going on for some time before the United States entered it, was subsequently written out of history and the United States declared it had "liberated" Cuba. The United States then took responsibility for Spain's other colonies. It invaded Puerto Rico and purchased the Phillippines for US$20 million. Guam and Puerto Rico were later ceded to the United States by Spain as "spoils of war."

One of the most important results of the Spanish-American War was to turn the United States into a world power with strategic frontiers in the Caribbean and interests across the Pacific Ocean. The scene was set for the American eagle to spread its wings still further. José Martí had foreseen the danger as early as 1895. Although he was at the time engaged in a struggle against Spain he saw his duty also "to prevent the United States with the independence of Cuba extending itself through the West Indies and falling with added weight upon our lands of America." Early in the twentieth century the Nicaraguan poet, Rubén Darío, speculated on what "that Cuban [José Martí] would say today in seeing that under cover of aid to the grief-stricken pearl of the West Indies, the 'monster' gobbles it up, oyster and all."

The Big Stick

Theodore Roosevelt had been the United States' hero of the Spanish-American War, it made his political career and in 1901 he became President.

Roosevelt's particularly truculent use of power in Central America and the Caribbean—invasions, threats and treaties made at gunpoint characterized his presidency though they were not exclusive to it—has associated his period in office with the use of the "big stick."

Roosevelt stressed the strategic importance of the region to United States interests and frequently expressed his impatience with the unstable governments which threatened them. Behind his impatience was a thinly disguised racism which maintained that the Anglo-Saxon was duty bound to help backward races who were incapable of governing themselves. Such views clearly lie behind Roosevelt's famous 1904 addition to the Monroe Doctrine known as the Roosevelt Corollary:

> Chronic wrongdoing or an impotence which results in a general loosening of the ties of civilized society, may in America, as elsewhere, ultimately require intervention by some civilized nation, and in the Western Hemisphere the adherence of the United States to the Monroe Doctrine may force the United States, however reluctantly, in flagrant cases of such wrong doing or impotence, to the exercise of an international police power.

Once again the pursuit of national self-interest was disguised by appeals to moral obligations and United States destiny.

The Panama Canal was completed in 1914 and became an important symbol of growing United States power in the Western Hemisphere. But the United States was not the only imperial power in the Caribbean. Rivalry between the United States and the European powers for control of the Caribbean was intense in these years. Great Britain, France, the Netherlands and even Denmark, until it sold the Virgin Islands to the United States in 1917, all had colonies in the region, and in these years America had to assert its right to defend its "backyard." It would often portray its interventions as well-intentioned acts to prevent more sinister European incursions and in this way tried to conceal its own imperial objectives.

Most of the intervention at this time involved the collection of debt by gunboat. Many countries of the region had borrowed heavily from European and United States creditors in order to build railroads and ports, pledging their customs duties as security. When a country defaulted on interest repayments and the creditors were unable to collect the customs duties they would call on their own governments to help. Thus in 1904 the government of the Dominican Republic defaulted on its payments to a United States financial company. The United States took over the collection of customs duties before any European government who was owed money could do likewise and then distributed the proceeds amongst foreign creditors. At the same time it imposed the United States dollar as the national currency thus opening the door to American business interests. In 1912 the US National Bank was established in the country.

In 1909 the Liberal government of José Santos Zelaya in Nicaragua defied the United States by negotiating a loan with a London syndicate and opening negotiations with the Japanese over a canal through its territory. The United States backed an insurrection against his regime and once it was overthrown appointed its own representative to collect and retain customs revenues, while US bankers Brown Brothers and Seligman negotiated new loans. The Americans were particularly anxious to secure control over rival canal routes in the region.

Sugar Satellites and Banana Republics

Coffee and bananas were to Central America what sugar was to the Caribbean.

As European and North American demand for coffee grew towards the end of the nineteenth century changes took place within the region which would lock it into a system of dependency on the export of one or two crops. The needs of the indigenous population suffered total neglect as the local landowning elites—often referred to as oligarchies, for indeed they were—were encouraged to produce solely for the consumption of Europe and North American markets.

The so-called Liberal reforms of this period paved the way for the expansion of coffee production by permitting the further concentration of land ownership, mostly at the expense of communally-owned Indian lands, and by creating a labour force. As Indians lost their land they were forced to work on the coffee plantations in conditions of semi-slavery. In El Salvador, Honduras and Nicaragua the land itself remained mostly in the hands of the local elite though the processing and marketing of production was in foreign hands. In Guatemala German immigrants as well as the local oligarchy came to own land, and by 1914 nearly 50 percent of Guatemala's coffee production was grown on German-owned lands. In Costa Rica the large rural estates or *latifundios* characteristic of the other countries in the region did not emerge, mostly due to Spanish lack of interest in the country during the colonial period as it lacked both Indians and mineral resources. However, the opportunities offered by the coffee export trade enabled the wealthiest agricultural producers to enrich themselves and this elite consolidated both its political and economic power in this period.

The early twentieth century thus saw on the one hand the emergence of the United States as an imperial power in Central America and the Caribbean, prepared to back up its authority and protect its interests with brute force. On the other, it saw the beginnings of the penetration of United States capital into economies which were already weak, export-oriented and dependent. The effect on political and social developments in the region was as profound as the economic impact.

Dollar Diplomacy

William Howard Taft, who followed Roosevelt as US President, is said by one historian to have replaced bullets with dollars in his policy towards the region, although use of military force was never, in fact, totally abandoned. The basic objectives remained the same, however, as Taft himself made clear in 1912: "The day is not far distant when three Stars and Stripes at three equidistant points will mark our territory: one at the North Pole, another at the Panama Canal, and the third at the South Pole. The whole hemisphere will be ours in fact as, by virtue of our superiority of race, it already is ours morally."

Taft's policy of safeguarding United States financial interests and promoting United States investments, partly to counteract European penetration of the region, was reinforced with even greater vigour by Woodrow Wilson. The United States was now seriously challenging British capital within the hemisphere. In 1914 the United States held 17 percent of all investments in Latin America; by 1929 the figure was 40 percent. Between 1914 and 1929 United States investment in Central

America and the Caribbean tripled, though the majority was still concentrated in Mexico and Cuba. On the Central American mainland United States investment was greatest in Guatemala and least in Nicaragua.

The growing United States economic stake in the region received United States government protection. In the 1920s the Evart Doctrine developed under President Coolidge justified intervention in the internal affairs of Latin American countries to protect the foreign holdings of United States nationals.

The marines were sent into Cuba in 1917 and they stayed until 1923 putting down strikes and protecting United States property. A United States governor virtually managed the finances of the Cuban government and representatives of American sugar interests became leading political figures. The United States was thus able to ensure that the Cuban government pursued policies such as free trade, which suited its own needs for markets for its manufactured goods and cheap sugar imports, at the expense of Cuban national development.

Using the pretext of a civil war, the United States occupied the Dominican Republic in 1916 and stayed until 1924. It claimed it was responsible for maintaining order in the country and it established martial law and a United States military government. Shortly afterwards two American companies set up business in the country: the Central Romana Sugar Refinery and the Grenada Fruit Company; and in 1917 the International Banking Company of New York arrived.

Haiti had assumed considerable strategic importance to the United States after the building of the Panama Canal; the sixty-mile stretch of water between Haiti and Cuba, known as the Windward Passage, was part of the only direct water link between the eastern coast of the United States and the Panama Canal. Political instability, economic bankruptcy and increasing French and German involvement in the country convinced the United States of the need to take direct action to defend its interests. In December 1914 a contingent of marines arrived to occupy the country, they took over the customs houses and established martial law. They were mostly from the deep south and they exacerbated racial and social divisions between the negroes and mulattos on the island and reinforced the rigid social structure. When they finally withdrew in 1934 their only contribution to the country was a few roads and sewers and a pro–United States local militia; the American presence in these years has been described as "socially and politically sterile."

United States marines occupied Nicaragua from 1912 until 1925 and returned again in 1926 after a civil war had broken out, provoked by the results of a United States–supervised election. This second intervention was "to protect American lives and property" and maintain United States supremacy in the region, which the Secretary of State at the time claimed was threatened by "Mexican fostered Bolshevik hegemony between the United States and the Panama Canal." At the time the Mexican government was supporting the Liberals in Nicaragua while the United States backed the Conservatives. This time, however, the United States did face a serious challenge. Augusto César Sandino refused to accept a United States imposed political solution to Nicaragua's civil war. He was a nationalist, opposed to foreign intervention and to the concentration of land in the hands of a tiny oligarchy, and he drew the Americans into the first anti-guerrilla war they had to face in Latin America. 4,000 United States marines were sent to the country and the techniques used against Sandino's forces included aerial bombing.

However, the involvement of United States troops in the struggle brought strong criticism at home and no outright victory in Nicaragua. In 1931 the United States began a gradual withdrawal but not before it had solved the problem of maintaining order in the country. The Americans created a local Nicaraguan military force—the National Guard—trained, equipped and advised by the United States, and when they finally withdrew in 1933 they crowned their legacy to the country by selecting the National Guard's commander: Anastasio Somoza. Somoza, who subsequently became President, as did his two sons after him, gave the first indication of the perfidy which characterized his dynasty's forty-three year rule in Nicaragua. Sandino had been persuaded to accept a gradual disarmament and in 1934, in good faith, he came to Managua to negotiate with the government, where he was murdered on Somoza's orders.

General Smedley D. Butler, who headed many of the American interventions in the region in the early part of the twentieth century gives a frank account of his achievements in his writings in 1935:

I spent thirty-three years and four months in active service as a member of our country's most agile military force—the Marine corps. I served in all commissioned ranks from a second lieutenant to major-general. And during that period I spent most of my time being a high-class muscle man for Big Business, for Wall Street, and for the bankers. In short, I was a racketeer for capitalism... Thus I helped make Mexico and especially Tampico safe for American oil interests in 1914. I helped make Haiti and Cuba a decent place for the National City Bank to collect revenues in ... I helped purify Nicaragua for the international banking house of Brown Brothers in 1909-1912. I brought light to the Dominican Republic for American sugar interests in 1916. I helped make Honduras "right" for American fruit companies in 1903.

The Dictators

As the 1920s progressed there was a growing feeling in United States government circles that the frequent use of the services of General Smedley D. Butler and Co. were becoming too costly. The Nicaraguan experience reinforced this doubt; over one hundred marines were killed in that escapade. The United States sought means of avoiding direct intervention while safeguarding their interests.

The "Somoza" solution seemed ideal and had already been successfully tried out in the Dominican Republic. Before their final withdrawal from that country, the United States had created a National Guard and placed at its head a man called Rafael Trujillo. In 1930, backed by American companies, Trujillo ousted the incumbent President and began a tyrannical rule which was to last 31 years. A United States–trained army and a friendly dictator became the established and favoured means of maintaining order in the region and protecting American interests. It was only a minor embarrassment that these dictators shared basic characteristics of extreme cruelty, corruption and megalomania and that their rule reinforced the already grinding poverty in which the majority of the people lived.

Even when the United States was not directly responsible for the installation of dictatorial regimes, the desire to protect American interests led to tacit support when such regimes appeared all over Central America in the early 1930s. These were years of the Great Depression. The world economic crisis affected the vulnerable Central American economies with particular severity due to their dependence on external markets and United States investment, both of which contracted with the crisis.

Coffee and banana prices plummeted as demand slumped. Peasants, unable to pay their debts, were evicted from their land, while workers were thrown out of their jobs or had their wages slashed. The result was a wave of social unrest in city and countryside throughout the region. Strikes broke out on the American-owned plantations and, as in Costa Rica in 1934, were ruthlessly suppressed by the local armed forces. The oligarchies, alarmed by the course of events, looked to the military as the only way to suppress the social conflicts and maintain their domination. In this way the workers and peasants were forced to bear the brunt of the Depression.

A series of strongmen emerged to dominate the political scene throughout the Depression: Jorge Ubico in Guatemala (1931–44), Tiburcio Carías Andino in Honduras (1931–48) and Maximiliano Hernández Martínez in El Salvador (1931–44). Although the latter did not enjoy immediate support from the United States— the banana companies had not established themselves in El Salvador and the country had not yet come as directly into the American orbit as the other countries—the United States sent a cruiser and two destroyers to stand by during the peasant rebellion of 1932 (two Canadian destroyers were also sent at the behest of the British). Though the revolt was eventually crushed without their help and with the massacre of some 30,000 peasants, the Americans had shown themselves to be "good neighbours."

Good Neighbour Policy

President Franklin D. Roosevelt declared in his inaugural address in March 1933 that United States foreign policy towards Latin America would henceforth follow the policies of the "good neighbour" and that it was opposed to armed intervention.

In practice this policy meant the temporary abandonment of direct intervention at a time when the Depression preoccupied the government at home. United States investment in the region also declined in these years as there was little surplus capital. Investment did not begin to rise again until the 1940s by which time the relative importance of Central America to American business had declined as it turned increasingly to South American oil and to manufacturing industry.

The new policy did not mean that the United States entirely gave up interference in the affairs of its backyard, nor did it abandon the threat of force. In September 1933 United States warships were stationed in every harbour of Cuba as a hint that events there did not please Uncle Sam.

The War Years

The United States military presence in the Caribbean increased considerably during the Second World War when it expanded its installations in Panama, Puerto Rico and the Virgin Islands. In Puerto Rico, for instance, US$200 million were spent on military building projects. Roosevelt Roads, a huge naval complex, and Ramsey air force base were built in these years.

But the United States now began to assert a claim to the Caribbean basin as a whole, much of which was still under British, Dutch and French colonial rule. The immediate aim was to defend the area from the German menace. In return for fifty obsolete destroyers Britain allowed the United States to set up bases in Trinidad, Barbados, St. Lucia and British Guiana. As Gordon Lewis, author of *The Growth of the Modern West Indies*, has written: "The kaleidoscope fortunes of the islands have been made and unmade by the treaty arrangements of European congresses or, more latterly as with the 1940 Anglo-American bases-destroyers deal, of British Prime Ministers and American Presidents." The American presence was to have a profound impact on the countries concerned, particularly Trinidad. American culture penetrated the country through the occupying troops, and US dollars amassed by local operators servicing the Americans' needs helped create the financial basis for local politics.

Roosevelt also made clear to the British in these years that the Americans would no longer accept their colonial presence in the region. The Commonwealth Caribbean was not only strategically part of the American "sphere of influence," it was also of growing economic importance. Large United States corporations had begun to penetrate the West Indies: United Fruit, W.R. Grace, Standard Oil and Texaco, the Chase Manhattan and First National City Banks, and, of particular importance, the bauxite companies. Alcoa and its sister company Alcan had secured an almost complete monopoly over bauxite deposits in the British and Dutch Guianas between 1912 and 1925, mostly through double dealing and trickery. The companies did not process the low-value ore in the Guianas, however, but shipped it back to North America to be smelted into aluminium, so that the Guianas never reaped the benefit of locally produced, high-value aluminium. Aluminium is used in the aircraft and arms industry and Guianese bauxite made a substantial contribution to the Anglo-American victory in the Second World War. There was no reward for the impoverished Guianese people, however. When Arthur Vining Davis of Alcan Aluminium died in 1962 he left a fortune of US$400 million, most of which he gave to a foundation on condition that its funds could not be used to benefit the citizens of the Caribbean bauxite-producing countries or any country other than the United States and its possessions.

During the war an Anglo-American Caribbean Commission was set up with headquarters in Trinidad. Its purpose was to maintain "stability" in the region during the war but also to consolidate the growing United States influence in the area. The results of British and American collaboration in these years was the emergence of a joint strategy for the post-colonial Commonwealth Caribbean which rested on the establishment of a West Indian Federation. The Federation, which was set up in 1958, was virtually imposed by the British and took almost no account of the real needs and interests of the people of the region: it collapsed in 1961. Instead of the Federation becoming independent as a unit as planned, the individual countries became independent on their own. The United States was forced to think again.

This increasing American involvement in the Commonwealth Caribbean reflected the gradual emergence throughout the war years of United States economic and political supremacy over Europe as a whole. In Central America the United States pressured governments to confiscate German investments and property and as European markets were closed the countries of the region came to depend on the single market of the United States. Between 1930 and 1934 Central America sold 20 percent of its total coffee harvest to the United States and 75 percent to Europe; between 1940 and 1944 the United States share increased to 87 percent. As coffee represented 70 percent-80 percent of the region's total exports its dependence on the United States was consolidated still further.

The Post-War World

Throughout the war the United States was planning and preparing for its future role in the post-war world. The United States was in a unique position to impose its world view; it emerged from the war unrivalled economically and militarily. The new order it would help shape would centre around its need for large export markets and unrestricted access to key raw materials. United States planners identified three separate areas—the Western Hemisphere, the Far East and the British Empire—which had to be economically integrated and militarily defended in order to safeguard America's interests.

The United States therefore planned for a cooperative and stable world-wide economic system based on the elimination of trade restrictions, the creation of international financial bodies to stabilize currencies, the establishment of international banking institutions to aid investment, and the development of backward areas. In the words of Cordell Hull, Roosevelt's Secretary of State:

> Through international investment, capital must be made available for the sound development of latent natural resources and productive capacity in relatively undeveloped areas . . . Leadership towards a new system of international relationships in trade and other economic affairs will devolve largely on the United States because of our great economic strength. We should assume this leadership and the responsibility which goes with it, primarily for reasons of pure national self-interest.

Short Chronology of US Activities in Central America and the Caribbean

1823	Monroe Doctrine pronounced
1850	Clayton-Bulwer Treaty
1898	Spanish-American War
1898–1902	US troops occupy Cuba
1901	US acquires Puerto Rico
1903	Panama becomes independent from Colombia
1905	US marines land at Puerto Cortes, Honduras
1906–1909	US troops occupy Cuba
1908	US troops sent to Panama
1909	US-backed overthrow of Zelaya in Nicaragua
1910	US troops land in Honduras
1912	US troops sent to Panama
1912	US troops occupy Cuba
1912	US troops briefly occupy Puerto Cortes, Honduras
1912–25	US marines occupy Nicaragua
1914	Panama Canal is completed
1914–34	US marines occupy Haiti
1916–24	US marines occupy Dominican Republic
1917–23	US marines occupy Cuba
1918	US troops sent to Panama
1919	US marines occupy Honduras' ports
1926–33	US marines occupy Nicaragua and set up National Guard under Somoza. Sandino defeated and assassinated
1924	US marines land in Honduras
1932	US warships stand by during El Salvador *matanza*
1933	Franklin Roosevelt declares "good neighbour" policy
1944	Bretton Woods conference sets up World Bank and International Monetary Fund
1947	The Truman Doctrine signals the beginning of the Cold War
1948	Organization of American States is founded
1954	CIA-backed invasion of Guatemala
1959	Cuban Revolution
1961	Abortive CIA-backed Bay of Pigs invasion of Cuba
1962	Cuban missile crisis

The institutional bases of the new order were elaborated by the Bretton Woods conference in 1944 which was followed by the establishment of the World Bank and the International Monetary Fund. The overseas expansion of United States capital which took place subsequently was unprecedented and centered round the emergence on a grand scale of giant companies with interests in all parts of the globe. These multinational corporations came to dominate the United States economy and that of many regions of the world.

The United States was thus instrumental in establishing an integrated international economic system which for many years it was able to dominate and which it was committed to defending. The emergence of the socialist bloc and the Cold War provided the rationale for United States economic aggression. United States capital was in the vanguard of a crusade: to stem the tide of international communist subversion; "manifest destiny" re-emerged in a new form and to meet new needs. American capital would bring development to backward regions and Latin American elites came to see it as the key to progress. The years following the Second World War saw a huge inflow of United States capital into Latin America. Direct investment grew from US$3 billion in 1946 to US$8 billion in 1961. In Central America direct investment increased from US$173 million in 1943 to US$389 million in 1959 (see Table). The economic importance of Central America to the United States was slight, but the region's dependence on virtually one source of foreign investment consolidated the United States' hold over its economic development.

US Direct Investment in Central America 1936–1959
(in millions of US dollars)

Country	1936	1940	1943	1950	1959
Costa Rica	13.0	24.0	30.0	60.0	73.2
El Salvador	17.0	11.0	15.0	17.0	43.9
Guatemala	50.0	68.0	87.0	106.0	137.6
Honduras	36.0	38.0	37.0	62.0	115.5
Nicaragua	5.0	8.0	4.0	9.0	18.9
Total	121.0	149.0	173.0	254.0	389.1

Source: *Donald Castillo Rivas,* Acumulación de Capital y Empresas Transnacionales en Centroamérica, *Siglo XXI, Mexico, 1980.*

The United States encouraged the belief that there was an identity of interests between the two regions, an inter-American system based on mutually compatible objectives. In 1948 the ninth Pan-American conference set up the Organization of American States (OAS); one of its aims was "to provide facilities for United States investors wishing to exploit the resources of Latin America." It was also to be used by the United States as a means of isolating regimes which tried to withdraw from the inter-American fraternity or to challenge its ideological basis. In 1954 a resolution passed by the OAS "updating" the Monroe Doctrine became known as the Caracas Declaration:

The domination or control of the political institutions of any American state by the international communist movement, extending to this Hemisphere the political system of an extracontinental power, would constitute a threat to the sovereignty and political independence of the American states, endangering the peace of America, and would call for a meeting of consultation to consider the adoption of appropriate action in accordance with existing treaties.

The Cold War had reached Latin America.

19. Play It Again, Ron*

By Ilene O'Malley

Ilene O'Malley recently received her Ph.D. in Latin American History from the University of Michigan.

In his address to Congress, the President of the United States warned of the threat of communism:

> I have the most conclusive evidence that arms and munitions in large quantities ... have been shipped to the revolutionists ... The United States cannot fail to view with deep concern any serious threat to stability and constitutional government ... tending toward anarchy and jeopardizing American interests, especially if such a state of affairs is contributed to or brought about by outside influence or by a foreign power.[1]

Are these the words of Ronald Reagan speaking about the USSR in El Salvador? No. The country referred to is Nicaragua, but the year is not 1980 or 1981. The year is 1927, and the president is Calvin Coolidge. Many of us are shaken to find the US seemingly headed for "another Vietnam," but we should contemplate the response that the Mexican novelist Carlos Fuentes gave to the question of whether El Salvador would be another Vietnam: "No," he said, "it's another Latin America."[2]

Although we are loath to remember, Latin Americans cannot afford to forget the long history of US intervention in their affairs. One of the most instructive examples of this long history is the six-year war (1927–1933) the US waged to stamp out the guerrilla movement led by Augusto Sandino, a man impudent enough to think that Nicaraguans should run their own country. To understand that war, as well as current affairs in Central America, we must begin with the roots of US interventionist policy: the Monroe Doctrine formulated some 160 years ago.

---

*Reprinted from *The Alternative Review of Literature and Politics*, September, 1981.

Grade school history aside, the Monroe Doctrine was not a brotherly act to protect the fledgling nations of the newly independent Spanish American colonies. It was a move to procure for our own enrichment the resources and markets formerly monopolized by Spain, and to scare off our competitors, especially Britain, who already had a foot in the door in the Caribbean. The Monroe Doctrine declared our intention to dominate the hemisphere.

Mexico was the first to fall victim to the expansionism we called our "Manifest Destiny." In 1847 we invaded Mexico City—later memorialized in the Marine Corps Hymn, "From the Halls of Montezuma"—with the result that Mexico was forced to "sell" one half of its territory to the US: what is now Texas, New Mexico, Arizona, California, Nevada, and part of Colorado. These events were to have great repercussions on the fate of Nicaragua.

When the great gold rush of the 1850's occurred in the newly acquired but rather inaccessible California, the US cast entrepreneurial eyes upon Nicaragua, the easiest place to traverse the Central American isthmus before the Panama Canal was built. The Golden West promised fortunes to merchants as well as prospectors, *if* they could get there. US shipping magnate Cornelius Vanderbilt constructed a ferry system across Nicaragua, stepping on the toes of the British, who had a protectorate along the Atlantic coast. "Firm" US policy eventually supplanted the British, and throughout the rest of the 1800's Yankee business interests dominated the strategic and lucrative inter-oceanic transportation system as well as the banana, coffee, mahogany, and gold industries.

By 1909 the nationalist dictator Zelaya decided to break up some of the US control. Although weak and small, Nicaragua could acquire more autonomy by diversifying its foreign creditors. Zelaya negotiated a loan with the British, and considered granting canal rights to Japan, whose imperialist ventures on its side of the Pacific made the US anxious about its intentions on this side. Secretary of State Philander Knox began denouncing Zelaya as a tyrant, and the US may have promoted the Conservative revolt, led by the hitherto unknown Adolfo Díaz, which broke out against Zelaya. Rafael de Nogales writes:

> Zelaya had committed the indiscretion of trying to cancel the concession of the La Luz and Los Angeles Mining Company, in which . . . Knox was the principal stockholder, while a nephew of his was the manager of the Company . . . and was, therefore, also the "boss" of Adolfo Díaz . . . a minor clerk at a salary of twenty or twenty-five dollars a week . . . [3]

When the revolt broke out, Díaz suddenly had $600,000 to contribute to the cause.[4] The revolt was on the verge of defeat when the US Marines landed on the Atlantic coast to save it. Conservative general Estrada became president of a government which, according to the US commander in Nicaragua was

> . . . not in power by the will of the people; the elections were in their greater part fraudulent . . . [T]he present government . . . is in power because of the United States troops . . . [5]

When Estrada proved to be too independent-minded, he was pressured by the US to resign. He was succeeded by his vice-president Adolfo Díaz. The US then moved to secure the financial interests which Zelaya had jeopardized. The Nicaraguan canal zone was sold to the US for $3 million but the money could be used by Nicaragua only with US consent. That sale was ratified by the Nicaraguan Congress while it was surrounded by US Marines and the terms of the sale were read to the congressmen in English.[6] Nicaragua was forced to replace its British loans with loans from US banks, which took half the national railroad, full control of customs duties and the currency system as "security."[7] A legation guard of 100 marines remained in Nicaragua to assure that peace would prevail.

After World War I, the US no longer had to worry about a Japanese or British competition in Central America; Nicaragua was paying off its loans to Wall Street.[8] The US began to think about withdrawing from Nicaragua, but not before setting up a National Guard which was to be manned with US troops until they trained Nicaraguan personnel to take over. In 1925 the US supervised an election which made a Conservative, Solárzano, president, and a Liberal, Sacasa, vice-president.

Within weeks Solárzano was ousted by a right-wing coup and replaced by Emiliano Chamorro, who purged the Liberals from the government. The Liberals resisted the coup in the name of Sacasa, the legal successor to Solárzano. Civil war ensued, and the US Marines returned to Nicaragua. The US "settled" the war by replacing both contenders with a third, "neutral" president, the old quisling Adolfo Díaz. The Liberals, the traditionally more nationalistic party, nevertheless continued to fight against the imposition of Díaz. More marines were sent in to quell the growing opposition.

In the 1920s the State Department feared not that communism would spread from Nicaragua north, but from Mexico south to Nicaragua. After a decade of revolution, Mexico had a government which took a turn to the left in 1924, threatening to expropriate the large US oil companies there.

There was strong sentiment in the US for invading our southern neighbor, and relations between the two countries were extremely tense. Thus, when the US discovered that war matériel was being shipped from Mexico to the Liberals in Nicaragua, the reaction was hysterical. Mexican ships were blown up in a Nicaraguan harbor by the US, and Sacasa was branded an agent of Mexico "bolshevikism," which had to be stopped before it tainted the rest of Central America red. When Calvin Coolidge warned about "outside influence" in Nicaragua, he was speaking of Mexico.

By July 1927, military and diplomatic pressure laced with offers of wealth and position, reconciled the Liberal generals to the new "supervised" government—with one exception. While Anastasio Somoza hastened to ingratiate himself with the US supervisors, Augusto Sandino, a liberal officer, decided to fight to rid Nicaragua of the US presence once and for all. He took to the hills with 400 followers, and defied the Yankees to come and get him. The war with Sandino was on.

The US, as well as Nicaraguan leaders, tried to pass Sandino off as a bandit and to deny his political stance. The campaign to defame his character was as futile as the campaign to catch him. As one marine officer remembered:

> By . . . 1929 it was becoming more and more evident that the marines . . . had
> been called upon to perform an almost impossible task . . . Neither the people
> nor their [local] officials stood behind the marines in their attempt to put down
> lawlessness . . . So long as the people would not assist the marines, the bandits
> could continue to operate . . . and carry on their depredations in spite of
> everything the marines could do.[9]

The heart of the US problem was that the common people did not suffer from
sandinista depredations and lawlessness, and the only ones in need of protection
were the marines themselves and collaborators. The presence of so many soldiers
(about 1 for every 100 Nicaraguans) inflamed anti-Yankee sentiment, and many
Nicaraguans who might otherwise have never supported Sandino did so in reaction
against the often brutal behavior of the Yankee soldiers. One lieutenant was
photographed holding a human head. A marine historian claimed that the officer
had not personally performed the decapitation, yet admitted that US soldiers shot
and abused prisoners, used the "water torture" and mutilated the bodies of their
victims.[10] US troops abused Nicaraguan women, a practice cavalierly dismissed by
the same marine historian as the "natural concomitants of military occupation."[11]

In contrast, it is generally agreed that the Sandinistas avoided victimizing the
people.[12] Sandino prided himself on the discipline of his men, instinctively following the principles of a conscientious and sincere guerrilla. "Do you think," asked
Sandino,

> that we could have existed . . . half a year with all the might of the United States
> against us, if we had been merely bandits? If we were bandits, every man's hand
> would be against us; every man would be a secret enemy. Instead, every home
> harbors a friend.[13]
>
> We have taken up arms from the love of our country because all other leaders
> have betrayed it and sold themselves out to the foreigner . . . What right have
> foreign troops to call us outlaws and bandits and to say we are the aggressors? . . .
> We declare we will never live in cowardly peace under a government installed by
> a foreign power.[14]
>
> . . . We are no more bandits than was [George] Washington. If the American
> public had not become calloused to justice and to the elemental rights of
> mankind, it would not so easily forget its own past . . . If their consciences had
> not become dulled by their scramble for wealth, Americans would not so easily
> forget the lesson that, sooner or later, every nation, however weak, achieves
> freedom, and that every abuse of power hastens the destruction of the one who
> wields it.[15]

Sandino promised to lay down his arms if and only if the US withdrew completely from Nicaragua.

Opposition to US policy ran high abroad and at home. One paper denounced it as "murder"; the US, it said, " . . . created the anarchy she is now trying to suppress . . . . American marines are doing police work for a government which would collapse in sixty seconds" if they withdrew.[16] The news filled up with stories and photos of US atrocities, civilian populations bombed by US planes, refugees fleeing not only the guerrillas, but the Yankees. As official explanations wore thin, *The Nation* complained that throughout the course of the war, the government had "deliberately and persistently lied to the North American people."[17]

Montana Senator Burton K. Wheeler summed up US intervention with these words:

Reduced to the simplest terms, the . . . Coolidge policy has led to armed intervention . . . in behalf of an American-made puppet president foisted upon the people against their own will for the simple reason that he is ready, at whatever cost . . . , to serve the New York bankers who are, and for seventeen years have been, mercilessly exploiting Nicaragua under the aegis of the State Department[18]

Government criticism of such opposition to its policies provoked more popular outrage. The *St. Louis Post Dispatch* wrote:

Apparently, the American people have made a great mistake in believing that the protests of conscience have any place in the council of the Coolidge administration. The story of Nicaragua belies it. We may think ourselves better or more merciful than that, but in truth we are not. These are the transports, the warships, the marines, the cannons, the troop trains, the airplanes and the Stars and Stripes—all testifying to the terror of the Empire.[19]

The *New Leader* warned:

The American government cannot be a despot abroad without becoming a despot at home. Despotism cannot stand criticism. It always commands obedience . . . All that remains is Federal Legislation to square with the reality of the American mailed fist in the Caribbean and Central America. Once having made us all intellectual conscripts of American imperialism the bureaucracy will have an excellent machine to hurl at trade unions and their struggles, to fill the nation with peace-time spies and informers, to penalize all who dissent . . . [20]

Nevertheless, the US forged ahead with the war. But it was a war we were not winning, and by 1930 Washington began looking for a way out. A plan—which would be seen again in Vietnam—was devised for replacing the US soldiers who comprised the Nicaraguan National Guard with natives, and to expand the Guard so that it and not Yankees, could kill sandinistas. The plan took pressure off the US without jeopardizing US interests, for the Guard was under the command of the pro-Yankee enthusiast Anastasio Somoza. Officers were selected through political appointments, distributed as favors to the upper classes of the nation, thereby assuring that the Guard function not as a "neutral" policing agent, but the military arm of the elite. The Guard's distance from the common people was soon recognized. Somoza jailed the man who wrote:

> The Yankee Marines taught the Nicaraguan solider to be cruel . . . They gave him lessons so he could break the holy law of brotherhood, killing compatriots. They taught the Guardsmen to behave like mercenaries in their own land.[21]

As the "Nicaraguaization" went ahead, the US prepared for its exit, permitting an election in late 1932. Sacasa became president. In early 1933, the last Marine left and Sandino, true to his word, ceased hostilities. He was given a grandiose hero's welcome in Managua and then retired with his men to farm in the countryside.

Somoza, who had wanted to destroy Sandino, was displeased with Sacasa's conciliatory attitude toward him. Rumors began to circulate that Somoza was planning a coup. Sacasa therefore had to depend all the more on Sandino's support in order to shore up his government, which increased tension with Somoza. Somoza, however, did not have a coup in mind.

On February 21, 1934, Somoza's men picked Sandino up as he left a dinner at the National Palace. He was machine-gunned to death in a field not far away. The Guard crushed sandinista resistance throughout the country. Although Sacasa finished the rest of term in office, Somoza was thenceforth the real power in Nicaragua. He enjoyed full US support. As Franklin Roosevelt said, "He's a sonofabitch, but he's ours."[22]

Notes

[1]Quoted in Belden Bell, *Nicaragua: An Ally under Siege* (Council on American Affairs, 1978), p. 17.
[2]"Murder by Proxies," *Nation,* April 25, 1981, p. 481.
[3]Rafael de Nogales, *The Looting of Nicaragua* (Robert McBride & Co., 1928), pp. 7-8.
[4]Ibid.
[5]Quoted by Senator Elihu Root in Nogales, p. 10.
[6]Nogales, p. 11.
[7]Mary Helms, *Middle America: A Culture History of the Heartlands and Frontiers* (Prentice-Hall, 1975), p. 256.
[8]Bell, p. 16.
[9]Neil Macauley, *The Sandino Affair* (Quadrangle Books, 1967), p. 135.
[10]Macauley, pp. 228-229.
[11]Macauley, p. 45.
[12]Carleton Beals, "With Sandino in Nicaragua, V: 'Send the Bill to Mr. Coolidge,'" *Nation,* March 21, 1928, p. 317.
[13]Beals, *Nation,* March 21, 1928, p. 316.
[14]Beals, "With Sandino in Nicaragua, IV: 'Sandino Himself,' " *Nation,* March 14, 1928, p. 289.
[15]Beals, "With Sandino in Nicaragua, VI: 'Sandino—Bandit or Patriot?' " *Nation,* March 28, 1928, p. 341.
[16]*Nation,* July 27, 1927, p. 75.
[17]*Nation,* November 2, 1927.

[18]Speech by Senator Wheeler given in Boston on March 6, 1927. Quoted in Nogales, p. 57.
[19]*St. Louis Post Dispatch*, March 15, 1927.
[20]Nogales, p. 126.
[21]Santos López, quoted in Gregorio Selser, *Sandino: General de Hombres Libres,* vol. 1 (Editorial Triángulo, 1959), p. 313. My translation.
[22]*Time,* November 15, 1948, p. 43.

20. *A Dictatorship "Made in the USA"**

By Edmundo Jarquin C. and Pablo Emilio Barreto

With the assassination of General Sandino in 1934 and the subsequent *coup* d'etat against President Sacasa in 1936, Somoza García initiated the longest, most corrupt dictatorship in Latin American history, a dictatorship continually supplied and supported by the United States.

Sustained by his family's monopolistic control of the economy and by the military power of the National Guard, the Somoza dictatorship passed through several stages. Until the mid-1940's, the dictator held relative legitimacy among those sectors of the society who, in their own self-interest, cloaked their leader with an image of "pacifier" and "innovator." By the mid-1940's, Somoza's intentions to establish himself in perpetuity became clear, thus betraying the nationalist recovery goals of the Liberal Party, which Somoza now dominated. Furthermore, because of the democratic surge developing in Central America (emerging from the struggle against fascism during World War II), Somoza entered a period of total isolation. The dictatorship lost its legitimacy and maintained its control only through the coercion and power of the National Guard. By this time large numbers of liberals abandoned Somoza and formed the Independent Liberal Party, which together with the Conservative Party, subsequently constituted a solid bloc of opposition against the dictatorship.

Once the crisis of the second half of the 1940's had passed, a new stage developed. Worldwide economic recovery in the postwar period and technological developments in the area of agricultural chemicals facilitated the development of cotton cultivation. The rapid expansion of cotton production gave Nicaragua a primarily agrarian export economy. The resulting profits had a major impact on the overall economy, extending and diversifying the productive potential of the country.

Based primarily on cotton production and secondarily on the expansion of coffee and beef exports, significant economic growth led to the rapid modernization of the economy. Capital accumulation, mainly agrarian based, was transferred to

---

*Reprinted from *Nicaragua: A People's Revolution* (Washington, D.C., EPICA Task Force, 1980).

other economic sectors such as industry, finance and commerce. This new wealth was dominated by the Somoza family, which had become synonomous with "the State." With this control over the expansion and diversification process, Somoza greatly increased his impact upon the social life of the country.

As a result of these economic changes, new social sectors emerged while others rapidly deteriorated. Cotton cultivation, developed primarily in the departments of Managua, Masaya and along the West Coast, accelerated a process of concentrating vast agrarian properties into a few hands. This same process converted large numbers of small farmers into plantation peasants and produced a significant migration of other *campesinos* off the land. These migrants converged particularly on the cities of the Pacific coast (Lén and Chinandega) and on Managua, the capital, overloaded the urban employment market and put a tremendous strain on the weak social service structures (housing, schools, hospitals). This created those sociological imbalances commonly called "marginalization."

At the same time, because of the expansion of employment in the industrial, financial and state bureaucracy sectors, a new salaried middle class emerged. Social and economic success came to this middle class so rapidly that it failed to question the roots of its development. This created, intentionally or not, a new social strata which legitimized the dictatorship. This strata together with the emerging capitalist class—the cotton producers, who also were completely dependent on the financial and technical assistance apparatus of the State—further strengthened Somoza's political control.

Despite the growing political legitimation by these new and ascending sectors, the vitality of the traditional liberal-conservative conflict was sustained during the 1950's. The conservative oligarchy maintained its economic independence from the State with the production and sale of coffee and beef inside and outside the country. This translated into their political autonomy from the Somoza regime.

In 1956 the founder of the dynasty was killed by a young poet and patriot, Rigoberto López Pérez. Following Somoza García's death a conflict developed between the traditional opposition and Somoza's sons during the election campaign to select his successor. At that moment United States Ambassador Whelan came to the rescue of the dynasty by giving total support to the succession of the dynasty through Luis Somoza Debayle, Anastasio's eldest son.

The creation of the Central American Common Market in the early 1960's stimulated the process of industrialization and thus accelerated the pace of modernization. However, this industrial expansion did not lead to any independence from Somoza. The state bureaucracy and the agrarian-export market, which developed at a parallel pace with industry, kept the Somoza interests in control of this expansion. The exploitative agrarian structure remained untouched, however, and this weakened the potential for industrial expansion.

> The seed of Sandino's blood
> lashes the murderous rooftops;
> multiplied, in torrents

it will cover exposed rooftops;
and will insure, inevitable apocalypse.
It will exterminate all of the murderers,
and each and every one
of the murderers' seed.

Their treacherous embrace of Sandino
is pregnant with biblical premonitions
like the crime of Cain
like the kiss of Judas.

And then peace will reign . . .
and Nicaragua will fill with olive branches and voices
that loft to the heavens
an everlasting psalm of love.

Rigoberto López Pérez
patriot and executioner of Anastasio I

At the same time, the portion of Nicaraguan capital in the Conservative Party was finally forced into dependency upon the State apparatus (i.e., upon Somoza) because all industry in Nicaragua functioned under the control of the State through its fiscal, credit and commerical concessions and privileges. The conservative faction, unable to gain control over this apparatus through election, rebellion or *coup d'etat*, could only obtain services from the State apparatus through coming to an *understanding* with Somoza. This ended the independence of the conservatives and thus the vitality of the old liberal-conservative conflict. This *understanding* was formalized in a pact between the conservative leader, Fernando Aguero and President Anastasio Somoza Debayle (Tacho), who inherited the dynasty following the death of his brother Luis in 1967. The pact was the product of the increasing concentration of control by those few economic groups in the parasitic bureaucracy linked to Somoza.

The decade of the 1960's was, without doubt, the period of Somoza's greatest power and social legitimation. The expanding State apparatus and the growing economy gave Somoza an unprecedented degree of influence among the upper class sectors—through coercion, blackmail and fraud. His secure position was guaranteed by the accumulation of family assets, multiple links with North American capital, and close associations with the Central American bourgeoisie, a factor that consolidated his borders. And, when none of these factors was able to resolve any domestic controversy, there was always the National Guard.

History Will Never Forgive You

But history creates its own contradictions. The Somoza model of growth during the two previous decades, while producing wealth, modernization and political consolidation, also produced incredible social injustices and inequalities. As both the old and new social elites enriched themselves and prospered under Somoza, broad sections of the population became ever poorer and were swallowed up by the most brutal misery.

Urban development was incapable of absorbing the growing unemployed work force that emerged from natural population growth as well as from the enormous migration of people expelled from the land. Within the poor rural population, a third of the *campesinos* were landless while another third subsisted on tiny farm plots located on marginally productive land. Administrative corruption—induced and encouraged by the dictatorship—prevented an adequate or planned expansion of social services, despite a growing economy and increased foreign investment.

This increasingly unequal distribution of wealth placed a brake on the expansion potential of the internal market and in turn on the growth of the entire economy. Despite agrarian and industrial diversification, Nicaragua's economy continued to depend largely on exported agricultural products, which suffered from constantly fluctuating world prices.

In summary, these inequalities represented a profound and growing social contradiction on top of an extremely fragile model of growth. These two factors ultimately precipitated the irreversible crisis of the Somoza dictatorship.

The Struggle against the Dictatorship

Despite the expanding control of the dictatorship, a pro-democratic spirit persisted in the country—holding fast to its goals of justice and freedom.

This spirit was present in all the rebellions, resistance, protests and martyrdoms of young people from 1959 onward, including the struggle of the Sandinista Front for National Liberation (FSLN).

The weakening of the liberal-conservative conflict which became obvious during the second half of the 1960's created a political vacuum that was not immediately filled by the FSLN. While the FSLN was accumulating experience, the Sandinistas remained politically and strategically isolated. But the reformist tendencies also lacked a social base from which to fill this vacuum. The middle class, where such reforms traditionally arise, did not recognize the crisis because it was caught up in the process of social and economic self-improvement.

Gradually, the contradictions in the model of economic and social growth created the conditions for a final crisis of the dynasty. The struggle for freedom and justice merged out of new organizational molds, with new content and perspectives, and with a greater intensity than ever seen before in Nicaragua. These forms began to appear after 1972.

The Crisis on the March

The crisis in the Central American Common Market—precipitated by the armed conflict between Honduras and El Salvador in 1969—coincided with a decline in international prices for primary agricultural and beef products. Together, these two factors induced a market deceleration in the level of economic growth and a decline in the level of private investment.

Somoza was unable to adjust to the economic crisis. He tried to compensate for this decline through increased public spending, but his methods only increased unemployment while decreasing real income, especially of the popular sectors. This led to economic stagnation in general.

Then, in December 1972, an earthquake destroyed a large part of Managua. But, despite its tragic human consequences—10,000 died and over 100,000 were dislocated—the quake actually stimulated the economy. The destruction of housing, buildings, roads, furniture, and inventories created new opportunites for investment and production to replace the items lost. In addition, a huge influx of international and public and private funds for reconstruction and insurance created the financing needed for the new investments. When this influx of funds was followed by favorable prices for sugar and beef in 1974-75 and for coffee in 1975, a significant reactivation of the Nicaraguan economy occurred.

However, the earthquake and its consequences led to a profound conflict between the bureaucratic bourgeoisie (Somoza and his friends) and the traditional bourgeoisie. The Somoza bloc, sustained by State power, exacerbated the existing administrative corruption by excluding other sectors of the bourgeoisie from the opportunities for investment created by the earthquake. Somoza enriched himself personally in the process by organizing his own bank, insurance company, finance and construction firms. Overstepping the traditional ethical bounds of capitalist competition, Somoza took over the most dynamic areas of capital accumulation.

At the same time, the government's failure to respond to the critical needs of the people following the earthquake precipitated a crisis of support among the middle class and especially among the masses of suffering poor. The exaggerated administrative corruption had led to an alarming decline in the level of public administration. The government's inability to adequately administer the reconstruction process increased the already sharp social inequalities. In turn, Somoza's failure to act, coupled by his selfish exploitation of the quake, led to a widespread political radicalization of the people.

Given this fraud, and in order to finance some post-quake reconstruction. Somoza borrowed large sums of money, leading to a sharp increase in foreign indebtedness. This practice, in time, further reduced the dictator's space for political and economic maneuvering. Incurring debts, by itself, might not be questionable if the new funds are destined to finance productive investments which will generate income to repay the loans. But such borrowing is dubious when it is done at such an accelerated rate (from $200 million dollars at the beginning of 1973 to $800 million by the end of 1977) and on the basis of repayment terms that are incompatible with the development project supposedly being financed. Above all, such borrowing is suspect when the institutions that are to administer the foreign debt (such as Somoza's *Banco de Vivienda* and *Instituto de Fomento Nacional*) are inefficient, dishonest and already without capital assets as a result of corruption.

But to fully understand the depth of Somoza's crisis one must also look at the other significant developments of the post-quake period. First, as a result of Vatican Council II, and the Latin American Episcopal Conference in Medellín in 1968, the Catholic church had been redefining its goals and reorganizing its hierarchy. This was particularly true of the church in Nicaragua. This process led to a gradual divorce of the church from the dictatorship, especially as Somoza lost public support. Initially, the church only reduced its official support of Somoza, but later it began to take overt actions challenging the regime.

Second, in the strictly political arena, organizational and ideological opposition to the dictatorship arose from the non-traditional parties. In December 1974, the Democratic Union of Liberation (UDEL) was created, led by Pedro Joaquín Chamorro. UDEL represented a broadly pluralistic convergence of political forces, including conservatives, liberal democrats, Christian and social democrats, and even the Nicaraguan Socialist Party. These forces united around a platform calling for the recovery of democratic rights and a social and economic transformation of the society.

In addition, the Sandinista Front was becoming more closely associated with the struggle for democratic renewal, and especially with the immediate problems and demands of the masses. Toward this end, the FSLN established bases among the people which in time helped the organization overcome its political and strategic isolation.

Finally, with the ascendancy of the Carter administration, the dimension of human rights appeared as a new strategy in North American politics. Whether or not this strategy implied any fundamental change towards Latin American problems, the overwhelming proof and continued denunciations of human rights violations in Nicaragua weakened the support of Somoza by the U.S. government—the creator and patron of the dictatorship during its entire existence. Thus, the United States relationship passed from one of unconditional support for Somoza to one that took on an ambiguous stance.

Chapter II:

Building the Revolution

Editors' Introduction

This chapter covers the Sandinista revolution. "Nicaragua: Zero Hour" written in 1969 by FSLN cofounder Carlos Fonseca Amador, was the first major analysis put forth by the FSLN. In it Fonseca analyzed the Nicaraguan situation as it was in those years, and examined previous FSLN efforts in a critical light. The future strategy of the FSLN was to a large extent based on this important work. This is followed by the "Historic Program of the FSLN," in which the framework for a revolutionary government was first articulated. One can see in this 1969 document the theoretical roots of the policy being implemented by the present government of Nicaragua.

Description of the final buildup and triumph of the revolutionary forces begins with an excerpt by George Black about the ever deepening crisis of the Somoza dictatorship following the 1972 earthquake. Henri Weber then describes the final struggle for power, including the organization and unification of the major tendencies or factions of the FSLN and the critical differences among them. Finally, a short statement on revolutionary justice by Tomás Borge, the last surviving original member of the FSLN and current Minister of the Interior, reflects the moral tone of those who led the overthrow of Somoza.

21. Nicaragua: Zero Hour*

By Carlos Fonseca Amador

Carlos Fonseca Amador was the central leader of the FSLN from the time he helped found it in July 1961 until his death at the hands of Somoza's National Guard on November 7, 1976. Today an eternal flame burns for him at the Plaza de la Revolución *in Managua, where in November 1979, 100,000 people gathered to mark the anniversary of his death. The following article first appeared in the Spanish language edition of* Tricontinental, *No. 14, 1969. This translation is by Michael Taber and Will Reissner, and is based on a 1979 reprint in Managua.*

The Economic Situation

The people of Nicaragua have been suffering under the yoke of a reactionary clique imposed by Yankee imperialism virtually since 1932, the year in which Anastasio Somoza G. was named commander in chief of the so-called National Guard (GN), a post that had previously been filled by Yankee officials. This clique has reduced Nicaragua to the status of a neocolony—exploited by the Yankee monopolies and the local capitalist class.

At the present time, the economic crisis that the country has been suffering has gotten worse. In the years immediately preceding 1966, the national economy grew at an annual rate of 8 percent. By contrast, in the years 1966 and 1967 the growth rate declined to 3.1 and 4.6 percent respectively.

The production of cotton, which has been increasing since 1950, will increase only slightly in the future. This is due, on the one hand, to a saturation of the foreign capitalist market supplied by national production. And in addition, it is due to the growing competition from synthetic fibers. There has, in fact, been a major drop in the prices offered by the foreign capitalist market for the harvest from the 1968 planting. This last fact has persuaded the country's government to establish commercial relations with some socialist countries, which will take part of the cotton harvest. This crop amounts to 26 percent of the cultivated land in Nicaragua.

Regarding coffee, which is the second largest export product, there is already overproduction, which cannot be sold on the capitalist market. Regarding sugar production, official sources state that it is unlikely that the pace of growth can be maintained in the immediate future.

The exploitation of minerals such as gold and copper, which is directly in the hands of foreign investors, pays ridiculously small sums to the national treasury through taxes. Parallel with this, the handing over of the national riches to the Yankee monopolies has continued to increase. In 1967, for example, a law went into

*Reprinted from a pamphlet published by Pathfinder Press, New York, 1982.

effect that gave Magnavox, a company specializing in the exploitation of forest, absolute ownership of a million hectares of national territory.

At the same time, the ruling clique handles the funds of the state banks as if they were personal funds, while fraud and smuggling reach staggering dimensions. The Somoza family, which had very limited economic resources when it took power, has obtained a vast fiefdom, whose domains go beyond Nicaragua's borders and extend into the other countries of Central America.

In Nicaragua, moreover, there is an unjust distribution of land. Statistical reports for the year 1952 show that a few proprietors control 55 percent of the total area of privately owned farms.

Nicaragua offers exceptional conditions for the development of cattle raising. Nevertheless, the consumption of products derived from cattle has declined and the increase in exports has largely been due to foreign sales of cows that would have contributed to an increase in the quantity of animals.

The advantages provided to producers of products for foreign markets—in this case for growing cotton—has led to a situation where food products are grown on the worst lands, which also means that imports are needed to satisfy this important sector.

Nicaragua is among the countries that have been hurt most by the so-called Central American economic integration. It is well known that this integration has been simply a plan to increase the economic hold of the Yankee monopolies over Central America. This scandalous fact has reached such a magnitude that even spokesmen of the Nicaraguan regime itself have been put in the situation of publicly stating that the industries established as a result of this integration do not enhance national economic development.

As with the other countries of Central America, there is no oil production in Nicaragua. It has been stated, however, that if there were possibilities for oil exploitation in Central America, the Yankee monopolies would have an interest in hiding it, in order to maintain it as a reserve in case revolutionary governments were established in the countries that currently produce oil.

Although the governmental capitalist sector represents the dominant segment of the country's capitalist class, it must be pointed out that the sector of capitalists who call themselves "oppositionists" are also involved in exploiting the Nicaraguan people. Many times, the governing and "opposition" groups jointly exploit important sectors of the national economy, as is the case regarding sugar, milk, the press, banking, liquor distilleries, etc.

The economic system described above turns the other classes making up Nicaragua's population into victims of exploitation and oppression. The poor diet of the working classes has caused numerous deaths through hunger. It's known that in 1964 hundreds of peasants died of hunger in the Tempisque area, in the department of Matagalpa. In various regions in the north, the incidence of goiters is very high. In the Malacaguas area, there have been cases of collective dementia provoked by poor diet; night blindness resulting from Vitamin A and protein deficiencies has occurred in areas around the town of Darío.

A few years ago, some tests carried out in a school in Jinotepe, a region located near the country's capital, indicated that every one of the 200 students suffered from tuberculosis.

Only 1.1 percent of the Nicaraguan population has completed primary school. Fifty percent of the population has had no schooling whatever. The proportion of students that leave school in the first grade or repeat grades is extremely high (73 percent). Only 21 percent of the student population comes from the sector of society with income levels at or below the country's average. Out of 200,000 young people from fourteen to nineteen years of age, barely 20,000 are enrolled in high school or commercial, vocational, or agricultural education.

Infant mortality reaches dreadful levels in Nicaragua. More than 50 percent of the deaths in the country occur among persons under fourteen years of age. Out of every thousand children born, 102 die. Six out of every ten deaths are caused by infectious—meaning curable—diseases. In recent investigations 9.28 percent of the population had a positive reaction in tests for malaria, while in Costa Rica it is 0.96 percent, and in Panama, 4.98 percent.

A Tradition of Rebellion

A notable feature of Nicaraguan history, particularly during the stage that began with independence from Spanish rule in 1821, is the use of violence by different political forces within the exploiting classes, fighting over control of the government. Peaceful changes between different factions of the ruling classes, which have been rather frequent in other Latin American countries, have not taken place in Nicaragua. This traditional experience predisposed the Nicaraguan people against electoral farces and in favor of armed struggle. There is no doubt, then, that the Nicaraguan people have a rich tradition of rebellion.

It is a fact that the Nicaraguan people have taken up arms to fight specific forms of oppression many times through movements headed by individuals, movements that in no sense could lead to progressive revolutionary change. This represents another characteristic of the Nicaraguan people throughout their history. This characteristic relates to the lack of a deepgoing revolutionary consciousness.

The ideological obscurantism inherited from the colonial epoch has continued to weigh heavily in preventing the people from marching with full consciousness toward struggle for social change. It is indisputable that throughout their history the Nicaraguan people have endured numerous battles in which they have demonstrated their courage. But they have marched to these struggles more by instinct than through consciousness. Perhaps it is useful to repeat in the case of Nicaragua the words that Marx wrote in relation to Spain. Marx pointed out that the Spanish people had traditionally been a rebel people, but not a revolutionary people.

The national and international conditions that currently prevail make it possible for at least a sector of the Nicaraguan people to initiate armed struggle, conscious that they are trying not simply to achieve a change of men in power, but a change of the system—the overthrow of the exploiting classes and the victory of the exploited classes.

Origin and Prolongation of the Present Regime

It is not possible to analyze the conditions that have permitted the ruling clique to remain in power for more than three decades without stopping to study the country's situation at the time this regime was installed, as well as the situation that has been developing for more than thirty years.

From 1926 to 1936 the Nicaraguan people went through one of the most intense periods in their history. The armed struggle, through which the people sought change, produced more than 20,000 deaths. The struggle began as a fight against a Conservative government imposed by the North Americans, went through the Sandinista resistance, and concluded with Anastasio Somoza's military coup against Juan B. Sacasa.

The struggle was carried out without an industrial proletariat existing. The incipient bourgeoisie betrayed the Nicaraguan people and sold out to the Yankee intervention. The bourgeoisie could not be immediately replaced as the vanguard of the people's struggle by a revolutionary proletariat. The Sandinista resistance, which became the heroic vanguard of the people, had an almost totally peasant composition, and therein lies the glory and the tragedy of that revolutionary movement.

It was a glory for the Nicaraguan people that the most humble class responded to the stains against the honor of the homeland, and at the same time a tragedy because it involved a peasantry lacking any political level whatsoever. Moreover, there were leaders of important guerrilla columns who were totally illiterate. As a result, once Sandino was assassinated his movement could not maintain its continuity.

The prolonged armed struggle, which ended in betrayal and frustration, exhausted the people's strength. The sector headed by Anastasio Somoza won hegemony over the traditional Liberal Party, while the opposition to Somoza's government came to be dominated by the traditional Conservative Party, a reactionary political force profoundly weakened because in the 1930s this party's sell-out to the Yankee interventionists was fresh in the people's memory.

An important factor that also seriously contributed to the interruption of the anti-imperialist struggle was the situation arising from the outbreak of the Second World War, which concentrated the focus of the world's reactionaries on Europe and Asia. Yankee imperialism, the traditional enemy of the Nicaraguan people, became an ally of the world antifascist front. The lack of a revolutionary leadership in Nicaragua prevented this reality from being interpreted correctly, and Somoza took advantage of the situation to consolidate the rule of his clique.

The Rise of the Old Marxist Sector

For many years, the influence of the Marxist sector in the opposition was almost completely under the control of the Conservative sector, the political force representing the interests of one sector of the capitalist class. One of the factors that contributed to the weakness of the Marxist sector originated in the conditions in which the Nicaraguan Socialist Party (the traditional Communist organization in Nicaragua) was formed. That organization was formed in June 1944, when the Second World War was still not over, and in a period when the views of Earl Browder were in full force. Browder, the general secretary of the Communist Party of the United States, proposed conciliation with the capitalist class and with North American imperialism in Latin America.

In those years, the Nicaraguan workers' movement was basically made up of artisans, and this provided a base for anti-working-class deviations. In addition, the leadership of the Socialist Party was also of artisan origin, and not of proletarian roots as the Nicaraguan Socialist Party demagogically asserts. It was a leadership that suffered from an extremely low ideological level.

For many years, the revolutionary intellectual was a rare exception in Nicaragua. The radical and free-thinking intellectuals of the years of the US armed intervention, who as a class represented a bourgeoisie that ended up capitulating, could not be replaced by intellectuals identified with the working class, for the reasons previously explained. As a result, the intellectual movement in Nicaragua came to be the monopoly of a Catholic element, who for a period even began to openly identify with fascism. In this way, the door of thought remained shut to the revolutionary movement.

The Nicaraguan Socialist Party was organized in a meeting whose objective was to proclaim support to Somoza's government. This took place on July 3, 1944, in the Managua gymnasium. To be rigorously objective, it's necessary to explain that this very grave error was not the result of simple bad faith by the leaders. We must look at the factors that brought it about.

The Marxist leadership did not possess the necessary clarity in the face of the Conservative sector's control over the anti-Somozaist opposition. It could not distinguish between the justice of the anti-Somozaist opposition and the manuevers of the Conservative sector.

Once Somoza had used the pseudo-Marxist sector for his own benefit, he unleashed repression against the workers' movement, which, due to the comfortable conditions in which it was born, did not know how to defend itself with the necessary revolutionary firmness.

Parallel to this, the capitalist sector of the opposition (Conservative Party, Liberal opposition grouping) carried out all kinds of compromises with the Somoza regime.

Role of the Cuban People's Struggle and Revolutionary Victories

The principal characteristic of the period from the assassination of Sandino in 1934 until the triumph of the Cuban revolution in 1959 was the interruption of the traditional armed struggle as a systematic tactic to fight the ruling regime. Another main characteristic was the almost total domination that the Conservative sector exerted over the anti-Somozaist opposition. That was the situation, lasting for twenty-five years, that preceded the new stage, which began with the armed struggle of the Cuban people and their victorious revolution.

There were a few exceptions to that long pacifistic period. But these were almost always insignificant actions by the Conservative sector, behind the backs of and against the people. In April 1954, an armed coup was foiled, which although under Conservative hegemony, involved elements that had revolutionary inclinations. The attitude of these revolutionary elements, along with the action of the patriot Rigoberto López Pérez, who gave his life in bringing Anastasio Somoza G. to justice on September 21, 1956, must be viewed as precursory events to the insurrectional stage that developed several years later.

The Cuban people's rebellion had an influence even before its victorious outcome. Thus, in October 1958, there was the guerrilla action in which the leader, the veteran Sandinista Ramón Raudales, was killed. There were a whole series of armed actions against the reactionary government of Nicaragua, including the following: Ramón Raudales, in the mountains of Jalapa, in October 1958; El Chaparral in June 1959; Manuel Díaz Sotelo, in Estelí, in August 1959; Carlos Haslam, in the mountains of Matagalpa, in the second half of 1959; Heriberto Reyes, in Yumale, in December 1959; Las Trojes and El Dorado, in early 1960; Orosí, on the southern border, in the second half of 1959; Luis Morales, on the San Juan River on the southern border, in January 1960; Poteca River on the northern border, January 1961; Bijao River, November 1962; the Coco River and Bocay River, in 1963; clash between peasants and local authorities in 1965 in the Uluse region of Matagalpa; economic actions against banks in 1966; actions in Managua, January 22, 1967; incursions in Panacasán in 1966 and 1967; economic bank action in Managua and certain revolutionary executions in some areas of the countryside in 1963; battle with the National Guard in Oaosca, Matagalpa, February 1969.

In some encounters, especially in the first months of the new stage, elements linked to the traditional capitalist parties were influential in the leadership of these actions. But in general, these efforts increasingly revealed the determination of the revolutionary sector to take up arms to win the country's liberation.

The period of gestation of the current revolutionary armed struggle has lasted almost ten years and this length of time is clearly a result of the characteristics of the revolutionary movement that have been explained.

The Rise of the Revolutionary Armed Organization

Especially in the first years of the new stage, the revolutionary leadership was obliged to take up arms with leaders who often lacked the political conviction needed to lead the struggle for national liberation. As the process has developed, these leaders have been replaced by comrades who possess a profound conviction and an unbreakable determination to defend the people arms in hand.

Another very prominent aspect of the first period of the new stage was the lack of an adequate revolutionary organization linked to the broad masses of the people, and especially to the peasants. It should be noted that the composition of what could be called the revolutionary groups was primarily made up of artisans and workers with a very low political and ideological level. At that time, revolutionary militants with a university student background were an exception. Students fell in different actions, but each group as such lacked the numbers needed to enable it to play a very important part in assimilating the experiences that the individual students were acquiring. The revolutionary groups lacked cadres who had the ability to solve the difficult problems that the situation posed.

One aspect that is worth looking at regarding the work that has been done over the last decade is that no one knew how to combine underground activity with work among the popular masses. In general, importance has been given only to underground activity, although after the defeat at the Bocay River in 1963 and the Coco River between 1964 and 1966 the error was committed of interrupting insurrectional work in order to pay attention to work among the masses.

It must be pointed out that for a period of time, more precisely up to 1962, each individual armed action came from a different group. That is, they reflected the total anarchy that the insurrectional revolutionary sector suffered from. The Sandinista National Liberation Front (FSLN) marked the overcoming of that problem, providing this sector with its political and military instrument.

Between 1959 and 1962, some of the components of the FSLN retained the illusion that it was possible to accomplish a change in the pacifistic line of the leadership of the Nicaraguan Socialist Party. In the year 1962 this illusion was dissolved in practice with the establishment of the Sandinista Front as an independent grouping, although for some time to come the idea was maintained that it was possible to arrive at specific unity with the Socialist Party, something which reality has refuted.

The movement that culminated at the Coco River and the Bocay River was the first action prepared by a more or less homogeneous revolutionary group. This first attempt was like a dry run for the revolutionary sector.

This first defeat led to a position marked with a reformist streak. It is true that armed struggle was not renounced and the conviction remained that this form of struggle would decide the unfolding of the Nicaraguan revolution. But the reality was that for some time the practical work of continuing the preparations for armed struggle was interrupted. It is also true that after the 1963 defeat our movement was seriously splintered, but we did not know how to adequately overcome the internal crisis that developed.

One factor that undoubtedly influenced the deviation was that our armed defeat coincided with a downturn in the anti-Somoza movement in Nicaragua. In 1963, the political ascent initiated by the struggle and victory of the Cuban people was interrupted. The basis for the downturn was that in February 1963 the Somozaist clique successfully carried out the maneuver of holding an electoral farce to impose the puppet René Schick.

In any case, although this downturn in the general situation took place, the FSLN leadership did not fully understand this to be no more than a partial phenomenon, inasmuch as the direction of the revolutionary movement was fundamentally toward progress and in transition toward maturity.

It was correct in that period to pass over to rebuilding the insurrectional organization and accumulating new forces with which to relaunch the armed struggle, but this goal naturally demanded an uninterrupted maintenance of a series of insurrectional-type tasks: accumulating material resources, training combatants, carrying out certain armed actions appropriate to the strategic defensive stage, etc.

This deviation in tactics was also expressed in the ideology that the Sandinista Front adopted. Although it raised the banner of anti-imperialism and the emancipation of the exploited classes, the Front vacillated in putting forward a clearly Marxist-Leninist ideology. The attitude that the traditional Marxist-Leninist sector had maintained in the Nicaraguan people's struggle contributed to this vacillation. As has been stated, this sector in practice has openly played the game of the Somozaist clique. This factor, together with the ideological backwardness prevailing in the revolutionary sector of the country, led to vacillation in adopting an ideology that on the national level was rooted in compromise. It can be said that at that time there was a lack of clear understanding that it was only a question of time before the youth and people of Nicaragua would begin to distinguish between the false Marxists and the true Marxists.

Consequently, in the years 1964 and 1965, practically all the emphasis was put on open work, which included legal work among the masses. Clandestine tasks were carried out, above all in the countryside, but the main emphasis of the work during that time was legal. Reality showed that legal work carried out in that manner did not serve to accumulate forces and that the progress achieved was minimal. Neither can it be overlooked that the legal work through the now-disappeared Republican Mobilization group, the student movement, and peasant movement suffered from lack of discipline, audacity, and organization.

One must also conclude that revolutionary work (whether it be public, legal, or clandestine), cannot be advanced in an accelerated way if the armed revolutionary force is lacking. It was the lack of such a force that determined the extreme limitations of the legal work carried out in the years 1964–65.

Our experience shows that the armed revolutionary force (urban and rural) is the motor force of the revolutionary movement in Nicaragua. The armed struggle is the only thing that can inspire the revolutionary combatant in Nicaragua to carry out the tasks decided on by the revolutionary leadership, whether they be armed or of any other revolutionary character.

Parenthetically, during the years 1964 and 1965 important contact with the peasant sector was developed. Comrades of urban extraction permanently established themselves in areas situated on both ends of the northern region of the country, and made trips to learn the peasants' problems firsthand and organize the revolutionary struggle in the countryside.

It must be said, however, that full advantage was not taken of the broad contact that was established with the peasants. In the countryside, some mass peasant meetings were held, some peasant delegations were sent to the city to expose the problems of the countryside, and the peasants occupied some lands, challenging the violence of the big landlords. However, an accelerated pace of peasant mobilization was not maintained. Contact was preserved at specific points and was not extended to other places where the peasants suffered terrible living and working conditions. In addition, if the few peasant marches to the city had been organized with more audacious methods, a much larger number of peasants would have participated, and at the same time a greater number of areas would have gone into action.

In various places, individual contact with certain peasants was prolonged for too long a time without proceeding to the mobilization of the peasant masses. Land invasions by the peasants who had been dispossessed were hardly ever carried out.

The lack of both adequately developed leading cadres and the necessary determination to organize the struggle of the popular masses played a decisive role in the fact that we did not fully utilize the possibilities that were presented. Lacking guerrilla camps, it was impossible to train cadres to organize the struggle of the diverse sectors of the Nicaraguan people.

The Armed Movement of Pancasán

In the course of 1966, practical steps were taken to relaunch armed actions. That year the Sandinista Front became conscious of the deviation that had occurred as a result of the blows of 1963 and it proceeded to prepare the Pancasán guerrilla base. Although this preparation showed organizational progress compared with the FSLN's armed movement in 1963, it did not represent serious progress in political and military tactics. It was a notable step forward organizationally because it did not follow the usual practice of preparing the armed movement in a neighboring country, which had provided distance from the enemy's observation; rather it was preparation of an armed movement in mountains situated in the very center of the country.

An extremely important factor that hindered the success of the Pancasán movement was the mistaken method used to get the peasants to participate in the struggle. The form used was to recruit a number of peasants to become part of the regular column. This means that these peasants were completely mixed in with the working-class and student fighters, i.e., combatants with an urban background.

The militants who came from urban areas generally possessed a higher revolutionary consciousness than the peasants as a whole, who became demoralized when faced with the first difficulties that we ran up against: scarcity of supplies, certain slow marches, and the first rumors of the presence of enemy soliders on nearby roads. This obligated the leadership to send back the majority of the peasants, although there were honorable exceptions of peasants who firmly refused to be let go and who are an example of the combative possibility of this sector.

In addition, in the first stage of the revolutionary war that was beginning, we did not find a way to incorporate the peasants in those areas some days distant, with whom contact had previously been established through organizing them in the struggle for land and for other demands. Some of the peasants who temporarily joined the guerrillas had been moved from their areas to the encampments.

When the break up of the Pancasán guerrilla movement had already taken place, it became known that once some of the peasants who had deserted the guerrillas arrived back in their own areas, they took part in armed assaults on local goverment posts or rural commercial establishments, as well as executions of known informers. This indicates that to a large extent some of the peasants who had become demoralized went through that crisis because they were not organized in the most appropriate manner. It means that they probably should have been irregular rather than regular guerrillas. This experience leads us to think about the possibility of organizing irregular guerrillas parallel to the regulars. We should not fail to point out that we can now evaluate the importance of work among the peasants much better, thanks to our own experience. We don't only base ourselves on the experiences of other Latin American guerrilla movements.

Another aspect that must be highlighted was the insufficient number of cadres to handle all tasks that the preparation of the work demanded, not only in the city and the countryside, but even outside of the country. For too long the leadership of the Sandinista Front tolerated sectarianism, which stood in the way of promoting a sufficient quantity of new cadres coming from politically advanced working-class backgrounds and from the university sector. Feverish attempts were made to achieve excessively big goals instead of always making progress in carrying out suitable, everyday tasks.

The insurrectionary work was not related to the general people's struggle—especially the peasant, student, working-class struggles. It was good that the Front put its principal emphasis on insurrectionary work, but it was an error to abandon other revolutionary forms of struggle. Sectarian tactics weighed heavily and these determined the course of activity in the preparation for the movement in the mountains.

The individualistic bad habits that leadership comrades often displayed was the factor that helped hold back the initiatives that could have resolved many problems; on different occasions individual problems were mixed with political problems. This may have decisively contributed to depriving certain initiatives of the seriousness that was due them.

In regard to placing cadres in charge of various tasks, it was a mistake to be confident that comrades who had not experienced the privations of guerrilla life would be able to work among the masses—for example, among the student masses. For some years now, our organization has been conscious of the ballast that the Nicaraguan revolutionary movement carries as a result of the stance of the capitalist parties, which for many years usurped the leadership of the anti-Somozaist opposition. However, at the time when the guerrilla base was established in the mountains, there was insufficient thought given to the fact that due to the prevailing conditions the tasks required by the work in the cities could not be attended to by militants who did not possess the necessary firmness and discipline. In view of this, the comrades in the forefront of urban resistance work could count on the practical collaboration of a very reduced number of militants. The situation of the urban resistance became more acute due to the sectarian attitude of those charged with responsibility.

Organized mass work (student, peasant, worker) was paralyzed. On the one hand, there were not enough cadres to handle this work, and on the other, there was an underestimation of the importance this activity could play in the development of the armed struggle. This weakness led to the situation where when the death of comrades in the mountains and in the cities was recorded, there was not consistent solidarity on the part of all the members of the Front.

In the cities, only violent actions of an individual nature were planned. And there was no attempt to develop a policy of using violence involving the participation of the popular masses in the cities—something that is possible mainly in Managua, the country's capital, which has a population of more than 300,000.

Under Nicaraguan conditions, as well as in most countries of Latin America, the center of action of the revolutionary war has to be the countryside. However, the cities must also play a role of particular importance, given that in the first stage of the war the city has to supply the countryside with the most developed cadres to lead the political and military detachment. In general, the revolutionary elements from the cities have a greater ability to develop themselves in the first stage. These elements are composed of the revolutionary sector of workers, students, and a certain layer of the petty bourgeoisie.

One must take into account the habits that the capitalist parties and their faithful servants have imposed on the popular masses through their electoral policy. These parties have conditioned broad sectors of the people to participate in the hustle and bustle of electoral rigamarole. This circumstance must be taken into account to fully understand why many sectors of the population, despite their sympathy with the revolutionary armed struggle, cannot demonstrate that sympathy through action. This forces us to consider the need to fully train a broad number of persons from among the population to have the material capacity to support the armed struggle. To seek out the people is not sufficient; they have to be trained to participate in the revolutionary war.

Some Current Tasks

Several months ago, work in the countryside was reestablished. The FSLN is simultaneously developing political and military work, with the objective of reorganizing the guerrilla struggle.

In the countryside a study of the peasants' problems is already under way, and this investigation has required militants to stay in the rural zones for several weeks. Militants with an urban background (workers and students) are participating in this political work. It has been said that the mountain (the guerrilla base) proletarianizes, and we agree with this statement. But as our experience has shown, it can be added that the countryside—political contact with the peasants—also proletarianizes. The urban militant, in contact with the countryside, including the zones where a guerrilla base is not organized, lives the abject poverty that the peasants suffer and feels their desire to struggle.

A phenomenon that has been seen in this country since the Pancasán movement is the growth of the Sandinista National Liberation Front's political authority over the broad sectors of the popular masses. Today the Sandinista Front can claim, and has obtained, a much greater degree of cooperation from the population than in the past. It must also be said that if we do not get greater cooperation than we actually are receiving, it is because we lack cadres who are competent in asking for this type of help, and also because the cadres now active are not functioning systematically enough.

Simultaneously, new methods are being found so that we can gain the practical collaboration of new sectors of the population in the clandestine conditions under which we function (a small country with small cities). This has led us to not depend exclusively on the old militants and collaborators (a large proportion of whom are "jaded").

Furthermore, we have reestablished squads that are prepared to act in the cities, and they have carried out some actions.

We now have plans to undertake actions in harmony with the period of reestablishment we are now going through.

The Sandinista National Liberation Front believes that at the present time and for a certain period to come, Nicaragua will be going through a stage in which a radical political force will be developing its specific characteristics. Consequently, at the current time it is necessary for us to strongly emphasize that our major objective is the socialist revolution, a revolution that aims to defeat Yankee imperialism and its local agents, false oppositionists, and false revolutionaries. This propaganda, with the firm backing of armed action, will permit the Front to win the support of a sector of the popular masses that is conscious of the profound nature of the struggle we are carrying out.

In order to outline a strategy for the revolutionary movement, it is necessary to take into account the strength that the capitalist parties represent, due to the influence they still wield within the opposition. One must be alert to the danger that the reactionary force in the opposition to the Somoza regime could climb on the back of the revolutionary insurrection. The revolutionary movement has a dual goal. On the one hand, to overthrow the criminal and traitorous clique that has usurped the power for so many years; and on the other, to prevent the capitalist opposition—of proven submission to Yankee imperialism—from taking advantage of the situation which the guerrilla struggle has unleashed, and grabbing power. In the task of barring the way to the traitorous capitalist forces, a revolutionary political and military force rooted in the broad sectors of the people has a unique role to play. Sinking these roots is dependent on the organization's ability to drive out the Liberal and Conservative influences from this broad sector.

The policy we follow later on regarding the old parties that now have a capitalist leadership will be determined by the attitude that the people as a whole have toward these parties.

Relating to the situation of the Nicaraguan Socialist Party, it can be stated that the changes that have taken place in that political organization's leadership are purely changes in form. The old leadership builds illusions regarding the Conservative sector, and calls for building a political front in which these stubborn agents of imperialism participate. The so-called new leadership currently justifies having participated in the electoral farce of 1967, supporting the pseudo-oppositional candidacy of the Conservative politician Fernando Aguero. Like the old leadership, the so-called new leadership keeps talking about the armed struggle, while in practice it concentrates its energies on petty legal work.

The above statements do not contradict the possibility of developing a certain unity with the anti-Somozaist sector in general. But this is unity at the base, with the most honest sectors of the various anti-Somozaist tendencies. This is all the more possible due to the increase in the prestige of the Sandinista National Liberation Front and the discrediting and splintering of the leadership of the capitalist parties and the like.

The Sandinista National Liberation Front understands how hard the guerrilla road is. But it is not prepared to retreat. We know that we are confronting a bloody, reactionary armed force like the National Guard, the ferocious GN, which maintains intact the practices of cruelty that were inculcated in it by its creator, the U.S. Marines. Bombardment of villages, cutting of children's throats, violation of women, burning huts with peasants inside of them, mutilation as a torture—these were the study courses that the U.S. professors of civilization taught the GN during the period of the guerrilla resistance (1927–1932) led by Augusto César Sandino.

The frustration that followed the period of the Sandinista resistance does not have to be repeated today. Now the times are different. The current days are not like those in which Sandino and his guerrilla brothers battled alone against the Yankee empire. Today revolutionaries of all the subjugated countries are rising up or preparing to go into the battle against the empire of the dollar. At the apex of this battle is indominatable Vietnam, which with its example of heroism, is repulsing the aggression of the blond beasts.

The combative example of our fallen brothers carries us forward. It is the example of Casimiro Sotelo, Danilo Rosales, Jorge Navarro, Francisco Buitrago, Silvio Mayorga, Otto Casco, Modesto Duarte, Robert Amaya, Edmundo Pérez, Hugo Medina, René Carríon, Rigoberto Cruz (Pablo Ubeda), Fermín Díaz, Selín, Shible, Ernesto Fernandez, Oscar Florez, Felipe Gaitán, Fausto García, Elías Moncada, Franscisco Moreno, Carlos Reyna, David Tejada, Carlos Tinoco, Francisco Córdoba, Faustino Ruíz, Boanerges Santamaría, Iván Sanchez.

We will faithfully fulfill our oath: "Before the image of Augusto César Sandino and Ernesto Che Guevara; before the memory of the heroes and martyrs of Nicaragua, Latin America, and humanity as a whole; before history: I place my hand on the black and red flag that signifies 'Free Homeland or Death,' and I swear to defend the national honor with arms in hand and to fight for the redemption of the oppressed and exploited in Nicaragua and the world. If I fulfill this oath, the freedom of Nicaragua and all the peoples will be the reward; if I betray this oath, death in disgrace and dishonor will be my punishment."

22. The Historic Program of the FSLN*

By the Sandinista National Liberation Front (FSLN)

This document was first presented to the Nicaraguan people in 1969. It was reprinted by the FSLN in June 1981. This translation from that edition is by Will Reissner.

The Sandinista National Liberation Front (FSLN) arose out of the Nicaraguan people's need to have a "vanguard organization" capable of taking political power through direct stuggle against its enemies and establishing a social system that wipes out the exploitation and poverty that our people have been subjected to in past history.

The FSLN is a politico-military organization, whose strategic objective is to take political power by destroying the military and bureaucratic apparatus of the dictatorship and to establish a revolutionary government based on the worker-peasant alliance and the convergence of all the patriotic anti-imperialist and anti-oligarchic forces in the country.

The people of Nicaragua suffer under subjugation to a reactionary and fascist clique imposed by Yankee imperialism in 1932, the year Anastasio Somoza García was named commander in chief of the so-called National Guard (GN).

The Somozaist clique has reduced Nicaragua to the status of a neocolony exploited by the Yankee monopolies and the country's oligarchic groups.

The present regime is politically unpopular and juridically illegal. The recognition and aid it gets from the North Americans is irrefutable proof of foreign interference in the affairs of Nicaragua.

The FSLN has seriously and with great responsibility analyzed the national reality and has resolved to confront the dictatorship with arms in hand. We have concluded that the triumph of the Sandinista people's revolution and the overthrow of the regime that is an enemy of the people will take place through the development of a hard-fought and prolonged people's war.

Whatever maneuvers and resources Yankee imperialism deploys, the Somozaist dictatorship is condemned to total failure in the face of the rapid advance and development of the people's forces, headed by the Sandinista National Liberation Front.

Given this historic conjuncture the FSLN has worked out this political program with an eye to strengthening and developing our organization, inspiring and stimulating the people of Nicaragua to march forward with the resolve to fight until the dictatorship is overthrown and to resist the intervention of Yankee imperialism, in order to forge a free, prosperous, and revolutionary homeland.

---

*Reprinted from *Sandinistas Speak* (New York, Pathfinder Press, 1982).

I. A Revolutionary Government

The Sandinista people's revolution will establish a revolutionary government that will eliminate the reactionary structure that arose from rigged elections and military coups, and the people's power will create a Nicaragua that is free of exploitation, oppression, backwardness; a free, progressive, and independent country.

The revolutionary government will apply the following measures of a political character:

A. It will endow revolutionary power with a structure that allows the full participation of the entire people, on the national level as well as the local level (departmental, municipal, neighborhood).

B. It will guarantee that all citizens can fully exercise all individual freedoms and it will respect human rights.

C. It will guarantee the free exchange of ideas, which above all leads to vigorously broadening the people's rights and national rights.

D. It will guarantee freedom for the worker-union movement to organize in the city and countryside; and freedom to organize peasant, youth, student, women's, cultural, sporting, and similar groups.

E. It will guarantee the right of emigrant and exiled Nicaraguans to return to their native soil.

F. It will guarantee the right to asylum for citizens of other countries who are persecuted for participation in the revolutionary struggle.

G. It will severely punish the gangsters who are guilty of persecuting, informing on, abusing, torturing, or murdering revolutionaries and the people.

H. Those individuals who occupy high political posts as a result of rigged elections and military coups will be stripped of their political rights.

The revolutionary government will apply the following measures of an economic character:

A. It will expropriate the landed estates, factories, companies, buildings, means of transportation, and other wealth usurped by the Somoza family and accumulated through the misappropriation and plunder of the nation's wealth.

B. It will expropriate the landed estates, factories, companies, means of transportation, and other wealth usurped by the politicians and military officers, and all other accomplices, who have taken advantage of the present regime's administrative corruption.

C. It will nationalize the wealth of all the foreign companies that exploit the mineral, forest, maritime, and other kinds of resources.

D. It will establish workers' control over the administrative management of the factories and other wealth that are expropriated and nationalized.

E. It will centralize the mass transit service.

F. It will nationalize the banking system, which will be placed at the exclusive service of the country's economic development.

G. It will establish an independent currency.

H. It will refuse to honor the loans imposed on the country by the Yankee monopolies or those of any other power.

I. It will establish commercial relations with all countries, whatever their system, to benefit the country's economic development.

J. It will establish a suitable taxation policy, which will be applied with strict justice.

K. It will prohibit usury. This prohibition will apply to Nicaraguan nationals as well as foreigners.

L. It will protect the small and medium-size owners (producers, merchants) while restricting the excesses that lead to the exploitation of the workers.

M. It will establish state control over foreign trade, with an eye to diversifying it and making it independent.

N. It will rigorously restrict the importation of luxury items.

O. It will plan the national economy, putting an end to the anarchy characteristic of the capitalist system of production. An important part of this planning will focus on the industrialization and electrification of the country.

II. The Agrarian Revolution

The Sandinista people's revolution will work out an agrarian policy that achieves an authentic agrarian reform; a reform that will, in the immediate term, carry out massive distribution of the land, eliminating the land grabs by the large landlords in favor of the workers (small producers) who labor on the land.

A. It will expropriate and eliminate the capitalist and feudal estates.

B. It will turn over the land to the peasants, free of charge, in accordance with the principle that the land should belong to those who work it.

C. It will carry out a development plan for livestock raising aimed at diversifying and increasing the productivity of that sector.

D. It will guarantee the peasants the following rights:

1. Timely and adequate agricultural credit.

2. Marketability (a guaranteed market for their production).

3. Technical assistance.

E. It will protect the patriotic landowners who collaborate with the guerrilla struggle, by paying them for their landholdings that exceed the limit established by the revolutionary government.

F. It will stimulate and encourage the peasants to organize themselves in cooperatives, so they can take their destiny into their own hands and directly participate in the development of the country.

G. It will abolish the debts the peasantry incurred to the landlord and any type of usurer.

H. It will eliminate the forced idleness that exists for most of the year in the countryside, and it will be attentive to creating sources of jobs for the peasant population.

III. Revolution in Culture and Education

The Sandinista people's revolution will establish the bases for the development of the national culture, the people's education, and university reform.

A. It will push forward a massive campaign to immediately wipe out "illiteracy."

B. It will develop the national culture and will root out the neocolonial penetration in our culture.

C. It will rescue the progressive intellectuals, and their works that have arisen throughout our history, from the neglect in which they have been maintained by the anti-people's regimes.

D. It will give attention to the development and progress of education at the various levels (primary, intermediate, technical, university, etc.), and education will be free at all levels and obligatory at some.

E. It will grant scholarships at various levels of education to students who have limited economic resources. The scholarships will include housing, food, clothing, books, and transportation.

F. It will train more and better teachers who have the scientific knowledge that the present era requires, to satisfy the needs of our entire student population.

G. It will nationalize the centers of private education that have been immorally turned into industries by merchants who hypocritically invoke religious principles.

H. It will adapt the teaching programs to the needs of the country; it will apply teaching methods to the scientific and research needs of the country.

I. It will carry out a university reform that will include, among other things, the following measures:

1. It will rescue the university from the domination of the exploiting classes, so it can serve the real creators and shapers of our culture: the people. University instruction must be oriented around man, around the people. The university must stop being a breeding ground for bureaucratic egotists.

2. Eliminate the discrimination in access to university classes suffered by youth from the working class and peasantry.

3. Increase the state budget for the university so there are the economic resources to solve the various problems confronting it.

4. Majority student representation on the boards of departments, keeping in mind that the student body is the main segment of the university population.

5. Eliminate the neo-colonial penetration of the university, especially the penetration by the North American monopolies through the charity donations of the pseudophilanthropic foundations.

6. Promotion of free, experimental, scientific investigation that must contribute to dealing with national and universal questions.

7. Strengthen the unity of the students, faculty, and investigators with the whole people, by perpetuating the selfless example of the students and intellectuals who have offered their lives for the sake of the patriotic ideal.

IV. Labor Legislation and Social Security

The Sandinista people's revolution will eliminate the injustice of the living and working conditions suffered by the working class under the brutal exploitation, and will institute labor legislation and social assistance.

A. It will enact a labor code that will regulate, among other things, the following rights:

1. It will adopt the principle that "those who don't work don't eat," of course making exceptions for those who are unable to participate in the process of production due to age (children, old people), medical condition, or other reasons beyond their control.

2. Strict enforcement of the eight-hour work day.

3. The income of the workers (wages and other benefits) must be sufficient to satisfy their daily needs.

4. Respect for the dignity of the worker, prohibiting and punishing unjust treatment of workers in the course of their labor.

5. Abolition of unjustified firings.

6. Obligation to pay wages in the period required by law.

7. Right of all workers to periodic vacations.

B. It will eliminate the scourge of unemployment.

C. It will extend the scope of the social security system to all the workers and public employees in the country. The scope will include coverage for illness, physical incapacity, and retirement.

D. It will provide free medical assistance to the entire population. It will set up clinics and hospitals throughout the national territory.

E. It will undertake massive campaigns to eradicate endemic illnesses and prevent epidemics.

F. It will carry out urban reform, which will provide each family with adequate shelter. It will put an end to profiteering speculation in urban land (subdivisions, urban construction, rental housing) that exploits the need that working families in the cities have for an adequate roof over their heads in order to live.

G. It will initiate and expand the construction of adequate housing for the peasant population.

H. It will reduce the charges for water, light, sewers, urban beautification; it will apply programs to extend all these services to the entire urban and rural population.

I. It will encourage participation in sports of all types and categories.

J. It will eliminate the humiliation of begging by putting the above mentioned practices into practice.

V. Administrative Honesty

The Sandinista people's revolution will root out administrative governmental corruption, and will establish strict administrative honesty.

A. It will abolish the criminal vice industry (prostitution, gambling, drug use, etc.), which the privileged sector of the National Guard and the foreign parasites exploit.

B. It will establish strict control over the collection of taxes to prevent government functionaries from profiting, putting an end to the normal practice of the present regime's official agencies.

C. It will end the arbitrary actions of the members of the GN, who plunder the population through the subterfuge of local taxes.

D. It will put an end to the situation wherein military commanders appropriate the budget that is supposed to go to take care of common prisoners, and it will establish centers designed to rehabilitate these wrongdoers.

E. It will abolish the smuggling that is practiced on a large scale by the gang of politicians, officers, and foreigners who are the regime's accomplices.

F. It will severely punish persons who engage in crimes against administrative honesty (embezzlement, smuggling, trafficking in vices, etc.), using greatest severity when it involves elements active in the revolutionary movement.

VI. Reincorporation of the Atlantic Coast

The Sandinista people's revolution will put into practice a special plan for the Atlantic Coast, which has been abandoned to total neglect, in order to incorporate this area into the nation's life.

A. It will end the unjust exploitation the Atlantic Coast has suffered throughout history by the foreign monopolies, especially Yankee imperialism.

B. It will prepare suitable lands in the zone for the development of agriculture and ranching.

C. It will establish conditions that encourage the development of the fishing and forest industries.

D. It will encourage the flourishing of this region's local cultural values, which flow from the specific aspects of its historic tradition.

E. It will wipe out the odious discrimination to which the indigenous Miskitos, Sumos, Ramas, and Blacks of this region are subjected.

VII. Emancipation of Women

The Sandinista people's revolution will abolish the odious discrimination that women have been subjected to compared to men; it will establish economic, political, and cultural equality between woman and man.

A. It will pay special attention to the mother and child.

B. It will eliminate prostitution and other social vices, through which the dignity of women will be raised.

C. It will put an end to the system of servitude that women suffer, which is reflected in the tragedy of the abandoned working mother.

D. It will establish for children born out of wedlock the right to equal protection by the revolutionary institutions.

E. It will establish day-care centers for the care and attention of the children of working women.

F. It will establish a two-month maternity leave before and after birth for women who work.

G. It will raise women's political, cultural, and vocational levels through their participation in the revolutionary process.

VIII. Respect for Religious Beliefs

The Sandinista people's revolution will guarantee the population of believers the freedom to profess any religion.

A. It will respect the right of citizens to profess and practice any religious belief.

B. It will support the work of priests and other religious figures who defend the working people.

IX. Independent Foreign Policy

The Sandinista people's revolution will eliminate the foreign policy of submission to Yankee imperialism, and will establish a patriotic foreign policy of absolute national independence and one that is for authentic universal peace.

A. It will put an end to the Yankee interference in the internal problems of Nicaragua and will practice a policy of mutual respect with other countries and fraternal collaboration between peoples.

B. It will expel the Yankee military mission, the so-called Peace Corps (spies in the guise of technicians), and military and similar political elements who constitute a bare-faced intervention in the country.

C. It will accept economic and technical aid from any country, but always and only when this does not involve political compromises.

D. Together with other peoples of the world it will promote a campaign in favor of authentic universal peace.

E. It will abrogate all treaties, signed with any foreign power, that damage national sovereignty.

X. Central American People's Unity

The Sandinista people's revolution is for the true union of the Central American peoples in a single country.

A. It will support authentic unity with the fraternal peoples of Central America. This unity will lead the way to coordinating the efforts to achieve national liberation and establish a new system without imperialist domination or national betrayal.

B. It will eliminate the so-called integration, whose aim is to increase Central America's submission to the North American monopolies and the local reactionary forces.

XI. Solidarity among Peoples

The Sandinista people's revolution will put an end to the use of the national
territory as a base for Yankee aggression against other fraternal peoples and will put
into practice militant solidarity with fraternal peoples fighting for their liberation.

A. It will actively support the struggle of the peoples of Asia, Africa, and Latin
America against the new and old colonialism and against the common enemy:
Yankee imperialism.

B. It will support the struggle of the Black people and all the people of the
United States for an authentic democracy and equal rights.

C. It will support the struggle of all peoples against the establishment of Yankee
military bases in foreign countries.

XII. People's Patriotic Army

The Sandinista people's revolution will abolish the armed force called the
National Guard, which is an enemy of the people, and will create a patriotic,
revolutionary, and people's army.

A. It will abolish the National Guard, a force that is an enemy of the people,
created by the North American occupation forces in 1927 to pursue, torture, and
murder the Sandinista patriots.

B. In the new people's army, professional soldiers who are members of the old
army will be able to play a role providing they have observed the following conduct:

1. They have supported the guerrilla struggle.

2. They have not participated in murder, plunder, torture, and persecution of
the people and the revolutionary activists.

3. They have rebelled against the despotic and dynastic regime of the
Somozas.

C. It will strengthen the new people's army, raising its fighting ability and its
tactical and technical level.

D. It will inculcate in the consciousness of the members of the people's army the
principle of basing themselves on their own forces in the fulfillment of their duties
and the development of all their creative activity.

E. It will deepen the revolutionary ideals of the members of the people's army
with an eye toward strengthening their patriotic spirit and their firm conviction to
fight until victory is achieved, overcoming obstacles and correcting errors.

F. It will forge a conscious discipline in the ranks of the people's army and will
encourage the close ties that must exist between the combatants and the people.

G. It will establish obligatory military service and will arm the students,
workers, and farmers, who—organized in people's militias—will defend the rights
won against the inevitable attack by the reactionary forces of the country and
Yankee imperialism.

XIII. Veneration of Our Martyrs

The Sandinista people's revolution will maintain eternal gratitude to and veneration of our homelands martyrs and will continue the shining example of heroism and selflessness they have bequeathed to us.

A. It will educate the new generations in eternal gratitude and veneration toward those who have fallen in the struggle to make Nicaragua a free homeland.

B. It will establish a secondary school to educate the children of our people's martyrs.

C. It will inculcate in the entire people the imperishable example of our martyrs, defending the revolutionary ideal: Ever onward to victory!

23. The 1972 Earthquake and After: Somocismo in Crisis

By George Black

George Black is a writer and researcher specializing in Central American affairs. He is on the staff of the North American Congress on Latin America where he is responsible for research on Nicaragua and Guatemala. He is a frequent contributor to The Guardian *(London),* United Nations Development Forum, Latin America Weekly Report, Latin America Regional Report *(London), among other journals.*

A little after midnight on December 23, 1972, the centre of Managua was torn apart by a massive earthquake. Up to 20,000 died, 75 percent of the city's housing and 90 percent of its commercial capacity was destroyed beyond repair, and damage was conservatively estimated by the United Nations at $772 million. Every contradiction of the Somoza regime was immediately heightened. Overnight, patterns of economic control and Somoza's relationship with the bourgeoisie were transformed. A boom in the construction industry brought new opportunities for speculation as well as an explosion in the size and militancy of the urban working class. In the aftermath of the earthquake, National Guard corruption was seen at its ugliest. The importance of the earthquake as a pivotal moment in the disintegration of *Somocismo* can hardly be overstated.

The true nature of the *Guardia* stood exposed. Officers led their men in systematic looting of the ruined capital and a complete breakdown of discipline meant that Somoza was unable to guarantee public order without the prompt arrival of

*Reprinted from *Triumph of the People: The Sandinista Revolution in Nicaragua* (London: Zed Press, 1981), pp. 58–62.

600 US soldiers and other Central American troops. Any remaining public respect for the military evaporated. Until the *Guardia* recovered its discipline, Managua residents described the city as under virtual American occupation, leaving an indelible impression of US troops storming through the devastated streets, shouting orders in English to a bewildered population and incinerating corpses with flame-throwers. In its rush to get rich, the *Guardia* forgot all about guerrillas. A thriving black market sprang up, filled with stolen property and medical and food aid from overseas. One observer described the sale of goods donated by Catholic relief agencies and foreign governments in hastily opened shops staffed by the National Guard: "Tinned food, clothing . . . you can even buy anything from a small electric generator to a water purifier, electric torches, pickaxes and spades, complete factory-sealed blood transfusion equipment. There are also shops selling goods from looted warehouses: in Chichigalpa, for example, where the military commander's wife looks after marketing goods stolen from the *Casa Mantica* in Managua. *Guardia* demolition crews directed by Anastasio Somoza Portocarrero made off with anything they could shift: toilet fittings, furniture, street-lights, electric wiring. And unemployed rural laborers of Carazo and the north were pressganged to help in the so-called "Civil Reconstruction Corps."

Somoza described the earthquake as a "revolution of possibilities," and certainly for members of the ruling elite the phrase was accurate enough. Paradoxically, the earthquake was a means of pulling the country out of its stagnation and inducing immediate economic growth, but at the cost of new economic distortion and an insoluble political crisis which went to the heart of bourgeois rule. The loans contracted for reconstruction projects brought an escalating foreign debt, and Somoza's increased tendency to stave off economic disaster by resorting to foreign loans was reflected in an external debt which shot up from $255 million in 1972 to more than $1 billion by 1978, half of it at interest rates above 8 percent.

Somoza himself cornered the reconstruction of Managua. His company ESPESA took charge of demolition work; *Inmuebles SA* of real estate speculation; a host of other companies, generally with a monopoly, took on contracts for concrete, building materials, metal structures, roofing, asbestos, and plastics. Fifty new construction companies mushroomed, the most prominent controlled by the Somoza clan, and speculative property corporations threw together cheap housing (11,132 temporary homes in 1973 and 4,033 permanent ones), which they resold at four or five times their original value. The streets were no longer paved with the traditional asphalt but with paving-stones (*adoquines*) from a Somoza factory using Somoza-produced cement. The quality of new housing was scarcely better than what had gone before. "Our climate lends itself to good living without our needing to make massive investments in housing," Somoza was later to tell *Le Monde* in a cynical 1978 interview.

Politicians like Alfonso Lovo Cordero of the ruling triumvirate* were awarded

<hr>

*The "triumvirate" was composed of the Conservative leader Fernando Aguero plus two Somoza appointees. It was part of a deal in which a Constituent Assembly was to reform the Constitution yet again and pave the way for Somoza's reelection in 1974. It ruled from May, 1972 to December 1974.

building contracts even when lower tenders were submitted, and speculation with prime housing land became a national scandal. In one incident, Cornelio Hueck—President of the Constituent Assembly—bought up empty land earmarked for temporary housing for the homeless. Having paid $17,000, he resold the land two days later to the state housing bank for $1.2 million—the funds having been received from USAID. But whatever private doubts the USA may have had, it was no time for niceties. Above all, the strong man had to be pulled out of the chaos. Although some of the aid which arrived was disinterested—like a Cuban hospital in Managua—the purpose of the vast American aid effort was clear: to shore up the dictatorship; and there was evidence that a large part of ostensibly humanitarian funds was placed at the disposal of the Pentagon. Even AID money not expressly designed to prop up the dictatorship ended up in Somoza's pockets because of the monopoly control he exercised over the reconstruction projects which that money paid for. The sums were large: $78 million from AID ($12.7 million in emergency grant assistance and a further $65.3 million in reconstruction loans) plus $54 million from the Inter-American Development Bank (IDB)—a striking contrast to the USA's later meager initial response to the devastation of the 1979 war.

The earthquake accelerated the class struggle in Nicaragua. It came in the middle of a two-year drought which wrecked the production of staple food crops, bringing hunger to the countryside and a wave of peasant migration to the capital. The rapid growth in construction and related industries absorbed many of Managua's unemployed, causing a dramatic rise in numbers of the urban proletariat. Rampant government corruption, coupled with longer working hours, lower wages, a generalized attack on working-class living standards, and the agitational work of the FSLN, all brought a corresponding rise in class consciousness. Organized working-class activity was on the increase, highlighted by *campesino* land invasions in the north and the big 1973 construction workers' strike led by the CGT, the trade union federation of the Socialist Party. The aftermath of the earthquake also introduced a new phrase into the vocabulary of the bourgeois opposition: *competencia desleal*, unfair or disloyal competition. The rules of the capitalist game, and with it the fragile consensus which held the dictatoral state together, had been broken.

A new phase of absolute power opened. The triumvirate survived in name but Somoza ruled by decree from the newly invented position of President of the National Emergency Committee. To comply with the new constitution ruling that no serving military officer could stand for the presidency, Somoza gave up the title of *Jefe Director* of the National Guard and instead took the title of *Jefe Supremo* of the Armed Forces. The September 1974 election, which Somoza won with the traditional overwhelming majority over the traditional hand-picked Conservative opponent, was boycotted by a number of dissident bourgeois politicians including Pedro Joaquín Chamorro, who by now had organized an opposition coalition, UDEL. For their pains, 27 leaders of the boycott were arrested and deprived of their political rights until March the following year. But they did not give up. They filed charges with the Supreme Electoral Tribunal, a body composed of one representative of Somoza's Supreme Court, two of the Liberal Party and the guaranteed 40 percent minority of two Conservatives. The charge of fraud, bribery and coercion was dismissed out of hand, but the Tribunal's replies to the two charges of constitutional violation were remarkable for their candor. The accusation that Somoza's rule had been continuous, thereby infringing the Constitution, was quashed by citing the two-year rule of the figurehead triumvirate, and the Tribunal ruled that Somoza's new post as *Jefe Supremo* of the *Guardia* was purely administrative, and did not disqualify him from the presidency on the grounds of active military service. The Tribunal even admitted that the *Junta*'s February decree creating the post of *Jefe Supremo* had been specifically designed to allow Somoza's candidacy in September. It was a bizarre attempt to provide a legal fiction for a wholly discredited regime.

The *Frente Sandinista* had other more impressive ways of registering its disgust with *Somocismo*. On December 27, 1974, it launched a spectacular commando raid in Managua. This was the catalyst for a new chapter of institutionalized repression. Within hours, Somoza decreed a state of siege, martial law, permanent military courts and press censorship, just as much to smash trade union militancy as to drive the FSLN into clandestinity and prevent the raid from having its desired impact on class consciousness and perhaps fusing two hitherto unconnected facets of the popular struggle—the guerrilla war and the open trade-union work of the PSN. The new repressive legislation might also allow all Nicaraguan capitalists to increase their profits by permitting super-exploitation of the workforce, a calculated move by Somoza to woo back some of the bourgeois support forfeited after the earthquake.

The emergency press laws were draconian. All newspaper copy had to be submitted to the National guard before publication, and was sent back with all offending articles blocked out in red ink. An offending article was any which made reference to trade unions, labor disputes, allegations of defective public services, including transport, roads, and housing conditions, precisely the issues which the mass movement was beginning to mobilize around in the *barrios*. The Church, whose acceptance of Somoza was fast waning, protested vigorously about the peasant massacres which were taking place under the blanket of press censorship: Somoza's only response was to extend censorship to include Church publications and radio broadcasts. Even US Ambassador Theberge acknowledged the scale of human rights violations, and with the election of Jimmy Carter in November 1976 and the ensuing "Human Rights" policy of the US government, Somoza's attempts to dismember the popular opposition led to grave doubts in Washington about the future viability of the dictatorship.

Somoza's repression of the mass movement was designed in part to restore favorable conditions for the capitalist class as a whole, but the result was the opposite. Within the bourgeoisie, contradictions merely deepened, and institutionalized terror frightened off every bourgeois group which preferred government by consensus. At the same time, the reign of terror of the mid 1970s failed to root out the popular movement led by the FSLN, and the basis for mass radicalization grew.

New possibilities for economic growth, by contrast, contracted. By the end of 1977, the combination of these three factors threw *Somocismo* into its acute final crisis.

24. The Struggle for Power*

By Henri Weber

The truth is that we always thought of the masses, seeing them, however, as a prop for the guerrilla campaign that would enable it to deal some blows at the National Guard. Reality was quite different: guerrilla activity served as a prop for the masses, who crushed the enemy by means of insurrection.

Comandante Humberto Ortega

In the early 1970s, all the contradictions of Nicaraguan society took a turn for the worse, and the economy began to suffer the harsh effects of the world crisis. According to official statistics, which generally softened the reality, the rate of inflation increased from an annual average of 1.7 percent before 1970 to 9.7 percent between 1971 and 1975, remaining high at 9.4 percent in 1976 and 11 percent in 1977. Industry was hard hit by the wave of factory closures and lay-offs, the crisis being especially severe in construction. Sharply contested strikes broke out in the building, health, and education sectors. The state debt rose to a record level. Savage repression struck on a mass scale.

Exasperated by the way the Somozist regime profited from the Managua earthquake, the bourgeois oppositions began to assert themselves and sought to unify their efforts. In late 1970, when Conservative Party leader Fernando Aguero announced his intention to sign a pact with Somoza, a wing headed by *La Prensa* director Pedro Joaquín Chamorro split to form the Conservative National Action (ANC). In Somoza's Nationalist Liberal Party, another split produced the Constitutionalist Movement (MC) under Ramiro Sacasa. And in 1973, the newly-formed "National Mobilization" and "National Salvation" movements sought to relaunch an opposition based on leading personalities. On July 8, 1974, twenty-seven notables, representing seven political movements and two trade unions, called for a boycott of the elections. Somoza was, of course, re-elected in September with the help of the *Magnifica* and the National Guard. But the rate of abstention reached an all-time high.

On December 15, 1974, a Democratic Liberation Union (UDEL) was officially formed by the groups that had supported a boycott: the Christian Social Party, Independent Liberal Party, Socialist Party of Nicaragua, Conservative National

*Reprinted from *Nicaragua: The Sandinist Revolution* (London, Verso Editions and NLB, 1981).

Action, Constitutionalist Movement, National Mobilization, National Salvation, General Confederation of Labor, and National Workers Federation. It was a Popular Front alliance against the dictatorship, bringing together on a moderate democratic program both liberal bourgeois formations and organizations representing the workers' movement. Bourgeois hegemony was evident in the Union's programme, methods of struggle, and leadership. But it was nevertheless not appreciated by broad sections of the employers, including the giant BANIC and BANAMERICA groups, who saw the UDEL notables as sorcerers' apprentices.

The UDEL Constitution, which called for respect for political and trade-union freedoms, marked a further stage in the anti-Somoza radicalization of a portion of the ruling class, and hence a narrowing of the dictatorship's social base.[1] On December 27, 1974, less than two weeks after the UDEL was proclaimed, the FSLN recommenced military operations, kidnapping two high figures in the regime, later exchanged for the release of a number of political prisoners and the publication in the press of long communiqués denouncing official corruption.

Somoza saw a growing risk that the apparently sectoralized and unrelated movements of protest and opposition might converge politically, especially since UDEL and its president, enjoying solid support in the United States, now represented a liberal alternative to the dictatorship.

His reply was a good example of the tactics he would adopt throughout the revolutionary crisis, though they contributed to his own downfall. Far from trying to splinter his opponents by reaching an agreement with the least determined of them, he simply tried to terrorize them all into silence. Thus, in winter 1975, on the pretext that the FSLN had revived its activity, a state of emergency was declared, martial law and press censorship imposed. UDEL was paralyzed. The strikes and student movement were brutally suppressed. And an annihilation campaign, Operation *Aguila Sexta,* was launched against the FSLN.

By September 1977, Anastasio Somoza Debayle seemed to have won: "social peace" had been restored on the basis of a cut in real wages; the FSLN, bled white in the military campaign, was split into three factions; and UDEL had given proof of its lack of consistency. Believing he had achieved his objectives, the dictator now agreed to comply with Washington's injunctions. But no sooner had he lifted the state of emergency in exchange for US military credits, than the opposition movements re-surfaced with even greater vigor.

In October 1977, a month after the state of emergency was lifted, the *Tercerista* tendency of the FSLN launched a series of assaults on National Guard barracks in the northern town of Ocotal, in Masaya, and in San Carlos near the Costa Rican border. The operation was a military failure, but it had a resounding political echo. By showing that repression had solved nothing, it acted as a spur to the popular opposition.

In November *La Prensa* published a full-page appeal in which twelve well-known figures from economic, cultural, and religious life called for a democratic alternative to the regime. Significantly, this was the first declaration of its kind to include the FSLN among the suggested participants in such an alternative. Somoza refused to make any concessions to this renewal of oppositional activity. On the contrary, he raised the stakes still higher, and on January 10, 1978, Pedro Joaquín Chamorro, *La Prensa* director and UDEL leader, was assassinated in Managua. By eliminating the very man who embodied the liberal solution, Somoza attempted to place the Nicaraguan bourgeoisie and the Carter administration before a dire choice: "Either Somoza or the Sandino-communists." Once again, he had deliberately opted for catastrophist politics.

The Revolutionary Crisis: January 1978 to July 1979

The assassination of Chamorro was the spark that lit the prairie fire. The resulting outrage coalesced all opposition to the regime into a single movement. Henceforth there would be a continual succession of mass demonstrations, general strikes, and partial insurrections, gradually leading to a situation of dual power. The oppositional bourgeoisie, working first through UDEL and later the *Frente Amplio de Oposición* (FAO), managed to stay at the head of the movement until January 1979. But as the masses grew increasingly radical, the leadership gradually slipped away to the FSLN.

On January 13, 1978, some 120,000 demonstrators attended the funeral procession of the liberal leader. The COSEP employers' federation, speaking for medium capital if not for the BANIC and BANAMERICA groups, called for a "civil stoppage" to demand punishment of the assassins and the resignation of Somoza. The mass strike, virtually total by January 24, was punctuated by huge demonstrations and bloody clashes with the National Guard.

The FSLN took advantage of this formidable popular mobilization to step up its level of activity, attacking the garrison at Rivas and Granada on 1 and 2 February. "It was the first great blow we had struck since the outbreak of the crisis," stated Humberto Ortega, the strategist of victory. "These large-scale operations encouraged the masses and strengthened their determination to fight against Somozism. This time, the people saw that the vanguard was more solid, capable of fighting, capable of hitting the enemy, capable of seizing towns . . . The February actions had an impact that reached its highest expression in the insurrection of Monimbo Indians."[2] Afraid that they were being outflanked, UDEL and COSEP appealed for a return to work on February 6. And although the labor federations tried to continue the strike, the call was generally observed.

Strictly in terms of its immediate objectives, the *paro cívico*, or civil stoppage, was a failure. Yet this first massive mobilization of the urban population, lasting for a considerable period, had an enormous impact upon the political maturation of the movement. It was crucial, too, that petty-bourgeois layers in the commercial and service sectors stood shoulder to shoulder with industrial workers and sub-proletarians.

The toiling population became aware of its own strength, learning to confront the ever-active police collectively at a time when divisions within the ruling class were nearing the breaking point. The FSLN grew in prestige and authority, while its project of a definitive, armed overthrow of the regime gained much greater credibility. The popular movement now took a decisive step towards political autonomy of the bourgeoisie.

Characteristically for a period of revolutionary upsurge, partial defeats and even savage repression did not cause demoralization or demobilization. On the contrary, the population increasingly met the *Guardia*'s actions with forms of mass violence, spontaneously seeking the road of armed resistance. Thus, on February 20, 1978 the local inhabitants of Monimbo, in Masaya, broke out in open rebellion. For nearly a week, they held their own against the National Guard, backed by artillery and aerial bombing. On the 26th, however, the uprising was drowned in blood.

The Broad Opposition Front (FAO)

Deeply affected by the scope and determination of the movement, Somoza finally decided to make some concessions: a one-month annual bonus and a rise in the minimum wage for the industrial workers; social security provisions for the agricultural laborers; and a "national dialogue" for the oppositional bourgeoisie.

But it was too late. The people now called for the ouster of "the little Nero." In any case, after the extremely costly general strike of January-February, the dictator no longer had the wherewithal to grant social concessions. The civil-war climate was hardly propitious for a business recovery, and capital was fleeing to more clement skies. Official sources placed the outflow of foreign currency in 1979 at $315 million, or 75 percent of the total value of exports. GDP fell by 25 percent, while inflation soared past 75 percent and unemployment hit 42 percent of the work-force.[3]

In a spiral characteristic of revolutionary situations, political agitation fueled the economic crisis, while economic decline maintained and extended political agitation.

It was a sign of the times when the Nicaraguan Democratic Movement (MDN), based on the cotton-growers of the North-West, was formed within the bourgeois opposition. Led by millionaire industrialist Alfonso Robelo, former president of the Nicaraguan Chamber of Industry (1972 to 1975), the Nicaraguan Development Institute, and COSEP (1975 to 1978), this new movement brought together a number of young company directors who had stood in the forefront of the employers' strike of January-February. The MDN called for the immediate dismissal of Somoza, the involvement of the FSLN in a future government, and the enactment of a number of democratic reforms.

In order to impose a political solution that would still afford it control, the anti-Somoza bourgeoisie finally agreed to establish a broad alliance of all forces hostile to the dictatorship, even including the FSLN *Terceristas* by way of "the Group of Twelve." The *Frente Amplio de Oposición* (FAO), enjoying Church support that counted for a great deal in this intensely Catholic country, was accordingly proclaimed in July 1978. Prominent among its sixteen demands was a call for the withdrawal of Somoza—a point publicly endorsed on August 3 by Monseigneur Miguel Obando y Bravo, Archbishop of Managua.

The oppositional bourgeoisie had devised a clear strategy: it would exploit the mass mobilization and the Carter administration's support so as to force a negotiated compromise on Somoza, removing him from power in accordance with the Constitution. There was to be no question of nationalizing the clan's property or of dissolving the National Guard.

The phase of bourgeois hegemony over the movement, lasting from the creation of UDEL in July 1974 to the disintegration of the FAO in January-February 1979, was marked by moderate goals and methods of struggle. The goal was to end the usurpation of power by a narrow *camarilla* that had systematically abused office—not, however, by force of arms, but by intensifying the converging pressures that would eventually force the dictator to yield.

For its part, the FSLN was far from inactive during this period. The "proletarian tendency" and the advocates of "protracted people's war" carried out wide-ranging agitation and political organization in the *barrios*, the factories, and the plantations. Work stoppages, street demonstrations, and riots succeeded one another in an unbroken chain: the strike of municipal and health workers in June-July 1978; the student strike to win the reopening of *"Mi Preferida"* radio station; the huge demonstrations celebrating the return of "the twelve" to Managua; the protest general strike against the murder of eight students by the National Guard in Jinotepe and San Marcos on July 19, 1978; another, FAO-sponsored general strike on August 27.

At the same time, the FSLN *Terceristas* stepped up their acts of war. On July 20, they fired rockets from the upper floors of the Hotel Intercontinental at National Guard headquarters and Somoza's famous "bunker." On August 22, guerrilla comandante Edén Pastora took over the National Palace and imprisoned more than five hundred leading figures of the regime, including sixty deputies, several ministers, and Somoza's own cousin. All these lights of high society were eventually exchanged for five million dollars, the publication of a press communiqué, and the release of Tomás Borge and eighty-two other FSLN prisoners. On 24 August, the commando group and the Sandinist prisoners left for Panama to popular acclaim.

The Limits of Peaceful Forms of Struggle

Despite the broad strikes and mass demonstrations, the daring guerrilla activity, and the pressures exerted by the bourgeoisie, the dictator still refused to yield. Apparently convinced that no one could oust him so long as the National Guard was under his control, Somoza set out to drown the popular movement in blood and to persuade the liberal bourgeoisie to come to terms. Once they tired of the chaos, they would eventually accept his orders. Time seemed to be on Somoza's side, provided he maintained a ruthless attitude and kept careful watch over the loyalty of his praetorians. With this in mind, he relieved thirty National Guard officers of their functions and on 27 August ordered the arrest on conspiracy charges of a number of army officers, whose "brain" was Lieutenant-Colonel Bernardino Larios.

Somoza's obstinacy exposed the limitations of FAO strategy. A general strike and street demonstrations, however massive, could not alone oust an opponent who clung to power through naked violence and did not flinch even from bombing his own towns. An enemy bent upon civil war could be vanquished only by the methods of civil war, and only an armed movement could overcome the National Guard. Unless it culminated in an insurrection, any general strike would inevitably be defeated.

The strategic superiority of the FSLN, which enabled it to wrest the leadership of the popular movement from the bourgeois opposition in less than a year, lay in its clear understanding of these necessities. Far from counterposing mass struggle to armed combat, the FSLN asserted and organized their convergence. Strikes and demonstrations would pave the way for armed insurrection as the climax of the general strike.

The Regime's Last Chance

By early September, two other features typical of a revolutionary situation were in evidence in Nicaragua. First, there was an *uneven development* of popular radicalization: in some sectors and regions, the mass of workers were urging an immediate insurrection, while in others they still had confidence in the FAO. Second, the combativity of the most radicalized sectors had outstripped the preparedness of the revolutionary forces. Unless the latter could effectively assume their political-military functions, however, any mass insurrection would be doomed to end in a bloodbath.

Sensing that the tradtionally radical North-West was approaching an inevitable conflagration, the FSLN *Terceristas* decided to press ahead. They hoped in this way at least to restrict the damage and to retain the leadership of the armed struggle.

On 9 September 1978 FSLN columns attacked León, Estelí, Chinandega, Masaya, and several other towns, unleashing a general uprising of the local populations. The National Guard replied by bombing the insurgent towns and intensifying its ferocious repression in the rest of the country.

On 20 September, when the Sandinists were compelled to withdraw, imposing columns of civilians fled in their wake to escape the savage reprisals that followed. Somoza set out to make an example of León and Estelí. The National Guard tortured and executed anyone "suspected of sympathy with the Sandino-communists," concentrating especially on teenagers. The September insurrection cost a total of 6,000 lives.

When Humberto Ortega was later asked if the action had been a mistake, he answered:

. We could not say no to the insurrection. The mass movement had grown to such a size that the vanguard was incapable of leading it. We could not oppose this torrent-like movement; all we could do was stand at its head, so as to lead it as much as possible and give it some direction. In this sense the vanguard, aware of its limitations, bowed to the general decision of the masses and took up a position at their head. Their decision and resolve stemmed from the example of Monimbo. . . .

If we had not given form to this mass movement, it would have lapsed into general anarchy. In other words, the vanguard's decision to call for the September insurrection made it possible to channel the torrent, giving form to the insurrection so that victory could subsequently be achieved.

I would like to repeat that we threw ourselves into the insurrection because of the prevailing political situation. Our aim was not to abandon the people to a massacre, for, as in Monimbo, the people were already plunging into action.[4]

That this fresh defeat was not a serious blow to the popular movement revealed the depth of the accumulated potential for revolt.

Somoza seemed jubiliant, convinced that he had won a decisive victory. But the bourgeois opposition, too, thought that its hour had come. The defeat of the September insurrection would surely force the FSLN to retreat, weakening the revolutionary wing of the movement, and would also demonstrate its dangerous potential in a situation of prolonged polarization. The Carter administration, aware of this peril, would be bound to step up its pressure on Somoza to abdicate.

Both pro- and anti-Somoza sections of the bourgeoisie, then, believed their own position stronger and therefore agreed to negotiate under an international "commission of mediation" composed of representatives of the United States, Guatemala, and the Dominican Republic.

The talks dragged on for several months. The idea was to force the dictator to accept "Somozism without Somoza": a conservative government, from which the FSLN would be excluded; maintenance of the National Guard; guarantees for Somoza property.

The FSLN—the "national leadership," or *Tercerista* tendency which had gone furthest in a policy of alliance with the bourgeoisie—could not agree to such a compromise. Too much blood had flowed for the people to be content with a mere refurbishing of the system.

The FAO program now lagged behind the state of mind of the masses, including the petty-bourgeoisie, which wanted an end to the regime and the root-and-branch destruction of Somozism. Evidence of this new awareness could be seen in their growing combativity against extremely fierce repression. The FSLN slogans— expropriation of the Somozists, dissolution of the National Guard—gave accurate expression to the people's aspirations at this point.

Overtaken by the new course of the class struggle, the FAO lost its political authority and suffered progressive dislocation. In November 1978 the "Group of Twelve," a cover for the FSLN *Terceristas*, announced its break from the FAO in protest against direct US interference in the talks. Other organizations followed suit.

On January 10, 1979, a gigantic demonstration took place in Managua to mark the first anniversary of the assassination of Pedro Joaquín Chamorro. Dozens of people were killed, and five days later health workers began a hunger strike. But the *coup de grâce* came on 19 January, when Somoza rejected the proposals of the "commission of mediation," reaffirming that he would remain in power until his mandate expired in 1981. The FAO, with American support, continued to advocate "moderate" solutions to the crisis, but it met with growing indifference and frustration on the part of the population.

Towards the "Final Offensive"

The breakup of the FAO opened a new and deeper phase of the revolution. It removed a major obstacle to the unification of the FSLN, since *Tercerista* participation in a bourgeois-dominated front striving for a bourgeois solution of the crisis had been one of the main points of contention with the other two tendencies. On 9 December 1978, all three set up a unified command structure, and organizational fusion followed on 26 March 1979.

Most crucially, the course of the FAO compelled the Sandinists to promote a new alliance policy, one independent of the bourgeoisie and in line with the FSLN's own revolutionary goals.

Greater effort was now put into the "United People's Movement" (MPU), an umbrella structure of twenty-two popular organizations that had been formed in mid-July 1978. Neighborhood committees, trade unions, women's and youth associations were strengthened and reorganized. The aim of the FSLN was to augment the capacity for initiative and organization in all sectors of the mass movement and to fortify their independence of the FAO bourgeois opposition, now more concerned with keeping the revolutionaries out of power than with sealing the fate of the dictatorship. On 1 February 1979 a new structure, the National Patriotic Front (FPN), brought together the MPU, the Twelve, the trade unions, and a few minor bourgeois formations. *It was an alliance under Sandinist hegemony that was to assume the task of organizing a general strike. The leadership of the mass movement had now changed hands. The bourgeoisie and imperialists had lost the initiative.*

On 8 February, the United States suspended military and economic aid to Somoza in retaliation for his rejection of the mediating commision's proposals. But the pro-Somoza lobby remained a powerful force in Washington, and money withdrawn with one hand was restored with the other. Thus, on 14 May the International Monetary Fund, whose sensitivity to American behests needs no elaboration, granted the Nicaraguan government a $65 million loan. Among those voting in favor was the representative of the United States. Somoza retained the support of many Latin American dictatorships, and continued to receive arms from Argentina and Israel. However, Costa Rica, Panama, Mexico, and Venezuela grew increasingly hostile in their public statements and their attitude within international bodies, thereby contributing to the dictator's isolation. On 20 May Mexico broke diplomatic relations with Managua. On 28 May the heads of state of the five Andean Pact countries condemned the Somoza government at a meeting in Colombia, and on 16 June they recognized the Sandinists' status as "belligerent."

On 24 June, the Organization of American States rejected Cyrus Vance's proposal to send a "peacekeeping force" to Nicaragua, demanding the resignation of Somoza instead. All these measures, in varying degree, lent real aid to the FSLN.

On 6 April 1979, a 42 percent devaluation of the córdoba relative to the dollar, the first since 1932, confirmed the regime's economic catastrophe. Galloping inflation deepened popular discontent, while hitherto neutral sections of the bourgeoisie and petty-bourgeoisie joined the ranks of the opposition. Entirely divested of its social base, the Somoza dictatorship was reduced to its quintessence: the National Guard.

Dual Power: March to July 1979

The FSLN resumed its military offensive in March 1979, occupying the town of Estelí between the 8th and the 14th. But the "final offensive" really began on 21 May in Jinotega and elsewhere. Unlike the Batista forces in Cuba, however, the National Guard continued to mount determined resistance.

Drawing inspiration from the Vietnamese experience, the FSLN sought to compensate for its military inferiority by forcing the *Guardia* to spread itself thinly. Its tactic was to create an indefinite number of operational zones through combinations of strike movements, local uprisings, and the activity of its own military units. The 15,000-strong repressive forces, only half of them seasoned National Guardsmen, would be unable to control a country of 132,000 square kilometers and 2,300,000 inhabitants. If they tried to do so, they would suffer dispersion, thus losing strategic superiority at many points that could then be attacked by the guerrillas. But if they set themselves a more limited objective, concentrating their forces at a few strong-points, the FSLN could use the surrendered territory to prepare a fresh assault. This is how Humberto Ortega later described the development of FSLN thinking:

We realized that our principal strength lay in our capacity to maintain total mobilization at the social, economic, and political levels, thereby dispersing the enemy's technico-military capacity. . . . We saw that if we were to win, we had not only to move our own guerrilla contingents into combat, but also ensure through our actions that the masses would take an active part in the struggle. . . .

The truth is that we always thought of the masses, seeing them, however, as a prop for the guerrilla campaign that would enable it to deal some blows at the National Guard. Reality was quite different: guerrilla activity served as a prop for the masses, who crushed the enemy by means of insurrection. . . .

After the September events, we saw the need to combine, at the same time and in the same strategic space, a nation-wide mass uprising, a frontal offensive by our military forces, and a general strike which the employers actively supported or approved. . . .

Had we not combined these three factors in a single time and space, victory would not have been possible. Several calls for a national strike had already been issued, but without being linked to a mass offensive. The masses had already risen up, but their action had not been combined with a strike and had taken place at a time when the vanguard's military capacity was too weak. Finally, the vanguard had already inflicted blows on the enemy, but at a time when the other two factors were not present.[5]

This strategy determined the specific character of dual power in Nicaragua. Despite the great heterogeneity of forms and situations, the basic units of people's counter-power were civil defence committees (CDS) in the localities and joint union committees in the factories. Where the Somozists still controlled a town, these committees carried out the task of preparing an insurrection and giving logistic support. In the liberated towns, they came together in a "central committee of civil defence committees" (Estelí) or a "junta of reconstruction" (Matagalpa), assuming all the civil functions connected with public safety, health, material supplies, distribution, and so on.[6]

In the north and center of the country, similar bodies administered a kind of "war communism." And sometimes when they did not function satisfactorily, additional bodies like the "Fabio Martínez Labor Unit" in Matagalpa were created alongside them.

But the real center of revolutionary power, recognized as such by the population, was the local FSLN headquarters. It appointed members of the "central committeess" or "municipal juntas," and it embodied the new legitimacy and the new political authority.

In the conditions of dual power in Nicaragua, then, which were embryonic and sectoralized after January 1978 but became fully-fledged after the May 1979 FSLN offensive, the Somozist state apparatus, essentially reduced to the National Guard, stood opposed to the Sandinist Front resting on a dense network of mass organizations.

"The Insurrectional General Strike"

Three fronts were opened between May and June: to the north in El Jicaro, Estelí and later Jinotega; to the south in El Naranjo, Peñas Blanca, and Sapoa; to the west in Masaya, Granada and Carazo. The southern front, reinforced by many internationalist fighters from the whole of Latin America, tied down one of the regime's two elite units, the EEBI.

At every level, women were involved in the struggle to an exceptionally high degree. They made up 25 percent of the ranks of guerrilla columns. There were a number of women commanders: Mónica Blateono and Leticia Herrera, to name but two. And Dora Téllez "Comandante No. 29," directed operations on the Rigoberto López western front, one of the most important in the war.

On 4 June, the FSLN issued a call for an "insurrectional general strike," and the next day the country was totally paralyzed. One after another, the main towns received their insurrection orders. On 10 June, the people of Managua rose up spontaneously, well before the date scheduled by the Sandinists. Elite troops had to move back to the capital urgently, thereby relieving the other fronts.

On 12 June, Mexico and Venezuela informed the US government that they would not tolerate a "hot-pursuit" incursion by Somozist troops into Costa Rica. Four days later, a provisional government was actually formed in the Costa Rican town of San José. It included Sergio Ramírez from the Group of Twelve; Alfonso Robelo, leader of the MDN; Violetta Chamorro, widow of the murdered liberal-conservative leader; Moisés Hassan from the MPU; and Daniel Ortega from the FSLN. Despite appearances, the FSLN had a majority in virtue of the support it enjoyed from the Group of Twelve and MPU representatives.

One hundred and thirty US congressmen now demanded the restoration of military aid to Somoza. At the Assembly of the Organization of American States, called by the United States on 22 June, Cyrus Vance formally proposed that a "peace-keeping force" be sent to Nicaragua. But only Argentina supported the idea. Almost unanimously, the OAS firmly opposed any North American interference in the Nicaraguan civil war.

As James Petras has pointed out, this virtual unanimity was the fruit of a curious combination of opposites. The military dictatorships, incensed by Carter's "human rights" doctrine, wanted no truck with a precedent that might later be used against them. For although an OAS military intervention might have blocked the FSLN, it would also have brought down a regime with many analogous to the south. By contrast, the hostile regimes held that the OAS should not compromise itself alongside Somoza, and should refrain from interfering in a purely internal affair of the Republic of Nicaragua. Somoza's dictatorship had been condemned by the Andean Pact countries, several of which were openly aiding its enemies. It had been abandoned by the OAS, deprived of direct intervention by US marines and confronted with a general insurrection. Somoza now saw that the game was up.

Paradoxically, even the unbelievable savagery of repression began to tell against him. For in this atrocious war, people had greater chances of survival fighting in the FSLN than remaining at home at the mercy of a *Guardia* raid. Most of the 50,000 dead—two per cent of the population—were civilians who fell under the machine-gun fire of hate-crazed Guardsmen. Whenever the FSLN had to abandon a position, thousands of young men and women would follow in its train. On 27 June, for example, a convoy of 6,000 civilians left Managua.

By 16 July, the major towns in Nicaragua (León, Estelí, Matagalpa, Masaya, Diriamba) were in FSLN hands. On the 17th, Anastasio Somoza Debayle fled the country, leaving to Francisco Urcuyo, after agreement with Washington, the task of negotiating a "provisional government" take-over. In the US government view, a cease-fire should have come into force, freezing each side in its positions and allowing as much as possible to be salvaged from the Somozist state apparatus. A fusion of "healthy" *Guardia* elements with the Sandinist columns would then have constituted the armed power of the new regime. Above all, the relationship of forces liberal bourgeoisie and the Sandinist revolutionaries would have become less unfavorable.

Unfortunately for the authors of this scheme, the National Guard began to disintegrate as soon as news of Somoza's flight had been confirmed. This praetorian militia, which unlike the usual national army had not fractured under the impact of crisis and class struggle, could not survive the downfall of its boss. And the crowning piece of ill luck was that even Urcuyo, no doubt secretly advised by Somoza, declined to respect Washington's scenario. Instead he renounced the agreement with the government junta and resolved to stay in office until expiration of the presidential mandate in 1981. The FSLN could scarcely have hoped for such a volte-face, but it immediately responded by calling the final assault.

On 19 July, then, the Sandinist columns triumphantly entered Managua. The National Guard evaporated, 7,000 men being taken prisoner and the rest trying to reach Honduras. Any prominent person or official with good reason to fear the people's vengeance packed his bags and left.

The FSLN had won a total victory, but it had cost 50,000 lives and incalculable destruction. To punish the oppositional bourgeoisie, Somoza had systematically bombed its factories. In the industrial zone of Managua, all along the north motorway, their burnt-out shells pointed accusing fingers to the heavens. Only the clan factories remained intact. On 20 July, they were all nationalized.

The FSLN: Three Unite into One

When Somoza's "*Aguila VI*" operation came to an end in 1976, the FSLN was reduced to a few dozen militants. Carlos Fonseca Amador had fallen in November in the Zelaya region. Tomás Borge, the only surviving founding leader, was in prison. Strategic differences, latent since the 1967 Pancasán defeat and fueled by the repression that followed the "Juan José Quezada" commando raid of 27 December 1974, were dividing the movement into three hostile factions.

The "protracted people's war" (GPP) tendency, as we have seen, was inspired by Maoist and Vietnamese conceptions, not a contradiction at the time. According to its strategy, centered on rural guerrilla activity, the creation of "liberated zones" in the mountains of the North would provide "support bases" from which to harry the towns and develop urban guerrilla warfare. The establishment of such zones was thus the strategic objective to which all else had to be subordinated. Mass work in the union and student movements was seen mainly as a means by which to recruit forces for rural guerrilla operations. Moreover, since it was overwhelmingly likely that US imperialism would intervene against a successful revolution, any strategy of armed struggle that did not entail the creation of such bases would be built on sand.

The "proletarian tendency," by contrast, laid claim to the classic Marxist tradition, locating itself among the urban working class, sub-proletariat, and youth as the driving forces of the revolution. In its view, the GPP strategy would lead to isolation in half-deserted regions, far from the active masses and nerve centers of the country. Holding that a powerful and independent mass movement was a precondition of victory, the "proletarian tendency" opposed not only "military adventures," that would substitute the violence of revolutionaries for mass violence as part of a private war against the dictatorship, but also alliances in which revolutionaries were subordinated to the anti-Somoza wing of the bourgeoisie. In 1978, it began talks with *Frente Obrero*, another revolutionary splinter from the FSLN deeply involved in mass organizing work in the towns.

The *Tercerista* "insurrectional" or "national leadership" tendency developed as a reaction to both the GPP and the "proletarian tendency." It accused them both of upholding strategies based on "passive accumulation of forces": the idea that there is an interruption between preparation for combat and the combat itself, that it is possible coolly to accumulate militants, arms, and experience without systematically intervening in both the political and military arenas.

According to their alternative conception, defined as "active accumulation of forces," the contradictions of the regime were such that even a numerically weak revolutionary group, if it knew how to seize the initiative, could have a powerful impact on the depth of the crisis.

The *Tercerista* strategy combined the ideas of an FSLN-led armed offensive with a broad alliance policy that sought to exploit divisions within the bourgeoisie, to isolate the dictatorship, and to advance a credible government alternative.

Its military audacity, which earned it the label "insurrectional," was rooted in a conviction that the US army was not capable of direct intervention in Nicaragua. Its openness to a united course rested upon a closely-argued analysis of divisions within the ruling class[7] and upon a belief that, so long as freedom of political and military action was preserved, revolutionaries had nothing to lose and everything to gain from an alliance with the bourgeois opposition. The *Terceristas* therefore joined the FAO, at a time when they were already stepping up their attacks on *Guardia* barracks. Internationally, they managed to win political and material support from Social Democracy, and even from certain liberal forces. But it would require a peculiar blindness to accept James Petras' characterization of them as a Social Democratic tendency.[8] A strange Social Democracy indeed that engages in revolutionary war and an insurrectional general strike!

If we have to give the *Terceristas* an internationally known label, "Castroist" would seem to suit them much better.

Taken together, all three Sandinist tendencies numbered barely 200 in 1977, and no more than 500 when they entered Managua on 19 July 1979. Being a political-military organization, the FSLN was forced to exercise great selectiveness in its choice of recruits. But thousands of sympathizers were active in its mass organizations. And tens of thousands of people who fought against the dictatorship spontaneously recognized the political authority of the Sandinists.

The Question of Alliances

The *Tercerista* policy of alliance was denounced as opportunist and capitulationist by various far-left currents in Nicaragua and elsewhere. Some saw it as a relic of Stalinist popular frontism, involving the sacrifice of proletarian unity and class independence within a subordinate alliance with the "national" bourgeoisie, the natural leadership of the "democratic stage" of the revolution. These critics opposed the idea of an "anti-fascist front" against the dictatorship, putting forward the "workers' united front" for socialism as an alternative.

Now, it does seem that at least some of the *Terceristas* had illusions in the anti-imperialist potential of the Nicaraguan bourgeoisie.[9] These illusions were quickly destroyed in winter 1978, under the combined impact of the radicalization of the masses and the bourgeoisie's support for the commission of mediation. But in any case, the *Terceristas* never subordinated the development of their own strategy—armed confrontation with the regime—to their activity within the FAO. It would be quite wrong to identify their alliance policy with Stalinist-type popular or anti-fascist fronts.

From the point of view of class alliances, the Nicaraguan proletariat could triumph only on three conditions: if it was itself united around a revolutionary program and strategy; if its political alternative polarized the middle layers; and if the ruling class was deeply and lastingly divided.

Only an alliance strategy that related to all three conditions could enable an absolutely dominated class, weaker than its enemy in every respect, to gain the upper hand over not only the dictatorship but the whole of the ruling class as well. It was, to be sure, a complex strategy, for the three conditions contradict one another in part.

Whereas supporters of a popular or anti-fascist front sacrifice the first to the two other conditions, advocates of a "class against class" policy do exactly the opposite. They pay no heed to the tasks of exploiting contradictions within the ruling class and winning the broadest sectors of the petty-bourgeoisie to the side of the proletariat. They thus deny themselves any prospect of victory, as surely as if they deliberately placed themselves in the tow of the bourgeoisie.

The "anti-imperialist front" policy the FSLN applied immediately after its break with the FAO met all three conditions. As Adolfo Gilly has correctly argued: "If the FSLN had counterposed a socialist workers' front to the anti-imperialist front, treating the latter as an instrument of the bourgeoisie or as equivalent to a popular front . . . they would have taken a narrowly sectarian position which, on the false pretext of defending principles, would have been doomed to failure and would have forsaken any mobilization of the real mass movement as it first appeared under the dictatorship."[10]

The March 1979 Fusion

If the split in the FSLN had occurred during an ebb in the mass movement, it would doubtless have had disastrous consequences. But occurring as it did in a period of rising popular combativity and deepening crisis of the regime, it never had time to harden into an intractable rift. Indeed, within the context of a fruitful strategic debate, a kind of functional division of labor developed among the three groups. The *Terceristas* assumed responsibility for military initiatives and the policy of alliances, while the GPP and "proletarian" tendencies conducted mass organizational work in the *barrios,* the university, the factories, and the plantations.

This effectively complimentary activity gave a certain perspective to tendency differences. Above all, the concrete evolution of the revolutionary process, much more varied and complex than any of them had envisaged, swept away the old lines of division and gave each one a share of truth and a share of error.

GPP supporters admitted that they had underestimated the insurrectional character of the situation in the urban Pacific coast centers, and that on crucial days their columns had consequently been rather a long way from the theater of operations. At the same time, they correctly maintained that rural guerrilla activity had provided the FSLN with its most experienced cadres and established its moral authority among the population.

The "proletarians" also drew a self-critical balance sheet, but emphasized the key role of the urban mass organizations in preparing and accomplishing the insurrection.

The *Terceristas* naturally emerged the strongest from the comparison, since the course of events had essentially confirmed their analysis and strategy. But they readily agreed that, as mass insurrection was playing a decisive role in the struggle, the patient organizational work that alone made it effective had been as crucial as their military offensives and alliance policy.

Each tendency thus had reason for both pride and humility. Spurred by the enthusiasm of the offensive, the three leaderships first set up a joint command and then, in March 1979, smoothly effected an organizational fusion on the basis of equality. The new National Directorate comprised three representatives from each tendency: Daniel Ortega, Humberto Ortega, and Víctor Tirado (*Terceristas*); Tomás Borge, Henry Ruíz, and Bayardo Arce (GPP); Jaïme Wheelock, Luís Carríon, and Carlos Nuñez (Proletarian Tendency). Still, some did appear to be "more equal than others," for as Comandante Luís Carríon explained: "We have all made mistakes throughout our struggle, but in varying degrees. Hence some cadres are better prepared, having had the fullest experience of the process of war and revolution. This has undeniably played a role in the constitution of the army and the organization of its command structure."[11]

Notes

[1]See María Esperanza Valle Buitrago, "Unión democrática de Liberación: la expresión política de una alianza de clase en Nicaragua, 1974–78," *Estudios sociales centroamericanos,* Sept.–Dec., 1979.

[2]H. Ortega, "Interview with Martha Harnecker," *Granma*, French-language edition, January 27, 1978, reprinted *Nicaragua: du rêve a la réalité.*

[3]Oscar Rene Vargas, "La Crisis del Somocismo y el movimiento obrero nicaraguense," *Estudios Sociales Centro Americanos*, (April 1978).

[4]"Interview with Martha Harnecker," p. 31.

[5]"Interview with Martha Harnecker," pp. 28, 35.

⁶See Pisani's report on the situation in Estelí and Matagalpa, *Los Muchachos*, pp. 133–39 and 189–91. See also, for the whole period under consideration here, Charles Andre Udry, "Nicaragua: la revolution en marche," *Inprecor*, September 1979.

⁷See the series of articles in *Pensamiento Crítico*, many of which are reproduced in López, Nuñez, Chamorro, and Serres, *La caída del somocismo y la lucha sandinista*, Managua, 1980.

⁸James Petras, "Whither the Nicaraguan Revolution?" *Monthly Review*, October 1979, Vol. 31, No. 5, p. 14.

⁹See the programmatic document of March 1979, in which the newly unified leadership made a critique of the FAO. *Cuadernos Políticos,* no. 20, Mexico City, April–June 1979.

¹⁰Adolfo Gilly, *La Nueva Nicaragua: anti-imperialismo y lucha de clase,* Mexico, 1980.

¹¹See the interview in Pisani, p. 253.

25. Our Vengeance Toward Our Enemies Will Be the Pardon*

By Tomás Borge

Comandante Tomás Borge, the most charismatic and popular Nicaraguan leader, is currently Minister of the Interior and a member of the nine-person National Directorate of the FSLN. He is the only surviving original member of the FSLN, which he founded in 1961 with Carlos Fonseca Amador and Silvio Mayorga. Originally members of the Nicaraguan Socialist Party (PSN), they broke away from its traditional Latin American communist party dogmatism. When the FSLN split into factions, Borge and Henry Ruíz stayed "in the mountain" leading the Prolonged People's War (GPP) tendency. He spent many years in Somoza's prisons, reportedly suffering brutal torture.

What are we doing in the prisons?

"We are not interested in destroying the sinners, but rather in eliminating the sin," I said.

And what are we doing with these assassins [ex–National Guardsmen]? We are trying to convert them into something they have never been: true human beings. I believe that it is our moral obligation to raise them from their condition like beasts to the condition of human beings.

This then is the philosophy of our revolution, but clearly, they do not understand. When I was a prisoner I spoke with them. I told them that someday we would help them. They didn't believe me then, and they still doubt it.

---

*Excerpts from *No pedimos que elogien la revolución, sino que digan y divulgen la verdad*, 1981. Translated by Peter Rosset.

A few days ago my wife's murderer was captured. When he saw me coming—that woman had been savagely tortured, she had been raped, her fingernails had been pulled out—he thought that I was going to kill him, or at least hit him. He was totally terrified when we arrived, but we treated him like a human being. He did not understand then, nor can he understand now. I think he may never understand.

We once said, "Our vengeance towards our enemies will be the pardon, it is the best of all vengeances."

Part Three

U.S. INTERVENTION

Editors' Introduction

As early as 1980 the new Nicaraguan government was reporting various forms of economic and military intervention by the United States. Shortly thereafter the international press began to recognize what was happening, *Newsweek* reported it in 1982, and by early 1983 the Reagan administration was no longer attempting to deny it. It is now widely known that the United States is intervening in Nicaragua's internal affairs in an effort to overthrow the government.

One aspect of the intervention had reportedly been orchestrated directly from the script provided by the influential "Di Giovanni Report" of the Heritage Foundation, in which it is stated

> ... although the Marxist government in Nicaragua might fall eventually of its own failures, the security of El Salvador requires the acceleration of the removal of the government in Managua. . . . [1]

> In a well-orchestrated program targeted against the Marxist Sandinista government we should use our limited resources to support the free labor unions, the Church, the private sector, the independent political parties, the free press, and those who truly defend human rights. [2]

Curiously, military intervention was discarded as counterproductive by the same report:

> It will not be possible to dislodge the current communist government . . . except through military action. Under the proper circumstances, the Nicaraguans themselves are prepared to initiate that action, and any US military or paramilitary involvement would be unnecessary and counterproductive. [3]

Subsequently, intervention by the United States escalated on both levels, thus initiating "America's Secret War." Chapter I includes the famous *Newsweek* article that "broke the story" in the mainstream media. Raymond Bonner's *New York Times* article then treats US involvement more deeply. The chapter concludes with several readings on the *"contras,"* as the counterrevolutionaries are called.

The response to the exposure of US involvement is covered in Chapter II, including several editorial pieces by well-known analysts. Robert White, former US ambassador to El Salvador, makes the gloomy prediction that the Reagan administration will try to expand the current conflicts in Central America into regional war.

Notes

[1] Cleto Di Giovanni, Jr., *The Heritage Foundation Backgrounder,* No. 128, October 15, 1980.
[2] *Ibid.* and Reading 26.
[3] *Ibid.*

Chapter I:

America's Secret War

Editors' Introduction

U nited States intervention in the internal affairs of post-revolutionary Nicaragua has ranged from subtle "destabilization" activities to overt support of
former National Guardsmen attacking from havens in Honduras. The first reading
in this chapter provides an overview of the US response to the Nicaraguan revolution, from President Carter's initial efforts to the Reagan administration's more
direct action.

Following this are the policy recommendations from the influential "Di Gio-
vanni" or "Heritage Foundation Report," widely viewed as the blueprint for later
Reagan policy. Excerpts from the North American Congress on Latin America
(NACLA) report, *Target Nicaragua*, further elaborate the theme of destabilization.

Reading 29 shows how antigovernment guerrillas were being trained on US soil
long before the counterrevolutionary attacks were openly acknowledged. This piece
gives some insight into the motives of those being trained, and casts doubt on the
Reagan administration's earlier assertions that the actions were planned for the
interdiction of arms shipments to El Salvador.

As we have pointed out earlier, United States intervention in Nicaragua had
been going on for some time before it was reported in the mainstream media.
Because the "breaking of the story" is in a real sense a part of the story itself, we have
included the pivotal *Newsweek* piece, "A Secret War for Nicaragua." It was the
publication of this story, more than any other event, that galvanized opposition to
the US policy towards Nicaragua, among the American people and in Congress.

The remaining readings in this chapter present analyses of what might be called
the armed opposition. One can generally divide the counterrevolutionary forces
into two groups: those in Honduras, who are composed mainly of former National
Guardsmen under Somoza, and those in Costa Rica, led by ex-Sandinista Edén

Pastora ("Commander Zero") and former Junta member Alfonso Robelo. Pastora's Democratic Revolutionary Alliance (ARDE) has apparently refused to cooperate with the Democratic Force (FDN) in Honduras, although this may change by the time this book goes to press. US representatives are reportedly expending a great deal of effort trying to forge an alliance.

Though he appears to have little support within Nicaragua, and despite the relatively small size of his forces (compared to those in Honduras), Pastora nevertheless enjoys a high profile in the US press. Since he may prove to be an important player in the future, we have included two readings about him.

The next article describes the different groups that make up the counterrevolution—*contras* as they are popularly known in Nicaragua. This is followed by "Reagan's Freedom Fighters," excerpted from a lawsuit filed by the Center for Constitutional Rights and the National Lawyers Guild. It is a complaint against President Reagan, members of his administration, and various counterrevolutionary organizations, on behalf of Nicaraguans who have suffered from *contra* attacks. It includes descriptions of the actual activities of the counterrevolutionary groups. Because of space limitations, we have arbitrarily included only 25 of the 86 incidents in the brief. However, it will be clear to anyone reading this piece that the ex–National Guard still behaves as it did when it was in power, terrorizing the population and committing bizarre atrocities. They do not appear to be trying to "win the hearts and minds" of Nicaraguans, as several glorified newswpaper and magazine accounts would have us believe.* It seems, rather, that their strategy is to create a general climate of terror, attempting to make it difficult if not impossible for people in remote areas to participate in government programs. It is widely rumored in Nicaragua that government workers, lay religious leaders, and peasants who join cooperatives are singled out for attacks.

This chapter concludes with an interview of "Commander Mack," a *contra* leader of one of the FDN's "task forces." In it he expresses his thanks to the United States because "overnight we got help and now we are a force."

---

*For example, Peter McCormick, "With Nicaraguan Rebels: Rosaries and Rifles," *New York Times*, May 13, 1983.

26. *Counterrevolution in Nicaragua: the US Connection**

By Jeff McConnell

Jeff McConnell is the author of a forthcoming book, The CIA in America *to be published by Lawrence Hill & Co.*

In spite of official claims to the contrary, the United States has never had a noninterventionist position toward the Nicaraguan revolution. Since the assassination of newspaper publisher Pedro Chamorro in January 1978, when the revolution became a large-scale insurrection, the US government has viewed developments in Nicaragua as a difficult dilemma that required some kind of US manipulation. Both the Carter and Reagan administrations have tried to influence events in Nicaragua by building up two social groups there: the so-called "private sector" (the bourgeoisie) and the military (that is, the National Guard while it existed, and later, its remnants). What is surprising about these American efforts is not *that* they have been occurring, but the *openness* with which they are occurring, compared with the true covertness of similar efforts in the Philippines, in Greece, in Brazil, and in Chile in the years from Truman through Nixon. In Nicaragua, Americans have kept a high profile while trying to manipulate events to suit US government ends. This is a new trend in the history of US intervention.

The Carter-Vance-Brzezinksi policy, both before the Sandinista victory and after, was to *contain* the revolution: to maintain a favorable climate for US business and to keep "radicals" out of power—in short, to block the creation of "another Cuba." The method they adopted was to "foster pluralism," Washington's code words for bolstering two minor sectors of Nicaraguan society: the business sector and the National Guard. Ronald Reagan has continued this policy. He has also expanded it into a policy intended to *roll back* the revolution. The revelations since early 1982 about CIA involvement only reflect the Reagan administration's latest refinements of this rollback policy.

I. Carter's Policy toward the Nicaraguan Insurrection

Carter's approach to the Sandinista insurrection went through four phases.[1] Initially, in response to growing unrest in Nicaragua in 1977, the US pressured Nicaragua's dictator Anastasio Somoza to lift the state of martial law under which he had governed the country for three years. It also encouraged Somoza to negotiate with centrist opposition groups.

---

*Reprinted from a revised version of an article which appeared in *CounterSpy* May-June 1982, pp. 11–23.

The administration's strategy was to cut losses—by channeling the new political currents in Nicaragua in ways the US could accept. But President Carter was not ready to abandon Somoza, since there were no guarantees that Somoza's successor would adequately support US aims in the region. US ties were closest to the most pro-American sectors of the FAO: business groups, American Institute for Free Labor Development (AIFLD)— established labor unions, and conservative political parties. When even these groups had abandoned Somoza, however, (largely because of his stranglehold on the economy through corruption and his vast wealth) it signaled to Carter that a government centered around Somoza was no longer in America's "national interest."

In January 1978, Pedro Joaquín Chamorro, editor of Nicaragua's leading daily *La Prensa* and an important opposition figure, was assassinated. This event signaled the start of the general insurrection against the Somoza government. There were demonstrations and a general strike. The Sandinista guerrillas made their broadest attacks yet against National Guard garrisons. The National Guard responded with savagery.

As the year progressed, all the opposition forces, including some sectors of the Sandinistas, came increasingly to hope that Carter, the "human rights" president, would abandon Somoza. But although he cut back most military aid, Carter released economic aid to Somoza in May 1978. When Carter sent a letter to Somoza in August 1978 praising Somoza's efforts to improve the human rights situation in Nicaragua, the opposition's hope vanished. The guerrillas launched their largest offensive, and the National Guard responded by bombing several Nicaraguan cities into rubble. Thousands of civilians died.

By late 1979 it was no longer politically possible for Carter to openly support Somoza. US policy entered a new phase. In conjunction with the Organization of American States (OAS), the US put together so-called "mediation" talks between Somoza and the Broad Opposition Front (FAO), a centrist coalition of opposition groups. The talks excluded the Sandinistas and their broad-based political fronts. The eventual outcome of these negotiations was envisioned by the US to be a plebiscite, and the replacement of Somoza by a government of private-sector moderates still loyal to the US. Somoza rejected the plebiscite in January 1979. When the US responded by proposing a compromise acceptable to Somoza, the FAO walked out.

Still, the Assistant Secretary of State for Inter-American Affairs, Viron Vaky, later wrote that the mediation effort had a very positive effect, by helping to "strengthen contacts among important moderate sectors of the Nicaraguan polity. It is true that some of the member groups of the FAO quit the organization during the negotiation process, but the fact is that most of them stayed the course. Indeed, the FAO picked up additional support from a broad cross section of the private sector (COSEP) [Superior Council of Private Enterprise, the congress leading Nicaraguan business organizations; today at the forefront of opposition in Nicaragua and once heavily funded through AID], which, while not formally joining the FAO, did provide broad support to their negotiating effort and endorsed the mediators' final proposal with the FAO. Thus," Vaky wrote, "the effort in effect catalyzed the moderate opposition elements into a relatively cohesive group capable of functioning."[2]

In early 1979, the several Sandinista factions united and joined a wide spectrum of Nicaraguan groups to form a very broad political front which approved a political program for a pluralist post-Somoza Nicaragua, and carried out more crippling strikes. The Sandinistas achieved significant military victories in late spring of 1979 as the entire country rose against Somoza. In an OAS meeting in Washington, Cyrus Vance initiated the Carter administration's third strategem for Nicaragua: he proposed that the OAS call for an interim government drawn from all segments of Nicaragua (including the supporters of Somoza) and consider deploying a "peacekeeping" force that would in effect block a Sandinista victory. The OAS overwhelmingly rejected Vance's proposal and called for Somoza's ouster and an interim government drawn from the opposition.

By now, the opposition front had formed a provisional government. The Carter administration, in its final gambit, tried to arrange a cease-fire. It proposed that Somoza resign and that a successor picked by the Somoza-dominated National Assembly appoint a group of prominent Nicaraguans to mediate among Somoza's Liberal Party, Somoza's National Guard, and the opposition forces to form an interim government. The opposition rejected this. Then Washington attempted to force the opposition to add more conservatives to the provisional government and to guarantee the survival of the National Guard. In exchange, Carter offered Somoza's resignation and threatened to hold back postwar reconstruction assistance. Again, the opposition refused. Finally on July 17, Somoza saw that defeat was inevitable. He resigned and fled to Miami.

II. Carter's Policy Directly after the War

The high command of the National Guard fled to Miami with Somoza. The National Guard itself disintegrated and its members fled to foreign embassies in Managua, to Red Cross centers through the country, and into Honduras and Costa Rica. Many who did not succeed in finding refuge were arrested. Although Somoza was encouraged to leave the US and did, the US government offered political asylum to many National Guard officers.[3] These officers were not subjected to criminal proceedings for the hundreds of My Lais in which they had been involved. These same people were soon carrying out terrorist acts once again against the Nicaraguan people and plotting a counterrevolution to be planned and financed from the United States.

In late 1979 and early 1980, the House Committee on Foreign Affairs held hearings on Carter's plan to give Nicaragua $75 million in postwar aid. Several witnesses argued against the plan. One witness was Dr. Cleto Di Giovanni, introduced respectfully as a "special consultant on foreign affairs to the private sector in Central America."[4] Three months later when his testimony was published, Di Giovanni's biographical sketch indicated that after leaving college, he "served three years with the US Navy in the Special Operations Group in Vietnam, then entered the Central Intellingence Agency. With CIA, he served in the Far East, in Europe, and in South America in a variety of operational and managerial assignments, including station chief abroad and clandestine operations chief of one of the geographical divisions at the headquarters levels. He left CIA at the end of 1978, and since early 1979 he has spent considerable time in Central America" as consultant.

Di Giovanni testified that he did not think it "realistic to believe that unconditional aid given Nicaragua, even if it should reach . . . moderate elements, would be used by them in any way not consistent with the goals and traditional orientation of the *frente* [Nicaragua's ruling body] and its members," which Di Giovanni viewed as Marxist. "Under these circumstances . . . why not withdraw aid . . . rather than provide money to [the government] which would help it solidify its power within the country . . . The credibility of anti-Somoza, anti-Communist Nicaraguan exile forces seeking to overthrow the Sandinista government has yet to be established. What could happen in the foreseeable future is that the population within the country, without outside intervention, becomes disenchanted with its government's policies, and we should be prepared to take advantage of that situation should it occur."

But Di Giovanni's recommendations were not immediately followed by the US. After intense White House lobbying, Congress eventually followed the line advocated by Viron Vaky.[5] Vaky argued that aid was the best leverage available to the US for keeping Nicaragua nonaligned, "pluralistic" and "moderate." He testified that the assistance "will go a long way toward strengthening the survival, and the capacity to operate, of elements which can contribute to pluralism. That is, the private sector . . . If we do not participate and assist those elements, such as the private sector, such as many of the moderate democratic elements in the government itself . . . , we will abandon the field to other nations, such as Cuba and the Soviet Union . . . "

The administration was not yet proposing direct subsidies of those private sector organizations, such as COSEP, with direct political objectives, but instead was requiring that 60 percent of its loan money to the Nicaraguan government be channeled through private companies rather than public agencies. At this point, private sector organizations were exercising restraint in criticizing the new government and, in fact, were still participating in the government. To assure Congress that these center-right groups would continue to wield political leverage, the administration stated it had privileged information of exchanges between COSEP and the Nicaraguan government, probably obtained from COSEP contacts, in which COSEP voiced concerns and which were said to have been "frank and [have] covered a wide variety of subjects, both of a political and economic nature."[6]

Agency for International Development (AID) documents repeat Vaky's themes. The "US interests" in offering the $75 million reconstruction package to Nicaragua were put this way: "Nicaragua's government of National Reconstruction faces enormous problems as it attempts to rebuild and restructure its shattered economy.

US assistance can accelerate reconstruction, bolster moderate economic policies, and help to create a positive relationship with the new government."[7] The package consisted of $70 million in long-term, low-interest loans, and a $5 million grant. The AID director for Nicaragua testified that over 60 percent, or about $45 million, would be "made available to private sector enterprises for the purposes of importing equipment, raw materials, farm machinery, and so forth from the United States"— that is, as export subsidies to US companies. The remaining loan money would be channeled by the Central Bank "into various construction and agricultural projects throughout the country."[8]

Even more interesting, though, is the $5 million grant, about which little has been said publicly. The allocations from this $5 million grant appear in Table 1. The funds from this grant represented the first overt attempt to build up groups friendly to the US. The scholarships under category 6 were administered under the LAS-PAU program, a Harvard-based effort that has brought Latin American scholars to the US since the 1960's for further training. Prior to this, LASPAU funding had come entirely out of a regional program for Central America and the Caribbean. AID used an ongoing program in this case to create a special program for Nicaragua. Notice also the "operational program grants" under category 2. The money for "agricultural cooperatives" was intended to offer "technical and financial assistance . . . [to] benefit 96,000 small farmer cooperative members." Of particular importance is the $300,000 grant to the Social Action Committee of the Moravian Chruch (headquartered in Bethlehem, Pennsylvania) which would "reach some 40,000 low-income people in the Atlantic Zone"—that is, Miskitu Indians. These points will gain importance when compared with later AID grants.

The final part of the AID package was a "publicity campaign." AID documents state: "Extensive publicity will be given to the program loan and the activities it will finance. In addition to television, radio, and press coverage of the basic loan agreement, there will be similar coverage of sub-agreement signings. Forms and contracts used in the various program will identify the US government as the source of the funds.

The $5 Million Grant

The $5 million grant will finance:
1. Agricultural technical assistance (title XII) _____ $1,500,000
2. Operational program grants for private and voluntary agencies __ 1,400,000
   a. Rivas Agricultural School (CARE) _____ (440,000)
   b. Agricultural cooperatives:
      (Moravian Church) _____ (300,000)
      (CARE) _____ (235,000)
      (Technoserve) _____ (210,000)
   c. Preschool education: (CEPAD—Church World Services) __ (130,000)
   d. Salvation Army activities _____ (85,000)
2. Technical assistance in municipal development _____ 1,000,000

4. Technical assistance fund to finance U.S. experts ———————— 500,000
5. Assistance to the Central American Institute of
    Business Administration (INCAE) ———————————— 300,000
6. Scholarships for poor students at the American School ———————— 300,000

    Total ————————————————————————————— 5,000,000

Signs will be placed at all construction activities identifying the project as US-financed. And plaques will be affixed to public buildings (e.g., the agricultural school)."[9]

III. Nicaragua Recovery Program II: A Shift in US Policy

It has been reported that even before the ouster of the Somoza regime, Jimmy Carter had signed a presidential "finding" that covert action by the CIA was needed in Nicaragua for the "national security" of the United States. According to *Newsweek*, this "finding" authorized the CIA to fund groups in Nicaragua friendly to the US, such as newspapers and labor unions. *Newsweek* has also reported that CIA funds have gone to businessmen and political parties. The specifics of these CIA funds are not yet known, but we can perhaps get some idea of the overall US effort, both overt and covert, by looking closely at the shift in AID funding to Nicaragua that occurred in 1980.

By November 1980, when AID's Congressional presentation for fiscal year 1982 was written, US policy toward Nicaragua had undergone a marked shift. Aid to the private sector was now to become more focused. And its aim was no longer simply companies but also business organizations. It had become clear that US leverage over the Nicaraguan revolution was not sufficient as yet to force subservience to US policy in El Salvador and elsewhere. The "US strategy and interests" for Nicaragua were now put this way: The principal US interest "is the evolution of a pluralistic society with a mixed economy, not hostile to the United States . . . The AID strategy is to assist in establishing the economic framework within which Nicaragua's forces of moderation can operate and prosper . . . The program also supports the private sector, which is the strongest force of democratic pluralism in Nicaragua, activities of other private and voluntary organizations (PVOs) and people-to-people projects which strengthen contacts between the United States and Nicaragua."[10]

According to the document, the FY1980 AID program, detailed above and now coming to an end, "concentrated on the recovery of the economy through support of both private and public sector organizations (including PVOs) which encouraged political and economic moderation . . . The $5 million grant for the Nicaraguan Recovery Program . . . provides support to private sector organizations for cooperative development, agricultural institutional development, scholarships for low-income students, and technical assistance and training." AID was continuing this strategy for the next fiscal year, but now starting to place "a greater emphasis on support to key private sector organizations."

The new $7.5 million Nicaragua Recovery Program II grant planned for FY1981 was designed to "strengthen private sector organizations by funding technical assistance to the confederation of business associations [COSEP] and its member organizations, lending capital to the independent cooperative associations [FUNDE], assisting Red Cross and church community development projects, supporting independent labor unions through the American Institute for Free Labor Development [AIFLD], reinforcing the Central American Business School [INCAE], and funding US professional exchange activities [LASPAU] . . ." It is important to note that AIFLD, like LASPAU, was an ongoing program under the Latin American and Caribbean Regional Program. These new funds under Nicaragua Recovery Program II were funds targeted toward Nicaragua over and above the traditional share of AIFLD money going to Nicaragua.

Carter administration planners were certainly aware that many organizations they were targeting for assistance were now *political* organizations—not simply organizations with business interests. After all, US officials had been in contact with COSEP for well over a year, and the Managua embassy had been substantially upgraded. Ambassador Pezullo's testimony in Congress revealed detailed knowledge of Nicaraguan organizations and trends.

The Reagan administration quickly became aware of this fact. Although Reagan had called for a cutoff of aid to Nicaragua during his campaign, when the new administration did suspend assistance several days after assuming office, it spared the $7.5 million grant program. No better testimony of its importance could have been made than that of Alfonso Robelo, a business executive and leader of the Nicaraguan opposition party, MDN, in a Caracas speech on January 25, 1981. "The US government," he said, "should continue trying to aid the Nicaraguan people, and should be creative in looking for channels parallel to the Sandinista government, such as cooperatives and other private sector groups."[11]

Perhaps playing a key role in the Reagan plan is Constantine Menges who, according to a public relations officer at CIA headquarters, is the National Intelligence Officer for Latin America at the CIA and formerly of the Hudson Institute.[12] In early 1981 he wrote, citing the "lessons of Portugal," that there is "an urgent need for a program of increased support for the genuine democratic groups in Nicaragua,"[13] and that throughout Central America there is "a need to work with transnational groups such as parties, trade unions, civic, business, and religious organizations to strengthen those genuinely democratic and moderate forces which exist within each country."[14]

Menges claimed that although "the Communist and radical left groups have made a hidden but nevertheless intense effort" to consolidate power in the Sandinista ruling council, "the much more loosely organized democratic groups represented by various independent political parties, non-Communist business and labor associations, most of the Catholic Church, and most of the population have been steadily weakened by a strategy of ambiguous but unremitting harassment and persecution. As a result, Nicaragua today is nearly under the control of the Communist groups."

After the revolutionary victory in July 1979, Menges wrote, the "obvious next question was whether the Cuban-supported Marxist-Leninist groups or the genuinely democratic forces would prevail in Nicaragua." Menges derided Mexico and the social democratic parties for ignoring their "revolutionary experiences." "Many Latin American social democrats also shared in the 'Cuban mistake': endorsing Castro without establishing a separate power base . . . and many European social democrats . . . would have cause to remember . . . the Portuguese experience. There, following the 1974 revolution which ended the five-decades long Salazar/Caetano regime, the Communist Party with strong covert Soviet support moved quickly to dominate most government organizations, trade unions, and communications, and seemed to be heading inexorably toward dictatorial power. Only the failure of a Communist coup attempt in 1975 and a concerted effort by democratic parties and governments in Europe to help both the Christian Democrats and the social democrats and oppose the Communists resulted in the free elections of 1976 and the functioning democracy that Portugal has today." Paying heed to their "revolutionary experiences" would have meant, "in Nicaragua, an effort on the part of Mexico and the social-democratic parties to strengthen the genuinely democratic groups and to prevent the covert Cuban strengthening of the Marxist-Leninist groups."

"This did not happen," Menges concluded. But the US appears willing to put its hand in the pie if Mexico and the social democrats do not. Importantly, Menges neglects to mention the right-wing political domination in present-day Portugal. Nor does he mention the crucial role that Western intelligence agencies, including the CIA, played in rolling back the Portuguese revolution.

IV. Our Men in Nicaragua

Much as the US embassy in Tehran became an important hub for espionage against the new government after the Iranian revolution, so the Managua embassy took on a new importance after the Nicaraguan revolution. In the rating of embassy assignments by the State Department, the Managua embassy went from lowest to highest. The CIA moved a large number of officers into the embassy, and the fact that the Subcommittee on Evaluation of the House Intelligence Committee has had an ongoing study of intelligence on Nicaragua since late 1978 reveals a high level of US concern.[15]

The AID grant money was distributed out of the Managua embassy. The Nicaraguan government stopped it in late 1982 because of the uses to which it was being put. It is instructive to look at several of the former recipients.

• FUNDE, the independent association of cooperatives in Nicaragua, received "operational support." US officials hoped the money to FUNDE would offset the power of the Sandinista organization of cooperatives.

• COSEP also received "operational support." It is unknown how these funds were used. In November 1980, the Vice President of COSEP, Jorge Salazar, was killed by security officials when he resisted arrest for involvement in a conspiracy to overthrow the government. In late 1981, four top officials of COSEP were arrested for agitating and violating civil emergency laws when they accused the government of adhering to "a plan to transform this revolution into a Marxist-Leninist adventure" and of "preparing a new genocide," even though 60 percent of the economy remains private and 80 percent of foreign credit and exchange goes into private hands.[16] They were released in early February 1982. Nicaraguan government officials regard COSEP as counterrevolutionary. Yet as it represents Nicaragua's business community, they need its cooperation in rebuilding Nicaragua. An official at the US embassy in Managua says that "COSEP is the internal bellwether for our policy. Its survival is key to our role here."

• The Chamber of Industry was another business organization which received AID "operational support." Then–vice president Leonardo Somarriba was implicated in the plot broken up in November 1980.

• AIFLD has represented the AFL-CIO in Nicaragua since 1965. Most of its funds have come from AID, about $1.6 million between 1965 and 1979; $824,000 of that between 1973 and 1979.[17] AIFLD was involved in setting up the Confederation of Labor Unification (CUS), which received AIFLD money before and after the war. It has taken public positions against government policy. More importantly, it is an alternative to the urban and rural workers, which are by far the strongest in the country. US-sponsored unions have clashed head-to-head with Sandinista unions in many council elections and thus represent a source of nongovernment power. In late 1981, Richard Martinez, who once organized Brazilian workers in preparation for the 1964 CIA coup there, identified an AIFLD representative in Nicaragua as a "conscious CIA agent."[18] He also found the activities of AIFLD and the unions it sponsors to be similar to activities he had organized in Brazil.[19] Thereafter the Nicaraguans refused to renew the visa of the AIFLD representative, and AIFLD and the AFL-CIO gradually pulled out of Nicaragua. Nevertheless, *Diario Las Americas* in February 1982 reported that a Nicaraguan exile by the name of Frank Jiménez, who was identified as the Assistant Secretary General of CUS, had taken part in creating a "CUS in exile" and had pledged the support of CUS in overthrowing the Sandinistas.

• The Wisconsin Partners is a program of the Partners of the Americas. It received a $450,000 grant from AID in November 1980 for work throughout Nicaragua, the only Partners program to receive government funds. Among the projects funded was an exchange program with the Nicaraguan paper *La Prensa* , believed to be one of the newspapers *Newsweek* reported to be receiving CIA assistance.

• Another controversial program has been the health and educational program of the Social Action Committee of the Moravian Church with the Miskitu Indians in eastern Nicaragua. The Social Action Committee has received AID money for this program since 1980. A clergyman arrested for aiding some Miskitus and Somocistas in insurgent activities testified that he had obtained money for arms and supplies from the Social Action Committee. The US embassy maintains close contacts with these Americans in the isolated Atlantic coastal region.

V. Military Pressures in September and October 1981

Reagan's position paper during the Presidential campaign called the Nicaraguan government a "totalitarian Marxist regime." Clearly, Reagan and his advisors did not see themselves as "containing" the revolution by continuing the grant money but rather by rolling it back. In fact, officials of several of the organizations that have received US money were taken into custody by Nicaraguan security forces in late 1980 and charged with plotting to overthrow the government.

Reagan's program quickly came to have three facets. Underlying the economic facet of cutting off loans to the government, and blocking loans from international lending institutions of which the US was a part, was the rationale that Nicaragua supported "terrorism" in El Salvador and was thus not eligible for US economic aid under the law. The military facet of the program consisted in ignoring the camps in Florida and, later, California in which Nicaraguan counterrevolutionaries were being trained. There were also reports that administration officials made contact with counterrevolutionaries based in Honduras. The political facet was to bring new faces and much money to the US embassy in Managua to bolster America's friends in Nicaragua.

Military threats were made to the Sandinista government throughout the first year of the Reagan administration, often disguised as diplomatic initiatives. In mid-August 1981, the State Department's chief of Latin American affairs, Thomas Enders, proposed in Managua that the US and Nicaragua hold discussions to overcome differences. According to the *Washington Post*, the Reagan administration asked that the Sandinistas stop funneling arms to the guerrillas in El Salvador; that the size of the Nicaraguan army be expanded no further than the 15,000 to 17,000 troops that the Sandinistas officially acknowledged to be in uniform, and that Nicaragua stop importing heavy weapons from Cuba and the Soviet Union and permit some international body to verify this.

In return the US made two offers. First, the administration would enter into a nonaggression pact with Nicaragua. Second, it would close down the camps in Florida where Nicaraguan exiles were training to overthrow the Sandinistas.

Not surprisingly, the US offers were not well-received. The Sandinistas responded that the US was merely offering to do what it ought already to be doing: to refrain from attacking Nicaragua and to close down the training camps. The Sandinistas themselves unilaterally pledged not to attack the US, independently of any pact. They pointed out the administration's past public statements that it did not have jurisdiction over the training camps under US laws. Either it did or it did not, and if it did, it should enforce the laws.

The Nicaraguan government further stated that what equipment Nicaragua was receiving and what efforts were being undertaken to expand its army and militia were necessary to protect the revolution from the United States, from Nicaragua's Central American neighbors, and from the former National Guard members in Honduras. Moreover, the US was told that Nicaragua was not helping the guerrillas in El Salvador militarily, although it was Nicaragua's duty to aid the revolution in ways short of military aid.

Finally, in responding to the US, the Sandinistas listed several complaints: that the US was joining Honduras in naval maneuvers to practice intercepting arms coming into Central America for Nicaragua and the Salvadoran guerrillas; that the columnists Evans and Novak had been fed the lie that 600 Cuban soldiers had arrived in Nicaragua; that the State Department had not repudiated the lie; and that the Reagan administration opposed the Nicaraguan proposal for a negotiated settlement of the Salvadoran conflict.

VI. The National Security Council Decisions

Secretary of State Alexander Haig took these Sandinista responses of late October 1981 to be a rejection of the US proposals and revived public attacks by accusing Nicaragua of renewing its support for the guerrillas in El Salvador. The Nicaraguan government responded that the US administration was inventing the evidence and doing so to justify American military intervention in El Salvador. About a week later, Haig spoke publicly for the first time about mounting evidence of the "totalitarian character of the Sandinista regime." Testifying before the House Foreign Affairs Committee in late November, Haig refused to rule out a military blockade of Nicaragua or assistance to Nicaraguan exiles trying to overthrow the Sandinistas.

Haig's remarks were carefully orchestrated and immediately followed the first decision by the National Security Council (NSC) in mid-November to implement a large-scale program to deal with opposition to US policies in the "Caribbean Basin." The program included increased subversive operations inside Nicaragua, support for paramilitary operations against the Sandinistas from the outside, economic pressures, military threats, contingency planning for military intervention, increased intelligence activity, propaganda efforts, more military aid to El Salvador and more pressures on Cuba, and joint planning with America's friends in Latin America.

The Reagan administration had already canceled direct loans to Nicaragua, but even greater economic pressures were possible. The US could oppose loans and debt renegotiations for Nicaragua by international lending bodies. Nicaragua reportedly received several hundred million dollars in such loans during Carter's last year and renegotiated a debt of about $490 million. The Reagan administration has already attempted to block several multilateral loans to Nicaragua. It is also known to have considered certain trade sanctions against Nicaragua.

A number of direct US military measures were approved. The Pentagon reportedly began contingency planning against Nicaragua in August and was ordered to continue.[20] These plans were said to involve naval blockades to stop arms shipments to Nicaragua or to strangle its economy. In addition to the maneuvers with Honduras, in November the US and other NATO countries held large Caribbean maneuvers code-named READEX-1 as a warning to Nicaragua and Cuba.[21] Haig continued to refuse to rule out direct military actions against Nicaragua, although it was generally acknowledged that actions like blockades would be ineffective. More maneuvers like READEX-1 were planned.

To make more intelligence activity possible, it was reported in mid-February 1982 that CIA stations in the region had been increased in strength.[22] Aerial reconnaissance was increased. The destroyer *Deyo* carrying surveillance equipment was deployed off the western coast of Nicaragua and El Salvador in November and has since been replaced by another such ship.[23] The Pentagon was making plans to reopen the Naval Air Station in Key West, Florida, as a command center for intelligence gathering in the Caribbean Basin,[24] and Defense Secretary Caspar Weinberger secretly negotiated with the governments of Honduras and Colombia to establish US bases there for use in "regional emergencies."[25]

Propaganda efforts were approved to create a perception in the US of a threat from Nicaragua to the rest of Central America. To this end, the State Department has released "facts and figures," said to have been classified, to bolster Haig's accusations about growing "militarization" in Nicaragua.[26] A campaign of "disinformation" was also reportedly approved by the NSC.[27] Accusations that the Sandinistas are aiding the rebels in El Salvador have been part of this campaign.

The Nicaragua decisions, apart from their long-term aims of making Nicaragua more amenable to US policies, have the important short-term aim of assisting the increasingly unsuccessful US policy in El Salvador. American planners hope that intimidating Nicaragua, and perhaps gaining some concessions, will demoralize the guerrillas in El Salvador. The elections there, not surprisingly, were said to be jeopardized by the ongoing war, and the CIA informed Reagan that the Salvadoran government cannot win without outside troops.

Argentina and the US were reportedly training Salvadoran soldiers in "infiltration" techniques that sound a bit like Operation Phoenix techniques of the Vietnam war.[28] And although Leopoldo Galtieri, Argentina's new president, denied that he made any offers, El Salvador's Defense Minister García stated that he would accept Argentine troops in El Salvador.[29] It has been reliably reported that Galtieri made the offer to traveling ambassador Gen. Vernon Walters, former deputy director of the CIA in September 1981.[30]

Another joint effort being pushed by the US was the creation of the "Central American Democratic Community," consisting of Costa Rica, Honduras and El Salvador, which Nicaraguans and many other observers believed would take on a military character. Venezuela, Colombia and the US have become observer members. It was reported that Guatemala will be asked to join.[31] Already there have been joint meetings of military representatives from Guatemala, Honduras and El Salvador that indicate coordinated military planning. The US has reportedly backed these meetings.[32]

VII. US Backing for Paramilitary Actions against Nicaragua

In mid-December 1981, the Reagan administration reportedly informed Congress that the CIA was involved in paramilitary covert action aimed at Nicaragua.

The US was also providing assistance to Argentine advisors, perhaps fifty of them, working with the Somocista counterrevolutionaries in Honduras.[33] About this time attacks on Sandinista positions escalated dramatically. Exile leaders in Honduras told reporters that "the war against Nicaragua has begun."[34] A number of sources indicate that the Somocistas are being aided by the Honduran military, which has essentially regained power in Honduras despite the recent cosmetic election there in which civilians were elected to government offices.[35] Nicaraguan Foreign Minister Miguel D'Escoto alleged that the US was arming 6,000 Somocistas in twenty camps in collusion with Honduras, Guatemala and Argentina.

About this same time, a possible scenario for a naval blockade was reported. Contingency plans were said to have been drawn up to support Somocista attackers in Honduras and Costa Rica. If they succeeded in controlling a small piece of territory, the US could set up a blockade around Nicaragua in conjunction with other Latin American nations to "prevent foreign interference." White House officials predicted this would be possible within several months. "Senior intelligence sources" were said to expect support from Chile, Argentina, Colombia and Venezuela. One official reported that "Venezuela would like to see the government of Nicaragua removed. Venezuela already is supporting a [rebel] group in Costa Rica."[36]

It was seen early that the CIA would be devoting much energy to recruiting Nicaragua's Indian population against the Sandinistas. The Indians of eastern Nicaragua have traditionally been isolated from the rest of the society. The Sandinistas tried to impose central authority on the east, upgraded their military presence, and brought Cuban doctors, teachers and soldiers into the area. These measures created much hostility. Relations with the central government plunged when it was disclosed that the Indians' representative on the national governing council, Steadman Fagoth, had been an informer for Somoza and he was arrested. He was released after demonstrations by Indian supporters. The belief that Fagoth thereafter began to plot with Somocista counterrevolutionaries was confirmed when Fagoth was discovered to be among the survivors of the crash last year of a Honduran military plane transporting top Honduran military leaders. The Sandinistas thereafter charged that Indian groups were joining Somocistas in raids from Honduras. After 26 people were said by the government to have been killed in these raids around the first of the year, Sandinista soldiers began evacuating Indians from the border area, sometimes forcibly.[37]

As has been shown, the Moravian Church project with the Miskitus has been funded through AID. The latest disaster relief plan put out by AID indicates that there are fifty "locals" of the Moravian Church on the Atlantic Coast. Not surprisingly, former US Ambassador to Nicaragua, Lawrence Pezullo stated: "We have very close communication with our people over there.[38]

Nicaraguan officials charged that Moravian Church leaders were working with Fagoth, Somocistas, Honduran officer Major Leonél Luque Jiménez and unnamed Argentine officers, to foment an uprising and declare independence for the eastern part of Nicaragua.[39] Ten clergymen were arrested or were being sought in mid-

February 1982. Vice Interior Minister Rene Rivas stated: "The Moravian Church, as a church, was involved in counterrevolutionary action. The pastors persuaded the young people to go over into the [training] camps, preaching a primitive brand of anti-communism.[40] As stated above, the Social Action Committee, funded by AID, was used by these clergymen as a souce of money for the insurgency.

Fagoth reportedly sought contact with US officials in Miami and Washington immediately upon being released from jail in early 1981. It is not known what contacts took place. However, it was reported soon afterwards that "in recent weeks" several United States military officers stationed [in Honduras] have visited the Honduran Army command post in Puerto Lempira [where exile groups provided paramilitary training for Miskitus], while the local United States mission [in Honduras] appears to have established direct contact with Mr. Fagoth and other anti-Sandinista leaders.[41]

Fagoth came to Washington on February 22, 1982, to speak with the press and the government. His trip was sponsored by the American Security Council, but his schedule was handled by the State Department. He was introduced at an American Security Council briefing by an aide to US Ambassador to the U.N., Jeane Kirkpatrick. In his appearances Fagoth falsely charged that the Sandinistas are guilty of genocide, had set up concentration camps, and had carried out massacres and other atrocities against the Miskitus. In response to questions about his spying for Somoza and being on the Honduran military aircraft, he demanded proof that he had done these things. He claimed to be involved in a political and not a military struggle. When asked why then he had in a January 1, 1982, radio address over Radio 15 September (a clandestine radio station operated for Miskitus from Honduras) praised those who had in 1981 died "fulfilling a noble mission for the liberation of our fatherland" and had vowed that 1982 would be the year of liberation, he denied having made the address. However, the speech was translated and printed in the US *Foreign Broadcast Information Service*.[42] Fagoth later repeated his charges to a US Congressional Committee.

"Sandinista repression of the Miskitus" is now a recurring theme in US government statements about Nicaragua. President Reagan used it in his February 1982 speech to the OAS; Jeane Kirkpatrick told the Senate Foreign Relations Committee in March 1982 that the Sandinista "assault" on the Miskitus is "more massive than any other human rights violation that I'm aware of in Central America today," and assured the Senators that Somoza, even though a "perfectly clear-cut dictator," was less repressive than the Sandinistas. Secretary of State Haig cited a photograph of burning bodies published in the right-wing French *Le Figaro* as evidence of "atrocious genocidal actions" against the Miskitus. The photo was captioned "The massacre of fiercely anti-Castro Miskitu Indians . . . last December." Steadman Fagoth had used the same photograph in his Washington press conferences. However, as it turns out, in reality the photo was taken in 1978, when Somoza was still in power, and depicts Red Cross workers burning bodies of war dead as a hygienic measure. *Figaro* editor Henrí-Christian Giraud later acknowledged that the caption under the photograph had been a "deplorable mistake."

An American Indian Movement (AIM) delegation which visited the Miskitu region in late 1981 publicly supports the relocation of the Miskitus away from the border area, for their own safety. This is the first time that AIM has endorsed the relocation of an indigenous people. AIM charges that the real danger to the Miskitus comes from the US government which wants to use the Miskitus in its war against Nicaragua, as the CIA used the Hmong tribe to fight the US war in Laos.[43]

VIII. The War Will Go On

Nicaragua should be prepared for a long fight. For the stakes are quite high for the Reagan administration, should it give in. As a "senior State Department policy maker" explained in December 1981: "We're on a collision course . . . If we do nothing there will be another communist regime in this hemisphere and they [the Republicans] won't be reelected. If we do something it undoubtedly will cause a negative public reaction, particularly among liberals in this country, who are still suffering from the post-Vietnam syndrome.

"The administration is going to have to face up to a fundamental decision in the next six months: whether to allow Nicaragua to consolidate its Marxist-Leninist regime, which already has become a base for subverting the whole hemisphere, or act to stop it."

Notes

[1]See Richard Fagen, "Dateline Nicaragua: The End of the Affair," *Foreign Policy,* Fall '79, pp. 178-191; Noam Chomsky and Edward Herman, *The Washington Connection and Third World Fascism,* Boston, South End Press, 1979, pp. 283-296. William LeoGrande, "The Revolution in Nicaragua: Another Cuba?," *Foreign Affairs,* Fall '79, pp. 28-50.

[2]House Committee on Foreign Affairs, *United States Foreign Policy toward Nicaragua,* June '79, pp. 59, 73.

[3]*New York Times* (NYT), 7/1/80.

[4]House Committee on Foreign Affairs, *Assessment of Conditions in Central America,* 5/20/80, pp. 77-89, see *CounterSpy,* vol.5, no. 2, pp. 54-55.

[5]House Committee on Foreign Affairs, *Special Central American Economic Assistance,* 11/27/79, pp. 43-44, 50.

[6]Ibid, p. 62.

[7]*AID Congressional Presentation for Fiscal Year 1981,* p. 260.

[8]cf supra, no. 5, p. 30.

[9]Ibid, pp. 32-33.

[10]*AID Congressional Presentation for Fiscal Year 1982,* pp. 208-210, 218.

[11]*NYT, 1/26/81.*

[12]*In a phone interview with the author on 3/82. Menges was also identified as a CIA officer in SAIS Review,* winter 1981-82, p. 229.

[13]*SAIS Review,* summer 1981, p. 31.

[14]*Commentary,* August 1981.

[15]House Committee on Foreign Affairs, *Review of the Presidential Certification of Nicaragua's Connection to Terrorism,* 9/30/80, p. 16.

[16]*NYT,* 11/17/81; 11/30/81.

[17]cf supra, no. 5, p. 26.
[18]*The Guardian* (New York), 12/2/81, p. 13.
[19]"La CIA es como un cancer," *Sobriania* (Managua), Oct. 1981, pp. 43–46.
[20]*Miami Herald*, 11/26/81.
[21]Ibid.
[22]*Washington Post* (WP), 2/14/82.
[23]*NYT*, 2/25/82.
[24]*WP*, 2/13/82.
[25]*WP*, 3/2/82.
[26]*Boston Globe* (BG), 12/4/81.
[27]*New York Post*, 2/15/82.
[28]*NYT*, 12/2/81.
[29]*NYT*, 2/23/82. *Los Angeles Times* (LAT), 2/1/82.
[30]*The Nation*, 1/30/82.
[31]*Latin America Weekly Review* (LAWR), 2/5/82.
[32]*WP*, 10/27/81.
[33]*LAT*, 2/5/82, p. 7.
[34]*The Nation*, 1/23/82, p. 70.
[35]*LAWR*, 2/5/82, p. 7.
[36]*San Francisco Examiner*, 12/20/81.
[37]*WP*, 2/5/82.
[38]Saul Landau memo on Nicaragua, Institute for Policy Studies, 1/25/82.
[39]*LAWR*, 2/12/82, p. 12; *FBIS*, 2/8/82 pp. 8-
[40]*WP*, 2/5/82.
[41]*NYT*, 2/21/82.
[42]*FBIS*, 1/4/82, p.
[43]"All Things Considered," National Public Radio, 3/4/82.

27. US Policy and the Marxist Threat to Central America*

By C. Di Giovanni, Jr.

Dr. Cleto Di Giovanni is a former employee of the Central Intelligence Agency. Since he left the Agency in 1979 he has spent considerable time in Central America. The following is excerpted from the "Di Giovanni" or "Heritage Foundation Report," which is widely viewed as the original blueprint for Reagan administration policy toward Nicaragua.

The United States should aid the aspirations of the Nicaraguan people to achieve the free society they have long sought. With regional security uppermost in our minds, we should be less concerned about the precise nature of that society and its

*Reprinted from *The Heritage Foundation Backgrounder,* No. 128, October 15, 1980.

government than about the inclinations and ability of that government to serve as a continuing source of support for Marxist revolutionaries elsewhere in Central America. In a well orchestrated program targeted against the Marxist Sandinista government, we should use our limited resources to support the free labor unions, the Church, the private sector, the independent political parties, the free press, and those who truly defend human rights. We should discontinue subsidizing a bankrupt government which clearly is planning on remaining in power through its police and security forces and whose interests are inimical to those of its neighbors and the US. The longer that government remains in power, the stronger its security apparatus will become, and the more difficult it will be to dislodge it. We should not abandon the Nicaraguan people, but we must abandon the Sandinista government.

Subsidizing this government through US financial aid which has little propaganda impact on the Nicaraguan people makes no sense. The US should terminate large-scale funding of the Sandinista government in order to send a clear signal to Central American revolutionaries that it does not plan to support leftist movements in the region. If the Soviets receive this message, they may realize that their unexpected opportunity to establish another communist country in this hemisphere has ended.

Sixty percent of the funds in the recently released $75 million aid bill is slotted for the private sector. The private sector doubts it will see all of this money, and whatever it does receive will have to be spent within parameters set by the Sandinistas. In any event, the remaining 40 percent will be used to help bail out the Sandinistas from their economic problems. Even to receive these funds under these restrictions, the private sector has advocated US financial aid to the Sandinista government because the Carter administration has not put forth any alternative formula of support for the private sector.

As long as private sector support has been linked by President Carter to Nicaraguan government support, the Carter administration has assured its policy of private sector blessing—which the administration has attempted to portray as private sector endorsement of the Sandinista government. Appropriately channeled assistance to the democratic institutions in Nicaragua could be far more effective and far less expensive than our currently structured official US aid program for the Sandinista government.

The Nicaraguans did not want Somoza, and they do not want the current Sandinista government. Despite its show of arms, that government is still weak and could be dislodged through a determined, coordinated, and targeted effort. But to assist the Nicaraguans in achieving that goal will require a much more realistic understanding about regional Marxist threats than the current administration has exhibited.

28. Target Nicaragua*

By George Black and Judy Butler

"**W**ere it not for imperialism," said an FSLN leader in November, as Haig was noisily refusing to rule out options against Nicaragua, "we could talk to the business sector, establish rates of profit based on their productive experience and say to them, this is the new situation of Nicaragua. And with the popular power that the revolution has, these businessmen could accept it as a real consequence of the political phenomenon that Nicaragua has lived through.

"But those that are trying to sabotage the revolution, that are boycotting it, that are decapitalizing the economy, do so because they are energized, supported and pushed from outside by a power that makes them feel confident. That is the imperialist policy."[1]

Indeed it is. In October 1980, the Heritage Foundation, a right-wing think tank, published policy recommendations for Nicaragua that have become a virtual blueprint for US policy. Author Cleto Di Giovanni, a former CIA officer in Latin America, identified real or possible allies that should be supported in a "well orchestrated program targeted against the Marxist Sandinista government [:] The Catholic Church is influential. There are many political parties . . . united in their opposition to the Sandinistas. There is one free newspaper in Nicaragua, *La Prensa* . . . Free labor unions are competing successfully for the loyalty of workers. The private sector is united under an umbrella organization, COSEP, which speaks authoritatively for it . . . Finally, among the free democratic forces in Nicaragua is the Permanent Commission on Human Rights, headed by José Esteban González."[2]

Conversely, these same sectors saw in the election of Ronald Reagan the opportunity to finally press their case with vehemence. They had been biding their time under Carter, but now the honeymoon with the Sandinistas was over.

Two weeks after the US elections, COSEP issued a 30-page document charging the regime with monopolizing political power, reneging on a promise to hold early elections and preparing to "implement in Nicaragua a Communist political-economic project, with totalitarian state capitalism [sic] and consequent restrictions on all civil liberties."[3] It was followed a few weeks later by the arrest and conviction of eight people, most of them business leaders, who admitted conspiring to overthrow the Nicaraguan Junta. In a press conference called by Interior Minister Tomás Borge, the president of the Chamber of Commerce and Industry—one of those arrested—admitted that the plotters had made contact with ex-Guardsmen and representatives of other Central American government and military officials.

*Reprinted from *NACLA Report on the Americas* Vol. XVI, No. 1, Jan–Feb. 1982.

Another testified that Jorge Salazar, a vice president of COSEP had given $50,000 to buy arms for the movement. The plot had been aborted a few days earlier with the killing of Salazar in a gun battle between his driver and Sandinista security police when they tried to stop his car, reportedly full of weapons.[4]

Only a month later, Managua's Archbishop Obando y Bravo risked splitting the Church by publicly demanding that four priests serving in ministerial posts in the government choose between politics and the Church. Obando y Bravo, no stranger to temporal politics, is an adversary the Sandinistas would prefer not to have. Widely identified with years of opposition to Somoza, he is still an important voice of authority in Nicaragua, even though a majority of priests and other religious workers have left his side to work within the revolutionary process. Initially subdued in his criticism of the Sandinistas, he suddenly became more outspoken. "In the long run, we could fall into Marxism," he said in an interview in early January 1981, "and by long run I don't mean 20 years, I mean three years."[5] In a conference sponsored by the Northeast Pastoral Center for Hispanics in New York City in January of this year, after blithely equating Marxism with totalitarianism, he even refused to admit that conditions of human rights were better than they had been under Somoza! On tha same trip, the archbishop received an award bestowed on him and the Nicaraguan Council of Catholic Bishops in July of last year by the Washington-based Institute on Religion and Democracy (IRD), a new organization of the neo-conservative stripe. The first recipient of IRD's Religious Freedom Award, Obando was praised for his "fight for human rights against both the Right and the Left," according to the Institute. IRD, which recently published and widely distributed a pamphlet called "Nicaragua—a Revolution Against the Church?" has as one of its main objectives to isolate progressive sectors within the US religious community.

Then there was the action of Heritage Foundation darling, José Esteban González. González' Permanent Human Rights Commission in Managua had received substantial international funding toward the end of the Somoza regime. But after the victory the money dried up and many of the early members of the executive committee took high posts in the new government.[6] González was clearly sidelined. In February 1981, after an audience with Pope John Paul II, González captured international headlines with the news that he had delivered a document to Vatican officials charging that there were 8,000 political prisoners in Nicaragua, that the "Sandinista regime applies methods of torture and repression very similar to those applied in the past by the Somoza dictatorship," and that he had compiled figures showing that 800 people in Nicaragua had mysteriously "disappeared" since Somoza was overthrown.

In fact, the Sandinistas had abolished the death penalty and had just concluded laboriously trying over 6,000 followers of Somoza, mainly National Guardsmen, as war criminals, convicting some 4,000 to sentences ranging from one to thirty years. The government, as well as much of the population which had wanted to avenge the brutal murders of friends and relatives at the hands of the Guard in a less generous way, was enraged, and González was arrested on his return for spreading false and dangerous propaganda. At his trial, González backed off, saying that his remarks in Rome had been "misinterpreted." But of course, as is the case with such headlines, the damage was done both internationally and internally among those already primed to be suspicious of the Sandinistas.

The Battle for Hearts and Minds

This rash of overt attacks, all within the space of a few months, does not mean that Nicaragua is polarized between revolutionaries and counterrevolutionaries. But a revolution is by definition the profound rupturing of an existing system. The period which follows is necessarily an unstable one in which contending forces struggle for control of the process by which a new ideology, a new social, political and economic system is forged. In Nicaragua, many people are simply confused by the speed of events—by the schism in the Church, by the stark inability of the revolution to bring the quick benefits they thought would come, by charges against the Sandinistas coming from paternalistic figures like Obando y Bravo. In the ideological struggle that has sharpened since Reagan's election, the so-called "free" trade unions, or the "free" newspapers, La Prensa, are hardly independent and neutral forces. Together with the opposition parties, and the international movements to which some are affiliated, they have played a concerted role. The objective has not been to put forth an alternative model that would improve the lot of the Nicaraguan people. It has been, purely and simply, to undermine the popular support of the FSLN.

Pressing the Battle

Far and away the greatest tool in the battle for hearts and minds in Nicaragua is La Prensa. Analogies to the CIA-financed precoup role of Chile's El Mercurio are now commonplace, but in fact La Prensa's value to the destabilization effort is proportionately greater, as it capitalizes on its prerevolutionary prestige and holds a monopoly on opposition news.

La Prensa is also Nicaragua's best know bourgeois institution internationally. It has received a $500,000 grant from West Germany's right-wing Friedrich Neumann Foundation, and was the focus of concern at the October 1981 conference of the US-dominated Inter-American Press Association (IAPA) in Rio de Janeiro.

The following month, a delegation led by IAPA president Charles E. Scripps arrived in Managua to discuss the treatment of La Prensa and challenge the government on the very idea of having media laws requiring responsible reporting. In a meeting with the directors of Nicaragua's three dailies, all members of the Chamorro family, Scripps was treated to a taste of the La Prensa style. "The Sandinistas are like the Nazis," exploded La Prensa's Jaime Chamorro to his nephew Carlos, director of the FSLN's Barricada, "because the leftist commanders control the government of Nicaragua like the followers of Hitler controlled Germany." An angered Carlos Chamorro stiffly suggested that the meeting had just come to an end.[7]

La Prensa also chose the IAPA visit to publish the results of its public opinion poll. Based on a sample of 900 respondents, the survey drew scathing conclusions about public opposition to the government's harassment of *La Prensa* and right-wing *Radio Corporación,* and asserted that popular support for the FSLN was running at a mere 28 percent.

La Prensa's oppositional stance has become both more blatant and more crude since a policy dispute with editor Xavier Chamorro caused him and a large portion of the staff to leave the paper and start *El Nuevo Diario,* which defines itself as "critically supportive" of the revolutionary government.

In a paper adapted from a briefing for the new US ambassador to Nicaragua, journalism professor John Spicer Nichols points out that freedom of the press is always a relative concept, having much to do with a country's level of national development and social tranquility. Given the conditions in Nicaragua today, professor Nichols points out, "the amount of dissenting ideas and discussion of unsettling topics flowing from the Nicaraguan media is remarkable."[8]

The vigorous championing of *La Prensa* by IAPA and the administration contrasts starkly with their indifference to the repression of the media elsewhere in Central America today. The bombing and closure of El Salvador's *El Indepen-diente,* the elimination of *La Crónica del Pueblo* after Salvadoran death squads had disposed of its editor and chief photographer, the killing of the editor of Guatemala's third largest daily, *La Nación,* and the murder and disappearance of 28 journalists in that country since the beginning of 1980, have all been met with a resounding silence from Washington.[9] So, for that matter, was the news that *La Prensa* employees recently fired directly into a crowd of demonstrators in front of their offices, wounding three.[10]

Turning the Economic Screws

The private sector derives its greatest muscle from majority control of the economy—75 percent of industrial and 80 percent of agricultural production.[11] Institutionally, this strength shows in COSEP, not in any of the myriad political parties of the Right and Center. "Our political influence derives from our entrepreneurial ability," claimed COSEP's Jaime Montealegre.[12] With the exception of a few properties confiscated on grounds of decapitalization, the FSLN has restricted state control to former Somoza properties, natural resources and the financial system.

These entrepreneurs have been happy to take their risks with state-supplied investment capital. In fact, since 1979, the great majority of government credits have flowed into private business.

But the terms of economic coexistence provided for guaranteed profit margins in exchange for uninterrupted production, and the agreement has faltered. Private investment has plummeted to an all-time low, from 80 percent of total investment in 1978 to only 10 percent in 1981. It is business' way to serve notice of its discontent with the FSLN's conscious strategy of not letting economic influence be translated into corresponding political power. The *Guardian Weekly* reported that "what Robelo cannot pardon is that wealth no longer brings with it power."[13]

What does this mean in practice? One young executive, who boasts that he has salted away $80,000 abroad since the revolution, made it clear: "Why shouldn't I? The government gives us economic incentives, but what we want is a climate of political confidence."

The bourgeoisie's periodic engineering of confrontations to coerce greater political clout from the Sandinistas has netted it the opposite. When Alfonso Robelo resigned from the Junta, together with Violeta Chamorro, in April 1980, his goal was to create a political crisis. Instead, they were simply replaced by two other representatives of the private sector who were more cooperative. A mass walkout from the Council of State by COSEP, the bourgeois parties and opposition trade unions in November 1980 simply meant they lost the only voice in government they had, albeit a minority one.

Masters of Economic War

But the battle is not going on at the ideological and political levels alone, and it is not being fought out primarily among Nicaraguans with merely aid and comfort from the Reagan administration. Underpinning all these attempts to break the fragile national unity in Nicaragua is the first and most basic level of the US assault: economic warfare. The hoped for sequence of events is that the disruption of economic activities will lead to social unrest, which in turn will induce political turmoil.

The Heritage Foundation had put it in a nutshell: "Nicaraguan workers continue to have an emotional attachment to the revolutionary movement. This attachment can be expected to weaken as the economy deteriorates . . . There are some indications of growing broadly based support to take to arms to overthrow the Sandinist government, and this support could increase as further economic problems develop."[14]

Sixty percent of the $75 million fiscal 1981 US foreign aid had been designated for the private sector. Of the balance, $30 million, only half actually made it to the Nicaraguan government before being suspended just as the reins were handed over to Reagan.

Following the suggestion of the Heritage Foundation—"economic shortcomings might provoke at least limited civil unrest by the end of the current harvest season (May–June 1981)"—Reagan turned the suspension into outright cancellation in April. In addition, Reagan also halted PL-480 credits for the purchase of $9.6 million worth of US wheat. But the maneuver backfired. There was civil unrest alright but it was aimed at Reagan, not the Sandinistas. Furthermore, western and socialist countries alike rushed to fill the wheat deficit.[15]

The Invisible Blockade Strikes Again

Given that all underdeveloped nations are structurally and dependently integrated in multiple ways into the capitalist world economy, economic warfare strikes at their Achilles heel. Like all of Central America, Nicaragua's economy is based on export crops which have confronted plummeting world market prices, while the cost of machinery imports has increased. As Daniel Ortega explained in his speech to the United Nations, 47 percent more cotton was required to buy one tractor in 1981 than in 1977; or 54 percent more sugar; or 145 percent more coffee. This, coupled with the breakdown of regional markets and the resulting capital flight in all the countries, has left all near bankruptcy. In the case of Nicaragua, decapitalization has resulted in a capital flight of some $140 million.

Productivity has remained low (labor problems were estimated to have cost $100 million in 1981); unemployment and inflation, which had bottomed out at 18 percent and 25 percent respectively by 1980, both began to rise again; state bureaucracy had mushroomed from 33,000 to 61,000 employees. (Much, but not all, of the bureaucratic growth results from the expansion or creation of ministries which provide the vast new social services.) Reserves had hit rockbottom and it was impossible to generate any internal surplus without resorting to ever-increasing foreign aid.

These problems, most of which are shared regionally, and are even worse in Costa Rica and El Salvador than in Nicaragua, come on top of and are exacerbated by the situation the Sandinistas inherited from Somoza: a $1.6 billion foreign debt, the highest debt *per capita* in the Americas; wholesale destruction of the country's productive infrastructure (factories and croplands); the dislocation of export crop cycles and Somoza's looting of reserves (both by mortgaging Somocista properties to get liquid capital in the later period of the war and by the blatant robbery of all but $3.5 million from the Central Bank just before he fled).

In US policy, "doves" and "hawks" alike have exploited this weakness and dependency. Nicaragua's "integration into the international economic system is one of the greatest deterrents to the consolidation of a Marxist system," wrote former Assistant Secretary of State for Inter-American Affairs Viron Vaky (1978–80), adding in a footnote that the Sandinista government's agreement on the rescheduling of $600 million in debts contracted by Somoza with some 120 American, European and Japanese creditor banks "locked Nicaragua into the private money market."[16] To be thus locked means to be subjected to international interest rates, exchange rates, loans procedures, creditor ratings, etc. Tied, in short, to a set of objective conditions determined by western finance capital, and above all by the United States.

But not to be tied is even rougher. Forgetting the medium- and long-term investment loans which carry high interest rates, there are also the crucial short-term credits which allow a country to carry on daily international trade. A US blockade of external financing (imposed against Cuba, Allende's Chile, Grenada and now Nicaragua), which in turn implies a blockade of foreign investment, is thus one of the deadliest weapons in the economic arsenal.

Despite the fact that the Sandinistas agreed to accept Somoza's debts, and actually received favorable rescheduling terms, both private credits and investments were effectively halted when the administration cut off aid. It is automatic in such situations that Ex-Im-Bank trade guarantees and Overseas Private Investment Corporation (OPIC) investment guarantees are halted as well. Without them, banks and investors are loath to take risks.

Because the major US banks have inordinate influence on the international banking community, the Sandinistas have received virtually no private credits, even short term ones, since the triumph. And in what can only be viewed as overkill, the State Department is now rumored to be directly pressuring the banks not to change their minds.

In effect, this means that the Nicaraguan government must put up cash for all import purchases, from food to tractors to horseshoe nails. Since Nicaragua has few manufacturing plants for spare parts and most of the machinery is from the United States, it only takes a few breakdowns before an entire fishing fleet is docked, buses and taxis are out of commission and factory production is operating at less than full capacity. Not only does this decrease production, but it puts workers out of jobs. Impesca, the state fishing industry, had to close one of its processing plants because so many boats were not operating.

The Reagan administration has now begun to move on the multilateral lending institutions. First, in early November, the newly appointed US representative, Cuban exile José Manuel Casanova, forced Nicaragua to withdraw a loan application to the Inter-American Development Bank for $40 million to renovate and invest in Nicaragua's fishing industry, centered mainly along the Atlantic Coast. While the stated reasons for opposing the loan were "technical," US sources revealed that the United States and some other countries had an "overall political problem with the direction" of the Nicaraguan government.[17]

In the World Bank, where the United States holds fewer votes, its "no" did not prevent other members from approving a $16 million loan for the improvement of Managua slum districts in January 1982.[18] State Department spokesperson Sue Pittmann confirmed in that month that the Reagan administration would oppose any Nicaraguan credit or aid request to any international lending institution.[19] It did not appear to matter that the social impact on the Nicaraguan poor is immediate. The IDB still has seven loan and technical assistance projects worth $87.6 million under consideration for Nicaragua, and the World Bank more than $70 million.[20]

Underdeveloped countries are also locked into world capitalist commodity markets, opening a further structural vulnerability easily exploited through trade embargoes. A country's principal export product may be boycotted, as happened with Cuba's sugar after the revolution, Chile's copper after Allende's electoral victory and Jamaica's bauxite after Manley imposed higher taxes on US aluminum corporations.

In Nicaragua's case, the embargoes will be more selective. Nicaragua's two leading export crops (coffee and cotton) have relatively diversified markets, but its next highest earners are wide open to US pressures; 75 percent of Nicaragua's meat goes to the United States, with virtually all the rest going to Puerto Rico, while the US market also accounts for 82.7 percent of sugar exports.[21] Early threats were waved at beef exports, but lifted when Nicaragua cancelled the planned purchase of high-grade, low-cost breeding bulls from Cuba. The Cuban connection also lay behind threats to suspend US export of resins used in Nicaragua's PVC manufacturing industry—because Nicaragua might sell Cuba its surplus stocks of plastics.

An all-out blockade would, however, make little sense. Widely held to have been a political failure against Cuba, it would be harder to apply against a country with long, permeable land borders and a wider spread of trading partners.

A final, and more dramatic facet of economic warfare is direct sabotage. Here, the forms of attack are multiple. At one extreme, sabotage is the withdrawal of industrial capital through any number of difficult-to-detect means. The Philadelphia-based chemicals corporation, Pennwalt, and the Sears Roebuck department store are two US multinationals accused by their Nicaraguan workers of decapitalization.[22] At the other extreme lies the bombing of a Nicaraguan state-owned passenger jet in Mexico City in December 1981.

Economic Emergency, Political Confrontation

By mid-1981, the economic situation was headed from bad to worse. By the end of the year, some analysts suggested that Nicaragua would need $500 million over and above currently predicted export earnings and foreign aid receipts simply to maintain current levels of economic activity in 1982.[23] Exports for 1981 were predicted at $540 million and imports at $900 million, a full 20 percent higher than first expected.[24]

The crisis presented the FSLN with an acute political dilemma. Even without calling in the International Monetary Fund (IMF) and their infamous restrictions, the Nicaraguan people were seeing liberation followed by austerity. The redistributive reforms put into effect by the government had yet to hit the middle class really hard. (Alan Riding wrote that "except for the occasional shortage of imported liquor . . . the quality of life for the middle class is largely unchanged.")[25] Treading a tightrope by trying to keep alliances alive while not alienating mass support, the FSLN decided to share the load evenly and visibly among all classes. On September 9 the government decreed a state of Economic and Social Emergency. The decree set out to cut government expenditure, raise tax revenues, halt capital flight and increase productivity—the latter by means of a controversial no-strike clause. The strike freeze, as well as seven other restrictions, made it illegal to carry out any act that would affect the precarious economic situation, whether by sabotage, land invasions, speculation, or spreading of false information. Violation carried penalties of one to three years in prison.[26]

The World Bank, in an unpulished report dated October 9, 1981, endorsed the Nicaraguan economic reforms which it said are "expected to define a framework wherein private sector business can satisfactorily operate." Within Nicaragua, the only initial complaint came from some who felt the step might have been taken earlier, COSEP welcomed the decree as "the first step toward solving the national crisis."[27]

Yet hard on the heels of the decree came a four-week sequence of events which convinced the FSLN that a major coordinated US plan of destabilization was finally falling into place, and that the opposition had gained enough confidence from external attacks to force the economic crisis onto a political battleground.

On September 29 and October 1, *La Prensa* was twice closed for its most serious provocation yet: the publication of false allegations by a convicted "decapitalizer." Days later, COSEP heard its complaints of Junta mismanagement cited in the US Senate as the FY82 Foreign Aid Amendment approving the $33.3 million to the Nicaraguan private sector was passed.[28]

Over the first three weeks of the month, an unprecedented 16 cross-border raids by Somocista terrorists from Honduras were registered and on October 7–9, the United States and Honduras staged two days of joint military maneuvers off Puerto Cortez on Honduras' Atlantic Coast. As of October 5, the details of the maneuvers involving patrol boats and aircraft "had not been concretized," and would therefore not become public information, but the exercise involved training in ocean search and interception. The objective, according to a Navy memo, was to train 130 US military personnel and their Honduran counterparts in sea and air tactics, communications and joint command. Samuel Dickens, past staff member of the Inter-American Defense Board, said at the time that the maneuvers were a signal of US support in case Honduras goes to war with Nicaragua.[29]

Three weeks later the US military carried out an unusually large exercise with 38 ships and 200 aircraft, with maneuvers running from Norfolk, Virginia, headquarters of the Second Fleet, to the Caribbean Sea. The operations, involving the aircraft carriers Kennedy and Eisenhower, were designed to "improve fleet readiness in coordinated dual carrier battle ground operations with Navy and Marine Corps personnel on weapons systems under realistic conditions."[30]

Meanwhile, on October 8, the US Deputy Ambassador to the United Nations leveled a vicious attack against Nicaragua in the General Assembly; on October 12, the IAPA arrived in Managua and received *La Prensa*'s accusations of sharply falling FSLN support and on October 19, a column in the *Washington Post* by Evans and Novak insinuated Cuba had sent troops via Nicaragua to blow up an important Salvadoran bridge: "Exactly 26 days [after 500–600 Cuban troops had supposedly arrived in Nicaragua masquerading as civilians], in the pre-dawn morning of October 15th, the most important bridge over the Lempa River that cuts El Salvador in two was blown up ... The action betrayed a made-in-Cuba professionalism." Administration officials reportedly used this as part of their arsenal to convince other governments of the dangers of Nicaragua to regional security. And finally, the end of the month saw the first signs of a radical new propaganda initiative from Washington which would target Nicaragua.

The climax of mounting domestic dissent had come on October 19. Six COSEP leaders signed an open letter to Junta coordinator Daniel Ortega denouncing government policies.

Far from simply "accusing the Sandinista Junta of Marxist-Leninist tendencies" as the US press would have us believe, the signatories accused the FSLN of creating the economic crisis, "preparing a new genocide" and leading the country to the verge of disaster. The letter was not only widely disseminated within Nicaragua, but was forwarded to a number of international organizations, including the UN, the OAS and the International Labor Organization, a direct challenge to stipulations of the Emergency Decree. The change of political climate the private sector demanded was nothing less than gaining state power.

Even Nicaraguan ambassador to the United States Arturo Cruz, who resigned in part because of disagreement with the actions taken by the government against his COSEP friends, was the first to admit that the letter had had a destabilizing effect. "If they wanted to criticize the government, they could have sent the letter directly to the Junta," he said to a group of journalists at the Center for Inter-American Relations.[31]

Facing the most serious political challenge to date, the FSLN moved swiftly to assert its authority, knowing in advance that to do so would have clear international consequences. Junta member Sergio Ramírez had already pointed out that, "We can't decide everything in terms of international opinion while we are being destabilized. There are times when it is better to show that the authority of the revolution does exist and that it can hit back at its foes. Our reactions are going to get harder as the harassment gets more aggressive."[32] The three COSEP signatories who did not go into hiding were tried and sentenced to seven months in jail (though this was commuted after four months).

The reassertion of authority was validated by impressive mass mobilization. Nationwide anti-intervention rallies in October brought 250,000 Nicaraguans onto the streets, the target of their wrath as much domestic enemies of the revolution as the Halcon Vista naval maneuvers which they saw as a dry run for intervention.

Signs are that this newest crisis has left the opposition, as before, in some disarray. Retreating from the brink, *La Prensa* changed tack in mid-November, denouncing Haig's "interfering and threatening attitude" in an editorial.[33] Even Róbelo positioned himself as far from the US administration as he could. With a new law governing the activities of political parties on the table for debate, some opposition groups found their way back to the Council of State, while others remained adrift. The new COSEP board took a conciliatory tone. And the FSLN, in no doubt about the most pressing task at hand, dubbed 1982 the "Year of National Unity Against Aggression." The Reagan administration was taking giant steps forward in its attacks against Nicaragua from which there would be no easy retreat. Some would call it just saber rattling. Others, remembering that Reagan's hero, Calvin Coolidge, had sent 50,000 Marines to Nicaragua, were not so sure.

In the Propaganda War, the Battle Is International

The whole issue of running the presidency is control of the agenda. We deal with what ought to be the buildup of things six to nine months out. It's a process question.

—Richard S. Beal, survey research expert for Reagan's political management team.[34]

There has been a distinct "buildup of things" in the propaganda war carried out by the US government against Nicaragua. In its content and ferocity, it bears a canny relationship to the rhythm of struggle waged by the insurgents in El Salvador.

On January 10, 1981, just as President Carter was preparing to cede the Oval Office to his successor, the Farabundo Martí Forces of National Liberation launched a major offensive in El Salvador. Within five days there were reports in the press of a 100-strong guerrilla force, reputedly Nicaraguan, which had landed by boat on a Salvadoran beach. A week later, on the eve of Carter's departures, US aid to Nicaragua was suspended in order to review "evidence" that the Sandinista government had been supplying the Salvadoran guerrilla force with arms.[35] This move came as a surprise to many, since even Haig was saying that the supposed weapons shipments had "slowed to a trickle."

Although the Nicaraguan government has categorically and consistently denied involvement in such activities, the Reagan administration fastened on the theme, using it as a rationale to cut off aid definitively in April.

Despite the administration's accusatory litany, the effort to coalesce active Congressional concern, international allies and public opinion against Nicaragua on these grounds showed few appreciable results. It hadn't helped that the boat story was exposed as a hoax and that the administration's "White Paper on Communist Interference in El Salvador" first met lukewarm response in Europe and was ultimately discredited by both the *Washington Post* and the *Wall Street Journal.* It was time to try something new.

"Drifting toward Totalitarianism"

It began offshore, like a Caribbean twister not significant enough to cause a stir in the mainland press. Only the *Miami Herald* carried the story that Sen. Thomas Eagleton (McGovern's original running mate in the 1972 presidential elections) called Nicaragua a dictatorship on his visit to Central America in April 1981.[36]

In October, the charge acquired official government status. It was inaugurated in the United Nations by deputy US representative Kenneth Adelman in a bristling response to Nicaragua's address to the General Assembly. In addition to labeling Nicaragua a dictatorship, Adelman accused it of being "a base for the export of violence to other countries." This two-pronged attack was simultaneous with a reporter's revelation in the *Washington Post* that the civil war in El Salvador was stalemated, guerrilla forces controlling an estimated 25 percent of the country.[37]

Within another month, the now hurricane force propaganda storm swept the

US media, reaching deep into public and private discussions about the fate of Central America and playing havoc with liberal sympathizers in Congress. On November 12, speaking before the House Foreign Affairs Committee, Secretary of State Haig moved from accusation to a threat of action. There is "mounting evidence in Nicaragua of the totalitarian character of the Sandinista regime," he claimed, and warned that policy-makers would exclude no options to deal with it.

Throughout November and December (roughly until Congress adjourned for Christmas recess) the charge of totalitarianism became a leitmotif as Haig and other administration officials hammered away daily at Nicaragua in interviews, press conferences, congressional hearings, television panels and trips to other countries. The rhetoric escalated at a geometric rate.

Nicaragua suddenly became a "forward base of operations for Cuba," which in turn is a "puppet of the expansionist Soviet Union" which is carrying out a "strategy to turn all of Central America into a Marxist enclave." Their conclusion: Nicaragua's military buildup can only be seen as offensive—the creation of "a superpower in Central American terms." Random quotations such as these by administration officials and conservative allies in Congress made their way incessantly into the network news and the front pages of the mainstream press. As examples of alarmist rhetoric, they were only topped by Sen. Jesse Helms, in a December hearing by his Subcommittee on Western Hemispheric Affairs: "If we don't fight this now, south of El Salvador, we will have to fight it in a decade, north of Mexico."[38]

Managing the Message

Why has the propaganda offensive become such a key tool of Reagan's destabilization efforts against Nicaragua? Once again, reference to the Heritage Foundation provides the clue. "In the near future," advises Di Giovanni, "the US must revert to a more traditional view of Central America if the spread of Marxism is to be contained . . . As long as it exists in any great strength in any one of [the countries], the others will be in danger. Thus, although the Marxist government in Nicaragua might fall eventually of its own failures, the security of El Salvador requires the acceleration of the removal of the government in Managua."[39] The favorable David and Goliath image the Sandinistas enjoyed for overthrowing the tyrant Somoza and carrying out attractive reforms such as the literarcy crusade would have to be broken if the administration wanted a free hand to accelerate.

Furthermore, it had become clear that the administration was opting for a military solution to the situation in El Salvador, and with the gains of the insurgents that would mean far greater US involvement. The hitch was that close to half of the US population feared a war under Reagan, and an effective solidarity movement had prevented Reagan from making any dent in that statistic with regard to El Salvador.

The campaign portraying Nicaragua as a totalitarian bastion carrying out the bidding of the Soviet Union in El Salvador would thus serve several ends. It could hope to explain away the successes of the Salvadoran insurgents, help mobilize

public opinion in support of increased US involvement and begin to construct a
rationale for the eventual regionalization of the conflict. Most importantly, it could
drive a wedge between support for the struggle in El Salvador and the triumphant
Sandinistas. Haig pushed at this in a speech in Palm Beach, Florida, in mid-
November: "The Reagan administration is very worried about the totalitarian
course the Nicaraguan regime is adopting. El Salvador is going to follow that same
road if the United States doesn't increase economic and military assistance to the
Durate junta."[40]

The campaign has all the qualities of a water torture theory of opinion building:
where basic proof is unavailable, the steady drip, drip, drip of repetition shall make
it true.

It is not a subtle technique, but Reagan's propaganda team does not pride itself
on subtlety. It prides itself on winning. While few Americans are still naive enough
to believe that public opinion is a major determinant of government policy, a recent
article by Sidney Blumenthal called "The Marketing of the President" captures the
cynicism with which Reagan's media masters regard such democratic silliness. To
them, public opinion only determines how government policy is "packaged," and
when it is presented.

The example is El Salvador; the time, February 1981. After a carefully planned,
full-scale campaign portraying El Salvador as a crucial East-West confrontation,
Reagan's strategists were stunned to see a drop in his support in the polls. They
quickly decided to "low key the issue," allowing it to "recede in the public mind"
until the polls changed. "What was wrong with El Salvador," offered Richard S.
Beal, a public opinion pollster who reports to political manager Edwin Meese III,
"was the packaging of the activity in terms of policy and presentation to the public.
It wasn't well staged or sequenced."[41]

Reagan's strategists, by November, had clearly concluded that the East-West
campaign would fly better if the ideological component were brought more into
play. If people were not warming to the idea of a Central American war in the name
of stopping Soviet expansionism, they could surely be motivated to defend the
region's great democratic traditions against totalitarianism. Trumped-up elections
in El Salvador were scheduled for March to shore up its dubious image of
democracy.

Within Congress the effort took its toll. Liberal members of Congress who had
fought on behalf of the $75 million aid package to Nicaragua during Carter's last
year began to speak of being betrayed by the Sandinistas. In debate over Senator
Zorinsky's proposed amendment to the fiscal 1982 foreign aid request that all $33
million for Nicaragua go to the private sector, Senator Kennedy endorsed it with the
following remark: "Nicaragua has experienced the lion's share of social and political injustice under two regimes—including first a corrupt tyrant of the right and
now an authoritarian regime of the left."[42]

A Slight Case of Exaggeration

A trigger-word like totalitarianism sets off dark, unthinking fears in the public mind. The association is Hitler's Germany or Soviet society under Stalin. Yet by applying the criteria associated with this concept in a static way, not taking the context into account, the early period of the American revolution could easily have qualified as "drifting toward totalitarianism." National elections were not held for 13 years, opposition presses were smashed, and Tories were expelled from public office, imprisoned without trial, forcibly exiled or summarily shot. Their property was confiscated as a general practice.[43] As one essayist succinctly put it, "The success of the Revolution was impossible without a revolutionary government which could enforce its will."[44]

The administration's charge against revolutionary Nicaragua uses as its rationale far less serious or pervasive events. Among the most often repeated are the Nicaraguan government's decision not to hold early national elections, the series of punitive closings of *La Prensa* and the arrest and conviction of the three business leaders. By the historic standards of revolutionary consolidation, these acts hardly qualify Nicaragua as totalitarian.

While it is to be expected that these and other decisions by the Nicaraguan government will be subject to critical evaluation from a variety of perspectives, the hypocritical posturing of the Reagan administration is beyond the pale. It is on particularly shaky grounds when it indignantly pushes for elections, while remaining unperturbed that Argentina has not had real elections in six years of military dictatorship, Chile in eight, Uruguay in ten or Paraguay in nearly half a century. Not very good at recent history, the administration has forgotten altogether that the US press was severely curtailed during both the Civil War and World War I.[45] And as for the COSEP prisoners, Norman Bailey of the National Security Council revealed the true extent of the Reagan administration's concern when he said, "If Nicaragua would change its foreign policy toward the United States . . . we would take a much different attitude about the arrest of the businessmen."[46]

Notes

[1] Interview with Bayardo Arce (Managua), November 1981.

[2] Cleto Di Giovanni, "US Policy and the Marxist Threat to Central America," *Heritage Foundation Backgrounder* (October 15, 1980), pp. 4–5.

[3] *New York Times*, November 28, 1980.

[4] *Miami Herald*, November 23, 1980.

[5] *Miami Herald*, January 2, 1981.

[6] *Miami Herald*, January 3, 1981.

[7] *Diario Las Americas*, November 14, 1981.

[8] John Spicer Nichols, "The Principles and Realities of Press Freedom in Nicaragua and Beyond," paper presented to the 10th National Meeting of LASA, Washington, D.C., March 3–6, 1982.

[9] *Columbia Journalism Review*, January–February 1982.

[10] *Diario Las Americas*, Janaury 15 and 16, 1981.

[11] *Plan Económico 1981,* Ministry of Planning (Managua).

[12] *New York Times,* August 16, 1981.

[13] *Guardian Weekly* (England), August 2, 1981.

[14] Di Giovanni, "US Policy and the Marxist Threat," p. 3.

[15] "Central America, No Road Back," *NACLA Report on the Americas* (Vol. XV, No. 3), May–June 1981.

[16] Viron P. Vaky, "Hemispheric Relations: 'Everything Is Part of Everything Else,' " *Foreign Affairs* (Vol. 59, No. 3), 1980, p. 621.

[17] Center for International Policy (CIP) *Aid Memo,* November 12, 1981.

[18] *World Bank News Release,* No. 82-41, January 14, 1982.

[19] *Uno Mas Uno* (Mexico), January 17, 1982.

[20] *CIP Memo,* undated.

[21] InterPress Service (Managua), November 27, 1981.

[22] *Multinational Monitor* (Vol. 2, No. 5), May 1981.

[23] *Washington Post,* November 23, 1981.

[24] Interview with Xavier Gorostiaga, reprinted in Instituto Histórico Centroamericano bulletin (Managua), 1981.

[25] *New York Times,* August 23, 1981.

[26] *Barricada Internacional* (Managua), September 15, 1981.

[27] *Miami Herald,* September 15, 1981.

[28] *Washington Post,* November 9, 1981.

[29] *Diario Las Americas,* October 6, 1981.

[30] US Navy Press Release and *Miami Herald,* November 26, 1981.

[31] Presentation by former Nicaraguan ambassador to the United States Arturo Cruz to the Center for Inter-American Relations, December 1, 1981.

[32] *Le Monde Diplomatique,* July 19, 1981.

[33] *La Prensa* (Managua), November 15, 1981.

[34] Sidney Blumenthal, "Marketing the President," *New York Times Magazine,* September 13, 1981.

[35] *Financial Times* (London), January 27, 1981, and *New York Times,* January 23, 1981.

[36] *Miami Herald,* April 26, 1981.

[37] *Washington Post,* November 10, 1981.

[38] "The Security Threat in the Caribbean and Central America," by Fred C. Iklé, under Secretary of Defense for Policy, Subcommittee on Western Hemisphere Affairs of Senate Foreign Relations Committee (December 15, 1981).

[39] Di Giovanni, "US Policy and the Marxist Threat," p. 2.
Las Americas, November 15, 1981.

[41] Blumenthal, "Marketing the President."

[42] *Congressional Record—Senate,* October 20, 1981. p. S11665.

[43] Herbert Aptheker, *The American Revolution, 1763-1783* (New York: International Publishers, 1960), pp. 125-128.

[44] Richard C. Haskett, "Prosecuting the Revolution," *American Historical Review,* April 1954.

[45] Nichols, "Principles and Realities."

[46] Presentation by Norman Bailey, Director of Planning and Evaluation, National Security Council, to the Center for Inter-American Relations, December 1, 1981.

29. *How Latin Guerrillas Train on Our Soil**

By Eddie Adams

I could hardly believe my eyes when the two men who came to call for me at the Holiday Inn in Coral Gables, Florida, walked into the lobby wearing US Army-type camouflage uniforms and bayonets and canteens strapped around their waists. They were there to take me to a nearby military camp where Cuban and Nicaraguan exiles are training and practicing to invade their former homelands in a supreme effort to overthrow the leftist regimes that rule them.

Until I encountered my two guides, I had no idea of how openly and extensively these displaced Latins are operating throughout southern Florida, including Miami, the Everglades and the Keys. Some of them use code names, like Condor and Bombillo (Spanish for light bulb), but most make no attempt to conceal their identities—or their purpose. They are determined to liberate their homelands from the Castro regime in Cuba and the Sandinista junta in Nicaragua—or die in the process.

The Nicaraguans are a new element in the invasion-plan picture. Since the replacement of the dictatorial Somoza regime by what they regard as an equally repressive regime of the left, they have swelled the ranks of the anti-Castro Cubans already undergoing training. One of the biggest and busiest guerrilla camps in Florida flies a trio of flags at its inner gates—American, Cuban and Nicaraguan.

Says José Francisco Cardenal, who used to be vice president of the Council of State in Nicaragua but now is among the refugees, "In the beginning, 95 percent of my people were for the revolution, but now the reverse is true."

Right now, there are at least 10 paramilitary organizations composed of Cuban and Nicaraguan exiles operating in Florida. Some of them advertise for recruits over Spanish-language Miami radio stations and speak freely about their aims. "We Nicaraguans are back-to-back with Cuba," says Max Vargas. "They confiscated my family's trucking company," he adds bitterly. "I was successful. I made money, a million dollars a month. They told me the people would own the company, but now only the government owns everything. I want Nicaragua to be the way I remember it. We're training people not only here in Florida, but in Guatemala, Honduras, El Salvador and Costa Rica. We have training camps in California, too."

At the camps, the prospective invaders work vigorously at their maneuvers and preparations. The newest base to open is a 68-acre flatland surrounded by 6-foot-high elephant grass and workmen building a new housing development. This guerrilla "boot camp" is about 20 minutes by car from Miami's International Airport. Some of the recruits working out there have enough of an income to enjoy

*Reprinted from *Parade Magazine,* March 15, 1981.

the Miami Beach resorts. Instead they spend every weekend clad in fatigues, firing automatic weapons or running the obstacle course.

Security is tight at camps like this. Visitors are scrupulously checked out. The guerrillas say they're armed to the teeth with an arsenal of weapons that even includes amphibious assault boats. But they won't say who supplies them. Many members of the groups are US citizens whose pasts are tied to Latin America. Some have families still there.

Another possible problem is rivalry between groups. The various units have been holding secret meetings with the objective of uniting. Said one of the guerrillas, clad in his battle fatigues, "One of our biggest problems is: Who will be the leader?"

The exiles insist that they don't want direct US intervention. They're not expecting the US marines or the 101st Airborne to support their liberation mission. But they say they would like a "green light" and possibly some hardware to help them do "the dirty work."

How much US assistance they may actually receive, however, remains problematical. Said one State Department spokesman when asked to comment:

"The new administration is not going to turn back the clock 21 years in Cuba or 17 months in Nicaragua and support any exile groups. It's illegal. It's a breach of international law. It's also stupid."

Nevertheless, the prospective invaders persist in regarding Ronald Reagan as their possible savior because, they think, he is unafraid of armed confrontation.

"With Carter, we knew we couldn't do anything inside Cuba," sums up Bombillo. "Now, maybe. This nation will be saved with the help of God and Reagan."

30. A Secret War for Nicaragua*

By John Brecher, John Walcott, David Martin, and Beth Nissen

The smoky bar in Tegucigalpa was a cousin to Rick's Café in "Casablanca," a nightly gathering place for the dangerous and the desperate in Honduras. Squeezed into a corner one evening last week were four Argentine military advisers speaking machine-gun Spanish and occasionally stealing furtive glances around the room. A half-dozen Americans stood in a loose line at the bar, drinking beer and talking too loudly about guns. In the center of the room, grouped around a table that listed far right, were seven men drinking rum. One of them wore a gold earring. He explained that the seven men were Nicaraguan exiles who belonged to various factions of *la contra,* a band of counterrevolutionaries trying to topple the leftist Sandinista regime. They were ready to move toward Managua, one of men said.

---

*Reprinted from *Newsweek,* November 8, 1982.

"We just need to hear from The Boss that it's time to go." Who was The Boss? The man with the earring was impatient with stupid questions. "He's the man you call 'Mr. Ambassador.' "

The envoy in question was John D. Negroponte, the American ambassador in Honduras. Official sources told *Newsweek* last week that Negroponte is overseeing an ambitious covert campaign to arm, train and direct Nicaraguan exiles to intercept the flow of arms to leftist guerrillas in El Salvador. But the operation has another objective: to harass and undermine the Cuban-backed government of Nicaragua. The project traces back to Jimmy Carter's efforts to support Nicaraguan moderates. Ronald Reagan added the task of cutting the Cuban-Nicaraguan arms pipeline to El Salvador. The plot, launched mostly with popguns and *machismo,* now threatens instead to destabilize Honduras, to fortify the Marxists in Nicaragua and to waste US prestige along the tangled banks of the Coco River. Worse, US officials concede there is a danger that the operation could provoke a Nicaraguan counterattack on Honduras that could drag the United States directly into the conflict. "This is the big fiasco of this administration," says one US official. "This is our Bay of Pigs."

Reports of secret operations along the Nicaraguan-Honduran border have circulated for months. But *Newsweek* has uncovered extensive details of a campaign that has escalated far beyond Washington's original intentions. Administration sources told *Newsweek* that there are now almost 50 CIA personnel serving in Honduras—certainly the longest manifest in Central America. That team is supplemented by dozens of operatives including a number of retired military and intelligence officers. Argentine military advisers are supporting the operation in Honduras; separate anti-Sandinista activities are underway in Mexico and Venezuela.

Camps

The fighting forces are drawn from 2,000 Miskitu Indians, an estimated 10,000 anti-Sandinistas in Nicaragua itself and an assorted group of former Nicaraguan National Guardsmen and supporters of deposed dictator Anastasio Somoza. They have set up 10 training camps divided between Honduran and Nicaraguan territory. Their hit-and-run forays against Nicaraguan bridges, construction sites and patrols are designed to harass the Sandinistas while CIA operatives cast around for a moderate new Nicaraguan leadership. Among others, the United States tried to cultivate Edén Pastora—the former Sandinista hero known as Commander Zero—after he resigned from the government in July 1981. That effort failed. "Pastora is a man who would not accept a penny from the CIA," swears one associate. "If he did, I would kill him."

The operation posed some very disturbing questions: did it violate the spirit if not the letter of congressional restrictions on dirty tricks—and would it only make a bad situation in Central America even worse? A congressional-committee spokesman said that CIA Director William Casey (who personally inspected the operation in Honduras) had adequately briefed congressional oversight committees. But some congressional sources complained that the CIA's briefings had been bland and disingenuous. And others wondered pointedly whether the administration had used approval for plans to cut off the flow of Cuban arms to rebels in El Salvador as a cover for a more reckless plot to topple the Sandinistas. "This operation's just about out of control and people are getting panicky," said one source. According to one US official, Secretary of State George Shultz was "fuming" over the mess. Said another, "Only Schultz can change it—if there is still time."

Moderates

Washington's covert involvement in Nicaragua began even before Somoza fled the country. In 1978, with the dynasty nearing collapse, Jimmy Carter signed a "finding," as required by post-Watergate law, authorizing under-the-table CIA support for democratic elements in Nicaraguan society, such as the press and labor unions. The Carter administration correctly recognized that with the Somoza regime crumbling, Cuban-backed leftist forces would try to squeeze out more moderate elements. American financial support for Nicaragua's opposition forces has continued, and it remains one of the many items on the CIA's yearly "Classified Schedule of Authorizations."

After the Sandinistas seized power anyway, the Reagan administration took office worried that Nicaragua would become a platform for Cuban-sponsored subversion. Ronald Reagan's first national security adviser, Richard Allen, set to work on plans to harass the Sandinistas. Former Secretary of State Alexander Haig and Thomas O. Enders, assistant secretary of state, became increasingly concerned that the Sandinistas were providing weapons to leftist rebels in El Salvador—much of the hardware shipped across Honduras. In several meetings, a well-placed administration source says, Enders spoke about the need to "get rid of the Sandinis-tas." "The driving forces behind this operation were Haig and Enders," said one insider. "Both the agency and the Pentagon had qualms."

Joint Action

At first, the administration's planning focused entirely on how to cut the Salvadoran rebels' supply lines from Cuba and other communist nations through Nicaragua and Honduras into El Salvador, Haig directed then State Department counselor Robert McFarlane to prepare a series of option papers. Senior Defense Department officials rejected a blockade of Cuba or Nicaragua, pointing out that much of the arms traffic moved by air. Administration officials say McFarlane then asked the CIA to explore possible covert action against the rebels' supply lines, an option that proved more promising and less politically risky than the direct use of US forces. Early on, Haig's ambassador at large, Gen. Vernon Walters, and other officials discussed possible joint covert operations with conservative Latin American governments, including Argentina, Guatemala and Honduras.

Last December Reagan signed his own "finding," expanding on Carter's and authorizing the CIA to contact dissident Nicaraguans in exile and to conduct political and paramilitary operations to inderdict weapons shipments from Nicaragua to Salvadoran guerrillas. A second document, known as a "scope paper," outlined permissible operations and their estimated cost. In its first stage, the plan was to create a 500-man, US-trained paramilitary force at a cost of $19.9 million. Argentina would train an additional 1,000-man force. "The focus was an action which would interdict the flow of arms to guerrillas in the friendly countries," said one source who has read both documents. "Nowhere does it talk about overthrow." But one senior official involved in the decisions conceded that "there are secondary and tertiary consequences which you can't countrol"—such as the fall of the Sandinista government.

As US officials tell it, the size of the CIA station in Honduras doubled, bringing it to about 50, with orders to help interdict the arms supplies by training the Honduran intelligence and security forces in intelligence gathering and interrogation, providing logistical support for raids into Nicaragua, aiding the Honduran coast guard and helping the Argentines and other non-Nicaraguans train anti-Sandinista Nicaraguans in sabotage operations using small arms supplied by the Americans.

Washington had used Honduras once before as a base for a destabilization program: in 1954, when the United States toppled the reformist government of Jacobo Arbenz in Guatemala. In the view of the Reagan administration, Honduras itself had become dangerously vulnerable to the Cuban-backed spread of communism. Honduras had managed to remain relatively calm and largely unaffected after the 1979 Nicaraguan revolution by simply looking the other way as Cuban-Nicaraguan arms passed through to El Salvador. "There was a kind of understanding that if we looked the other way, the *subversivos* wouldn't look our way," said one Honduran Army officer.

Spearhead

That changed when John Negroponte arrived. He was handpicked for the job and reported to Enders, with whom he had worked in Southeast Asia during the Vietman War and later under then national-security adviser Henry Kissinger. "Negroponte is the spearhead," said one Washington insider. "He was sent down there by Haig and Enders to carry out the operation without any qualms of conscience."

Negroponte forged close ties with powerful Hondurans, especially the commander of the armed forces, Gen. Gustavo Áldolfo Alvarez, who is still the most powerful Honduran in the country despite the election in January of President Roberto Suazo Córdova, the first civilian president in nine years. "They discuss what should be done, and then Álvarez does what Negroponte tells him to," a member of the military high command said matter-of-factly. The two appear to dislike each other personally, said one aide to Álvarez, because "they both run the army, although only one of them has the title for that job." Álvarez's G-2 military-intelligence agents act as liaisons to the *contras* and Álvarez himself reports to Negroponte. In addition, two officials in Washington said, Álvarez's military is the main conduit for small arms being delivered to the Nicaraguan exiles and is the main link to Argentine military advisers in Honduras. Álvarez has reason to cooperate: in the past two years, total US assistance to Honduras has totaled $187 million. A $78.3 million aid package has been proposed for 1983.

The interdiction project proved more difficult than expected. The rebel supply lines were elusive: as the Honduran army cracked down on arms shipments across land, the leftists began receiving aid by sea and air. At the same time, the Sandinistas undertook a massive military buildup. Under the new pressures, the plan spread beyond its original bounds. "It became clear that cutting the roads from Nicaragua wasn't enough," said one source. "It was necessary to raise the cost to the Sandinistas and the Cubans of meddling in El Salvador."

Problems

That meant, at the least, cross-border harassment—and that, too, proved more difficult than Washington planned. First, according to sources in Honduras, the Argentines reduced their participation in the covert training program and in the overt training of the Honduran Army after the outbreak of the Falklands War. (Washington officials said, however, that there were about 20 Argentine trainers in the country last week and that the numbers had not changed appreciably during the Falklands War.) Then the Mikitu Indians, who had been forcibly driven from their homes along the Honduran-Nicaraguan border, proved eager but unpromising modern soldiers. "The Indians aren't very quick learners," says one knowledgeable source.

Such problems soon led to strange bedfellows. When the covert policy was first developed, direct US dealings with exiled Somocistas were officially ruled out. "Our guidelines are pretty damn firm," says one senior US official. "At no time has there been any authorization to deal with the Somoza people." But Negroponte, under pressure from Haig and Enders to produce some successes against the Sandinistas, turned to the only promising group available—the Somocistas. "It was Negroponte who began dealing with the guardsmen and the Somocistas," says one US official. "That wasn't the original plan. He had to improvise." Sources in both Washington and Honduras say the ambassador has been careful to deal with the Somocistas through intermediaries to preserve his deniability. Asked about US support for Somocistas or other *contras* last week, Negroponte said: "No comment, no comment and a big fat no comment." Of his own contacts, he said, "The only Nicaraguan I know personally is the Nicaraguan ambassador to Honduras. The only Nicaraguan I deal with in any official way is the ambassador."

At the same time, the Reagan administration looked for a leader around whom to build the opposition. No one connected with the hated Somocistas would do. The most attractive candidate was Pastora—Commander Zero. After leaving the government in 1981, he suddenly surfaced in Costa Rica last April, denounced his former comrades as "traitors and assassins" and announced: "I will drag them with bullets from their mansions and Mercedes-Benzes." The CIA first tried to cultivate Pastora after he left the Sandinista government, but he would not cooperate. After Negroponte began to deal with the Somocistas, any chance of recruiting Pastora probably was lost.

Alienated

Negroponte now has frozen him out of the action. Pastora and other disillusioned Sandinistas, such as former junta member Alfonso Róbelo, have been told that "Honduras is closed to us, we cannot work here," says one of them. *Newsweek* has learned that Pastora has made two clandestine trips to Honduras since spring to try to win support and establish base camps. Both times he was kept under virtual house arrest by the military. "He couldn't make a phone call, let alone organize a *contra* group," says one Honduran military officer. "The orders came from Álvarez himself that our American friends did not want this guy to have any part of the game." As a result, despite Washington's intentions, Negroponte has alienated the only group likely to attract widespread support inside Nicaragua. "There's no question that Nicaragua is ripe for a change," said one European observer in the region. "But the US is supporting the only wrong, the only truly evil alternative."

After Negroponte and the Somocistas became partners, the new American allies began to force Washington's hand. The Somocistas bivouacked in Honduras were already trained soldiers, backed by wealthy exiles in Miami. With the added boost of tacit US support, they soon took a commanding position among competing contra groups. They also developed their own private plan numero uno: to move the contra camps that remain in Honduras across the border into Nicaragua, then move the camps already established in Nicaragua farther down toward Managua and, finally, past the capital into the south. When the time is right, the Somocistas say, they will draw their loose circle of camps together toward Managua and force the Sandinistas out. And then? "Come the counterrevolution, there will be a massacre in Nicaragua," promises one contra officer. "We have a lot of scores to settle. There will be bodies from the border to Managua."

That obviously was not what Washington had in mind. Despite the dirty little war on the ground, there is little support in Washington either for a massive contra invasion or for a border war between Nicaragua and Honduras. Instead, the constant pressure on Nicaragua from the border areas is designed to keep the four-year-old Sandinista government in a jumpy state of alert. While US officials maintain that the primary objective of the operation remains cutting off the supply routes, they also hope that a threatened Sandinista government will bring itself down by further repressing its internal opposition, thereby strengthening the determination of moderate forces to resist. If that happens, says one US official in Central America, "then the Sandinistas will fall like a house of cards in a wind."

Thin Line

Although the Reagan administration and the Somocistas disagree on strategy, US involvement with the contras has escalated. When equipment—helicopters and radios, for example—breaks down, Americans repair it. Americans established the guerrillas' training regime, and arming the contras was easy: the massive American buildup of the Honduran military freed older Honduran equipment, which was shipped off to counterrevolutionary bases. The Americans were soon treading the thin line between instructing insurgents and plotting the missions they were being trained for. Though Americans are expressly forbidden to go out on operations, one veteran of other paramilitary operations said: "Inevitably that happens . . . You lose your credibility with the people you're training if you hole up entirely."

Negroponte insists that his strategy precisely follows Washington's orders. But other sources claim that Negroponte censors embassy cables so that Washington will only know what he wants it to know, and that he seems to operate with little interference or second-guessing from superiors. "Haig and Enders gave Negroponte full autonomy," said one high-level insider in Honduras. Added another: "A lot of us think the ambassador should have a little more E.T. in him—that he should phone home now and then. But I'm sure his contention would be that 'home would say, "Go ahead and do what you think is best." ' He only has to answer to himself."

In either case, virtually every knowledgeable official says that the operation needs firmer restraints. "It is reminiscent of the cable that went out, 'Order turkeys for the division' but got garbled so we ordered a division to Turkey," said one official.

The Hondurans themselves fear that their country might slip into the Central American line of fire. In September Honduran leftist guerrillas took more than 100 businessmen and officials hostage for eight days in San Pedro Sula. Tegucigalpa was blacked out after a power plant was dynamited. The Hondurans say they have evidence that both operations were masterminded by Salvadoran and Nicaraguan leftists. The Hondurans also claim to have cracked six safe houses in the past two months and found huge stocks of weapons and literature that connects the caches with the Sandinistas.

Any more violence could touch off a confrontation over security measures between General Álvarez and the still unsteady civilian government. Guerrilla attacks already have led to growing repression. For the first time in Honduras's modern history, right-wing death squads now appear to be operating. "There is a low level of violence and subversion now, and it would be an easy step to more aggressive government actions than are needed," worried a US official—"followed by more aggressive subversion." America's secret war might thus have the intended effect—in the wrong country.

The operation has stirred up its intended target as well. The Sandinistas have used the contra attacks as an excuse to spend an estimated $125 million on defense this year, beefing up the Army and civilian militia while attacking what remains of a free press and private business. But Sandinista repression has not led to a noticeable upsurge of anti-Sandinista activity inside the country—perhaps because Nicaraguans now only see a choice between the Sandinistas and the hated US-backed Somocistas. "Our operations along the Honduran border have only played into the hands of the Sandinistas," says one dismayed US official.

Terrified

But other American officials see light at the end of the tunnel. The Sandinista leaders are "terrified to their Marxist cores," says one. They have made their first attempts in months to try to re-establish communication with the private sector—and with the United States. US Ambassador to Nicaragua Anthony Quainton, who had been refused any official meetings with the Sandinista leaders, was astonished to find junta member Bayardo Arce waiting for him, unannounced, in the Foreign Ministry recently. On the verge of panic, one source said, Arce asked, in effect, "What is the price we have to pay to stay in power?"

Tensions could peak within the next few weeks. On December 5 the United States and Honduras will begin joint military maneuvers near one of the most sensitive stretches of the Nicaraguan-Honduran border. The five-day maneuvers will include the US Army, Navy and Air Force; they will simulate the freeing of an army garrison from cross-border invaders. A growing number of people on both sides of the border fear the simulation might preview a real war. Ronald Reagan will be visiting nearby Costa Rica on December 4. Two months after he authorized the operation against Nicaragua, Reagan was asked how he felt, generally, about covert action to destabilize regimes. His answer: "No comment."

31. US Ties to Anti-Sandinistas Are Reported to Be Extensive*

By Raymond Bonner

Washington, April 2—A Honduran who was directly involved in planning American covert activities reports that the United States has been giving intelligence assistance and military advice in Honduras to forces fighting the Sandinist government in Nicaragua.

According to this Honduran, the United States was extensively involved in training and arming the paramilitary forces before they recently entered Nicaragua from Honduras.

---

*Reprinted from *The New York Times,* April 3, 1983.

The information supplied by the Honduran in a series of interviews over the last few days was confirmed in large measure by two senators on the Senate Intelligence Committee and a highly placed Reagan administration official.

In its detail, the information supplied by the Honduran suggests a mosaic of American covert activities that administration officials acknowledge is apparently having the effect of supporting the current insurgency in Nicaragua. The political and military leaders of the anti-Sandinist forces have openly vowed to overthrow the government.

Administration officials say, however, that the United States' objective in Nicaragua is to harass, not overthrow the government. A law passed by Congress last year prohibits United States support of efforts to topple the Sandinist government.

Administration officials say the United States' involvement does not mark a shift in policy, and they maintain that the support for the anti-Sandinist forces, although increasing, remains consistent with the original intention of blocking arms shipments from Nicaragua to guerrillas in El Salvador.

The conflicting descriptions of the purpose of the American involvement may reflect the difficulty inherent in trying to manage foreign paramilitary forces in a highly volatile region.

Several senators on the Senate Intelligence Committee, reporting that their colleagues had grown increasingly uneasy in recent weeks about the American role in Honduras and Nicaragua, said the Central Intelligence Agency had overestimated its ability to control the anti-Sandinist forces. As a result, they said, it appeared to have been drawn into underwriting more ambitious operations than it intended.

The Honduran informant has close ties to the Honduran military as well as American diplomatic and military officials in Tegucigalpa and was directly involved in joint military planning until early this year. He said that to his knowledge no Americans were operating inside Nicaragua with the insurgents. He described these covert American activities:

• Providing frequent intelligence reports to the insurgent forces about the movement of Nicaraguan government soldiers as well as the location of Nicaraguan tanks and artillery.

• Training and arming the paramilitary forces, including the shipment of planeloads of arms and ammunitions in August 1982 to Miskitu Indian units in eastern Honduras. More than 50 United States military advisers, most of whom were of Hispanic background and did not dress in uniforms, trained paramilitary units in Honduras last year. The CIA and the Pentagon refused to comment on these matters.

• Providing underwater equipment and explosives to Argentine-trained sabotage teams that were infiltrated into Nicaragua earlier this year and blew up port installations in Puerto Cabezas in Nicaragua. The CIA and the Defense Department declined to comment.

The Honduran source said the intelligence reports are based in part on information collected by planes manned by United States Air Force personnel that make regular reconnaissance flights along the Nicaraguan-Honduran border as part of an intelligence-gathering operation with the code name Royal Duke.

The reports are given to the Honduran military with the understanding that they will be shared with the commanders of the paramilitary forces, he said. The CIA and the Defense Department refused to comment on the Air Force operation or other intelligence-gathering efforts.

"The Pretension Is Over"

The activities described by the Honduran source would indicate a far deeper level of American involvement in the Nicaraguan conflict than the Reagan administration has publicly acknowledged. The administration, while refusing to deny a covert American role in the fighting, has portrayed the conflict in Nicaragua as a factional dispute between different elements of the coalition that seized power from Gen. Anastasio Somoza Debayle in 1979.

The Honduran informant said the "real objective" of the operation in Nicaragua "is to overthrow" the Sandinists. He added that "the pretension is over" that the United States was interested only in harassing the Sandinist government.

Although he is troubled by the Marxist orientation of the Sandinists, he said, he is more concerned that the current hostilities in Nicaragua may expand into a war between Honduras and Nicaragua.

The Honduran said the United States Ambassador to Honduras, John D. Negroponte, and the chief of the Honduran military, Gen. Gustavo Adolfo Álvarez Martínez, were "the brains behind the operation."

"They were, and they still are," the informant said, referring to the role the two men played during the planning of the operation and its execution. He said the two met daily to discuss the progress of the war, including strategy. Mr. Negroponte has refused to comment on such reports.

Three Command Centers

The Honduran said the operation was being directed from three command centers. He said the rebels' command center was in the southern part of Honduras, and two or three liaison officers from the Honduran military were assigned there. The Honduran military high command directs the operation from its regular headquarters in Tegucigalpa and the United States participation is directed out of the American Embassy, he said.

The three-tier system is apparently part of an effort by the American mission in Honduras to remain insulated from direct contact with the anti-Sandinist forces now that the irregular troops are operating in Nicaragua. CIA officials have cited the system to Congress as an example of how the agency has organized its operations to remain in compliance with the law, according to two members of the Senate Intelligence Committee.

According to the Honduran informant, the United States is most active in gathering intelligence information about activities inside Nicaragua. He said the United States was supplying the Hondurans with surveillance photographs, tapes of intercepted communications between Nicaraguan leaders, and other raw intelligence information.

The official said 15 to 20 United States Air Force pilots and technicians based in Honduras frequently conducted reconnaissance flights as part of Operation Royal Duke. He said the men were not permitted to write their families or inform anyone about their activities or location.

Two Twin-Engine Planes

The men operate two Beechcraft Queen Air twin-engine airplanes, according to the official. He said these planes were loaded with electronic equipment, and the operation was part of the CIA's intelligence-gathering efforts in Central America.

The Defense Department declined to comment on whether Air Force pilots and technicians were present in Honduras. For the record, the Pentagon has stated that there are 43 military trainers and six support personnel in Honduras.

According to the Honduran, the rebels' military plan calls for them to gain control of either Jinotega, in the northwestern part of Nicaragua, or Puerto Cabezas, a Caribbean port, and then to install a provisional government.

He added that the Honduran military had plans to airlift supplies, troops and provisional government leaders into either of these cities.

An Indian Sabotage Raid

As a prelude to the effort to seize Puerto Cabezas, the official said, a team of Miskitu Indians trained as frogmen sabotaged the port installation last January. According to the source, the Miskitus had been trained in underwater demolition techniques at the island of Vivorillo off the east coast of Honduras. He said they had been trained by Argentines, and the equipment and explosives used for the sabotage mission had been supplied by the United States.

According to the Honduran, nearly all the weapons and equipment being used by the anti-Sandinist forces have been supplied by the United States.

He said, for example, that last August numerous United States C-130 cargo planes "full of weapons" landed at Puerto Lempira, an eastern Honduran city, and that the weapons were then distributed to the rebel forces. He said these planes had arrived after joint exercises in the area involving the United States and Honduran Armies. "Because of the exercise, they figured that the planes would not attract notice," he said. The Pentagon again declined to comment.

"We Just Opened the Doors"

In addition, he said, at the end of the exercises the United States forces left most of their equipment behind. In previous exercises, he said, the Americans took their equipment when they left. The official said this equipment also went to the anti-Sandinist forces. There was no comment from the Pentagon.

Other weapons were supplied to the rebels by the Honduran Army—"we just opened the doors" of warehouses, the official said—with the United States, in turn, resupplying the Honduran Army.

He said the rebels began moving weapons and supplies into Nicaragua last November. He said there were three phases to the movement of supplies. First, he said, the United States would deliver the supplies into Honduras primarily by air. Next, the Honduran armed forces would move them to the border by truck. And, finally, the rebels would pay individuals $10 a kilometer to carry them, sometimes loaded on mules, into Nicaragua.

According to the Honduran informant, American military personnel began training the anti-Sandinist rebels in late 1981. He said about 55 American soldiers were involved in the training, adding that they were not part of the regular United States military advisory group in Honduras.

He said the presence of the American military personnel went largely unnoticed because they blended in with the Honduran population. He said most were of Cuban, Mexican, Puerto Rican and other Hispanic backgrounds, spoke Spanish and did not wear uniforms.

US and Argentine Instructors

Most of the training the Americans provided was at Lepaterique, a few miles west of the capital, according to the source. He said this was the main camp for training the rebel commanders. Rebel soldiers were trained at five or six other camps in Honduras near the Nicaraguan border.

The source said Argentine soldiers provided the training in these other camps, which the Americans visited for short periods.

The Honduran source said the decision to shift the operation from one of harassment to one of trying to overthrow the Sandinists was made jointly by Honduran and American officials in Tegucigalpa.

According to the source, approximately 5,000 rebels have entered Nicaragua from training camps in Honduras. One of the largest infiltrations was on December 30, 1982, when, according to the source, five columns, each with 125 Miskitu Indians, crossed from Honduras into the eastern part of Nicaragua.

32. *"Commander Zero" Resurfaces**

By Charles Roberts

After nine months underground, Edén Pastora surfaced last April 15 in San
José, Costa Rica. The famed *Comandante Cero* (Commander Zero) of the
Sandinista-led insurrection that overthrew the Somoza dictatorship condemned the
nine-member FSLN leadership and threatened to "drag them out of their Mercedes
Benzes with bullets."

Two days later several thousand demonstrators gathered in Managua to condemn "the traitor Pastora." Militia members throughout the country burned their
membership cards, signed by Pastora, in repudiation of his counterrevolutionary
political position. Until he left Nicaragua last July, *Cero* had been National Chief of
the Militias.

The emerging alliance between the former Sandinista guerrilla leader and
Alfonso Robelo of the Nicaraguan Democratic Movement (MDN)—who went into
self-imposed exile in late March—constitutes perhaps the greatest external political
challenge to the Sandinista leadership to date. This is due both to the popularity
Pastora had enjoyed, and Robelo's history as a leader of the anti-Somoza struggle
among the business sector.

Who is Edén Pastora?

Pastora had first taken up arms against the Somoza dictatorship in 1959.
Between 1956 and 1959 some 20 armed movements of diverse ideological tendencies
unsuccessfully tried to dislodge the family dynasty, which had already been in
power 20 years. In 1969 the Sandinista National Liberation Front (FSLN) emerged
from the political activism of the late '50s.

During the '60s and '70s Pastora alternated collaborating with the FSLN,
working with more conservative political movements that opposed the Somoza
dictatorship, and leading the life of a private entrepreneur. In 1973, after breaking
away from FSLN leaders over strategic questions, Pastora moved to Costa Rica,
where he spent a few years running a fishing operation. In the late '70s the
Insurrectionalist tendency of the then-divided FSLN invited him to rejoin the
struggle.

Pastora gained fame in the August, 1978, takeover of the National Palace.
Commanding the 24 FSLN guerrillas who participated in the action, *Comandante
Cero* became famous as the image of him boarding the airplane that took the
triumphant Sandinistas to Panama appeared on pages around the world.

---

*Reprinted from *Nicaragua*, May–June 1982.

After the July, 1979, victory he first became Vice-Minister of Interior, and was later named Vice-Minister of Defense. Given his military capacity and wide popularity, he was made National Chief of the People's Militia.

In July, 1981, Pastora, who had led the southern front in the final year of the drive to oust Somoza, resigned his post. He wrote in a letter to FSLN leader and Defense Minister Humberto Ortega that he felt moved to fight in new trenches, "where the duty of being an internationalist fighter leads me."

On leaving Nicaragua Pastora was accompanied by Sandinista guerrilla leader José Valdivia. After the April 15 press conference in Costa Rica, Valdivia re-emerged in Managua and gave his own press conference, which served primarily to answer the question: Where had they been?

According to Valdivia, between July and December 1981, they had carried out a mission for the Guatemalan revolutionary movement. This mission involved traveling to Panama, Cuba, Algeria and Libya in order to raise money. But in December, Valdivia reported, Pastora began to have contact with US officials.

The Guatemalan revolutionary movement declared that it maintained contact with Pastora for ten months, during which it learned of his "political and ideological inconsistency, and his lack of revolutionary commitment." Pastora continuously kept in touch with what the Guatemalan revolutionaries called "individuals linked to the counterrevolution in the Central American area."

Why Did Pastora Leave Nicaragua?

While Pastora has leveled several criticisms at the FSLN leadership, the principal cause of his defection lies in his personal ambition. As far back as October, 1978, just after the palace takeover, he told the *Washington Post* that his aspiration was to be president of Nicaragua. *Central America Report* notes that "some believed he felt unappreciated, aspiring to be a member of the [FSLN] National Directorate." And the Mexico City daily *Excelsior* described him as "an innate guerrilla organizer, good, brave and bold. He is, however, incapable of working in a professional military capacity within a regular army, and his political training is deficient."

Valdivia pointed out that the combination of personal vanity and lack of political understanding have made it possible for Pastora to change his attitude toward the revolution. "Edén was influenced by some Latin American politicians who led him to believe that he was a popular and well-liked man in Nicaragua and that he should be the one leading the revolution."

Some of Pastora's criticisms echo charges already made by the Reagan administration, which include alleged Soviet-Cuban influence, including the presence of Cuban advisers in Nicaragua; an "excessive" military build-up; and the problematic way in which the government has dealt with the Miskitu people of the Atlantic Coast. While many Nicaraguans agree with some aspects of Pastora's criticisms, most disagree with his methods.

Valdivia noted that Pastora felt that in the face of the increasingly aggressive US policy and actions toward Central America, Nicaragua's defense preparations were counterproductive insofar as they might further provoke the US. According to Valdivia, "Pastora's is a defeatist analysis, under the criteria that war is decided only by arms." That analysis is consistent with the ex-Sandinista's recent declarations: "This time I will not only be on the southern front; I'm going to conspire from Honduras, I'm going to go to the Atlantic Coast, to the cities of the Pacific . . . We will carry out the military actions that are necessary to finish off the forces foreign to our psyche."

Pastora's Role in the Counterrevolution

Despite his use of both anti-Soviet and anti-US rhetoric, and his apparent admiration of Fidel Castro (with whom he has compared himself), Pastora's actions play directly into the hands of US policy for Nicaragua and Central America. Armed actions against Nicaragua have increased in number and sophistication since last December, when the Reagan administration formally approved a $19 million plan to subvert the Nicaraguan government. But in order for such counterrevolutionary actions to lead to a viable alternative to the FSLN leadership, political figures with some degree of legitimacy among the Nicaraguan masses must be found. In this sense, Pastora is a key asset for the counterrevolution.

During recent weeks another key figure—Alfonso Robelo of the Nicaraguan Democratic Movement (MDN)—has also gone into self-imposed exile. Robelo, who was a member of the revolutionary junta from the July 1979 victory until April 1980 when he resigned, is considered a "moderate" in Washington. MDN spokesperson Álvaro Jerez confirmed that Robelo and Pastora were holding talks. It is rumored that the two may have signed an agreement according to which Pastora would be the president of a new government for the first six months. The FSLN, denouncing the imminent formation of a government in exile in which both Pastora and Robelo would play key roles, noted that they may have some problems due to the personal ambitions of both men.

Pastora's presence in Costa Rica coincided with stepped-up attacks by anti-Sandinista forces operating there. In late May Costa Rica expelled Commander Zero. He has since traveled to Europe, where he is attempting to drum up support for the anti-Sandinista forces among social democratic parties. Some Latin American social democratic parties, most notably Venezuela's *Acción Democrática*, have adopted an increasingly negative attitude toward the FSLN. Yet the most powerful sectors of international social democracy, based in Europe, have continued to support both the FSLN and the FDR-FMLN of El Salvador.

The Reagan administration would like nothing more than to drive a wedge between the powerful social democrats (who currently govern France and West Germany) and the revolutionary movements in Central America. Pastora, whose confused ideological orientation is often characterized as social democratic, is attempting to do just that.

Right-wing columnists Evans and Novak note the key role that Pastora can play in galvanizing counterrevolutionary forces: "Anti-Sandinista forces in Managua believe Pastora is a sincere, if confused, patriot whose popularity must be utilized."

Such thinking is also reflected in the recent statements of a US diplomat in the region. "So we're really pulling for *Comandante Cero*. There's no doubt about it. I don't know if we're giving him money, but I wouldn't be surprised if we were. He's our boy."

33. Analysis of Edén Pastora*

By Humberto Ortega

Comandante *Humberto Ortega, brother of Junta Coordinator Daniel Ortega, is minister of defense and a member of the nine-person National Directorate of the FSLN. Along with his brother he was a leader of the insurrectionalist or* Tercerista *faction of the FSLN.*

Pastora's ideological and political weaknesses became evident in the 1960s, when he participated in the armed movements against Somoza and refused to join Carlos Fonseca, Santos López, Silvio Mayorga, Germán Pomares and Tomás Borge. He chose to become part of the rebel groups of conservative and rightist ideology like those of his relative Indalecio Pastora.

We see Pastora side-by-side with adventurer Alejandro Martínez, who now heads Somozist bands in Costa Rica. Martínez has rejoined Pastora, who has decided that his counterrevolutionary movement will bear the acronym which was borne by the movement of his former boss, Alejandro Martínez, back in 1959, i.e., the acronym of the Sandino Revolutionary Front.

These simple reasons lead one to see clearly why Pastora was not one of the founders or creators of our vanguard, the FSLN, during those years. Those rebel groups which had no clear-cut ideology or revolutionary consistency disappeared rapidly and only our FSLN survived as a truly revolutionary organization. However, a man like Pastora could not be a militant of an organization like ours which, since the 1960's, has advocated waging a long and harsh struggle of self-denial and sacrifice.

That is why Pastora abandoned the guerrilla struggle and took advantage of the guarantees which were offered to him by puppet President René Schick from 1961 to 1966.

Between 1966 and 1967, Pastora reappeared in the political life as a full activist of the conservative movement of Fernando Aguero Rocha, another traitor, again giving proof of his ideological and political inconsistency and wavering. Pastora

---

*Reprinted from a speech given at the Rubén Darío Theatre in Managua on April 28, 1982.

was held prisoner for one month following the bloody events of January 22, 1967. After his release, Daniel Ortega, head of the FSLN urban resistance movement, asked him in Managua to again join our clandestine organization. Again he hesitated and became a simple collaborator of our persecuted (and resolute) combat organization, allowing his farm to be used so some of our fighters could be trained by our organization in various conspiratorial and military techniques.

During that same year, 1967, a Sandinist squad led by Oscar Turcios, (Edmundo Pérez) and Daniel Ortega carried out an initial, and bold, execution. It executed Sgt. [Gonzalo Lacayo], hated Somozist henchman who was one of the leading members of the somber security office of the tyrannical regime. The National Guard then unleashed a fierce repression against our fighters. Pastora again hesitated. He took asylum in the Venezuelan Embassy and left the country but did not join revolutionary activities abroad.

In 1970, Pastora joined the FSLN again. Showing patience and confidence once more, our organization decided to admit Pastora again and to allow him to participate in the work it was doing in the mountains in northern Nicaragua under the direction of Henry Ruiz, Modesto, and Víctor Tirado López. However, Pastora became desperate. He did not see victory near, and deserted from the mountains. He reached Matagalpa and then Carazo, where he joined rightist anti-Somozists Edmundo and Fernando Chamorro Rappaccioli, who now head the armed counterrevolution operating in Honduras and Costa Rica under CIA orders.

This took place between late 1972 and early 1973. Pastora left for Costa Rica, forsaking the struggle once more. From 1973 to August 1977, he led a peaceful family life, working first as a poor fisherman, until he became a fishing entrepreneur.

In October 1977, and at the cost of valuable militants, the FSLN launched the uninterrupted struggle which was to culminate with the popular victory of July 19. Our brothers Pedro Arau, member of the FSLN leadership, and Juan Carlos Herrera and Israel Levite, among others, died during this campaign.

Pastora then began to feel that victory was more probable and near. He looked for us, and the FSLN, wishing to train and help him follow the line of a true Sandinist, again admitted him among its ranks.

During the year 1978, the people carried out great struggles for the FSLN. A significant and decisive event in this struggle was the great national insurrection of September, to the preparation of which the FSLN devoted most of its cadres and efforts. Prior to the September insurrection, it was decided to carry out the operation at the National Palace to further promote insurrection by the people.

Germán Pomares was the militant chosen to lead the operation. Unfortunately, however, during those days his state of health did not allow him to assume this responsibility. As a show of confidence and encouragement for Pastora, and so that he would strengthen his revolutionary attitudes, we decided that he would lead the commandos.

Others of the domestic front, such as martyr [Oscar Pérez César], or the Carlos Nuñez brothers, [words indistinct] Duarte and Joaquín Cuadra were key figures in the organization of this Sandinist operation. However, they did not receive any publicity.

We can say that the Sandinist front carried out the National Palace operation and it created the publicized figure. Today we understand why the transnational press agencies gave greater publicity to Pastora than to the operation itself.

The people triumph. Edén is a figure loved by the people, because the people believe that the FSLN had created Cero and that he was of the FSLN. Our people knew the figure of Cero but not Pastora. They knew it. We knew it and the leaders of the FSLN were confident that Pastora, within the triumphant revolutionary process, would overcome his limitations and weaknesses. To be frank, we never believed that he would betray the people's cause and take up the weapons of Somozist counterrevolution at the service of the CIA.

When worst came to worst, we never expected him to withdraw from the movement, as he had done so many times before, from revolutionary political activity, to dedicate himself to business matters in our country or abroad.

When he said that he was going into revolutionary internationalism, we were sincerely glad, because we thought that in the harsh struggle of the revolutionary brothers from other peoples, he would finally become a true revolutionary. However, it was all a great publicity show. Today, we see him as an instrument of the CIA serving the most somber and reactionary interests of imperialism as was done yesterday by Moncada, Emiliano Chamorro and other traitors of our people.

Generally speaking, this is the sorry case of traitor Pastora, who will be consumed by the flaming revolutionary ardor of the people, which today hates him more than it loved him yesterday. . . .

34. "The Contra"*

By the Instituto Histórico Centroamericano

Because the conflict in Nicaragua is frequently depicted in the exterior as a civil war, and the contra forces as a viable alternative to the Sandinista government, it is useful to look at who comprises the contra, and who backs them.

A. The FDN (Nicaraguan Democratic Forces).

This group has become the most prominent contra force which has now embraced several smaller groups such as the 15th of September Legion and Steadman Fagoth's MISURASATA followers among the Miskito people who are in

---

*Reprinted from Instituto Histórico Centroamericano, *Envío,* Number 22, April 1983.

Honduras. The FDN was organized in 1981 by José Francisco "Chicano" Cardenal. Under CIA instructions, the organization was restructured in an effort to make it more acceptable internationally. This new political directorate was first announced at a press conference in Miami and also in a paid ad in *La Tribuna* in Tegucigalpa on March 21. The political directorate includes: (1) Edgar Chamorro, public relations representative for the wealthy Pellas family until 1979. He lives in Miami. (2) Enrique Bermudez Varela, National Guard colonel, military attaché in Washington under Somoza. He lives in Honduras. (3) Lucía Cardenal, widow of Jorge Salazar, wealthy coffee grower killed in a shoot-out with Nicaraguan police while gun-running. Salazar is now a "martyr" of the internal opposition. Sra. Salazar has close ties with this internal opposition. (4) Alfonso Callejas Deshán, Vice-President under Somoza, uncle of Alfonso Robelo. He lives in Miami. (5) Adolfo Calero Portocarrero, former manager of Coca Cola franchise in Managua, former leader of Conservative Party and leader of the Chamber of Commerce. He lives in Honduras. (6) Indalecio Rodríguez, right wing intellectual and ex-rector of the UCA. He works for the FDN in Panama. (7) Marcos Zeledán, former leader of COSEP and INDE (private sector organizations). He lives in Miami.

Calero had substantial holdings in the Coca Cola plant (which is not US owned but only a franchise), the El Camino Hotel, and the Datsun distributorship. According to Nicaraguan law, the property of counterrevolutionaries is subject to confiscation. Thus these enterprises have been impounded while it is determined what percentage belonged to Calero. Once that is determined, that part will be confiscated and made part of the APP or state property.

In Rome recently, Callejas, Sra. Salazar, and Zeledán called themselves the "political arm" of the invasion forces.

The military high command and operations leaders are all ex-Guardia, many of them from the EEBI, the hated and feared special forces under Somoza who were responsible for the worst of the repression and terror of the Somoza regime. Many use the same nicknames that they used under Somoza and their infamous past is well-remembered by the Nicaraguans.

One Sandinista who fought on the Southern Front in the insurrection said recently, "And to think that we turned 'El Diablo' [one of the high command of the contra] over to Costa Rican authorities!" A *US News and World Report* article in the March 14 issue said, "Sandinista vengeance is lasting. The prisons still hold about 3,500 former National Guardsmen of the Somoza regime that ran the country for 46 years." If the Sandinistas had really practiced "vengence" many of the contra would not be alive to be invading the country. Instead the FSLN abolished the death penalty and tried to rehabilitate the Guardia. In spite of the current difficulties this policy has not changed.

The FDN claims it gets its weapons on the black market, mainly in Florida, with funds provided by unnamed sources. They say other weapons have been donated by the Honduran Army. Large-scale military maneuvers between US and Honduran forces, such as Halcón Vista in November 1981, and Big Pine in February 1983, are additional sources of supplies, both to Honduran military and to contra forces.

The FDN operates the clandestine Radio 15 de Septiembre out of Tegucigalpa and publishes *América Libre* in California.

One question mark in the new structure of the FDN is the absence from the new directorate of founder "Chicano" Cardenal. Apparently he was so openly associated with acts such as the killing of 15 in San Francisco del Norte in July, that a new image was sought. However, Cardenal is still making statements in the name of the FDN. He was quoted in *Tiempo* (Honduras) on March 24 as saying, "There is an agreement between the forces in the north and the south that this operation continue."

B. Costa Rican Groups.

Last fall four contra groups in Costa Rica formed an alliance which they called ARDE (Democratic Revolutionary Alliance). The groups included the MDN (Nicaraguan Democratic Movement) of Alfonso Róbelo; UDN-FARN of "Negro" Chamorro-Rappaccioli; Brooklyn Rivera's faction of MISURASATA; and Edén Pastora's FRS (Sandino Revolutionary Front). Pastora boasted that ARDE "has the support of 2.5 million Nicaraguans [the entire population]. The armed forces are behind us."

However the ARDE alliance cracked recently. Chamorro, in a paid ad in the Costa Rican papers on March 23, announced that his UDN-FARN [that was part of the FDN when it was formed but later broke away] was withdrawing from the alliance "for ideological differences." The ad said that the word "dialogue" does not exist in the UDN-FARN vocabulary. Chamorro's ad went on that the FDN had "cleaned out their ranks" of Somocistas in order to improve their image and there were moves toward uniting his group with the FDN, again. The ad also said they were maintaining close contact with Fagoth, whom it now called "the authentic leader of MISURASATA," and they hoped to consolidate their efforts.

Numbers of armed contra in Costa Rica are much less than in Honduras but Costa Rica authorities claim to have dismantled eight camps near the Nicaraguan border. The divisions within the Monge government are evident in the flip-flopping policy that one day turns a blind eye on the contra and the next raids and dismantles their camps. Observers in Costa Rica tell us that when Pastora called for a general insurrection for April 15, he seemed to overstep his welcome and has been less visible recently. Costa Rican Foreign Minister Volio said in Nicaragua on April 4 that Pastora had been expelled from Costa Rica on March 28 and left for Mexico in a private plane. Pastora had stated that he will not operate a southern front in Costa Rica but will work from inside; but he has also said he has nothing to do with the FDN. On his clandestine radio station on March 27, he claimed that the 25,000 (!) internationalists in Nicaragua are the Sandinista's only support.

C. Contradictions in the Contra.

As happened when the CIA mounted the Bay of Pigs operation, a major factor in what the *New York Times* refers to as the "Bay of Piglets" is the lack of unity among the various contra groups. Steadman Fagoth and Brooklyn Rivera both claim to be the maximum leader of the dissident Miskitu people and seem unable to work together. Hard as it tries, the FDN cannot rid itself of its Somocista image or its military leadership that depends on ex-Guardia and EEBI officers. This base will prevent it from ever having broad support within Nicaragua, even among people who are unhappy with the present government. The FDN, in its fanatical anti-Communism (its radio station frequently says, "With God and patriotism we are fighting communism"), distrusts Pastora who has a love-hate relationship with the Cuban revolution and an admitted admiration for Che Guevara. ARDE wants to disassociate itself from the Guardia and so cooperation with the FDN is unworkable, but it has no substantial military capabilities on its own.

In addition, many of the exiles in Miami, in Honduras and in Costa Rica are vain and ambitious and all want assurances of being on top in the unlikely event that the Sandinistas could be overthrown.

One other factor, the CIA's manipulations are so well-known and have been experienced first hand throughout Latin America, that the contra groups want to give a certain impression of independence—which is more and more difficult as CIA involvement becomes more open.

The presentation of the FDN as some sort of democratic force contradicts their own stated program. As summed up in a March 22 *Christian Science Monitor* article by Larry Boyd, "their program calls for a rollback of the Agrarian Reform in Nicaragua, including return of properties confiscated from Somoza, release of National Guardsmen now jailed by the Sandinistas, and condemns the literacy campaign as a Marxist-Leninist plot." These are the most popular Sandinista programs which have benefited thousands of Nicaragua's poor.

35. Reagan's "Freedom Fighters"*

By the Center for Constitutional Rights and the National Lawyers Guild

UNITED STATES DISTRICT COURT FOR THE DISTRICT OF COLUMBIA
Javier Sánchez-Espinoza, resident of the village of San Francisco de Guajiniquilapa, Department of Chinandega, Republic of Nicaragua;
Myrna Cunningham, resident of Bluefields, Department of Zelaya, Republic of Nicaragua;
Brenda Rocha, resident of the village of Bonanza, Department of Zelaya, Republic of Nicaragua;

---

*Excerpts from a lawsuit filed in US district court for the District of Columbia by Sánchez-Espinoza et. al.

María Espinal-Mondragón (Viuda de Guevara), individually and as personal representative of Victorino Guevara-Centeno, resident of the village of San Francisco de Guajiniquilapa, Department of Chinandega, Republic of Nicaragua;

Victorino Hernández-Aguilera, resident of the village of San Francisco de Guajiniquilapa, Department of Chinandega, Republic of Nicaragua;

José Santos-Barrera, individually and as personal representative of Evilio Baquedano-Barrera, resident of the village of San Francisco de Guajiniquilapa, Department of Chinandega, Republic of Nicaragua;

Elia María Espinoza (Viuda de Moncada), individually and as personal representative of Ramón Aristides Moncada, resident of the village of San Francisco de Guajiniquilapa, Department of Chinandega, Republic of Nicaragua;

Ronald V. Dellums, in his capacity as a member of the United States House of Representatives, 213 Rayburn House Office Building, Washington, D.C. 20515;

Eleanor Ginsberg, *ex rel.* State of Florida 9500 Southwest 60th Court, Miami, Florida, 33156; and

Larry O'Toole, *ex rel.* State of Florida, 15625 Southwest 102nd Place, Miami, Florida 33157,

Plaintiffs,
-against-

Ronald Wilson Reagan, individually and in his official capacity as President of the United States;

William Casey, individually and in his official capacity as Director of Central Intelligence;

Alexander M. Haig, Jr.;

George P. Schultz, individually and in his official capacity as United States Secretary of State;

Thomas O. Enders, individually and in his official capacity as United States Assistant Secretary of State;

Vernon Walters, individually and in his official capacity as United States Ambassador-at-Large;

Caspar Weinberger, individually and in his official capacity as United States Secretary of Defense;

Nestor Sánchez, individually and in his official capacity as United States Assistant Secretary of Defense;

John D. Negroponte, individually and in his official capacity as United States Ambassador to Honduras;

Frank Granizo, individually and in his capacity as an official of the Central Intelligence Agency;
Jorge González;
Hector Alfonso;
Inter-American Defense Force, an unincorporated association;
Edmundo Chamorro;
Fernando Chamorro;
Max Vargas;
David Stadthagen;
Nicaraguan Democratic Union — Revolutionary Armed Forces of Nicaragua, an unincorporated association;
Nicaraguan Democratic Front, an unincorporated association;
Steadman Fagoth-Mueller;
Pedro Ortega;
Nicaraguan Liberation Army, an unincorporated association;
Enrique Bermudez;
15th of September Legion, an unincorporated association;
José Francisco Cardenal;
Nicaraguan Democratic Force, an unincorporated association;
Alpha 66, an unincorporated association; and
Association of Bay of Pigs Veterans-Brigade 2506, an unincorporated association,

Defendants.

Introductory Statement

1. This action is brought *inter alia* on behalf of various Nicaraguan citizens who have been murdered, tortured, mutilated, wounded, kidnapped and/or raped as a result of US-sponsored paramilitary activities designed to ravage the civilian population of Nicaragua and to destroy its economy. Plaintiffs sue for damages caused by these acts of terror and for an injunction to prevent such attacks in the future. These United States sponsored raids against the people of Nicaragua violate fundamental principles of human rights established under international law and the Constitution of the United States.

2. This suit also seeks to enjoin the operation of US-sponsored and condoned paramilitary training camps operating in Florida, California and elsewhere. People trained in these camps engage in terrorist attacks on civilians in Nicaragua. The maintenance and sponsorship of these camps, which are in the United States and which violate US neutrality laws, constitute a nuisance under Florida law. Plaintiffs Eleanor Ginsberg and Larry O'Toole, residents of Dade County, Florida, sue under Florida law to close these camps.

3. Plaintiff Ronald V. Dellums, a member of Congress, sues to stop the unde-

clared war waged by defendants against the people of Nicaragua. Such an undeclared war conducted by the US government, sometimes using a proxy army, violates plaintiff's authority as a member of Congress to declare war under Article I, Section 8, Clause 11 of the United States Constitution and the Neutrality Act . . . .

Facts

40. United States government defendants, acting in conspiracy with other defendants and others unknown, have authorized, financed, trained and directed activities which terrorize and otherwise injure the civilian population of the Republic of Nicaragua. As an intended or foreseeable result of these activities, plaintiffs herein have suffered and continue to be threatened with torture, murder, kidnapping, mutilation, rape, wounding and other injuries.

41. In addition to harming individual civilians, the defendants' conspiracy and their activities include:

a. Destroying hospitals, bombing bridges, razing communities, destroying crops, stealing cattle, and cutting communications lines; and,

b. Destroying the livelihood of thousands of innocent Nicaraguan civilians and leaving them homeless refugees.

42. Among the goals of the defendants' conspiracy is the terrorizing of the civilian population of Nicaragua as a means of destabilizing the Nicaraguan government. In furtherance of this goal defendants are:

a. Supporting, arming and training former Somoza National Guardsmen and other terrorist groups to enable them to attack innocent civilians;

b. Assisting the Honduran armed forces to provide military assistance to such groups;

c. Utilizing economic means including withdrawal of promised US aid and discouraging financial aid by other countries;

d. Covertly supporting opposition parties; and,

e. Manipulating the press in Nicaragua and elsewhere.

43. This conspiracy is directed against the people of Nicaragua, a country with which the United States is at peace.

44. In November of 1981, as part of the conspiracy, pursuant to a Reagan administration request, the CIA presented an option plan covering covert activities which would result in terrorizing and otherwise harming the people of Nicaragua.

45. On information and belief, the plan set forth above was reviewed and aspects of it were approved by various members of the National Security Council and others, including, but not limited to defendant President Ronald Reagan, defendant Director of Central Intelligence William Casey, defendant former Secretary of State Alexander M. Haig, former National Security Adviser Richard Allen, defendant Assistant Secretary of State Thomas O. Enders, defendant Secretary of Defense Caspar Weinberger, defendant Deputy Assistant Secretary of Defense Nestor Sánchez, and Edwin Meese, Counsel to the President. The approved plan is hereinafter referred to as the "Plan. . . ."

52. Defendants acting in concert, support, train and direct terrorist training camps in Honduras (see Appendix I) and Nicaragua (see Appendix II). On information and belief, there are up to 10,000 terrorists operating out of these camps.

53. Defendants, acting in concert, launched hundreds of raids from these camps against innocent Nicaraguan civilians and against economic targets which had provided Nicaraguans with the basic necessities of life, causing grievous injury to the plaintiffs and other civilians.

54. On or about November 1, 1982, US defendants or their agents admitted that the US was supporting clandestine military operations against the people of Nicaragua. They admittted that the CIA provides money, military equipment and military training to the "anti-Nicaraguan" forces and that this support is part of the covert military operation plan approved by defendant Reagan.

55. Upon information and belief, the appropriate members of Congress have never been fully and accurately informed about the extent of the Plan, as required by law. . . .

Paramilitary Attacks on the Civilian Population of Nicaragua

84. The above-described terrorist organizations, financed, trained and otherwise supported by the US government defendants, have carried out, in furtherance of the conspiracy, scores of attacks upon innocent Nicaraguan civilians. These attacks, some of which are described below, resulted in summary execution, murder, abduction, torture, rape, wounding, and the destruction of private property and public facilities.

85. On November 22, 1981, terrorist forces kidnapped security officer Granicio Edén Tom in the community of Krasa. He was taken to Honduras, tortured and killed. The Nicaraguan Democratic Force claimed responsibility for his murder.

86. On November 23, 1981, four terrorists raided the Cerro Dorado mine and took three hostages to Honduras. The three, José Medina, Juan Spelman Zuniga and Norman Castro, were later murdered.

87. On November 30, 1981, terrorists attacked Nicaraguans near Asang. Julio César Granados and Edgard Espinoza González were killed. Ignacio Ortega Sequeira and Juan Rugama Duarte were taken to Honduras where they were assassinated.

88. On December 2, 1981, terrorists attacked San Jerónimo, kidnapped health official Benigno Romero, and abducted him to Honduras where he was tortured and murdered.

89. On December 7, 1981, terrorists from Honduras crossed the border and attacked several towns in Nicaragua. In Asang, stores were raided and Genaro Williams and Arles Escobar were kidnapped, taken to Honduras and tortured and murdered. The towns of Andrés and Tara were raided and Fabio Barrera, Bacíleo Barrera, and his son were murdered. In Ulwas, Agustín Brismon López was kidnapped and murdered. The terrorists then raided the community of Krasa kidnapping Elmos and Hernando Ralf, who were taken to Honduras and murdered.

90. On December 13, 1981, in a brutal attack on San Carlos, 12 Nicaraguans were kidnapped, taken to Honduras and murdered. On information and belief, Efraín Omier Wilson led this attack. Numerous other Nicaraguans were tortured.

91. On December 18, 1981, as Nicaraguans searched for those captured at San Carlos, four of the searchers were ambushed and murdered including Rafael Gómez Rios, José Antonio Torres and Bernabé Pérez Solís.

92. On December 21, 1981, several Nicaraguans were killed by terrorists at San Carlos. Others were wounded, tortured and mutilated. Naked bodies were thrown in a common grave, with hands tied behind backs. A man whose legs had been broken and who had been shot in the stomach was still alive, and was then taken by the terrorists, tied to a post, stabbed in the chest, and killed.

93. On December 28, 1981, the village of Bilwaskarma was attacked. Terrorist forces ransacked the hospital. Plaintiff Dr. Myrna Cunningham, Regina Lewis, a nurse, and two hospital administrators were kidnapped. The two women were raped as were 13 other women from the town.

94. On December 31, 1981, 25 terrorists attacked the village of Anorestara, kidnapping José Morales. Morales was subsequently found decapitated, with his eyes removed from their sockets.

95. On March 14, 1982, terrorists invading Nicaragua from camps in Honduras blew up a bridge on the Río Negro on the highway leading to El Guasaule, a town on the Nicaraguan-Honduran border. They also caused substantial damage to another bridge. After the explosions, a US made M-18 antipersonnel mine and US-made rolls of detonation cable were found. Defendant National Liberation Army claimed responsibility for destruction of the bridges.

96. On July 3, 1982, terrorists, with the support of the Honduran Army, attacked the village of Seven Benk, Province of Zelaya. There were 200 attackers armed with FAL and M-16 rifles, rocket launchers and M-79 grenade launchers. The attack lasted for three days and resulted in 30 civilian dead, 12 wounded and 11 kidnapped. Captured weapons included automatic rifles, disposable rocket launchers and grenades, all made in the United States.

97. On July 24, 1982, plaintiff Brenda Rocha was at the village of Salto, in the Province of Zelaya, about 20 kilometers from her home in the village of Bonanza. Salto was attacked by about 100 terrorists, and she and seven other townspeople took cover in a trench. The seven others were killed, and plaintiff Rocha was wounded in the arm. She pretended to be dead until the attackers departed. She was later rescued, but her wound was so serious that her arm had to be amputated.

98. On the same day, July 24, 1982, approximately 130 armed terrorists, who, upon information and belief, were members of defendant Nicaraguan Democratic Front, attacked the small rural farming town of San Francisco de Guajiniquilapa (norte), Province of Chinandega, Nicaragua, at about 6 A.M. The town is located about 12 kilometers from the Honduran border. On information and belief, the attacks were launched from camps in Honduras.

99. The attackers were dressed in two types of uniforms—some wore dark blue uniforms similar to those of FUSEP, a special unit of the Honduran Army, and

others wore olive green uniforms. They attacked the town with FAL and Galil rifles, mortars, rocket launchers and machine guns.

100. Townspeople tried to defend the town for about two and one half hours. Fifteen villagers were killed: Walter Baquedano-Espinoza, Reynaldo Barrera-Carrazco, Evelio Barrera-Baquedano, Justo Espinal-Moreno, Victorino Espinal-Moreno, Alfredo Espinoza-Aguilera, Luís Alberto Espinoza-Moncada (15 years old), Donald Espinoza, Victorino Guevara-Centeno, Reymundo García-Montenegro, Domingo Laínez, Hugo Martínez-Espinoza, Ramón Aristides Moncada, Ángel Sánchez-Pérez and Félix Pedro Sánchez-Guido. Four villagers were wounded: Aristides Espinoza-Aguilera, Armando Espinoza-Hernández, Arturo Espinoza-Sánchez and plaintiff Victorino Hernández-Aguilera.

101. After the battle, the attackers ran through the town painting "FDN" on buildings and shouting "Long Live the Nicaraguan Democratic Front," and "With God and Patriotism We'll Defeat Communism." People were told to come out of their houses or the soldiers would break down the doors.

102. Some of the attackers then ransacked homes, stores and the town's municipal building. They took food, clothing, money and horses and destroyed the telephone system.

103. Eight people were kidnapped, including a fifteen-year-old boy, plaintiff Javier Sánchez-Espinoza, who was seized from his home. The others were: Oscar Espinal Benavides, Constantino Espinoza, Santiago Espinoza-Betanco (who was wounded), José Santos Gómez, Ismael Meza Castellán, Timoteo Moreno (who is blind), and Félix Pedro Moncada-Neyra.

104. After the attackers left the town, plaintiff José Santos-Barrera found the body of his son, Evelio Baquedano-Barrera. He was lying face up, his legs destroyed, his chest bullet-ridden. His watch had been taken and his pockets turned inside out.

105. Plaintiff Elia María Espinoza discovered the body of her husband, Ramón Aristides Moncada. His head had been destroyed; his brains were falling out. His chest had a hole in it that appeared to have been made with a knife and a knife handle was protruding from his back. Plaintiff Espinoza lost seven members of her family in the attack, including her brother, nephew, uncle, and cousin, as well as her husband.

106. Plaintiff María Espinal Mondragón found the body of her husband, Victorino Guevara Centeno, with holes in his neck, stomach and right leg. His throat, as well as the throats of other victims lying near him, had been slit.

107. About 80 mortar shells were left behind bearing the marking "Made in USA." In one home, the attackers left matches and pills marked "Made in USA." The pills were later found to be poison.

108. On information and belief, this attack was carried out by defendant Nicaraguan Democratic Front, which took credit for the attack. . . .

127. The aforesaid conspiracy and acts of defendants constitute torts in violation of the law of nations and treaties of the United States including, but not limited to: the UN Charter, the Universal Declaration of Human Rights, the UN Declara-

tion against Torture, the American Declaration of the Rights and Duties of Man, the O.A.S. Charter, the American Convention on Human Rights, the Charter of International Military Tribunal (Nuremberg Charter), the General Assembly Resolution adopting the Nuremberg Charter Principles, the Geneva Convention (IV) Relative to the Protection of Civilian Persons, the Inter-American Treaty of Reciprocal Assistance, the General Assembly Resolution, "Declaration on Principles of International Law Concerning Friendly Relations and Cooperation among States," the Treaty of Friendship, Commerce and Navigation between the United States and Nicaragua, and other pertinent declarations, documents and practices constituting the customary international law of human rights and the law of nations. . . .

131. The aforesaid conspiracy and acts of the defendants are carried out in violation of the Fourth and Fifth Amendments to the United States Constitution; the National Security Act of 1947, 50 USC. §§401 *et seq.*; the Hughes-Ryan Amendment, 50 USC. §413; the Neutrality Act, 18 USC. §960; the War Powers Resolution, 50 USC. §§1541 *et seq.*; and Article I, section 8, Clause 11 of the United States Constitution, giving Congress the power to declare war. . . .

Appendix I: Border Training in Camps in Honduras

1. San Judas Base—14 kilometers west of San Pedro de Potrero Grande. Weaponry at the base includes hand grenades, M-79 grenade launchers, 60 and 81 mm mortars, bazookas and helicopters.
2. Cerro Baldoquin Base—11 kilometers northwest of San Pedro de Potrero Grande. Approximately 700 people at the camp. Armaments at the camp similar to San Judas camp.
3. San Marcos de Colán—400 to 600 people at the camp.
4. Cacamuya Base—600 ex-Somoza guardsmen at the camp led by Alcides Espinoza. Weapons similar to San Judas.
5. Trojes Base—10 kilometers northeast of Teoticaciente. 400 to 600 ex-Somoza guardsmen at the camp. Operations center on Jalapa area.
6. La Ladoza—(also called "Nicaragua" Military Training Base). This camp is a school for ex-Somoza guardsmen who are transferred to other camps or sent directly to Nicaragua to operate as paramilitary bands. Approximately 130 to 150 ex-guardsmen led by Benito Bravo. Weapons similar to San Judas.
7. Monte de Aguila Base—10 kilometers northeast of Jalapa. Approximately 250 guardsmen at the camp. Armaments similar to San Judas.
8. Hacienda La Estrella Base—12 kilometers southwest of Jalapa. Approximately 250 ex-guardsmen at this camp. Armaments similar to San Judas.
9. Cerro Los Nubarrones Base—10 kilometers west of Jalapa. Approximately 200 ex-guardsmen. Armaments similar to San Judas.
10. Auka Base—36 kilometers northeast of Leymus. Approximately 400 ex-guardsmen at the camp. Armaments include FAL and M-16 rifles, M-79 grenade launchers and rocket launchers.
11. Rus Base—37 kilometers northwest of Leymus. Approximately 400 ex-

guardsmen. Armaments similar to San Judas.
12. Mokoron Camp—35 kilometers north of Leymus. Approximately 400 ex-guardsmen. Armaments similar to San Judas.
13. Guasaula—Northeast of Somotillo.
14. Choluteca—Northeast of Somotillo.
15. Orocuina—Northeast of Somotillo.
16. San Antonio de Flores—West of Santa María.
17. Las Tunas—Northwest of Santa María.
18. El Pescadero—UDN camp near El Paraíso.
19. Tablazo
20. Arenales—near Tablazo.

Appendix II: Terrorist Bases within Nicaragua

1. Sandy Bay, Loma, Kaska and Dakora—200 persons.
2. Kukulaya—Lapan, Haulover—Southwest of Puerto Cabezas—200 persons.
3. Musawas—Northeast of Bonanza—100 persons.
4. Wina, Kuwali, El Ocote, Santa Rose de Tapaskon—In Department of Jinotega—200 persons.
5. Chachagua, Palo Prieto, Cerro Zacateras, Murra Cuidad Sandino—100-150 persons.
6. Labu, Kukinita, Tadasna, Waylawas—South of Sirina.
7. Wapi, Cerro El Cacao, Cerro El Pinol Okonwas, Cerro La Flor—100 persons.

36. We're Not Doing This to Solve the Problems of El Salvador*

By "Commander Mack"

"Commander Mack" is the nom de guerre of José Benito Bravo Centeno, a commander in the Nicaraguan Democratic Force (FDN), the largest counterrevolutionary organization and based in Honduras. He served previously in Somoza's National Guard from 1956 to 1979, reaching the rank of lieutenant. He was also a bodyguard for Somoza's son and was trained in counterinsurgency in Colombia and at the US army's School of the Americas in the Panama Canal Zone. After the 1979 Sandinista victory he fled to El Salvador, and later to Honduras. The following interview was conducted inside of Nicaraguan territory, in the department of

Nueva Segovia, by a film crew traveling with a clandestine counterrevolutionary group. The transcript is from a 16mm film being released by Skylight Pictures.

My name is José Benito Bravo Centeno. I am Comandante Mack of the Nicaraguan Democratic Force. I am commander of the operational force in Zone 1, Nueva Segovia, Nicaragua.

Q: What is the F.D.N.?

A: The F.D.N. is a political/military organization working for a change in Nicaragua. We are fighting against international communism.

My country paid for my training in the United States, the (Panama) Canal Zone, in South America and Central America. I took courses in Colombia, Chile, El Salvador and Lackland, Texas.

You could say that this is a sacred war because we believe in God and we're fighting an enemy who denies God's existence. Knowing this, yes, you can say it's a sacred war.

Of course, the United States can do a lot. Not just sending arms. It has economic power and persuasion. It has political and diplomatic influence to such a degree that it can help a great deal. We are very hopeful and we have a lot of faith in the United States. [We are] tremendously convinced that if anything is going to change in our country, it will be thanks to the combined effort of the US and the people here with rifles.

Q: Do you think that the economic pressure put on the Sandinista government by the United States has helped you?

A: Yes, I would say that it has been efficient, the economic pressure has helped bring us to the point that we're at today. It has helped so that we the Nicaraguans have had an opportunity to organize and confront communism in our country. Yes, I believe that the economic measures taken by the United States are efficient, are noble, against an enemy that is not noble, that is stupid. So the economic measures are good.

Q: Which measures?

A: For example, the economic measures that the United States has taken against Nicaragua withholding loans and a series of private institutions that haven't received aid from other US private institutions. This has created an economic conflict in Nicaragua. Although the people suffer from this, the government has to deal with it and this has national and international repercussions.

Many times, due to a small amount of aid [money], there are more deaths, so we have to fight harder. With more aid, there are more means and more persuasion and the struggle will be shorter. The aid at this time is good, but if we get more, it would be even better. If we have 1,000 FALs [rifles] then we are 1,000 rifles. If we have 3 pistols, then we'd be 3 pistols, and with 3 pistols, we can't negotiate. But with 1,000 FAL rifles, yes, we can be identified as being 1,000 rifles. And if there are 10,000 rifles, we have to be reckoned with. So we are thankful that there are 10,000 FAL rifles and more.

It doesn't bother us to admit this. There's nothing to hide. We're thankful to the

United States and I for one believe in the United States and I'm very happy that the people of the United States understand our situation because here are your dollars. (pats gun) And it's hard to let go of your dollars to give to somebody else. Even if it's a rifle—which is a war weapon—they're giving us the means to solve the problem that can't be solved in any other way because international communism doesn't negotiate with anyone. They don't solve the problems by talking. They force men to take this only alternative of taking up arms.

We've experienced an extraordinary change in a short period of time. At one time we carried hand guns and worthless rifles. To get a weapon from the enemy we had to fight a lot. Overnight we got help and now we are a force—that you have seen. Everyone who turns on a radio or reads a cable is going to know that we're fighting for the country.

We're not doing this to solve the problems in El Salvador or to save El Salvador. We're contributing to that, but we have to be clear that we're fighting for Nicaragua.

Chapter II:

Response to US Intervention

Editors' Introduction

The response to the Reagan administration's covert war against Nicaragua has been almost uniformly negative. We include as examples several short pieces by distinguished commentators that appeared in the *New York Times*. The following piece by Kevin J. Kelley responds not just to US actions, but also to the other responses by critics of the war. Finally, the analysis by Robert White, former US ambassador to El Salvador under Carter, predicts that the next Reagan administration strategy will be to regionalize the Central American conflicts.

37. *Shame in Nicaragua**

By Tom Wicker

Tom Wicker is an associate editor of the New York Times *and a regular contributor to the Op-Ed page.*

Unison Whiteman, the Foreign Minister of Grenada, said the other day that he had "evidence" that his nation was the target of an "imminent attack" by the United States.

"Ridiculous," said Alan Romberg, a State Department spokesman.

---

*Reprinted from the *New York Times,* April 1, 1983.

So it is, as seen from Washington or New York or Peoria or anywhere outside the Caribbean. But the charge will not seem so ridiculous in Grenada or elsewhere in the gulf and Central America.

Gringo intervention is part of the region's history. President Reagan just recently displayed photos of an airfield under construction on Grenada as "evidence" of threatening Soviet-Cuban intentions in the Caribbean. And American involvement in the "destabilization" of Nicaragua has been so authoritatively reported from so many sources that it seems hardly to be doubted.

"Diverse Nicaraguan exile groups," writes Alan Riding of the *New York Times*, "now concede that the Reagan administration, working through the Central Intelligence Agency, forged them into a single force, the Nicaraguan Democratic Force" (F.D.N., by its Spanish initials). American arms are openly displayed in insurgent camps along the Honduran border. CIA officials have testified about the Nicaraguan operation to the Congressional intelligence committees.

In UN debate, the Netherlands, Spain and Pakistan—allies all—openly doubted Washington's insistence that the insurgency is an internal affair motivated by Nicaraguans' disillusionment with the leftist Sandinist regime. Only Honduras, where the insurgents mount their raids, and El Salvador, a US client, supported that interpretation.

In the absence of credible refutation from Washington—the State Department neither confirms nor denies involvement, and neither did President Reagan during his mini-news-conference—it seems depressingly clear that the US *is* trying to destabilize Nicaragua. Whether the goal is to overthrow the Sandinists or merely make them more amenable to Reagan administration pressures is not so clear.

Either way, the CIA operation appears to be violating the Boland Amendment, which prohibits support of paramilitary forces "with the purpose" of overthrowing the Nicaraguan government. Philip Taubman of the *Times* reports that CIA officials claim they aren't trying to overthrow that government, hence are observing the letter of the Boland Amendment. That's like saying you're hitting a man with a hammer but not trying to kill him; and it's the kind of sleazy, hair-splitting "deniability" that debases language and credibility alike.

The parallel drawn in the UN debate and elsewhere between Nicaraguan intervention in El Salvador and that of the US in Nicaragua is sleazy, too. Aside from the disputed question how much the Salvadoran guerrillas are sponsored, armed and encouraged by the Sandinists, should the United States hold itself to no higher standards than those it rightly condemns in others? Is the covert, armed destabilization of even an obstreperous nation permissible to a democratic, lawabiding power?

We deny that right to the Soviet Union, Cuba, Nicaragua; what gives it to us? The pleas that they do it, so we can too, reflects the puerile ethic of the schoolyard: "You did it first!"

Even without a long history of intervention from the North—US power established and largely maintained the Somoza regime that the Sandinists ousted—the destabilization of Nicaragua alienates and alarms nonclient states in the hemisphere (witness Foreign Minister Whiteman); gives the Sandinist government opportunity to deflect Nicaraguans' attention from its failures, repressions and broken promises; confuses international opinion, which ought to be dubious about the direction of the Sandinists; probably drives them further in that direction, and tarnishes the good name of the United States, among allies as well as nonaligned nations.

But even if for some hard-nosed reason of power politics the destabilization of the Sandinist regime could be tenuously justified, the administration and the CIA appear to have learned nothing from past disasters, as in Southeast Asia or at the Bay of Pigs. Not only is this an undeclared war, subverting constitutional procedure and waged without leave from Congress or the public; but numerous supporters of the deposed Somoza regime are known to be prominent among the insurgents. One former officer of Somoza's hated National Guard is a member of the political directorate of the F.D.N.

How can the Reagan administration defend arming, training and supporting these surviving elements of the Somoza government, one of the most corrupt and repressive the hemisphere has experienced? How can Washington even pretend that an "insurgency" so tainted can develop anything like popular support among Nicaraguans? How can the people of the United States accept without protest a gangster operation that shames rather than defends democracy?

38. *To the People of the United States**

By Gabriel García Márquez et al.

Gabriel García Márquez is a Colombian writer who was awarded the 1982 Nobel Prize for Literature. Carlos Fuentes (Mexico), Günter Grass (Germany), Graham Greene (England), Julio Cortázar (Argentina), William Styron (United States), and Heinrich Böll (Germany) are all leading writers.

The present United States administration has gone to war against the people and government of Nicaragua.

It is an undeclared war, unauthorized by Congress and, therefore, unconstitutional. It is a covert war. The American people have not authorized the use of public funds for a war waged in the name of supposed intelligence operations.

It is an irrational war. It renounces diplomatic negotiations without giving them a serious try.

It is a reactionary war. The United States created and then supported the corrupt Somoza dictatorship during more than 40 years. Now it cannot tolerate an independent government in Nicaragua. It has armed the former guardsmen of the

---

*Reprinted from the *New York Times* (advertisement), April 17, 1983.

Somoza regime against the people of Nicaragua.

It is an inhuman war. It is destroying the modest but profound achievements of the Nicaraguan revolution. It is destroying the crops and schools of Nicaragua. It is killing the children and the peasants of Nicaragua.

It is a dangerous war. It wrenches the problems of Nicaragua and Central America out of their peculiar cultural and historical contexts and thrusts them onto the stage of east-west conflict. This distortion can internationalize the war and destroy opportunities for diplomacy, democracy and social advancements in the region.

It is a treacherous war. It is the fourth time in this century that the United States has invented pretexts to invade Nicaragua. This time, it is doing so by mercenary means, pitting brothers against brothers and countries against countries in the region. It is an immoral war. Once again, a superpower declares itself menaced by the independence of a small nation and attempts its submission by intimidation or its destruction by force.

We fear that the United States government is attempting to implement policy by "accomplished fact"—in Nicaragua, leaving no room for debate or opposition.

We are also confident that the people of the United States, their public opinion and their democratic institutions will speak out against this undeclared, covert, irrational, inhuman, dangerous and immoral adventure undertaken by the government of Ronald Reagan.

SPONSORED BY:
Gabriel García Márquez
Carlos Fuentes
Günter Grass
Graham Greene
Julio Cortázar
William Styron
Heinrich Böll

39. Illegally Aiding Latins*

By Kenneth E. Sharpe

Kenneth Sharpe is associate professor of political science at Swarthmore College.

Two members of the Senate Intelligence Committee, Daniel Patrick Moynihan and Patrick J. Leahy, have publicly suggested that the Reagan administration may be violating a December 1982 law forbidding the United States to support any attempt to overthrow the Nicaraguan government. But Jeane J. Kirkpatrick, America's chief delegate to the United Nations, has pleaded not guilty, claiming "absolutely that no law is being broken." Is the Administration breaking the law?

Evidence mounts that the Central Intelligence Agency is conducting operations against Nicaragua far larger than the abortive Bay of Pigs attempt to overthrow Fidel Castro in 1961, a landmark fiasco in United States foreign policy. The CIA has funded, trained and equipped paramilitary groups operating under the banner of the Nicaraguan Democratic Force, whose public aim is the overthrow of the Sandinist government. Other aid is diverted by the CIA, the United States Embassy in Honduras and the Honduran military from funds Congress approved for Honduras.

In December 1982, Congressional concern about these operations led to passage of an amendment offered by Representative Edward P. Boland, chairman of the House Intelligence Committee. In language initially worked out with the CIA, the amendment bans financial support for "military equipment, military training or advice, or other support for military activities . . . for the purpose of overthrowing the government of Nicaragua or provoking a military exchange between Nicaragua and Honduras."

Is the administration, then, breaking the law? The CIA, like Mrs. Kirkpatrick, would say no, claiming its purpose was not to "overthrow" the Nicaraguan government but merely to harass the Sandinists and interdict arms it claims are moving from Nicaragua to El Salvador.

Could the CIA be shown to be lying about its intent? Does Congress need proof that the CIA actually told the exiles to use its funds to overthrow the Sandinists? No. If the CIA continues supporting paramilitary groups it knows are actively seeking the overthrow of the Sandinists and whose activities risk triggering a conflict between Honduras and Nicaragua, there are reasonable grounds to establish intent.

The problem is not lack of evidence but Congressional willingness to accept such legal sophistry. The Boland language was initially chosen to block Representative

---

*Reprinted from the *New York Times,* April 9, 1983.

Thomas R. Harkin's unambiguous amendment that would have cut all funding for military activities "in or against Nicaragua." The House Intelligence Committee itself has maintained a timid, nonconfrontational stand, giving the CIA a free hand to bypass Congress and substitute covert action for policy and diplomacy.

Until now, Congressional leaders have been reticent to challenge the not-so-secret war, apparently choosing to split legal hairs in the interests of protecting our national security. This is a grave mistake—not least because the covert operations are likely to produce the very results Congress most fears.

CIA activities encourage Nicaragua to rely increasingly on Cuba for assistance and may even spur the Sandinists to request MIG fighter jets for defense against the Honduran Air Force. Hopes for stabilizing the region will be dashed if exile forces ignite a conflict between Honduras and Nicaragua—a war that could in turn draw in Guatemala, El Salvador and even the United States. Military threats will not discourage authoritarianism in Nicaragua; in fact, they make it rational for the Sandinists to maintain the state of emergency, continue press censorship, postpone elections and limit internal opposition.

Congress must take steps immediately to enforce the Boland Amendment by cutting all funding for covert operations, including military assistance to the Honduran government. The further hearings to question top administration officials called for by Senator Moynihan would be a good first step. The Congressional intelligence committees could also introduce new, unequivocal legislation prohibiting any direct or indirect support for irregular military forces or paramilitary groups operating in Central America.

Our most fundamental values are undermined when an administration breaks the law, lies to its citizens and supports the same kinds of subversive actions we accuse our enemies of taking. Its action in Nicaragua also endangers our national security by polarizing conflict in the region. Congress must tell the President that he cannot violate the law with impunity.

40. Liberals' Quibbles over Nicaragua*

By Kevin J. Kelley

Many media organs of the liberal establishment have lately been emitting critical noises about Washington's blatant attempt to overthrow the Sandinista regime in Nicaragua. These prestigious dailies and newsmagazines, which set the tenor for "respectable" dissent in the US, are generally urging the Reagan administration to reconsider the no longer secret war which the CIA is directing from Honduras and Costa Rica.

---

*Reprinted from *The Guardian,* April 27, 1983.

Why the sudden concern in Manhattan and Washington press boardrooms over proxy subversion of the Managua government?

Not because Nicaragua is a sovereign nation entitled to follow whatever political course it thinks appropriate. Not because the Sandinista revolution is a just and popular response to decades of poverty. And certainly not because the victorious rebels are striving, against increasingly awesome odds, to create a distinctively Nicaraguan form of socialism.

Instead, liberal editorialists repeatedly cite four basic reasons for reassessing the tactics being employed against what the *New York Times* (March 30) calls "the undesirable and offensive Managua regime."

First, and most importantly from that premise, there's the likelihood that the current scheme just isn't going to work. Several commentators have pointed out that the Somocista "contras," who are doing most of the raiding, are too few in number and too hated within Nicaragua to succeed in their aims. *Newsweek,* which blew the first widely heeded whistle on the covert *putsch* back in November, sounded this theme in its original exposé. Quoting the ever-reliable "European observer in the region," the *Washington Post*-owned weekly asserted: " 'There's no question that Nicaragua is ripe for a change. . . . But the US is supporting the only wrong, the only truly evil alternative.' "

A second major worry for these critics is that the whole operation may backfire, with fighting (and revolts) spilling over into "friendly" and "moderate" Honduras or Costa Rica.

As a corollary to their first two objections, liberal doubters suggest that the current tactics may ultimately harm the US strategy throughout the isthmus.

Here's what *New Republic* executive editor Morton Kondracke has to say on the subject: "The US is risking disaster—another Bay of Pigs and possibly worse— by giving aid to rightist guerrillas. . . ."

Noting that the Somocistas are too weak to seriously threaten the Sandinista government, Kondracke cautions that they are "large enough to give it an excuse for snuffing out what little is left of liberty in Nicaragua and perhaps launching 'retaliatory' raids into Honduras and Costa Rica." The *New Republic* pundit has here touched upon the fourth problem frequently cited by these critics. Somocista incursions are only going to strengthen the Sandinistas, thus thwarting our (laudable) purposes, warn Kondracke and his ilk.

The *New York Times* and *Washington Post* are both quite eloquent on this point. "One result [of the CIA offensive] may be to entrench rather than topple a revolutionary autocracy," the *Times* pontificated in a March 30 editorial. And "with foreign-backed insurgents at the gate," the paper of record continued, "Nicaragua's leftists have been given a pretext for further repression."

Agreeing that "it serves no American purpose to see Marxist power ensconced in Managua," the *Post* boldly urged the Reagan administration to take another look at its destabilization program. Why? Because it "helps to strengthen the Sandinistas' claim to be embattled nationalists and also helps them tighten their internal grip," concluded this March 24 editorial.

None of these commentaries contain any real objection to the notion of US covert operations aimed at a poor third world country. All the revelations of the past decade about CIA "dirty tricks" are willfully forgotten by *Times* editorialists who conclude (April 18): "If the Nicaragua regime is now lost to despotism, it is not necessarily wrong to encourage its enemies."

In a sidebar to its November exposure of the secret war, *Newsweek* set out to defend the notion of covert subversion. It helpfully provided some "rules" to obey when the US does decide to destroy progressive governments: "Don't violate your own principles. Don't make things worse. Don't get caught." And lest it be accused of not having shaken off the Vietnam syndrome, *Newsweek* concludes: "As a last resort, the destabilization or overthrow of a foreign government may be necessary, whether it involves subtle subversion or something nastier."

But wait; aren't I being too harsh? Didn't these very same organs expose the CIA war against Nicaragua in the first place?

They did, if one doesn't count the many earlier and detailed reports on US intrigue in Honduras appearing in the radical press. But the motives and purposes for these investigative accounts by liberal publications are not especially noble, as *Newsweek* itself conceded. Explaining why it was blowing the whistle last November, the magazine said: "Reporters know that the story will come out, and that if they don't print it, a competitor will. Even today, the news media will generally suppress a story if publication would put [US] lives at risk or expose a secret that is indisputably vital to the national interest."

It's a truism on the left that liberals aren't the enemy. But their views on the subversion of the Sandinistas should remind us that they aren't very good friends, either.

41. *Perilous Latin Policy**

By Robert E. White

Robert E. White, was US ambassador to El Salvador during the Carter administration and is presently a senior fellow at the Center for Development Policy.

Washington—President Reagan's speech to Congress last Wednesday signals his determination to pursue the course—based on a disastrous self-fulfilling prophecy—he has followed in Central America since coming to office. Instead of trying to contain unrest in Nicaragua and El Salvador, the administration is apparently going to continue to spread upheaval throughout the region.

---

*Reprinted from the *New York Times,* May 2, 1983.

The administration has made a definitive break with the diplomatic principles of respect for sovereignty, territorial integrity and nonintervention. Instead, it has directed its resources toward strengthening the Central American military and fighting an ill-defined "Communist threat" with huge Central Intelligence Agency stations and large numbers of military advisers. The result has been to encourage precisely the threat that the President hoped to stop.

To grasp why the administration sponsored an invasion of Nicaragua from Honduras, look to El Salvador. Many key foreign policy aides understand that the brutal and corrupt Salvadoran government is falling apart and that no amount of military assistance will enable it to contain the revolutionaries. Yet the White House firmly rejects any direct parleys with guerrillas. Instead, Washington is determined to create an ill-starred, region-wide military battle—hoping in the end to negotiate a region-wide solution on its own terms.

The campaign began in earnest this spring when the Pentagon conducted joint military exercises with Honduras along the Honduran-Nicaraguan frontier and the Honduran military strongman, Gen. Gustavo Álvarez Martínez, announced that co-existence with Nicaragua was no longer possible. By that time, several thousand Nicaraguan counterrevolutionaries, trained, armed and funded by the CIA, occupied camps on the Honduran side of the border. In early March, these forces, known as *contras,* invaded Nicaragua.

The true intent of the administration, in supporting the *contras,* may have been neither to overthrow the Sandinistas nor, as Mr. Reagan claimed, to interdict the negligible trickle of arms from Nicaragua to El Salvador. Rather, I believe, the invasion was part of a systematic plan to provoke the Sandinistas to cross the Honduran border and attack the counterrevolutionaries' base camps. Honduran troops were poised to repel the invaders and enter Nicaragua in hot pursuit—creating a border war. But even the hot-headed and inexperienced Sandinistas refused to fall into so obvious a trap. They ordered their troops to stay well clear of the Honduran border and reiterated their offer to negotiate with Honduras or the United States. Neither country has taken up the offer—and instead both have continued to aid the *contras.*

It is in Honduras, the poorest country in the region, that the worst effects of the Reagan policy may be seen. In the face of widespread misery and despair, many Hondurans oppose their government's militaristic policies, demanding deep political, economic and social changes. These dissidents are now treated as subversives and, for the first time in its history, the Honduran military has begun to abduct and kill labor union leaders, intellectuals and others who dissent from official policy. This is the way revolution took hold in El Salvador—with popular outrage against officially sponsored disappearances.

The administration accuses Nicaragua of exporting revolution to Honduras. In fact, the exact opposite is true. In obedience to our policy, Honduras has become embroiled in militaristic counterrevolution—and is attempting to export it.

The administration must learn that counterrevolution is precisely the wrong response to a people determined to take power and transform their countries. Our policy toward the region must take into account the security interests of the United States. But where is it written that the people of Central America must remain in bondage so that the United States can remain free?

Do the Reagan policy-makers truly fear that Nicaragua will end up identified with the Soviet Union and Cuba? Or do they fear precisely the opposite—that if we pursued a less aggressive policy, Nicaragua might emerge not as a Soviet lackey but as a nonaligned country? Do we reject negotiations in El Salvador because our policy is based on continued military domination of that country? Do we perhaps reject the consistent offers of good offices from Latin American democratic leaders to help bring peace to Central America because we seek primarily military solutions to political, economic and social problems?

As we examine our actions in Central America, we should recall Florence Nightingale's words: "The first responsibility of a hospital is not to spread disease."

Part Four

LIFE IN THE NEW NICARAGUA

Editors' Introduction

Despite *contra* attacks and other efforts at destabilization, some very important changes are taking place inside Nicaragua, changes which could signify a "new way" for the Third World. The following two chapters provide an introduction to some of those changes. Chapter I details the operation and organization of the government, how citizens participate in decision-making, the role of the church, and the trade union movement. Chapter II offers a description of Nicaragua's "New Society," including health, education, culture, and the role of women.

Chapter I:

Structures for Change

Editors' Introduction

The first three documents in this chapter outline the basic philosophical and operational elements of the government of Nicaragua: its philosophy, its administrative and political structure, and its unique version of grassroots democracy.

According to the government's plans, the trade union movement in Nicaragua must play a key role in both reconstruction and in combatting economic destabilization. This view is echoed by the major trade unions affiliated with the FSLN, which speak for close to 90 percent of organized labor.[1]

They are to de-emphasize wage demands and focus on worker participation and on what is called the "Social Wage" (noncash benefits like health care, food and transportation subsidies, and occupational safety). In addition, worker committees are expected to monitor management practices for evidence of decapitalization.

Reading 45 describes the friction that has developed between the government and unions not allied with the FSLN, particularly with regard to the temporary prohibition of strikes under the State of Emergency. While this has been used by some government critics as evidence of a lack of trade union freedom in Nicaragua, the record shows that the number of trade unions grew from 138 in July 1979, to 1,182 by March, 1982.[2] Reading 45, "The Trade Union Movement in Nicaragua," presents a detailed analysis of this and related issues, and includes interviews with members of three different unions, both FSLN and non-FSLN affiliated.

Nicaragua's Catholic church is "a church divided." Belief in "liberation theology[3] during the years leading up to the 1979 triumph has contributed to support for the present government. Several priests hold high governmental posts. Yet, the Catholic hierarchy, never entirely comfortable with liberation theology, is now one of the major antagonists of the government. It has essentially withdrawn its support for the government and demanded that the priests in office resign their posts.

It is clear that a key focus of the US destabilization campaign has been to exploit this rift. This strategy was originally layed out in the Heritage Foundation's "Di Giovanni Report."[4] Its justification comes from the influential "Santa Fe Document" prepared by a group of Reagan's advisors, which states

> US foreign policy must begin to counter (not react against) liberation theology as it is utilized in Latin America by the "liberation theology" clergy. The role of the church in Latin America is vital to the concept of political freedom. Unfortunately, Marxist-Leninist forces have utilized the church as a political weapon against private property and productive capitalism by infiltrating the religious community with ideas that are less Christian than Communist.[5]

Reading 46, "A Church Divided," gives the historical background to the current division within the church. Next, Elliott Abrams of the US State Department presents the Reagan administration's viewpoint on religion in Nicaragua. The final reading on the church outlines its role in destabilization.

In 1979, amid confusion and conflict, the youthful Nicaraguan government developed an economic program unique to Nicaragua, based on a "mixed economy." As described in our reading "The Somoza Legacy: Economic Bankruptcy," the Sandinistas inherited an economy devastated by the 1972 earthquake and mismanagement of relief funds, the destruction wrought by the war, and Somoza's looting of the Central Bank. The "Challenge of Reconstruction" deals with the government's economic response. "Nicaragua Debates New Rules for Foreign Companies" describes the current debate within Nicaragua on foreign investment.

Whatever form the economy eventually takes, its base will be agriculture. All questions concerning agriculture are crucial to at least the short-term development of the country. Reading 52 describes agrarian reform, the centerpiece of the government's program, and one of the most ambitious ever attempted in Latin America. In "Failed Partnership: Big Growers and the State," Joseph Collins examines some of the problems that have arisen in the government's attempt to accommodate both large-scale landholders and peasants in the agrarian reform.

Notes

[1]"The Trade Union Movement in Nicaragua, Part I," *Envio,* No. 12, pages 13–23, June, 1982 (see resource guide at end of book).

[2]*Ibid.*

[3]See Penny Lernoux, *Cry of the People* (N.Y.: Penguin, 1980).

[4]Reading 27.

[5]The Committee of Santa Fe, *A New Inter-American Policy for the Eighties,* Council for Inter-American Security, Inc., Washington, D.C. (1980).

42. The Philosophy and Policies of the Government of Nicaragua*

By the Junta for National Reconstruction

The following is an edited version of a pamphlet published by the Nicaraguan government.

Introduction:

A Government of National Unity

The government of Nicaragua was born in the midst of the struggle against the military dictatorship of Anastasio Somoza, a struggle in which the Sandinista Front for National Liberation played the leading role, supported by all of the democratic forces of the country.

The first declaration of the Junta of the Government of National Reconstruction in July 1979 assured a "broad representation of all the political, economic, and social forces that have contributed to the overthrow of the Somoza dictatorship." The diverse social forces and groups included:

1. The Sandinista Front for National Liberation
2. The National Patriotic Front (composed of seven political and trade union organizations)
3. The Broad Opposition Front (composed of seven political and trade union organizations)
4. The Superior Council of the Private Sector (composed of six trade and business organizations)
5. The National Autonomous University of Nicaragua
6. The National Association of Clergy.[1]

Among the many political parties and groups represented, one stood out because of its unifying role, because of its audacity, and because of its capacity to sum up within a single cause so many diverse groups.

The National Plan for Economic Reactivation in Benefit of the People issued in 1980 includes as one of its general objectives the strengthening of National Unity: "It's a question of bringing together wage workers with small producers and artisans, with professionals and technicians in a single unbreakable project of

---

* Reprinted from JGRN, *Dirección de divulgación y prensa* March, 1982.

National Unity. It also means integrating the patriotic businessmen and offering these businessmen the support of the government necessary to reactivate their sector of the economy, in order to achieve the goals in production which this plan has set for the private sector."[2]

Upon first taking power on July 19, 1979, the Nicaraguan government was composed of a Junta made up of five members, each of whom represented different social sectors in the country, as well as a cabinet where practically all of the political parties, religious and social organizations of the country were represented. If to this, we add the fact that the most important political force in the country (the FSLN) is led by a collective leadership of nine members, and that a Council of State has been formed in which almost all organized groups in Nicaragua are represented, we can safely assert that the political leadership of Nicaragua is one of the most collective and non-sectarian of any in the world.

The process of National Unity cannot be isolated from the objective contradictions which exist within Nicaraguan society. These form the basis of the dynamic of the revolutionary process, giving rise to new combinations and syntheses which are reflected and institutionalized in the political and judicial structures of the country.

The policy of National Unity is most clearly expressed by the Junta of the Government of National Reconstruction, the executive branch of government, and the Sandinista Front for National Liberation, which continues to be the leading force uniting a broad cross-section of social forces and political interests which exist in the country, whose leadership is legitimized by the fact that it has the support of the majority of the Nicaraguan population.

The goals of the Government of National Unity can be summarized in the following principles, which are its *raison d'etre*, and to whose development the government has pledged itself:

—the development and transformation of the economy
—sovereignty and self-determination.

At the same time the government has put into practice a form of republic which over the past three years has become more and more defined and which is characterized by:

- political pluralism
- a mixed economy
- popular participation and mobilization
- national defense and non-alignment.

These elements taken together constitute the political philosophy of the current government in Nicaragua.

The Government of National Unity expresses the common interests of the nation of Nicaragua in the face of the external and internal limitations imposed by our history and our plans. Accordingly we recognize the differences that exist in our

society as well as the right of the Junta of the Government of National Reconstruction to harmonize these differences between various interest groups through its
leadership and in alliance with others, in order to attain a system of unity, liberty
and social justice, thus realizing the dream of Sandino, the nightmare of the
Somocistas and the hope of the Nicaraguan people.

Our political pluralism has as its common denominator the development of the
revolution in accordance with its principles; the mixed economy in turn will be
linked with the economic development and social well-being of all Nicaraguans;
finally the participation-mobilization and the national defense and non-alignment
cannot be divorced from the context of the necessity to maintain and struggle for a
just peace for our people and for all the peoples of the world.

I. Democracy and Political Pluralism

The institutionalized and ongoing development of the democratic process, born
out of the revolutionary struggle and fundamentally based on the principles of
popular participation and political pluralism, constitutes one of the most important
objectives of the Nicaraguan government.

The first step towards democracy and political pluralism taken in Nicaragua was
the overthrow of the worst dictatorship in all of Latin America.

When the Sandinista Front for National Liberation took power and the Junta of
the Government of National Reconstruction was installed, one of its decisions was
not to impose the death penalty on any of the Somocistas imprisoned by the
revolutionary forces.

This in itself constitutes one of the most generous actions in the history of
revolutions, in that for the first time those parties guilty of crimes during the
previous regime were not executed. Together with this initial gesture the Government of National Reconstruction abolished all of the repressive and antidemocratic
institutions which existed under Somoza.

Political Parties and General Elections. February 22, 1982, a special commission of the Council of State presented a working document outlining a law concerning political parties. Among the principles concerning political parties expressed in
this document one finds such basic democratic ideals as: "the recognition of the
right of the people to social and historical self-determination, the concept of
pluralism, the recognition of the unhindered right of diverse ideological, social, and
political schools of thought to exist. . . ."

Among the functions of political parties mentioned we find: "participation in
the political and administrative process of government and promoting the economic, social, political and cultural reconstruction of the country for the benefit of
the Nicaraguan people."[3] This law concerning political parties, which will probably
be discussed in the coming months, signifies another step in the process of further
institutionalization of political pluralism.

Presently there exists in Nicaragua a coalition of political parties which support
the advance of the revolutionary process. The FSLN, the Popular Liberal Inde-

pendent Party (PLI), the Nicaraguan Socialist Party (PSN), the Popular Social Christian Party (PPSC) together make up the Patriotic Front of the Revolution (FPR). The Communist Party of Nicaragua (PCN) and the Movement for Popular Action (MAP), both of which consider themselves progressive members of the revolutionary movement, have manifested a series of differences and been involved in a series of conflicts with the new government over the past 30 months.

Another series of parties presently forms the opposition to the government. These parties include the Nicaraguan Democratic Movement (MDN), the Social Christian Party (PSC), the Democratic Conservative Party (PCD), and the Liberal Constitutionalist Movement (MLC). These parties have come together in the "Ramiro Sacasa Democratic Coordinating Committee."

In August of 1980, one year after the triumph, general elections were announced for 1985. This position was reiterated in February of 1982 on the occasion of the Congress of the Permanent Conference of Political Parties of Latin America. The statement issued in the Congress of COPPAL could not have been clearer. "Nicaragua maintains its complete disposition to develop its revolution within the framework of a mixed economy, political pluralism, and non-alignment, as well as to hold general democratic elections in 1985 at the latest."[4] The amount of time scheduled to pass between the triumph of the Revolution and the holding of the elections is actually rather short when compared with other international experiences. In the United States, for example, after the revolution of 1776–1781, it was not until 1800, 19 years after the triumph, that national elections were held where two political parties were allowed to participate.

Freedom of Press. Immediately after the triumph of the revolution all the regulations regarding radio and television which under Somoza had come to be known as the "Black Law" were abolished. They were replaced in August of 1979 by a law regulating the mass media. This law clearly states that "freedom of information is one of the basic principles of any authentic democracy. The government should assure that there is no possibility that the means of communications are restricted through the direct or indirect domination of the economic power of any given group. This is the only way to assure the independence of the press. . . . Also, under this law the Nicaraguan Union of Journalists is guaranteed representation on a special council which will review all decisions regarding the media."[5]

Presently there are three functioning newspapers in Nicaragua. The first, *Barricada,* is the official newspaper of the Sandinista Front, *El Nuevo Diario,* the second, is an independent newspaper which maintains an editorial policy of support for the revolution. The third, *La Prensa,* is also independent.

La Prensa maintains an editorial policy which is systematically opposed to the revolutionary political process. Besides the three newspapers there are 51 radio stations in the country, of which 34 are privately owned. The two television stations are public. A broad gamut of privately controlled magazines, publishing houses, and weeklies also exists in the new Nicaragua.

Nicaragua, it could be argued, is the country in our hemisphere which actually has a freer press than any other. In no other country will one find newspapers and radio stations which maintain a fierce opposition to the government being the principal sources of news in the country. What is taking place today in Nicaragua in this sense is a clear sign of both the vitality and pluralism of our revolution.

Other Freedoms. The Nicaraguan government's commitment to democracy and political pluralism is also reflected in the Declaration of Principles which the Sandinista Popular Revolution issued regarding the indigenous communities on the Atlantic Coast.

This Declaration states, "The Sandinista Popular Revolution will support and guarantee the participation of the communities of the Atlantic Coast in the resolution of all the social, economic, and political problems which affect not only them, but the entire nation. . . . All the different forms which communities develop to organize themselves will be supported, thus assuring a true representation of the population in the different social, political, and economic decisions that are made regarding the Atlantic Coast."[6]

The most important of all the liberties the Revolution has brought, however, has been the liberty which has come from abolishing the repression that Somoza's National Guard carried out against the people. The present social peace and political liberty which our citizens enjoy constitutes one of the most fundamental manifestations of the strength of our democracy.

II. Development and the Mixed Economy

General Goals. *(a)* To overcome the economic backwardness, which is expressed in our low level of agricultural and industrial development, and which impedes the rational utilization of our natural and human resources, by developing the basis for a viable process of industrialization whose foundations would be the transformation of raw materials produced within the country.

(b) To break our economic dependence on the transnational corporations and the countries that support these corporations to the extent possible given that we are a poor, underdeveloped, and small country. Nicaragua must strengthen its capacity to function in diverse markets and broaden the sources of credit and of technical cooperation on which it presently relies. It must promote joint investments with the private and public sectors of those countries which are interested in the development of our economy.

(c) To favor changes in the distribution of the national income in ways that benefit the majority of the population.

The Political Philosophy which Guides the Development of the Government of National Reconstruction. One of the basic elements of the policy of National Unity promoted by the Government of National Reconstruction is the strengthening of the mixed economy. The mixed economy is composed of four sectors:

a) businesses in the private sector
b) the state sector
c) production cooperatives in the city and the countryside
d) the peasant and artisanal sector.

The private sector as a whole produces 75 percent of the national product, leaving approximately 25 percent of all production in the Public Sector.

Public and Private Sectors of the Nicaraguan Economy 1980-1981 (in %)

Sector	Private	Public	Total
Agriculture	80	20	100
Industry	75	25	100
Total Production	75	25	100
Total GNP	59	41	100

If we compare the participation of the Nicaraguan government in material production or in the overall GNP we find that the participation of the government in the national economy is one of the lowest in Latin America. In Peru, for example, the state controls over 42 percent of the material goods produced in the country. Likewise, throughout Western Europe, state control over the economy is broader and stronger than in Nicaragua. In France, for example, the government produces more than 26 percent of all goods produced in the country.

Government Financial and Economic Policy in the Mixed Economy: (a) Internal and External Commerce. The immediate post-war period was characterized by a great scarcity of basic foodstuffs. This scarcity put pressure on price levels and created the conditions for dishonest merchants to speculate with the supply of these goods. The role of the National Basic Foods Corporation (ENABAS) has been, on the one hand, to promote an increase in prices for the producers, a measure which has resulted in higher levels of income for large numbers of poor peasants. At the same time, ENABAS' policy of subsidies has allowed the prices of basic goods paid by the consumer to remain relatively stable in 1980 and 1981. The state's role in performing these functions, operating as the most important middleman in the market (in spite of the fact that it only controls 30 percent of the internal market), has had positive effects, not only for the producers of grains and basic foodstuffs but for the urban consumer as well. The costs to the government of maintaining these policies have had a negative effect on efforts to balance the budget. Nevertheless, the Government of National Reconstruction has reiterated on various occasions its commitment to sustain and elevate if possible the income levels of the poorest strata of the population.

One of the most important achievements of the Government of National Reconstruction has been controlling the level of inflation. The World Bank and the International Monetary Fund have both noted the new government's sense of prudence and sound thinking in the area of monetary policy. In the period between July 1978 and July 1979 inflation in Nicaragua reached 80 percent. By 1980 this figure had been reduced to 35.3 percent and in 1981 to 23.9 percent. Complementing the food subsidies given to the majority of the population with an austere wage policy greatly contributed to achieving this stability in prices.

In the field of foreign commerce, the government took the measure of nationalizing all foreign trade in the principal agricultural products, thus carrying out one of its promises which had been included in the first government program upon taking power. The nationalization of the export of agricultural products has greatly benefited the producers of these products. Prior to this measure, because these markets were controlled by a few large exporters, Nicaraguan producers received prices that were markedly inferior to those on the international market.

(b) The Law of Economic and Social Emergency

On August 9, 1981 the Junta of the Government of National Reconstruction approved a law of economic emergency whose basic principles are:

• Control over the use of foreign exchange, restraining imports of luxury goods through a list specifying import priorities;
• A freeze on all government expenditures;
• Promotion of labor agreements and the temporary prohibition of strikes;
• Controls against the removal of capital from the country and the decapitalization of businesses.

(c) Credit

The Government of National Reconstruction has taken a wide variety of measures aimed at the recuperation of the economy including the waiver of interest payments and the restructuring of the private debt with long terms and low interest rates, as well as a general policy of facilitating the private sector's access to credit.
1) The public financial system in 1980 and 1981 financed 100 percent of the private sector's need for working capital and investment.

This is in stark contrast to the policies of the dictatorship, which never financed more than 70 percent of these needs.

Despite the fact that the private sector has made significant profits over the last two years, the producers in this sector have not been forced to use these profits to meet their own needs for working and investment capital.
2) Both for the restructuring of past debts and the financing of new credit the rates of interest which have been established are substantially below those which are presently available on the international market.
3) Credit for small and medium producers, an important group within the private sector, has increased notably.

The number of small and medium-sized recipients of credit has grown from 37,510 during the dictatorship to 97,350 under the Revolutionary Government.

(d) Foreign Currency

Of the $US 409.9 million assigned for imports during the period between January 1980 and August of 1981, 52.9 percent of this ($217.0 million) went to the private sector while only 27.3 percent ($112.2 million) went to the Area of People's Property and 19.4 percent ($79.5 million) went to the central government and decentralized public service corporations such as the Nicaraguan Energy Institute (INE) and the Nicaraguan Water and Sewage Institute.

(e) International Economic Relations

To begin to confront the basic necessities entailed in the reconstruction of the economy the Nicaraguan government appealed to the international community to renegotiate the national debt and provide additional financial assistance.

During the Government of National Reconstruction's three years of existence, it has been able to obtain some $1,200 million US dollars in external financing. At the same time donations have been received for some $260 million US dollars. Of all the aid received from the different countries 49 percent came from other nations of the Third World, 32 percent from the developed capitalist nations and 19 percent from the socialist countries.[7]

Loans and Donations to Nicaragua

Block/Countries	Bilateral Loans	Multilateral	Donations	Total Loans & Donations
Non-aligned Nations of the Third World	44%	71%	49%	49%
Developed Capitalist Countries	28%	29%	26%	32%
Socialist Block Countries	28%	09%	25%	19%
Total	100%	100%	100%	100%

The Junta of the Government of National Reconstruction also promotes the realization of joint investments with friendly governments. Presently agro-industrial projects are being jointly developed with different countries including Cuba, Bulgaria, Libya and Mexico. Other foreign investments will also be promoted through a new law regulating direct foreign investments.

(f) Incentives for Export

Finally, in February of 1982, an Export Incentive Plan was approved aimed at guaranteeing the profitability of export production and giving producers increased access for foreign currency.

These incentives allow exporters to continue to import capital and intermediate goods at the present exchange rate (10 córdobas/dollar) while at the same time allowing them to obtain a higher exchange rate for their exports, through a special system of import certificates.[8]

III. Participation and Socioeconomic Well-Being

In its first declaration, the Government of National Reconstruction included among its goals in the economic area "the substitution of the traditional paternalistic principles of government . . . with government actions that stimulate the participation, both individual and collective, of all Nicaraguans in the solutions to their problems."[9] Given the enormous problems and the tremendous deficit of resources which the present government has inherited, there is only one way to guarantee this individual and collective form of democracy: by consolidating and increasing the already high levels of popular mobilization, organization, and participation that were achieved during the struggle of our people against the dictatorship.

The Struggle for Literacy and Health. The first great campaign developed in this context was, without doubt, the National Literacy Crusade which went from February to August of 1980. The crusade succeeded in lowering the overall illiteracy rate in the country from 50.3 percent to 12 percent. Presently the campaign is being continued through the Popular Education Collectives (CEP), which daily bring together for two hours more than 200,000 recently educated Nicaraguans allowing them to continue their studies. In the CEP, just as with the campaign itself, the work is going ahead based on volunteers and involves minimal costs to the government. Presently in Nicaragua there are over 900,000 people (nearly 40 percent of the population) who are enrolled in some sort of education, or the university. It is clear that this massive process of democracy in the field of learning constitutes a basic pillar for the democratization of political power.[10]

Within the realm of formal education, a broad democratic process has also been occurring:

Previously pre-school education was practically non-existent. In 1978 only 918 preschoolers were enrolled in public programs. Today more than 26,000 participate in the Nicaraguan government's pre-school programs.

Enrollment in primary education grew from 369,640 in 1978 to 503,452 in 1980/1981, an increase of 36 percent. With this increase the percentage of school-age children attending school grew from 64.8 percent to 80 percent. Almost 1,100 new primary schools were constructed by the government in less than two years.

In secondary education, the percentage of adolescents attending was extremely low in 1978, 14.7 percent. Due to the efforts of the government, this percentage has risen to 20 percent with an absolute rise in the number of students from 98,874 enrolled in 1978 to 135,116 in 1980. It is estimated, however, that the total amount of resources dedicated to the students in the secondary education system actually increased even more than these figures indicate because the number of hours of classes daily in these programs was doubled.

Perhaps the clearest indicator of the democratization of education in Nicaragua is the fact that peasants who make up 65 percent of the population received only 30 percent of the educational resources in 1978 whereas the present government has given absolute priority to the rural areas. A full 95 percent of the new schools constructed were located in rural areas.

The government not only guarantees the right to private education but even subsidizes it. In Nicaragua, there are 574 centers of private education. Of these, 108 or almost 20 percent are subsidized by the government. Almost all these subsidized schools are religious centers.

The health sector is presently one of the top priorities for the government and for the mass organizations. One concrete result of health programs is the reduction of the infant mortality rate from 120/1,000 in 1978 to 94/1,000 last year. The Popular Health Campaigns in 1981 carried out programs of vaccinations, malaria and dengue fever control and prevention, and environmental sanitation. These campaigns mobilized over 80,000 volunteers.

The Rights of Trade Unions and Other Organizations. In the area of organization and participation of workers, the complete freedom to form unions which has been guaranteed by the Revolution is clearly reflected in the fact that between August of 1979 and December of 1981, more unions were created and registered with the Ministry of Labor than during the entire previous history of the country. In 1978 there were only 175 registered trade unions in the country with fewer than 5,000 members. Within one year after the victorious insurrection, the Ministry of Labor had certified the formation of more than 1,000 new unions with some 40,000 members. By 1982 the number of union members in the country had risen to 150,000.

In Nicaragua today there are seven different trade union federations. Four of these federations support the revolutionary process. Of these, the two federations connected with the Sandinista Front are by far the largest in Nicaragua. The Sandinista Workers' Federation (CST) includes 543 unions with 100,000 members and the farm Workers' Association (ATC) has some 1,100 unions with 35,000 organized members. The other three federations have disagreed consistently with the majority of the government's policies, sometimes taking positions to the left of the government, sometimes to the right. Internationally one of these federations (CUS) is affiliated with the Inter-American Regional Labor Organization (ORIT) controlled by the AFL-CIO of the United States, another (CTN) is affiliated with the Latin American Workers' Federation (CLAT). These three federations control 131 unions with 15,000 organized workers. In addition to the trade union organizations in the country, the National Union of Farmers and Ranchers (UNAG) and numerous other professional and trade associations play an important role in national life. This high level of trade union and professional organization has already produced notable benefits, contributing to the defense of the level of real wages, and the increase in productivity and production.

It can be safely affirmed that currently almost every single Nicaraguan in the country has been organized in one fashion or another. The proof can be seen in the countless activities carried on constantly by the diverse community, youth, womens', student, union, professional, political, and religious organizations that exist within the country.

The Freedom of Religion. Nicaragua is number one as far as Latin America is concerned with regard to the participation and integration of Christians both in the insurrectional period that led to the overthrow of the Somoza dictatorship and in the present period of national reconstruction. The Christians, priests, religious leaders, and lay people form a vital part of the national life carrying out their faith through important contributions of various types in the achievement of social welfare and a more democratic society. There are over 76 churches of different denominations in Nicaragua. Some 20 of these have come into existence since the

Revolution, a clear sign of the increase in religious activity which has accompanied the Revolution.

The leadership of the Sandinista Front has publicly recognized the permanent and crucial role that Christians have to play in Nicaragua. Three different priests have positions as ministers or ambassadors: the Minister of Culture, the Minister of Foreign Affairs, and Nicaragua's ambassador in the Organization of American States (OAS). Many other priests occupy important roles in the new government. Both the Catholic Church and the Evangelical Churches have their own representatives in the Council of State. In the judgment of a special commission sent by the Vatican and headed by the Italian Bishop Betazzi of the organization Pax Christi, "In Nicaragua there is absolute freedom of religion, of the preparation of priests, of evangelizing, of Christian education, to form new religious organizations, and of the Archbishop Obando to celebrate the Eucharist and give sermons each day."

The Atlantic Coast and the Struggle Against Discrimination. The same emphasis placed by Nicaraguans in the defense of religious freedom, applies as well to the struggle against any form of discrimination. The full recognition of the historical and cultural heritage of the inhabitants of the Atlantic Coast and the defense of their rights as Nicaraguans was made clear on August 12, 1981 with the publication of the "Declarations of the Philosophy of the Sandinista Popular Revolution regarding the Indigenous Communities of the Atlantic Coast." This document states, "The Government of National Reconstruction supports the retention of the different cultural expressions of the area and will provide to the Miskitu, Creole, Sumo, and Rama communities of the Atlantic Coast the necessary means to further their own cultural traditions including the preservation of their languages."

The same Declaration also affirms that the "Sandinista Popular Revolution will guarantee and support the participation of the Communities of the Atlantic Coast in all of the different political and economic decisions which concern them and the country as a whole."[11] One concrete expression of the political will of the government in this respect and its respect for the ethnic minorities was the enormous effort that was put into the carrying out of the Literacy Crusade in such a way that the Miskitus, Sumos, Ramas, and Creoles, could each be taught to read and write in their own language.

IV. Sovereignty and Self-Determination: National Defense and Non-Alignment

Another one of the Government of National Unity's basic goals is achieving national sovereignty and self-determination for Nicaragua. The desire to achieve this goal has translated itself into programmatic efforts to strengthen national defense and carry out a policy of non-alignment internationally. National sovereignty has become one of the most cherished values of the Nicaraguan people, carrying on in the anti-colonialist traditions of their ancestors who fought against the Spanish empire. On a wide variety of occasions the Nicaraguan people have had to defend their sovereignty from foreign interventions.

The government of Somoza had practically sold the sovereignty of Nicaragua with no money down and monthly payments at low rates. His National Guard was really no more than the continuation of US military presence. The struggle against Somoza, in this sense, was a struggle against foreign intervention and in favor of the sovereignty and self-determination of the Nicaraguan people.

After the revolutionary triumph on July 19th, 1979 Nicaragua became the object of threats, attacks on its border and terrorist attacks by bands of Somocistas and counterrevolutionaries, a campaign to isolate Nicaragua internationally, a financial boycott, sabotage against our economy, and destabilization and misinformation campaigns. But in spite of all these aggressions the positions of our government have not changed. The national liberation movement that made Nicaragua a free country has continued in its policy of non-alignment along with the majority of the nations of the Third World for whom our model of National Unity, of a Mixed Economy, of Political Pluralism and Participation constitute a model of understanding and supporting.

Comandante Daniel Ortega, coordinator of the Junta of the Government of National Reconstruction, in a speech delivered before the United Nations on October 7, 1981 declared, "We want peace but not at the cost of our freedom."[12] With these words he reminded the ambassadors present of the commitments that had been made in Nicaragua's first Government Program of July 1979.

This program was reiterated and fully endorsed by the Sandinista Assembly during the celebration of its 2nd National Conference on January 31, 1982. According to the Assembly, "The Popular Sandinista Revolution showed its foreign policy of non-alignment by maintaining relations with all countries interested in doing so within a framework of mutual respect and cooperation."[13]

This policy of defense of the nation's sovereignty and self-determination has meant carrying through a number of more specific programs, some of which are listed below:

The reorganization of the Armed Forces. The Popular Sandinista Army was created in November 1979. At the same time, the functions of the police were differentiated from those of the armed forces, with the Sandinista Police being delegated the function of guaranteeing public order and personal security. (Under the Somoza government there was no distinction between the National Guard and the Police.) In less than two years, the Sandinista Police succeeded in completely eradicating drug traffic, practically eliminated prostitution in the country, considerably lowered the rate of delinquency, and had begun to implement the various traffic regulations.

In February of 1980, the Sandinista Popular Militias were formed. Any man or woman from any social class or religion and in general anyone who wishes to participate in the defense of his country in the case of attack can join the Popular Militias. Participation in the Militias is completely voluntary unlike other countries where there is compulsory military service.

The Sandinista Popular Army, which is also completely voluntary, has a purely defensive character. Nicaragua does not participate in any military pacts.

In September 1979 Nicaragua became a member of the Movement of Nonaligned Nations and took up the ideals of this movement, making them its own.

In the United Nations, Nicaragua has always voted in favor of human rights, of limiting the arms race, of the struggles for decolonialization and movements of national liberation, and of the creation of multilateral agreements regulating international trade. In keeping with Nicaragua's interest in the creation of a just peace in Central America along with the necessary stability for the development of the Central American economies, a concrete proposal was brought before the United Nations aimed at finding a political solution to the conflict in El Salvador in which all of the forces involved in the Salvadoran conflict, including the Revolutionary Democratic Front of El Salvador, would participate. On this same basis Nicaragua looked favorably on the joint Mexican/French proposal regarding El Salvador, a proposal which the Nicaraguan government feels represents a real option for peace and bringing an end to the suffering of people in El Salvador.

Nicaragua, in its participation in international forums, and especially in the United Nations, has consistently followed its policy of non-alignment, not conforming to any world bloc. Rather, it has voted as it feels correct, based on the Popular Revolutionary Government's basic principle of respect for the self-determination of all nations. In the case of a motion calling for the suspension of nuclear experiments, Nicaragua voted in favor while the Soviet Union abstained, and the United States voted against. In the vote on Afghanistan, Nicaragua abstained, expressing its concern for world peace, while the United States sought the condemnation of the Soviet Union. In the case of Chad, Nicaragua voted with the United States for supporting the reconstruction of the war-wracked country while the Soviet Union voted against the motion. The same was the case on a vote concerning the installation of UN facilities in Nairobi.[14]

Finally it should be mentioned that the Sandinista Front in Nicaragua participates as an observer to the Socialist International in which the leading political parties are the Social Democratic Party of Germany, led by Willy Brandt, the Socialist Party of France, and the Democratic Action Party of Venezuela.

Abbreviations of the Organizations That Participate in the Social and Political Life of the Country.

1. Political Parties

FSLN — Sandinista Front for National Liberation
MAP — Popular Action Movement
MDN — Nicaraguan Democratic Movement
MLC — Liberal Constitutionalist Movement
PCD — Conservative Democratic Party
PCN — Nicaraguan Communist Party
PLI — Liberal Independent Party
PPSC — Popular Social Christian Party

PSC — Social Christian Party
PSN — Nicaraguan Socialist Party
PSD — Social Democratic Party

2. Trade Union Federations

ATC — Farm Workers' Association
CAUS — Federation of Trade Union Action and Unity
CGT(i) — Independent General Confederation of Workers
CST — Sandinista Trade Union Confederation
CTN — Nicaraguan Workers' Federation
FO — Workers' Front

3. Trade Unions

FETSALUD — Federation of Health Workers
SCAAS — Carpenters, Bricklayers, Fitters and Related Workers Union
STUCA — Central American University Workers Union
STRUD — University Workers Union of the Rubén Darío (main) Campus

4. Trade Associations

ANICS — Nicaraguan Association of Social Scientists
ANIA — National Association of Engineers and Architects
ANDEN — National Association of Nicaraguan Teachers
CONAPRO — National Confederation of Professional Associations (Martyrs and Heroes)
UPN — Union of Nicaraguan Journalists
UNE — National Union of Employees

5. Organizations of the Private Sector

COSEP — Superior Council of the Private Sector
CADIN — Nicaraguan Chamber of Industries
UNAG — National Union of Farmers and Ranchers
FECANIC — Nicaraguan Federation of Coffee Growers
FAGANIC — Nicaraguan Federation of Ranchers Associations
FUNDE — Nicaraguan Development Foundation
INDE — Nicaraguan Development Institute
UPANIC — National Union of Agricultural Producers
Cámara de Comercio de Nicaragua — Nicaraguan Chamber of Commerce
Cámara Nicaraguense de la Construcción — Nicaragua Chamber of Construction
CCC — Confederation of Chambers of Commerce

6. Religious Organizations

ACLEN — National Association of the Clergy
CEN — Nicaraguan Episcopal Confederation
CAV — Antonio Valdivieso Center
CEPA — Educational Center for Agrarian Promotion
CEPAD — Evangelical Committee to Aid Development
Caritas de Nicaragua — Charities of Nicaragua
IHCA — Central American Historical Institute

7. Youth and Student Organizations

JS July 19th — The 19th of July Sandinista Youth Movement
ERC — Revolutionary Christian Students
UCR — Revolutionary Christian University Students
UNEN — National Union of Nicaraguan Students
Juventud Democrática del MDN — MDN Democratic Youth
ANS — Association of Sandinista Children

8. Neighborhood and Mass Organizations

CDS — Sandinista Defense Committees
AMNLAE — Nicaraguan Womens' Association "Luisa Amanda Espinoza"
CEP — Popular Education Collective
CPC — Centers of Popular Culture
MPS — Sandinista Popular Militias

Notes

[1]First Proclamation of the Government of National Reconstruction to the People of Nicaragua, July 18, 1979, published by the Press Secretariat of the Government of National Reconstruction. Managua, Nicaragua.

[2]Economic Program of Austerity and Efficiency 1981, Ministry of Planning. Managua, Nicaragua.

[3]Report of the Special Commission of the Council of State on the Law Concerning Political Parties. *Barricada,* Feb. 22, 1982.

[4]Position Paper of the FSLN in the Meeting of the Permanent Commission of Latin American Political Parties. Feb. 19–20, 1982.

[5]*La Gaceta,* Official Newspaper of the State, Sept. 9, 1979. Managua, Nicaragua.

[6]Declaration of the Principles of the Sandinista Revolution on the Atlantic Coast. Nicaraguan Institute for the Atlantic Coast (INNICA), Bulletin No. 7, October, 1981.

[7]International Fund for Reconstruction (FIR), Feb., 1982. Managua, Nicaragua.

[8]Law Concerning Economic Incentives for the Private Export Producers, *Nuevo Diario,* Feb. 9, 1982.

[9]First Proclamation of the Government of National Reconstruction to the People of Nicaragua, July 18, 1979.

[10]Nicaragua's Triumph in Literacy. Ministry of Education and Ecumenical Department of Research. San Jose, Costa Rica, 1981.

[11]Declaration of the Principles of the Sandinista Revolution on the Atlantic Coast. Nicaraguan Institute for the Atlantic Coast (INNICA), Bulletin No. 7, October, 1981.

[12]Speech of Comandante Daniel Ortega Saavedra before the General Assembly of the United Nations, Oct. 7, 1981.

[13]Resolution of the Assembly of Sandinista National Liberation Front, Jan. 31, 1982, *Barricada,* Feb. 1, 1982.

[14]Official Documents of the Thirty-fourth, Thirty-fifth, and Thirty-sixth Conferences of the United Nations.

43. Popular Power*

By the North American Congress on Latin America (NACLA)

Popular Power—"The people have conquered their full right to the exercise of power."

The Nicaraguan revolution is nothing if it is not energy and motion, enthusiastic experimentation with creative new ways of doing things that have never been done before in five decades of dictatorship and US Marine occupation. This is particularly evident in the emergence of new mechanisms through which "the people" are exercising the power to determine the course of their own lives. This is occurring on three levels. First is the day-to-day level, within the community and workplace; second is in the transformation of the state; and the third is in the overall orientation of the revolutionary process, that is to say, in their relation to the FSLN.

The Community

Present in every neighborhood, from the city slums to rural towns, the Sandinista Defense Committees are the mass organizations with the flexibility to respond to the major social and economic problems facing the community. They hold weekly meetings to discuss outstanding problems and review their ongoing activities and projects. Although usually based only on volunteer labor, the results of CDS projects can be seen everywhere, in the form of cleaner and safer living areas, new potable water systems, health clinics and now the introduction of food distribution centers. CDS members are also activists in the broader tasks of the revolution: the Committees organize community participation in the Literacy Crusade, voluntary work brigades in the countryside and mass mobilizations for the political defense of the revolution.

Because the CDS are so much more all-encompassing in their composition than

*Reprinted from *NACLA Report on the Americas,* May–June, 1980.

the other organizations, they are often referred to as the primary, albeit embryonic, expressions of popular power.[1] They have become the main channel of communication for the Sandinista Front. As Comandante Dora María Tellez made clear to a meeting of the CDS, several months before the inauguration of the Council of State, ". . . The CDS permit us to communicate the preoccupations of the people to the state. If the CDS didn't exist, the FSLN wouldn't know what the people are thinking."[2]

The Workplace

Within the nationalized sector of the economy, the APP, workers are involved in plant administration through the participation of elected delegates on committees at both the production unit and plant levels. Also on the committees are administrators who stayed on the job after nationalization, and the plant manager, who is almost always a militant of the FSLN. All aspects of the factory's operations are discussed, ranging from production goals to problems of health and safety. Most plants now also have regular meetings of *all* the workers and administrators to further these discussions. Production councils, grouping together workers and administrators from several factories within the same manufacturing area, are now being set up to review the production goals of an entire sector, in furtherance of Plan 80.

Although workers' participation in these committees and councils implies only a preliminary form of workers' control (the final decisions still rest largely with the administrators), their influence is expected to grow as they gain experience.[3]

Workers at privately-owned plants, lacking such direct access to decision making, do play the crucial role of guaranteeing that the productivity of the factory is maintained. Economic Reactivation Assemblies are being organized, where workers have the opportunity to grill management. At the first Assembly, held at the 6,300-worker San Antonio sugar mill (Nicaragua's largest, and fourth largest in Latin America), the workers' questions ranged from whether several fires had been accidents or sabotage, to requesting further information on the state of the international sugar market, to demanding to know why replacement machinery was slow in arriving.[4]

Without waiting for a formal review, workers in over a dozen plants have taken over their factories in the past several months, after discovering that the owners had been draining away the profits. These workers have organized themselves to fulfill all administrative positions and make all decisions themselves, in some cases increasing production as much as 66 percent.[5] The government recently enacted a decree allowing for nationalization of factories and a fine for the former owners once charges are proven by the workers. To date the workers have been upheld in each case.

All this has not obviated the need for unions, which are being registered at the rate of 32 per month (still as single-plant unions, their organizational form under Somoza). The unions are responsible for seeing that their firms conform to the collective bargaining agreements, and every union has a representative to oversee safety and health conditions.

The Land

In the countryside, the ATC has organized the workers on state farms into trade union committees which, like their urban counterparts, are gradually assuming a greater participation—along with INRA administrators—in all facets of agricultural production, from production schedules and crop allocation, to the incorporation of new capital equipment. The ATC sees technical training programs as the key to more direct workers' control.

The State

With the inauguration on May 4th of the Council of State, the mass organizations have moved toward direct participation in decision making at the national level. Composed of 47 delegates from 29 national political, professional and mass organizations, the Council has a joint legislative function with the Junta, with the important exception that the Junta has veto power, and the Council does not. In all, 24 seats have been designated to the FSLN and its organizations, including three each for the CST and ATC, one each for AMNLAE, the women's organization, and JS-19, the student organization, six for the FSLN itself and one for the Sandinista Army.

The Council of State deals with major questions involving the overall direction of the revolution, both domestic and foreign. Already the mass organizations have petitioned the Council of State to condemn the US military maneuvers (Solid Shield-80) in the Caribbean.

Commenting on the character of the Council of State, Angel Sevilla, a small coffee producer and ATC activist from Matagalpa, went straight to the point: "The installation of the Council of State is no more than the participation of the people who already have power."[6]

Even when their participation is consultative rather than direct, the mass organizations wield enormous moral authority within the various new state structures. Speaking to the National Constituent Assembly of the ATC, Comandante Jaime Wheelock, Minister of Agriculture and Agrarian Reform, pointed out that, "The ATC has a permanent position in INRA, on its Council. And you are a power there. For us, what you say in INRA is practically law. . . . "[7]

One of the innovations that legitimizes this consultative role is the establishment of a Programmatic Coordinating Commission (CPC) for each ministry. Membership in each CPC includes representatives from other appropriate ministries as well as delegates from the mass organizations. Periodic reviews of all aspects of the ministries' operations give the delegates the chance to draw attention to bureaucratic failings or ineptitude.

What is often needed, however, is for the mass organizations to work more directly with a particular ministry at the operational level. For example, small agricultural producers complained that they were having difficulties obtaining credit from the National Development Bank (BND) and INRA, each of which were authorized to dispense loans, and whose technocrats were accustomed to working with large landowners. The answer was to coordinate the credit institutions through a joint credit commission of both BND and INRA, together with a third member from ATC. By representing the small producers, the ATC delegate would make sure that the institutions met their credit needs, answered questions thoroughly and patiently, etc.

The Vanguard

An integral element in the advance toward "popular power" is the relationship between the masses and the FSLN. "The FSLN," says Comandante Carlos Nuñez, "came to be and is the vanguard of the Nicaraguan people not only for having defined the correct way of struggle, but also for having clearly defined that the masses were the forces capable of moving the wheel of history. If yesterday, oriented and directed by their vanguard, they were the motor of the overthrow of the dictatorship, then today, directed by that vanguard, they are the motor of the revolution."[8]

Although to be a vanguard is to fulfill a leadership function for the masses, the relationship is not defined by the Front as a static one. "In Nicaragua the people are not isolated from the vanguard or vice versa," argues Ricardo Wheelock, a long-time FSLN member and currently ambassador to the USSR. "There's intercommunication between the two of them. That's an important dynamic. Neither is our vanguard thinking in terms of utopias, nor are our people making revolution independently of the vanguard."[9]

That dynamic, says Carlos Nuñez, requires a "permanent relationship" with the people through the mass organizations. That relationship is partially attained by means of all the FSLN activists and militants who work within the mass organizations, one of the criteria in fact for joining the FSLN.[10]

Maintaining the correct dynamic between the developed centralism of the FSLN and the more loosely organized mass groups is a major preoccupation of the organizations themselves. "Following the leadership of the FSLN," argues CST Secretary-General Iván García, "doesn't mean, for example, that the FSLN imposes its criteria over the workers in authoritarian fashion. To the contrary, the FSLN enriches its political conceptions and strengthens its position as vanguard by understanding the concerns of the workers and applying them to the real conditions in a way that aligns those concerns to the development of the revolutionary process."[11]

Thus, many different forms of popular participation are opening up, not only as the mass organizations evolve into stronger and more politically sophisticated entities, but also as the progressive socialization of the economy erodes the capitalist past. The ultimate direction of this dialectical growth of political consciousness, organizational forms and state transformation is the creation of "popular power." No one yet has a definitive vision of what popular power will look like. But everyone understands what it means: that the dispossessed popular classes, the majority, will have the determinant voice in establishing the future direction in Nicaragua.

Notes

1 *Barricada*, December 11, 1979.
2 *ibid.*, March 15, 1980.
3 *ibid.*, March 29, 1980.
4 *ibid.*, March 23, 29, 30, 1980.
5 *ibid.*, March 14, 21, 1980.
6 NACLA interview with Angel Sevilla, small coffee producer and ATC activist.
7 Asamblea Nacional Constitutiva, *Memorias* (Managua, Nicaragua, 1980), p. 38.
8 *El Brigadista* (Nicaragua), March 1980.
9 *Guardian*, February 13, 1980.
10 For specific membership preconditions, see *Barricada*, December 11, 1979.
11 Iván García, "Papel de los trabajadores en el cumplimiento del Plan '80," *Barricada*.

44. The Council of State and the Mass Organizations *

By the Institute for Central American Studies

On August 23, 1980, just over a year after the Sandinista victory over Somoza Commander Humberto Ortega announced that national elections would be postponed from the originally scheduled date in order to carry out a national census, register the hundreds of thousands who had never voted during scheduled date in order to carry Somoza's regime, and to move ahead with the literacy program so that people could make educated choices.

The postponement of elections brought cries of "totalitarianism" from Sandinista opponents such as Alfonso Robelo, a wealthy industrialist and member of COSEP (Higher Council for Private Enterprise). These cries have been echoed by others, inside and outside Nicaragua, the most recent critic being former ambassador to the US, Francisco Fiallos, who resigned in December after publicly airing his feelings that early elections were essential.[1]

It is important to note, however, that although national elections will not be held until 1985, hundreds of thousands of Nicaraguans are actively involved in an

*Reprinted from *Mesoamérica*, January, 1983.

electoral process, choosing local, regional, and national representatives to the Council of State.

Inaugurated May 4, 1980, the Council of State is the main legislative branch of the Government of National Reconstruction. In addition to approving (or disapproving) *Junta* legislation and presenting its own proposals to the *Junta* for new legislation, the Council of State serves as a forum for political and ideological debate.

Originally composed of 33 seats, the majority of which favored the interests of the private business sector, the FSLN directorate later added fourteen new delegates to the Council, which changed the balance of voting power to favor the interests of the peasant and working classes and other popular mass organizations. The addition of these fourteen delegates served to incorporate the majority of Nicaraguans into the decision-making process.

Critics, particularly the Nicaraguan Democratic Movement (MDN) headed by Alfonso Robelo, have charged that the addition of the fourteen delegates violated the original agreement established among a broad coalition of Nicaraguans prior to Somoza's fall. The Sandinistas have responded that to exclude the newly represented organizations, whose memberships have grown tremendously since the initial agreement was made, would mean the exclusion of the majority of Nicaraguans.

The new delegates of the Council of State represent the following organizations: the Association of Rural Workers' (ATC), Sandinista Workers' Union (CST), Sandinista Defense Committees (CDSs), Center for Union Action and Unity (CAUS), Federation of Health Workers (FETSALUD), Nicaraguan Womens' Association (AMNLAE), Teachers' Union (ANDEN), Higher Education Council (CNES), Journalists' Guild (UPN), Association of Clergy (ANCLEN), National Union of Farmers and Cattle Ranchers (UNAG), Sandinista Youth Organization (US), Union of Miskitu, Sumu and Rama Indians and Sandinistas (MIS-URASATA), and the Sandinista Armed Forces (EPS).

To understand the significance of the changes in the Council of State, it is necessary to take a closer look at the mass organizations. The most important are the ATC, UNAG, CST, the CDSs, and AMNLAE.

Table I. Composition of the Present Council of State.

Organizations	Number of Seats
Patriotic Front (FPN)	
FSLN	6
Independent Liberal party (PLI)	1
People's Social Christian party (PPSC)	1
Nicaraguan Democratic Movement (MDN)	1

Other parties
    Nicaraguan Democratic Conservative party   1
    Social Christian party   1

Popular organizations
    Sandinista Defense Committees (CDSs)   9
    July 19th Sandinista Youth   1
    Luisa Amanda Espinoza
        Nicaraguan Women's Association (AMNLAE)   1

Labor organizations
    Association of Rural Workers (ATC)   3
    Sandinista Workers' Central (CST)   3
    Independent General Workers' Confederation (CGTI)   2
    Rural Workers' Central   1
    Council for Union Unity (CUS)   1
    Center for Union Action and Unity (CAUS)   1
    Federation of Health Workers (FETSALUD)   1

Guilds and other social organizations
    Armed Forces   1
    National Association of Clergy   1
    National Council of Educators   1
    National Association of Educators   1
    Journalist Guild   1
    Unity of Miskitu, Sumu, Rama and Sandinistas
        (MISURASATA)   1
    National Association of Professionals   1

Private-sector groups
    Nicaraguan Development Institute (INDE)   1
    Chamber of Industries   1
    Confederation of Chambers of Commerce   1
    Chambers of Construction   1
    Union of Nicaraguan Agricultural Producers (UPANIC)   1
    National Union of Farmers and Cattle Ranchers (UNAG)   1

Total representation   47

Apportioned geographically

Source: Consejo de Estado, "Saludo al primer aniversario de nuestra revolución popular sandinista," Organo Informativo del Consejo de Estado, Press Release No. 1, Managua, July, 1980.

The origin of the ATC dates back to the '60s when Christian missionaries began bringing peasants into the organization "Delegates of the Word." The Delegates of the Word trained lay people in an attempt to raise people's consciousness about social problems. This organization later became the Committee of Rural Workers. By the mid-'70s it had joined forces with the Sandinistas, who supported the workers' demands for improved living conditions, better wages and access to social services such as sanitary facilities and medical care for themselves and their families.

At the time of the September Insurrection in 1978, there were a few thousand workers organized in the ATC. By December of the same year, membership had jumped to 50,000. Today, three years after the triumph, the ATC represents more than 120,000 workers.

The UNAG was formed in 1981 to represent the interests of the small and medium landholders, whose needs are very different from those of the landless peasants. Although it was formed quite recently, there are already 75,228 producers affiliated with UNAG. Many of these are organized into cooperatives to facilitate obtention of bank credit. Together with the members of the ATC, UNAG's members work in the formation and implementation of the agrarian reform program.

The CST evolved from the Insurrectional Workers' Fighting Committees (CLTS), which organized urban workers in the struggle against Somoza. Today the CST represents 70 percent of unionized labor. Under Somoza, the Labor Code prohibited the formation of national craft or industry-wide unions, permitting only the organization of plant based unions in order to prevent national unity among the working class. Although the Somoza Labor Code remains in operation, the Sandinista government immediately suspended the clause mentioned above. The elaboration of a new labor code is one of the urgent tasks facing the Council of State.

The largest (approximately 400,000 members) and most important of the mass organizations are the Sandinista Defense Committees (CDSs). With nine seats, the CDSs have more voting strength in the Council of State than any other organization including the FSLN, which has only six seats. Unlike other mass organizations which represent specific interest groups, the CDSs are not tied to any particular sector. Based on the smallest unit of the population—the urban block—the CDS is open to all Nicaraguans, young, old, men, women, party members and non-members, businessmen and workers, Catholics, Protestants and atheists.

The CDS has numerous functions, among them maintenance of neighborhood security, accomplished through 24-hour vigilance against delinquency and counter-revolutionary activity; organization of street cleaning, garbage disposal, tree-planting, building playgrounds, defense of the local economy by appointing "watchdog" committees who guard against over-pricing and hoarding, organization of literacy and vaccination campaigns in collaboration with the different government ministries in charge, and vigilance against state bureaucracy.

The involvement of women in the Nicaraguan Revolution in the armed struggle as well as in the defense and reconstruction of the country has been massive. In some provinces women make up as much as 40 percent of the voluntary Sandinista army (EPS).

AMNLAE—named after the first woman killed in the struggle against Somoza, Luisa Amanda Espinoza—today holds a seat on the Council of State. Composed of more than 25,000 women, AMNLAE has developed a structure of neighborhood committees, each headed by a coordinator, a promotional secretary and a political development secretary, elected by the local members. The committees serve as local forums for debates on issues such as literacy and social welfare programs, the role of women in the military and in trade unions, the politics of shared housework, child care, contraception and abortion.

AMNLAE's most recent accomplishment in the Council of State was the passing of the "Ley de Alimentación," (literally the "Law of Feeding"), which requires that a father provide financial support for offspring regardless of whether the couple is legally married or not.

Each mass organization follows a similar pattern in electing representatives to the Council of State. Beginning with the most basic unit, be it the work place or neighborhood committee, members elect secretaries who are in charge of different functions. In a CDS, for example, one secretary coordinates health programs for the *barrio,* another coordinates education programs, another cultural events and so on. The next level is the Zonal Council to which each work center or *barrio* elects two representatives. Finally, for the Council of State elections, zonal delegates select their representatives to the regional assemblies where nominations are made and delegates to the Council of State are elected.

Notes

[1] Many US critics seem to have forgotten American Revolutionary history. The first US elections were held April 30, 1789, thirteen years after the Declaration of Independence was signed and nearly eight years after Cornwallis' surrender at Yorktown 19 Oct 1781.

45. The Trade Union Movement in Nicaragua*(and list of Trade Union Confederations compiled by NACLA**)

By the Instituto Histórico Centroamericano.

Trade Union Confederations:

Sandinista Workers' Confederation "José Benito Escobar" (CST): Established

---

*Reprinted from *Envio,* June 1, 1982.
**Reprinted from *NACLA Report on the Americas,* May–June, 1982.

following the victory, initially incorporating the clandestine workers' committees and the National Union of Employees (UNE).

The CST now incorporates over 380 unions, organized nationally into 12 departments, with a membership exceeding 100,000. The CST is named after José Benito Escobar, a construction worker and member of the FSLN national leadership who was assassinated by the dictatorship in July 1978.

Association of Rural Workers (ATC): With roots that go back to radical church activists, the FSLN first organized landless peasants into Committees of Agricultural Workers in 1976. After two years of land invasions and protest marches, the committees in 1978 established the ATC. ATC membership was very active during the insurrection, ambushing National Guardsmen and cutting their communications, and setting up supply lines for the guerrillas. The ATC now takes in small producers as well as peasants and rural workers. Its steady growth has taken it past 100,000 members.

Nicaraguan Confederation of Workers (CTN): With a Social-Christian orientation, the CTN is an affiliate of the regional CLAT (Confederation of Latin American Workers) and its world organization, WCL (World Confederation of Labor). CTN is probably the largest confederation after CST. Before the victory it numbered about 20,000 and today boasts 105 unions with 65,000 members. Its largest affiliate, FETSALUD, however, a union of over 8,000 health workers, is in the process of moving away from the CTN.

General Confederation of Workers-Independent (CGT-I): CGT-I is a member of the regional CPUSTAL (Permanent Workers Council of Latin America) and its world organization, WFTU (World Federation of Trade Unions), both with a Communist orientation. Affiliated with it is the major construction union, SCAAS. Close to the Communist Party of Nicaragua (PSN), a pro-Moscow Communist Party, the CGT-I's unions reportedly have about 5,000 members, and its particular strength is in the textile sector. Some of its leadership has become hostile to the FSLN.

Action and Labor Union Federation (CAUS): Organized by the Socialist Party of Nicaragua (PSN), a pro-Moscow Communist Party, the CAUS's unions cooperated with the FSLN during the insurrection, and belonged to the MPU.

Confederation for Trade Union Unification (CUS): With only several thousand members, CUS is a member of ORIT (Inter-American Regional Organization of Workers) and its world organization, ICFTU (International Confederation of Free Trade Unions). ICFTU, with a Social-Democratic orientation, was created as an alternative to the WFTU. CUS is also a beneficiary of aid from AIFLD (American Institute for Free Labor Development), an agency closely linked in the past to the CIA. CUS was the least combative federation during the years of the dictatorship.

Workers Front (FO): Organized by Popular Action Movement (MAP), a small split from the FSLN in the early 1970s, originally with a pro-China position. FO has retained a belligerent attitude toward the government and the FSLN, although one small faction broke away and supported the Front.

For various reasons which we shall not analyze here, Nicaragua is suffering a serious economic crisis, which is having, and will continue to have, a notable effect upon the manufacturing sector, especially since the present economic strategy of the Government of Reconstruction places top priority upon the development of the agricultural sector.

Minister of Industry Emilio Baltodano, in an interview published May 10 by the Managua newspaper *Barricada,* stated that "given the serious shortage of foreign exchange, we have had to prioritize the needs of the manufacturing sector, and the harsh reality is that many companies will have to rely on their own resources." Baltodano explained that the industries which are considered priorities are "medicine, food, clothing, non-leather shoes, soap and detergent, and industrial metal which is essential for agro-industrial production and for construction," adding that "we had originally thought we would see one or two percent growth in the manufacturing sector, but we now see that this is not possible."

In his July 19th speech, Coordinator of the Government Junta Daniel Ortega pointed out that "we must invest more dollars in the productive sectors so as to develop our agricultural and livestock production, including our agro-industrial production, because these sectors represent the basis for our national development." This economic strategy will obviously have an impact upon the manufacturing sector. In the short run, some factories in non-priority industries which are losing money at the present time will have to close.

Despite the fundamental problems mentioned above, the labor movement has acquired a new dynamic in the last three years. A study of this dynamic can help answer many questions that are often asked outside Nicaragua: Is there trade union freedom in Nicaragua? What is the level of worker participation in the trade union movement and in the revolutionary process? Does one find different conceptions of trade unions and how are those differences manifested? Are there substantial differences between present-day trade union activity and that which existed under the Somoza regime?

1. Background Explanations

(A) Types of Unions. The Ministry of Labor groups unions under four different headings. The first is "One-Company Unions," which bring together different types of workers employed by the same company. Four-fifths of all unions and union members fall within this category. The second type is the "Guild Union," made up of workers of one profession or specialty.

"Multi-profession Unions" comprise workers participating in unrelated activities, when in a given location or a given company there are not enough workers of one type to meet the legal minimum. The last category, the "Multi-company Union," brings together different types of workers employed by two or more companies which engage in one type of economic activity.

(B) Size of Unions. The Ministry of Labor also classifies unions by size. Only three unions belong to the largest category, that of unions having more than 1,000

members. (For a complete classification by size, see *Envío* No. 12, June 1982, p. 15).

(C) Collective Agreements. Collective agreements between management and unions must be ratified by the Ministry of Labor. Most agreements are reached with the cooperation of the labor federation to which the individual union belongs. Thus, the number of agreements with which it is involved is an important measure of the activity of any given federation.

During the 45 years of the Somoza regime, only 160 collective agreements were signed. This compares with 546 agreements signed between August 1979 and December 1981, agreements which benefit 137,267 workers, most of whom are in the manufacturing sector.

Percentage Distribution of Collective Agreements by Labor Federation

Federation	Aug. '79–Dec. '80	Jan. '81–June '81	July '81–Dec. '81
CST	66.0%	63.1%	63.9%
ATC	3.0	11.5	24.6
CTN	8.2	6.6	7.0
CUS	10.2	4.1	1.5
CGT (i)	4.1	4.1	1.5
CAUS	7.5	8.2	1.5
Other	1.0	1.8	—

Source: Ministry of Labor, *Socio-Labor Statistics Bulletin,* No. 4, March 1982.
Note: For a description of each federation, see *Envío* No. 12, June 1982, pp. 16–17.

2.Aspects of the Life of Three Different Trade Unions

SOLKA Laboratories. On July 16 we attended a production meeting at SOLKA Laboratories, a pharmaceutical company located 16 km. south of Managua. A billboard placed at the factory entrance lists the workers' four commitments: *a)* to continue to increase production and productivity; *b)* to increase the level of worker organization; *c)* to eliminate lack of work discipline; *d)* more actively to participate in the militias and in the voluntary night-watch.

More than 300 workers were joined in the meeting by delegations from other companies. Presiding at the meeting were some members of the union's directorate, representatives of the Sandinista Workers' Federation (CST), to which the SOLKA Union belongs, a blind worker honored for being one of the best workers in the factory, and the mother of a former SOLKA worker who died in September 1981 during militia training. The union has named itself after this last worker, Basilio Cálix.

After a brief introduction by the union's General Secretary, representatives of the different divisions of the company (e.g., serums, pills, maintenance, cafeteria) presented divisional reports. Each of these reports, which, workers told us, were the fruit of much worker effort, contained two main sections: *a)* main problems which have an adverse effect upon production; *b)* suggested worker solutions. After two hours of presentation of these reports, the General Administrator of the company gave his report, which dealt with many of the workers' criticisms, explained other points, and presented for the consideration of the workers the future projects and plans of the company (plans for growth, changes, corrections, etc.).

An honest and critical, though orderly, discussion followed, open to all workers and administrators. The latter stated that 65 percent of the production goals had been met, and that the company had shown a 12 percent profit in the first half of 1982. Listening to the discussion, we appreciated the great significance of the goals listed on the billboard at the factory entrance.

Thus the production meeting was a collective evaluation, by workers, technicians and administrators, of all aspects of the company. The evaluation included self-criticism, as well as recognition of the most disciplined workers, who were honored for their sense of responsibility.

Interview. After the meeting we interviewed Julio González, a worker in the maintenance division and General Secretary of the union.

Q.: Did this sort of union participation occur before July 19, 1979?

A.: Not at all. Under the Somoza dynasty workers were manipulated by the "tranquilizer policies" of management. Little favors and gifts were occasionally distributed, which served as a diversion for the workers and prevented their organizing. This paternalism created a spirit of conformity, which made our work very difficult, almost clandestine.

At that time SOLKA belonged to the Solárzano family, which had close ties with Somoza, with whose help the company was set up. Salvadora Somoza, the sister of the dictator, was also a shareholder. At the time of the victory the Somoza share of the company was confiscated, and six months later, when the Solárzanos left the country, their part was also confiscated and the company became part of the People's Property Area with 100 percent state ownership.

Q.: Were there many problems immediately after the confiscation?

A.: At first there were some workers who had had special privileges under the former management, who resented the government. It was a difficult period because the workers had no experience in collective organization, and generally had a very traditional notion of the functions of a trade union, a notion which was not appropriate in the new situation.

Q.: And what is the present situation of the SOLKA Union?

A.: The union structure has been greatly consolidated. The workers have developed a high level of awareness and participation: they deal with the global questions of production and they understand the economic situation of the country. Our meetings now are different from those held right after July 19, 1979. Worker participation is very positive and has led to the improvement of some elements of production in the company. The innovations of workers, creating spare parts using their imagination and scarce resources, have been significant.

Q.: Even in this new situation, there could still be contradictions between the workers and management, which, after all, is still an employer. What is your opinion?

A.: This is very interesting. There have been many problems. After the triumph, many technicians who had been closely allied with the management left the country. Others took advantage of the situation, wrapping themselves in the mantle of Sandinismo while in fact refusing to cooperate. Technicians had been in a privileged position, but with the implementation of worker participation in decision making, they saw that they would now be on a more equal basis with the other workers. So there were confrontations, and some of the technicians who had stayed had to leave because of worker pressure. When I first became General Secretary of the union, the technicians didn't even show up at the production meetings. We made an effort to explain the new reality to them. The situation now is much better. Later other technicians who were also revolutionaries came to SOLKA, and this increased the participation of all sectors of the company in the common process.

The Nicaragua Machinery Company (NIMAC). Because many private companies operate in Nicaragua within the structure of the mixed economy, we decided to visit the Nicaragua Machinery Company, located just north of Managua. NIMAC repairs and sells John Deere farm equipment, and its present owners are Nicaraguans. The company employs 184 workers, of whom 140 belong to the Ricardo Membreño Union, named after a NIMAC worker who died in the insurrection. At the time of its creation a few months before the triumph, the union was pretty much underground. After July 19, it gained legal recognition and affiliated itself with the Sandinista Workers' Federation.

Interview. During our visit to NIMAC we interviewed Pablo Sánchez, in charge of the union militia, Bismark Colomer, Secretary of Culture and Publicity, Sergio Pérez, member of the "Grass-roots Committee" (an FSLN party structure within the company), and Miguel Jarquín, a company worker.

Q.: Can you describe the union's activity before the 19th of July, 1979?

P. Sánchez: We began discussing the creation of a union around the end of 1978. In line with Somoza's policy, the management at that time systematically blocked any efforts aimed at organizing the workers. So we had to meet at the university or in houses of different workers. But things were very hard, because many workers shared the management's point of view, and others came only to spy on us, and then reported to management.

S. Pérez: The Directorate of the union was formed at the beginning of 1979, with the support of 50 percent of the workers, but management repressed the union by firing the leadership. But the work continued, and after the triumph 80 percent of the workers joined the union.

P. Sánchez: Before July 1979, the general manager, José Cardenal, repressed and humiliated the workers. Paul Giordano, an American in charge of the spare parts department, was another example of pure and simple repression. By 1979, ten to fifteen workers were being fired every two weeks. When they fired the directorate we went on strike for a week. After the triumph, there was a massive mobilization of the workers, and the resulting political pressure forced Cardenal and Giordano to leave the company.

Q.: Where have you seen the most progress in the past three years?

M. Jarquín: There have been great advances. The first is the reactivation of union activity. Repressive and corrupt structures which hurt the working class have been eliminated. Most of the workers now belong to the union and are taking part in the revolutionary process. We have regular meetings in which everything is discussed, and within the union the workers participate and share their opinions. The workers have rid themselves of the complex which kept them repressed.

B. Colomer: We have also won the subsidization of transportation (the company pays 100 percent of the transit fares of those living in Managua, and 50 percent of the cost of those living outside the city). Workers receive new uniforms every six months. Meals are subsidized by 60 percent. The workers won company financing for a library which contains a wide variety of books. The union won the right to an office, and to a medical dispensary which is open for two hours a day, with a private doctor paid by the company. We receive the medicine from the Nicaraguan Social Security and Social Welfare Institute. The workers participate in the Literacy Crusade. Overall we can say that the greatest advance has been the signing of a contract which contains 48 clauses, all of which are 100 percent to the benefit of the workers. At the moment we are studying the contract to modify it and bring it up to date.

Q.: What is the present relationship between management, the union and the workers?

B. Colomer: Generally speaking, the Union Directorate meets every week with company management. We discuss everything. We also have access to the company books. In our in-service workshops we decided to cooperate with the company to increase production. At the same time as we were strengthening our union organization, we were searching for better methods that would reduce costs. We make suggestions to management concerning tensions which exist between them and the workers. The Directorate is always looking to resolve disagreements.

P. Sánchez: In the last few days we have had to deal with a controversial question. The company ordered three vehicles from the US, with a total cost of $24,000, despite the state of economic and social emergency in the country. Earlier, the administration halted the construction of a workers' cafeteria which would have cost 500,000 córdobas, giving the economic and social emergency as its reason. We are going to discuss the decision to buy the vehicles since no one consulted the union.

[*Editorial Note:* We do not outline the structure of the NIMAC union here, as it is quite similar to that of the SOLKA union.]

The Managua Gas Station Workers' Union (SITEGMA). SITEGMA, a "Guild Union" affiliated with the Nicaraguan Workers' Federation (CTN) brings together workers from 50 Managua gas stations, 48 of them privately owned. CTN officials claim that the union has 364 members, but the Ministry of Labor states that SITEGMA has only 51 members. This latter figure, officials in the Ministry's Department of Statistics told us, represents the number of signatures in the record of the meeting which elected the union's Directorate. In April 1981 the union gave the Ministry an official List of Claims, as part of the collective bargaining process, with

270 signatures. To be valid, this List must have the signatures of all union members, though non-members may also sign. Thus, the true number of SITEGMA members would appear to be between 51 and 270.

We met with representatives of SITEGMA in the office of the CTN. Present at the meeting were Alberto Alemán, union President, Julio Veliz, Secretary of Organization and Publicity, Earl Downs, Secretary of Culture and Education, José Zamora, Secretary of Finance, José López, Recording Secretary, and Antonio Jarquín, the CTN's union advisor, who is not a member of SITEGMA.

Interview. Q.: What have been the main advances of the past three years?

A. Jarquín: The first was the reorganization of the union (SITEGMA had operated before 1979 and was reactivated in July of that year). Another was the signing of a collective agreement by which certain rights were achieved which previously had been totally disregarded by the owners. We have also won partial subsidization of food and education, time off for education, and some improvement in health care.

Q.: What do you feel are the differences in union activity between the Somoza period and the present one?

A. Jarquín: We believe that there has been a marked difference. Before there was not the slightest expression of trade union freedom. Anyone connected to a union ran the risk of being killed. We think that the present situation in Nicaragua is critical, difficult, and that some uncontrollable events have had negative repercussions upon trade union freedom and pluralism.

Q.: Can you give some examples?

A. Jarquín: Our union has suffered assaults from the Marxist-Leninist sector of the CGT (i) (Independent General Federation of Labor), and from the Sandinista Workers' Federation. With respect to the state, under Somoza collective bargaining was held up, the granting of legal status was delayed, as were certifications of changes in the union Directorate. At this time we feel that it is irresponsible on the part of the government to allow these types of things to continue.

Q.: Then would you say that SITEGMA has problems or disagreements with the Ministry of Labor?

A. Jarquín: At the moment we don't have any disagreements, but we think they are coming, as the gas rationing could lead to unemployment in our sector.

Q.: In other unions the workers give great importance to the task of protecting the productive centers. What is your union's policy in this respect?

A. Jarquín: We have not implemented a policy on the militias at the union level. With respect to voluntary night-watch, we think that this is important, but we also think that it distorts the role which the workers should play. It seems to us to be a well-camouflaged tool for distorting the workers' struggle. We think that protection is not simply looking after the company's property, but has a wider sense which includes the participation of the workers in administrative decisions.

Q.: What do the workers at the grass-roots level of SITEGMA think about the participation of the CTN in the Democratic Coordinating Committee, whose positions coincide with those of the Superior Council of Private Enterprise (COSEP)?

A. Jarquín: The alliances of the CTN with certain political, guild, and private enterprise sectors were defined in the Fourth Congress of the CTN in which it was decided that, owing to the particular circumstances of the present moment, we should form non-organic alliances. The union's grass-roots understand perfectly that this is only a product of the present situation.

3. Points for Comparisons and Conclusions

We have presented three distinct trade union realities. We included the SOLKA Union as an example of a union within the People's Property Area. It is a relatively large union, with over 300 members, affiliated with the CST. We included the NIMAC Union, as it operates in the private sector, is a somewhat smaller union, with 140 members, and is also affiliated with the CST. The inclusion of SITEGMA reflects the fact that it is a "Guild Union" affiliated wth the CTN, and operates within companies 96 percent of which are privately owned.

Besides these three unions, we have studied several other types of unions. We can offer certain comparative reflections which emerge from our study of these distinct trade union realities:

(A) There is a high level of trade union activity, which indicates an important quantitative advance in the labor movement during the last three years.

(B) This union activity also represents progress in experience and organization, and an overcoming of the passivity imposed upon the movement during the Somoza years.

(C) In the trade unions which we visited, the concept of "union freedom" has a unique dimension which perhaps does not correspond to the more traditional criteria used in some countries. None of the persons interviewed even mentioned the suspension of the right to strike (one of the economic and social emergency measures decreed in September 1981), through outside Nicaragua this measure might be seen as a flagrant violation of union freedom. The concept of union freedom which we discovered in our interviews has three basic elements: the freedom to participate actively in the life of the union; the freedom and the right to participate actively in the running of the company and in its policy decisions; the negation of the climate of terror and anti-union persecution in the Somoza period.

(D) There is an evident increase in worker participation in the control and the running of both private and public companies. We were struck by the many structures and mechanisms established within the unions affiliated with the CST to implement this control and participation. We note that in the unions affiliated with the CST the union has a "watch-dog" role in the running of companies in the private sector, while workers enjoy a more integral participation in the management of public sector companies. Without a doubt this integral participation in companies of the People's Property Area reduces the impact of errors committed by technicians and administrators appointed by the People's Industry Corporation (COIP), errors which reflect either inexperience or incomprehension.

These limitations of COIP (e.g., lack of understanding of the lines of credit, or of the running of the state's administrative apparatus) have led in some cases to a reduction in production or even to a closing of some companies. The active control of the workers compensates for the improvisation which administrators must often confront in the public sector.

We saw less activity and less tendency in this direction in SITEGMA, though it is not easy to compare a company union in which the members work in one location and a service union in which the members are geographically separated. We also found a clear difference between CST and CTN affiliated unions with respect to the tasks of defense of the productive centers. CTN advisor A. Jarquín was quite ambiguous on this point, a clear attitude of nonparticipation.

(E) Within the CST unions there is significant encouragement of worker creativity, reflected in the stimulation of innovation: workers are creating spare parts and even machinery with very few resources and much determination, which saves foreign exchange and strengthens production. The first exhibit of innovators took place in Managua between July 9 and 14.

(F) The Directorate structures of CST and CTN unions differ considerably. SITEGMA has a traditional structure, with a Financial Secretary and a Recording Secretary, while the CST unions have new elements in their structures: Secretaries of Production, of Volunteer Work, Secretaries of the Militia. These new elements express a new conception of the roles of the trade union.

The different political-ideological conceptions of unions define to a large degree their concrete activity at the grass-roots level. The CTN unions express their Federation's mistrust of the Nicaraguan government and of the present socio-political process, a mistrust which leads to a certain nonparticipation in the tasks of the reconstruction, and to a policy of high-level alliances with elements of the Nicaraguan opposition (traditional political parties and owners of large private enterprises).

The unions affiliated with the CST, on the other hand, feel strengthened, not only by increased worker participation and control, but also by their participation in the revolutionary process and by their relation to a government which they feel favors workers.

46. A Church Divided*

By Jackie Reiter

Nearly two years into the Nicaraguan revolutionary process, the Church continues to be an arena of conflict between the country's social forces. While

*Reprinted from *NACLA Report on the Americas*, May–June, 1981, Vol. XV, No. 3 pp. 45-48.

most sectors, including the Church, were united in the struggle against Somoza, the Church hierarchy has become less cooperative in the face of the Sandinista government's clear commitment to true social revolution.

Last October, the bishops laid down an ultimatum to the three priests with government posts, attempting to force them to choose between the Church and politics. Expulsion from the priesthood was the penalty for the latter. The ultimatum was part of a strategy aimed at thwarting the power of the progressive Church. The hierarchy's efforts to maintain the traditional power structure by bringing grass-roots Christian organizations into line and challenging radical clergy, throws into relief the polarity of class interests encompassed by the Church.

A predominantly Catholic and devout people, the Nicaraguans' fight against tyranny took sustenance from their faith. This incorporation of faith into the liberation struggle must be considered in light of the 1968 Bishops' Conference in Medellín, which denounced the unjust distribution of wealth and victimization of the masses. The bishops called for a society where the poor were not *objects* but *agents* of history, a radical transformation which had as its corollary an alternative interpretation of Christian love. The virtues of stoicism, benign suffering and ability to forgive all were replaced by those of an active defense of the poor, a love expressed by commitment to and solidarity with the cause of the poor.

Although the bishops' appeal was not accompanied by strategy for action against the ruling class, for many believers it sanctioned the struggle for change. Eleven years later, at the Puebla Conference of Bishops, the principle was reinforced by the official proclamation of the Church's "preferential option for the poor." The concept of the kingdom of God, hitherto reserved for an afterlife where the poor would be rewarded and the rich punished, shifted to life on earth where, by means of structural changes, justice and equality for all would be safeguarded.

The impetus provided by this option for the poor manifested itself throughout Latin America. Grass-roots Christian organizations sprang up in poor neighborhoods and peasant lay preachers were appointed in the countryside. Gospel teachings were interpreted in light of the daily experiences of an oppressed people. Social issues, such as the need for health facilities and education, became their focus.

Grass-Roots Activism

In Nicaragua, this radicalization of Christian practice was an essential prelude to the struggle against Somoza and the National Guard. From the late 1960s, Christians became a dynamic force within the liberation movement, both ideologically and organizationally. They joined the other mass organizations—street defense committees, peasant, womens' and student bodies—as mainstays of the guerrilla movement.

In the early 1970s, a group of Christian students set up a community in a poor Managua neighborhood, Riguero, based upon the twin principles of socialism and Christianity. The group's integration into the community and commitment to its problems generated an advanced degree of politicization, manifested in hunger strikes and church occupations demanding the release of political prisoners. Luis Carríon and other members of the group later became leading FSLN representatives. In Estelí, known for its radical diocese, clergy and nuns organized clandestine street committees, supplying arms and combatants, as well as giving refuge, passing messages and distributing food during the insurrection.

In the countryside, peasants were also organized into Christian communities, served by lay ministers drawn from their ranks. The peasants' political consciousness was nurtured by the emphasis on a social interpretation of the gospel as well as the lay priests' participation in the peasant organization that was later to become the Rural Workers Association (ATC). This consciousness proved a prerequisite for cooperation with the Frente during the guerrillas' entrenchment in the countryside.

Clergy Join Armed Struggle

Many priests became radicalized by direct engagement between faith and social conditions. In 1977, priests and nuns, mainly of the Capuchin order, wrote to Somoza denouncing the disappearance and murder of 350 peasants in the Atlantic region. They also wrote to President Carter asking him to cease military aid to the Somoza regime, a measure which helped isolate the dictator. Monsignor Obando y Bravo, Archbishop of Managua and a figure associated with the forces seeking an alternative to the dictatorship, acted as a mediator between the Frente and Somoza. Members of the clergy joined the Frente, including internationally acclaimed poet Ernesto Cardenal, now Minister of Culture.

Others took up arms in defense of the people. One of the few who survived is the Spaniard Antonio Sanjines, who fought alongside Gaspar García Laviana, a priest also of Spanish origin who was killed in combat. Of the discrepancy between the armed struggle and Christian doctrine, Sanjines says: "As a Christian and a priest, I never had any doubts about joining Frente Sandinista and taking up arms in defense of the poor."

For many, any remaining qualms about armed struggle were resolved by the bombings of September 1978. All attempts at mediation with Somoza in hopes of mitigating the suffering had failed. In preparation for the shelling of major cities, civilians were threatened with arrest if they appeared on the street. Houses, full of men, women and children, were easy targets for Somoza's flying death squads.

The bishops of Nicaragua issued a document in early June 1979 condoning the armed struggle, based on what they called a "just war theory." First, war may be declared by an authority which is truly representative of the majority and not just of an elite group. Second, the leaders must have just intentions or goals leading to a more humane society, and not seek power to their own ends. Third, violence may only be used as a last resort when nonviolent means have failed. The bishops emphasized that violence is institutionalized in the Third World and in using violence to do away with violence, the good outweighed the bad. Although of marked significance to a religious people, the late appearance of the document, at the beginning of the final insurrection, indicated the hierarchy's begrudging support for the liberation movement.

Bishops Join Bourgeoisie

In the absence of a bishop of the stature of the late Archbishop Romero of El Salvador, the Nicaraguan Church hierarchy has, since the victory, adopted an at best cautious and at worst hostile attitude to the revolution. In November 1979 they issued a document proclaiming their "Christian commitment to the new Nicaragua," applauding measures leading to better living standards for the destitute and linking the gospel to the reigning spirit of solidarity with the poor. They have, however, recently become increasingly critical of the Frente's socialist program.

For many traditional clergy, the desire to eradicate poverty is based in paternalism and charity, sentiments incompatible with the mass mobilization for structural change and self-determination taking place in Nicaragua. The replacement of mass subjection to autocratic rule by mobilization around a materialist idea transcending personalities and rituals is, by its very nature, threatening to a traditionalist church. And the potency of the Christian championing of the poor, as a rallying cry for grass-roots Christians, reinforces the hierarchy's fear that control is slipping out of their hands.

Opposition to the Frente's political program has taken the form of public criticism by the hierarchy, along with some sectors of the bourgeoisie, of a new educational scheme. Called *Escuela Campo* (work study), the scheme is designed to introduce school children to productive work in industry or agriculture for short periods. As well as acquainting schoolgoers with working conditions, the plan reinforces the contact between workers and students established during the 1980 literacy campaign. The project has been denounced by the bourgeois opposition as a subterfuge to undermine the nuclear family by "forcing" (in spite of the declared voluntary character of the scheme) children to spend part of their school holidays in government-sponsored activities. Traditional elements within the Church share the fear that this work study program augurs the transfer of parental authority to the state.

That the Church hierarchy, with CELAM (Conference of Latin American Bishops) as its ideologue, should find a community of interests with the bourgeois "democratic" opposition is hardly surprising. The Latin American Church's predominant identification with concentrations of wealth is legion, and Nicaragua has been no exception. Since a popular church has become an organized force in the continent, CELAM has become the reactionary counterbalance. By various means, the bishops have expressed their discontent about Nicaragua's development. They prevented Obando y Bravo from speaking at Puebla in March 1979 to raise support for his harrowed country, and after the Sandinista victory, devised a plan of "aid" to Nicaragua, including an exhortation to pray for its salvation from totalitarianism.

Recently, CELAM, acting through the Nicaraguan bishops, has taken more serious measures. Starting with the dismissal of Father Ortiz of León for alleged neglect of his flock, a campaign has been unleashed to remove progressive clergy from their posts. Priests and nuns in San Judas, a Managua neighborhood noted for its radical Christian community, were given notice by the bishops of their transferral to other countries. After community protests, the hierarchy backed down, at least in part. The nuns were reinstated while the priests must leave when their assignments are completed.

The hierarchy's efforts to assert authority culminated in the ultimatum issued to the three priests in government—Ernesto Cardenal, Minister of Culture; Miguel d'Escoto, Foreign Minister; and Edgar Parrales, Minister of Social Welfare—to choose between Church and politics. But once again, the hierarchy had to back down, failing to enforce the conditions of the ultimatum. The deadline, December 31, 1980, went by with no response by either side. At a meeting at the end of January, the priests and bishops agreed to refer the matter to the Vatican, which is expected to approve the priests' continued participation in government. This capitulation to the progressive forces within the Church is an implicit recognition of the support which they command in the population.

Nicaraguan Christianity

For members of grass-roots communities who have both participated in the insurrection and in the process of reconstruction there is no doubt as to the compatibility of Christianity and *Sandinismo*. They have demonstrated that belief in this union overrides their allegiance to a traditional church. But the threat of a divided church is a dangerous one. While the revolution seeks a united church carrying out its mission in a spirit of communion with the political and ideological climate, a divided church can only serve imperialist interests as the hierarchy dissociates itself from its base, legitimizing the opposition's counterrevolutionary stand.

The Frente's statement on religion (October 7, 1980) reflects the unique breadth of the Nicaraguan revolution, which embraces the Church as an integral part of the new society. In it, the vital contribution of Christians to the fight for liberation and the construction of a revolutionary society is acknowledged. The Church's requirements—as laid out at Puebla and reiterated by Nicaraguan bishops in their post-victory document—for freedom to carry out their evangelical mission, to practice and teach their faith and its moral imperatives, have been guaranteed. "Our experience shows that when convinced Christians are able to respond to the needs of the people and of history, their beliefs lead them to revolutionary militancy," the Frente announced, spelling out the common ground shared by Christianity and Marxism. The statement marks a turning point for both Christians and Marxists throughout the world.

This challenge to the Church is an historic and transcendent one. As a spiritual and moral guide, it leaves no grounds for vacillation. The unreserved commitment and energetic activity of its grass-roots communities is evidence that the new Nicaragua provides fertile terrain for Christian values. But if the Church hierarchy spurns its popular base, obeying the interest of imperialism, it will not only isolate itself, but will also condemn itself to being an agent of alienation and abstraction, rather than a source of humanitarian values shared by the whole community.

47. The Silence on Nicaragua*

By Elliott Abrams

Elliott Abrams is assistant secretary of state for human rights.

Congress, the executive branch and the human rights organizations have just completed extensive reviews of the human rights situation in El Salvador, in connection with the "certification" of human rights progress there. Both the House and Senate foreign relations committees held hearings; several human rights groups issued reports, including a 272-page report produced jointly by two such groups; and all of this was important enough to be featured on television news programs.

The human rights picture in El Salvador warrants this attention. But an equally serious question in a nearby country—Nicaragua—has received only scant attention. This is true even though the last few weeks have seen an extraordinary deterioration there. The new developments come against a background of reports of torture, continuing government harassment of the Nicaraguan Human Rights Commission and continuing violence against Indian tribes, which has resulted in the flight from the country of several hundred Sumo Indians in recent weeks.

Now, here are some of the major incidents of the last few weeks alone:

• The bishop of the Atlantic Coast province, who has been harassed repeatedly by the Sandinistas, was once again detained.

• The Sandinistas prohibited publication of a pastoral letter from the pope to the bishops of Nicaragua, which had been read in churches throughout the country on August 1. For two weeks, *La Prensa* was forbidden to publish it, and the church's radio station was forbidden to read it on the air. Because of this dispute, *La Prensa* was not printed for several days.

• On August 9, more than 20 churches belonging to several Protestant sects were seized by the Sandinistas' "neighborhood committees," whose spokesmen said the churches were in contact with the CIA and working for the counterrevolution.

• When the Nicaraguan archbishop replaced a parish priest who was working closely with the regime, an organized mob gathered at the church. When the auxiliary bishop of Managua came to the scene, he was beaten up by the mob. The archbishop has excommunicated all those involved in the beating.

• The head of the church's radio station, a priest, was forced to disrobe at gunpoint by Sandinista police and was marched naked through the streets of Managua to jail. Pictures of the naked priest were shown on the government television station and printed in the Sandinista press. The Sandinistas said he had been caught in a love triangle; when *La Prensa* tried to print an interview with the priest, the story was censored.

---

*Reprinted from the *Washington Post*, August 22, 1982.

• In the last week, violent clashes in Masaya between Sandinista mobs and Catholic school students and their supporters have resulted in three deaths, and mobs have twice tried to attack Archbishop Obando y Bravo.

All of these events have taken place since the beginning of July, and no one can doubt the pattern that they form: the Sandinistas have decided on a tremendous increase in pressure on organized religion in Nicaragua. As the official Vatican newspaper, *L'Osservatore Romano*, has said: "The church and its institutions have become targets of offensiveness and violence by groups of Sandinistas, a situation that has never before come about in a nation where Catholic faith and tradition have been so firmly rooted."

Where are the protests? Does anyone doubt that a series of events half as serious in El Salvador would be front-page news? Does anyone doubt that human rights groups would be clamoring? They would be right to do so, and the silence over events in Nicaragua is deeply troubling. The State Department receives protests and inquiries regularly from human rights groups about events in countries such as El Salvador and Chile; to date we have not received one inquiry about this attack on religion in Nicaragua.

Now, some people in the human rights movement and in the churches are quite simply pro-Sandinista. They believe Nicaragua has a "progressive" regime. To judge by their behavior, many are simply unwilling to apply to "progressive" countries the same severe standard they apply to countries whose governments they do not support.

For the human rights movement, Nicaragua, where the Sandinistas have co-opted all of the language and symbols of social revolution and progress, is a crucial test. Those who insist on examining El Salvador with a microscope, while seeing no evil in Nicaragua, are undermining the claim of the human rights movement to be interested in people rather than in politics.

Yet this does not explain the attitude of the many who have no political bias toward the Sandinistas: their silence is a true mystery. Is it uninterest in a country not aligned with the United States? A desire to avoid criticizing a country other human rights activists excuse? Simple lack of information?

The fact remains that the silence is deafening. And while it continues, churches and clergy in Nicaragua will be subjected to increasing menace.

48. Discrediting Nicaragua: US Takes Aim at Religion*

By Jaime Peinado

During August, the American and world press gave extensive coverage to a series of incidents in Nicaragua religion which suggested that a confrontation was occurring between the government and the churches. The US State Department seized the opportunity to add repression of religion to its list of charges against "totalitarian" Nicaragua.

In an August 22 Op-Ed article written for the *Washington Post,* Assistant Secretary of State for Human Rights Elliott Abrams gave his version of the incidents and declared, " . . . no one can doubt the pattern they form: the Sandinistas have decided on a tremendous increase in pressure on organized religion in Nicaragua." He concluded his article by accusing the American human rights movement of selectively overlooking alleged human rights violations in Nicaragua.

The most obvious objective of Abrams's article was to justify the continuing aggressive policies of the Reagan administration towards Nicaragua.

The Events of July and August

A brief review of several of the incidents reveals how Abrams distorted the facts to make his case against the Sandinistas.

The Atlantic Coast Bishop. According to Abrams, "The Bishop of the Atlantic Coast, who has been repeatedly harassed by the Sandinistas, was once again detained."

This charge originated as a wire service report in a Brazilian newspaper. When Bishop Schlaefer learned of it, he issued a public statement in which he emphatically declared that he had never been arrested. What did occur was that the Sandinista military flew him out of Puerto Cabezas on July 17 for his safety; military intelligence had learned that a large unit of counter-revolutionaries intended to attack the city on July 19. It was also feared that an assassination attempt might occur which could be blamed on the Sandinistas.

The Santa Rosa Incident. Abrams wrote in the *Post,* "When the Nicaraguan Archbishop replaced a parish priest who was working closely with the regime, an organized mob gathered at the church. When the auxiliary bishop of Managua came to the scene, he was beaten up by the mob."

The editors of *Christianity and Crisis,* an American magazine on religion and social issues, sent a team to Nicaragua to investigate the situation. The following

Reprinted from *Nicaraguan Perspectives,* Number 5, Winter, 1983.

description of the incident is excerpted from their report in the magazine's September 20 issue.

Monsignor José Arias Caldera is one of the best loved priests of the poor in Managua, *una cura de barrio y no de salon* (a neighborhood priest, not a drawing room priest), as he recently described himself. The parish of Santa Rosa where he has worked for eight years was known during the insurrection as the "combative *barrio*," and it still quite obviously is. When the archbishop announced Father Caldera was to be transferred, the parishioners organized protests and briefly took over the church.

Auxiliary Bishop Vivas went to the church to remove the Blessed Sacrament, confronted the people (with harsh and threatening language, it is said), waded into the crowd that, arms locked, surrounded the altar, and fell—or was pushed—to the floor.

Not very edifying church behavior, perhaps, but the issue is essentially an internal church matter . . . and in no way was the Nicaraguan government directly involved.

The Father Carballo Incident. Abrams's next charge concerned a bizarre incident involving Archbishop Obando's press secretary, Father Carballo. Abrams said that "the head of the church's radio station, a priest, was forced at gunpoint by Sandinista police to disrobe and was marched naked through the streets of Managua to jail."

Columnist Jack McKinney of the *Philadelphia Daily News* was in Managua at the time and gave this explanation: "The police did not force Carballo to disrobe. He was in that state when they found him. But what the police did do is save his life from the outraged, pistol-wielding boyfriend of the young woman Carballo was visiting." The police had been accompanying a demonstration down a nearby street when they heard shots and saw a man with a gun chasing a man out of a house. The police covered up the naked man, who was later discovered to be Father Carballo, and took both away in a police jeep.

The Masaya Incident. This is the next piece of evidence presented by Abrams; according to his article, "violent clashes in Masaya between Sandinista mobs and Catholic school students and their supporters resulted in three deaths."

The following description of the events is taken from a September 16 *Latinamerica Press* article by Presbyterian minister James Goff:

On August 16, ex-Somocistas and students from the local high school run by the Salesian fathers ran through the streets of Masaya saying that the Sandinista government was trying to carry off an image of the Assumption of the Virgin Mary, the city's patroness. Later, they attacked the nearby Monimbó police station and the Sandinista Defense Committee (CDS) headquarters. Finally, reportedly armed with machetes, clubs, pistols, and M-16 rifles, they barricaded themselves in the Salesian school, with the acquiescence of five foreign priests, including the principal.

Over ten thousand Masaya residents organized a demonstration to repudiate the school takeover; as the march approached the school, "... it was fired upon from the second story of the school. Two young people, members of the Sandinista Youth Organization, were killed and six others wounded."

Sandinista police were able to clear the school without further injuries; 81 people were arrested. Comandante Tomás Borge came to Masaya and addressed a gathering estimated at 17,000 people; he asked people to remain calm in the face of the provocations being orchestrated against them.

The Hand of the CIA?

The bizarre nature of some of the incidents and the distortions contained in some wire-service reports strongly suggest CIA involvement; the dual purposes of covert action would be to create disunity within Nicaragua and to provide material for anti-Sandinista propoganda. In the April 11, 1981 issue of *The Nation*, ex-CIA agent Ralph McGehee described the propaganda-generating role of the CIA. "Where the necessary circumstances or proofs are lacking to support US intervention, the CIA creates the appropriate situations or else invents them and disseminates its distortions worldwide via its media operations."

Penny Lernoux makes a strong indictment of the CIA in her well-documented book, *Cry of the People*:

> There is conclusive proof that the CIA used religious groups in Latin America for its own secret ends. At the same time it contributed to the persecution and division of the Latin American Catholic Church by supporting right wing Catholic groups, and financed and trained police agencies responsible for the imprisonment, torture and murder of priests, nuns and bishops, some of them US citizens.

In his article in the Spring 1982 issue of *Covert Action*, researcher Fred Landis presented evidence suggesting that the CIA was using religion to destabilize Nicaragua via *La Prensa*:

> In April 1981 a major campaign of psychological warfare began in Nicaragua with an attempt to mobilize protests by Catholics against the government. The first step was to inflame the parents of students attending parochial schools. A *La Prensa* campaign attacked and polarized democratic nationwide forums to discuss educational reform by using such terms as "Marxist brainwashing," "turning children into guerrillas," "filling children with hatred."... Although the clear intention of the propaganda campaign was to polarize relations between Church and State, the religious tone which the political struggle acquired was not created by the Church.

Target: Monimbó

There is ample evidence to suggest that the Salesian school takeover in Monimbó was part of a CIA orchestrated plan to generate an anti-Sandinista insurrection. First of all, according to several independent sources, only 11 of those arrested when the school was cleared by the police were actually from Masaya (Monimbó is a *barrio* of Masaya). Furthermore, 31 of those arrested were members of the openly counter-revolutionary Nicaraguan Democratic Movement.

Secondly, according to the September *Bulletin* of the Managua-based Central American Historical Institute, there had been a rumor campaign throughout Masaya and Monimbó the weekend before the takeover. The message of the rumors was that, " 'The FSLN wants to do away with religion,' 'the FSLN is going to close down the churches,' 'the FSLN is going to outlaw the Catholic religion,' etc. . . . These rumors created an atmosphere of confusion and tension. . . ."

Finally, an August 17 AP wire service report about the school takeover clearly contained false information designed to project the image of a spontaneous uprising. The report's last paragraph states:

> In Monimbó some 2,000 residents built barricades. Many wore handkerchiefs over their faces and refused to give their names. Many of them carried home-made "contact bombs" consisting of gunpowder, nails and shards of glass.

Earlier in the report, an anonymous man on the barricades is conveniently quoted:

> "At this moment, as you can see, we're building barricades to keep out the police and government supporters. They will surely come and we'll be obliged to confront them," one armed resident told reporters.

In fact, fewer than 100 people were involved in the attempt to stir an uprising. No barricades were built in Monimbó, except for a small one constructed in front of the Salesian school by its occupiers.

This bit of journalistic embellishment is reminiscent of similar reports which surfaced during the CIA-sponsored Bay of Pigs invasion in 1961, which described how thousands had joined the invaders to overthrow Castro. Actually, nothing of the kind took place; the Cuban people rallied to defend their government and the invasion failed miserably.

The September *Bulletin* of the Historical Institute pinpointed why Monimbó and Masaya had been selected:

> Both within Nicaragua and abroad, Monimbó is a symbol of the fight against Somoza because of its extremely valiant conduct during the insurrection. For this reason, the celebration of the third anniversary of the revolution was held in Masaya. . . . If the plan to spark a popular uprising had been successful . . . the significance of the celebration slogan "Monimbó *is* Nicaragua" would have been totally changed to indicate that all of Nicaragua was rising up against the present government.

Evangelical Sects and Destabilization

In recent months, the Nicaraguan government has become concerned that some of the proliferating evangelical sects in the country were part of the destabilization campaign. Referring to the concern in Nicaragua about these groups, the *Christianity and Crisis* report noted that "throughout much of Latin America . . . both Catholic and Protestant leaders have expressed concern over the activities of fundamentalist groups, often well-financed and funded from the US. Throughout Central America especially, the sects are viewed as opportunistically supporting governmental authority in contrast to the Catholic Church's social concern. In Nicaragua, some of the sects . . . seem to have become rallying points for those opposed to the government."

Certain pastors of evangelical groups have discouraged followers from working in community projects or health campaigns, and have prohibited participation in the militias, armed forces or civil defense activities, often in areas where counter-revolutionary attacks have been most frequent. Some lay pastors have been identified as ex-Somoza national guardsmen, and have been linked to armed groups operating from Honduras.

The Historical Institute *Bulletin* gave this concrete example of such a connection:

Two days before the massacre at San Francisco del Norte [15 Nicaraguans were tortured and killed in the July 25 raid from Honduras], a group of Bible-carrying itinerant preachers came to the town and talked to the people, including those on duty at the militia post. No one knew these preachers. In the attack, just two days later, slogans such as "with God and patriotism we will drive out the Communists," were found on the walls of houses in the town.

US Policy and American Churches

The Abrams article fits into a pattern of attacks by conservatives and administration figures on progressive religious groups in the US for their opposition to US policy in Central America. In 1981, for example, Richard Nixon's ex-press secretary Patrick Buchanan wrote an article entitled "Maryknoll Order Blesses Castro," which portrayed the Maryknolls as willing agents of Castro in disseminating revolution throughout Central America.

Christianity and Crisis commented that

Abrams was wheeled out to blast the human rights organizations in this country—and indirectly the churches. . . . From what sector of the US community has come the most significant opposition to current US policy in Central America? Without any doubt it has been the church. If the American church could be drawn into the administration's war on Nicaragua, it could effectively be neutralized with regard to El Salvador, Honduras, Guatemala.

American religious leaders refused to be swayed by Abrams's arguments. According to *The Catholic Voice*, a fact-finding team led by Franciscan Father Alan McCoy "found no evidence of religious persecution by the Sandinista government, enthusiastic support of the Sandinistas by a majority of Nicaraguans, and a government structure and civil society based on a profoundly Christian value system."

The governing board of the National Council of Churches, a coordinating body of major Protestant denominations, released a statement which protested "the US government's involvement in activities designed to overthrow the government of Nicaragua." The statement went on to call upon Washington to "reverse its policy of seeking military solutions to the conflicts in Central America."

The Government's Response

In late August, the government made several moves to ease tensions. The government intervened to return some 20 temples of sects that had been taken over by CDSs in different Managua *barrios* to protest their activities against the revolution. In a speech to 300 members of CEPAD, the Protestant umbrella organization, Junta Coordinator Daniel Ortega assured them that "there is no confrontation between the state and religion. But what the state does oppose is the manipulation of religion."

CEPAD shared the government's preoccupation over the activities of the sects. The government and Protestant leaders also took steps to ensure that the attention on the manipulation of religion by a small minority of sects would not overshadow the excellent educational and health programs carried out by Protestant denominations. CEPAD made the commitment that in case of an invasion, its buildings could be used by the government as needed for shelters and refugee centers.

The government also took steps to initiate dialogue with the Catholic hierarchy, some of whose members are clearly identified with the political opposition; this initiative received a positive response from Managua's Archbishop Obando. Another member of the hierarchy, the newly appointed Bishop of Matagalpa, made clear his view of the situation: "Anyone who says there is no religious freedom in this country is a liar."

49. The Somoza Legacy: Economic Bankruptcy*

By the EPICA Task Force

Victory held a mixture of elation and suffering for the Nicaraguan people. They had paid an incredible price for their liberation: 40,000 dead—1.5 percent of the population, some 100,000 wounded, 40,000 children orphaned, 200,000 families left homeless, and 750,000 dependent on food assistance.[1] Without emergency international aid, the population faced imminent starvation. The major cities had been razed and the treasury systematically looted, leaving more than one-third of the labor force out of work. But the legacy of Somoza encompassed far more than the war's death and destruction. He left them an infant mortality rate higher than India's and an illiteracy rate of 53.3 percent.[2] He left a deeply depressed economy; a neglected social service system grossly deficient in housing, health care, basic services and general urban infrastructure; and an insurmountable external debt totalling $1.5 billion. The cumulative effect of these factors meant that every sector of the economy was in a state of crisis.

Agricultural, Industrial and Social Impact

Agriculture, the base of the Nicaraguan economy, suffered severe setbacks because the fighting extended into the 1979 planting season. Virtually 70 percent of the country's main export—cotton—went unplanted, severely cutting potential foreign exchange earnings. Farmers missed planting the year's first crops of corn, beans and rice—Nicaragua's staple diet. The principal sugar mill was destroyed as the sugar cane became ready for harvest. The war interruptd a crucial blight control program for the coffee plants. These setbacks promised to severely affect Nicaragua for at least two years.[3]

Industry and commerce suffered the most from direct losses caused by the war.[4] The economy had ground to a halt three times in one-and-a-half years—in January 1978, September 1978, and finally during June and July 1979—paralyzing domestic demand. Somoza's aerial bombardment destroyed buildings, machines, and other equipment, totaling some 1,500 million *córdobas*.[5] More than one-third of the manufacturing plants located on Managua's northern highway were completely destroyed, and others suffered major damage; the Guard had systematically destroyed industrial areas in virtually every city.

Somoza's legacy of bankruptcy to the industrial sector has an even longer history, its impact climaxing with the 1972 earthquake. Somoza's corruption and

---

*Reprinted from *Nicaragua: A People's Revolution* (Washington, D.C., EPICA Task Force, 1980).

mismanagement of the reconstruction funds created a crisis of confidence in the industrial sector. Production stagnated; employment never regained its 1972 level in the same eight year period.[6] By the time of victory the industrial/manufacturing sector faced the future with a destroyed infrastructure, completely depleted inventories, uncollectible outstanding accounts, lack of raw materials, a drop in domestic demand—especially for non-essential goods—and a technical vacuum due to the exodus of many professionals. Initial estimates placed the reduction in commerce's gross product at 47 percent.[7]

Social Services were also reeling under the impact of the war. Hospitals, schools, and housing had been hard hit in Somoza's "scorched earth" policy. The Rivas and Estelí hospitals lay in total ruin, while most others suffered partial physical damage and major loss of equipment totaling some 160 million *córdobas.*[8] Social services were totally inadequate for the needs of the wounded, malnourished, diseased, and psychologically traumatized persons requiring medical attention at the end of the war. The war caused a 15 percent decline in medical personnel; even before that loss there had been only 6.5 doctors for every 10,000 inhabitants.[9] Similarly, schools and housing—long neglected by Somoza and then ravaged by war—would require hundreds of thousands of dollars to meet the country's immediate needs.[10]

Somoza's Final Economic Rape: IMF Funds

Unable to physically take his private industries out of the country, Somoza came close to doing exactly that financially. He borrowed heavily from private foreign banks, double-mortgaged his businesses, left innumerable unpaid bills from multinational corporations—bills which the new government had to pay before receiving new credits. During the spring and early summer of 1979, Somoza slaughtered cattle from his immense ranch-holdings, using National Guard troops as meat processors when *campesino* workers refused to work. Illegal cattle exports during this war period amounted to 2.5 million head of cattle.[11] Somoza shipped the beef to cold storage in Miami for later sale, completely filling Nicaragua's 1979 beef quota to the United States before the war ended. Somoza's long-time allies also pillaged the country—stripping inventories from port warehouses and escaping with them in private boats to Honduras and El Salvador.[12]

Somoza's final act of vengeance emptied Nicaragua's cash drawers of all but $3.5 million.[13] His final pillage involved the "disappearance" of $33.2 million, the first half of the International Monetary Fund (IMF) credit awarded Somoza in May 1979. The IMF had granted Somoza a mixture of stand-by and compensatory loans on the basis of "economic" criteria established by an IMF delegation following its April 1979 study of the Nicaraguan situation. Despite protests against the loan from renowned Nicaraguan economists, the entire Nicaraguan business community, and numerous US organizations, the United States voted in favor of the credit to Somoza. The State Department feebly excused its position as one of "not opposing the loan." The IMF disclaimer that the decision was political was contradicted in a telegram issued by US Treasury Secretary Blumenthal, arguing that such a loan could only be given assuming it would rejuvenate the Nicaraguan economy.[14] Since by May 1979, Somoza's economy was bankrupt and could not be revived under his leadership, the US decision was obviously political in nature. The first half of the $66 million loan from the IMF was deposited in the Central Bank in Managua by June 1, 1979, and it was still there on June 9 when the bank closed down during the "Battle of Managua." But on July 20 when the second echelon officials returned, the money had disappeared, undoubtedly transferred to one of Somoza's foreign bank accounts.[15]

Notes

[1]Center for International Policy, statistics compiled from US AID, IDB and UN ECLA, Washington, September 1979.

[2]*Wall Street Journal*, New York, July 18, 1979.

[3]*Excelsior*, "Si occidente no ayuda irémos donde sea," Mexico, August 14, 1979, p. 2.

[4]United Nations Economic and Social Council, Economic Committee on Latin America (CEPAL), "Nicaragua: Economic Repercussions of Recent Political Events," September, 1978, p. 17.

[5]CEPAL, p. 36.

[6]Edmundo Jarquín, "The Nicaraguan Crisis and the International Monetary Fund," Washington, DC, mimeographed document, May 10, 1979.

[7]CEPAL, p. 42.

[8]CEPAL, p. 25.

[9]CEPAL, p. 20.

[10]CEPAL, pp. 21–23.

[11]CEPAL, p. 34.

[12]*Wall Street Journal*, July 18, 1979.

[13]*Washington Post*, July 26, 1979.

[14]Telegram to the National Network in Solidarity with Nicaragua (and to others), from Michael Blumenthal, May 1979.

[15]EPICA interview, Central Bank staff, Managua, September 1979.

50. *Challenge of Reconstruction**

By the National Network in Solidarity with the Nicaraguan People

When the Sandinistas took power in July 1979, they were faced with an economy crippled by years of dependency, unresponsive to the real needs of the people, and nearly bankrupt by foreign debt, corruption and outright theft. In addition to the 50,000 lives lost, the war cost $500 million in physical damage, $200 million in lost cotton exports, 25 percent reduction in the cattle herd, and $700 million in capital flight. Unemployment was 40 percent and inflation over 80 percent. Somoza sacked the National Treasury before fleeing, leaving only $3.5

*Reprinted from *Nicaragua*, May–June, 1982, pp. 1–2.

million in the bank and a national debt of $1.6 billion. The World Bank estimated it would take Nicaragua ten years to get back to prewar production levels.

Nicaragua's economy, like all of Central America, was designed to supply cheap raw materials to world markets. It was not Nicaragua which controlled the prices of cotton, coffee, sugar and beef, which account for 66 percent of export earnings. These products are vulnerable to the slumps and false booms engineered by commodity men in London and New York. Under Somoza, an increasing portion of the country's Gross National Product (GNP) came from foreign commerce. In 1950 foreign commerce from the productive sector alone accounted for 36.5 percent of GNP (and foreign debt was only $2 million). By 1977, it rose to 67 percent of GNP (and foreign debt was $900 million).

Falling prices of raw materials, increased costs of oil and materials necessary for agricultural production, and soaring interest rates from international financiers have created economic havoc throughout Central America. In 1970, 100 pounds of coffee bought 100 barrels of oil; today they buy three. In 1977, 4.4 tons of coffee bought a tractor; today 11.2 tons (145 percent more) buy a tractor. The falling prices of exports and rising prices of imports necessitated extensive foreign borrowing at escalating interest rates. In 1960, foreign credit for agriculture amounted to 43 percent of production; by 1971, 90 percent. From 1970–75 the amount borrowed for agricultural production was *greater* than agricultural export earnings. The extent to which Somoza sold the country to foreign bankers is indicated by the following chart:

	Debt service (millions)	% of export earnings	Oil as % of export earnings
'79	$ 94.7	15.4%	13.4%
'80	130.7	29.0	38.6
'81	230.0	40.1	35.5

This year Nicaragua is paying 52 cents on every dollar it earns for debt service alone. By 1985, unless the debt is renegotiated, all of Nicaragua's export earnings will be needed for debt service.

The Sandinista Strategy

How have the Sandinistas begun to tackle this economic nightmare? The confiscation of Somoza's economic empire brought some 100 factories and two million acres of farmland into state hands. The state also nationalized all natural resources and the finance system. But these were mixed blessings. Though government controlled 40 percent of GNP, many of Somoza's holdings were undercapitalized, often in debt, and rarely efficient. Opposition businessmen, on the other hand, had survived under a system of grossly unfair competition, and tended to manage industries which of necessity had become leaner and more efficient.

Continued coexistence with this anti-Somoza private sector was fundamental to the Sandinista strategy of economic recovery through national unity. The alliance was as much the child of necessity as commitment of honor. The chronic lack of technical skills and the Sandinistas' dependence on a broad range of international friendships prevented them from moving faster towards state control. From the beginning, the target of a mixed economy was fraught with pitfalls. Would businessmen be willing to abide by the revolution's new "rules of the game"? Would they keep their factories in full production and invest in agriculture if they complained that their economic weight was not translated into political power? Pragmatically, the FSLN knew that any hope of recovery rested on the effective contribution of a private sector which still controlled 75-80 percent of production.

Against the backdrop of debt and dependency, the new government aimed first of all to restore former production levels, become self-sufficient in staple foodstuffs for the first time through a National Food Program (PAN), and satisfy basic social needs, *before* moving on to develop new forms of earning foreign exchange. The economic situation at the end of the war meant that the country was incapable in the first years of the revolution of generating any internal surplus for reinvestment. Nicaragua relied heavily on foreign aid for both emergency relief programs and new investment.

The early targets set by the 1980 economic plan were largely met. Crops came in on schedule, new jobs were created, factories began to revive. But as US hostility grew, opposition business began to flex its muscles. Cracks began to show in the Capital alliance. flight reached worrying levels and COSEP, the association of large producers, with US backing became more strident in its criticisms and called for a complete return to the mechanisms of the free market. While small traders, artisans and some medium-sized businessmen remained loyal to the revolution (often due to the Sandinista's generous credit allocation to these sectors), COSEP pulled its six representatives out of the co-legislative Council of State in November 1980. Private investment slumped to 10 percent of total investment, with businessmen preferring to risk the state's capital rather than their own. Many businessmen complained that current profit margins—running at an average of 25 percent—were unacceptably low.

Changing People's Lives

In fact, middle-class living standards were not seriously eroded by the redistributive income and taxation policies or the heavy government social sector expenditure of the first two years. Their only real reverse was the "cost of imported liquor," wrote the *New York Times*. Visitors to Nicaragua today often register surprise that many children still go barefoot, that many houses still lack basic facilities, forgetting that revolutions cannot change living conditions overnight. The basic tension in any revolution is between the expectations it arouses and its capacity to fulfill them. For the impoverished majority of Nicaraguans, material change has come spectacularly in some areas like education and preventive medicine, but much more slowly in others.

With a ruined economy, "raise production" became the watchword. Major wage hikes were a wild dream. The Sandinistas opted instead for a series of measures reinforcing the "social wage," which they also hoped would hold off inflationary risks. Rents were halved, food prices regulated, public transport heavily subsidized, education and health care extended, land rentals slashed for small peasants. Job creation targets were met though the Sandinistas were criticized (and criticized themselves) for increasing jobs in the public sector and services rather than in the crucial area of production. Immediately on taking power, the FSLN began to sow the seeds of democracy and worker participation in the planning of production— fixing budgets and targets, understanding shortages and price fluctuations—to further enhance the purely economic benefits brought about by the revolution.

Above all, economic crisis forced the FSLN into a real political dilemma. The working class had to be convinced that a policy of austerity was unavoidable, that it was being applied equally to all social groups, and that it did not prejudice long-term popular interests. The task of winning public confidence for austerity was not made any easier by the latitude given to opposition propaganda by the revolution's framework of openness and pluralism. While dissident businessmen blamed admitted government inexperience for the uneven pace of economic recovery, left-wing groups hostile to the FSLN used the crisis to expand their own power base by leading workers in pursuit of impossible 100 percent-150 percent wage hikes.

The Crisis Deepens

Political conflicts over the direction of the economy built towards a climax during 1981, while the factors mentioned earlier in this article (falling export prices; rising prices of imports and oil; foreign debt) continued to worsen. During Reagan's first year, all economic aid was halted in April 1981 and PL-480 food credits suspended. Direct US assistance to the private sector ($42 million in 1981) has continued, however. The US has also interfered with Nicaragua's loan requests in international lending institutions, not to mention the millions it is spending to destabilize the country politically and militarily. . . .

Domestic factors made the crisis worse. Decapitalization—a series of crimes of economic sabotage by businessmen opposed to the revolution—had cost the country $140 million in 1981, and the Sandinistas put another $100 million lost during the same period down to labor problems and strikes. The FSLN now admits honestly that it made a costly political error in allowing industrial efficiency to slide. The rapid normalization of the economy during 1980, when GNP rose by 10.7 percent, and the dramatic change in worker-management relationships are two factors which the government now recognizes. Inflation, which had been cut from 84 percent to 17.5 percent, according to government figures, threatened to rise again. And so did unemployment, which had fallen from 40 percent to 16 percent.

Industrial workers in Managua were particularly vulnerable, their factories starved of vital stocks of raw materials.

Few were surprised in September 1981 when the Junta of National Reconstruction decreed a one-year state of national emergency. Coming after the July confiscation of 14 businesses for decapitalization, it was the first sign that the FSLN wanted to define once and for all the "rules of the game," to avoid any further ambiguity about how the mixed economy was designed to function. The message to private enterprise, in a nutshell, was this: "Invest and produce, and your profits will be assured, your future guaranteed. Undermine the economy by decapitalizing or by halting production, and your factory or farm will be taken over by the state."

The September emergency was designed to cut public expenditure, halt capital flight, increase productivity and raise tax revenues. A jobs freeze in all government departments was accompanied by stern limitations on current expenditures, aimed at $43.8 million by the end of 1981. A 10 percent reduction in state subsidies to service industries has also been imposed and new taxes ranging from 30 percent to 100 percent slapped on imported luxury goods from outside the Central American Common Market. All foreign exchange activities have been regulated and sanctions of up to three years in jail introduced for those convicted of speculation, hoarding or "disseminating false and damaging economic information." While taxation laws will hit middle-class consumption levels, with some luxury imports becoming unobtainable, the weight of the crisis is also being felt by the working class. In a drastic attempt to curb labor disputes, strikes, factory occupations and land takeovers have been temporarily outlawed, a measure criticized by many critics and even members of the government.

Although COSEP responded favorably at first, calling the measures "the first step towards resolving the national crisis," their tone soon changed. It became obvious that some private sector groups and opposition parties were intent on exploiting the economic crisis and the accompanying threats from the Reagan administration as a framework for their most direct confrontation to date with the FSLN. The US administration and its right-wing advisers know that the Nicaraguan economy is vulnerable, and that crises can be engineered and aggravated to cause the revolution maximum political damage.

Despite US actions and economic sabotage by some Nicaraguan businessmen, in February of this year the government provided further incentives to coffee, cotton and sugar producers. Credit is being made available over a 15-year period at 8 percent interest with a five-year grace period. Exporters may sell part of their crops at a higher dollar exchange rate, and the package as a whole will yield a 26 percent jump in profits on all exports. The governments of other Central American countries have provided no such cushion for their large exporters. The Sandinistas also have no interest in increasing the state sector of production. In fact, increasing numbers of peasant families are receiving title to state lands and being organized into cooperatives.

With moves like these, the Sandinistas have shown that the revolution's original commitments to a mixed economy are still alive. During the political confrontations of late 1981, they showed too that they are ready to act decisively to uphold the revolution's authority. The decision to let private enterprise survive, Sandinista leaders insist, has been reaffirmed, not abandoned. But that survival must be on terms compatible with the long-term goals of the revolution.

51. *Nicaragua Debates New Rules for Foreign Companies**

By Rose Marie Audette and David Kowalewski

In a bid to attract investment from multinational corporations, the Nicaraguan government is discussing liberalization of its foreign investment law. The proposed law is expected to be acted upon by the Council of State before summer.

Exact details of the law have not been made public. But last December the Nicaraguan Minister of Finance, Joaquín Cuadra, told the *New York Times* that the new regulations will allow 100 percent foreign ownership of Nicaraguan operations, and give investors the right to repatriate their profits. Foreign companies, said Cuadro, will also be taxed at the same rate as Nicaraguan businesses, a flat rate of 40 percent of profits.

Under the Somoza dictatorship, foreign investment in Nicaragua was not extensive; the highest level reached was $300 million. But since the Sandinista-led revolution in 1979, foreign investment has declined. Last year, for example, Standard Fruit, a division of Castle and Cooke, announced that it was pulling out of the country and would no longer market Nicaragua's bananas—as it had done exclusively for the past 12 years.

A Mixed Economy

Since coming to power, the Sandinistas have been trying to get their underdeveloped country on its economic feet. Their strategy has been to encourage a mixed economy of privately owned farms, factories and stores together with cooperatives and state ownership of some farms and major industries. But the obstacles have been great: war damage, the pillaging of the national treasury by Somoza and his allies, disinvestment by landowners and industrialists, continuing attacks by the "contras" (counterrevolutionaries), a depressed world market for Nicaragua's primary exports, the collapse of the Central American Common Market, and natural disasters.

According to preliminary figures released by the Nicaraguan embassy, Nicara-

*Reprinted from *Multinational Monitor*, March 1983, pp. 20–21.

gua's economy contracted by 2.5 percent in 1982 after two years of solid growth. Although a disappointment to the government, this was the best economic performance in Central America. In 1982, Costa Rica's economy dropped by 5.6 percent, El Salvador's by 10 percent and Guatemala's by 3 percent.

In December 1982, the Nicaraguan government moved on several fronts to attack its continuing economic problems. Minister of Finance Cuadro travelled to New York to make a plea for increased investment in the country, and made the first public presentation of the new investment law before the Council on Foreign Relations.

That same month, the government obtained a $25 million short term loan from a group of Western bankers led by the Bank of America—a significant event since Nicaragua has had trouble getting credit from foreign banks and multilateral lending institutions. The credits enabled Nicaragua to meet a $40 million interest payment on the $580 million commercial portion of the country's $2.5 billion external debt.

In another expression of its willingness to work with American companies, the Nicaraguan government has moved to settle a dispute with the Neptune Mining Co. of New York, 52 percent owned by ASARCO (American Smelting and Mining Co.), over issues raised by the 1979 nationalization of the company's gold mine. Neptune and the Nicaraguan government agreed in December to seek arbitration on tax and accounting questions resulting from the action; Nicaragua also agreed to pay Neptune $3.7 million, plus interest, over a six year period for the minerals seized during the nationalization.

The timing of the agreement was "fortunate," Justice Minister Carlos Arguello told *Business Week*. "It should show US businessmen that we want to deal with them in a fair way, in a responsible manner, to our mutual benefit."

Foreign Capital for a Strained Economy

"The [foreign investment] law is not a favor that we are doing for the multinationals to allow them to set the roots of their oppressive system in our country," Ruiz Caldera of the International Directorate of the Sandinista Front (FSLN) told *Multinational Monitor* in an interview in Managua last December. Caldera argued that the law will strengthen the Sandinistas' hand in dealing with multinationals and "will only be beneficial for the people." Because of "the way we will apply this law," he said, "it will strengthen Nicaragua's currency, broaden our commerce throughout the world, and combat unemployment."

Many Nicaraguans interviewed about the law felt it would ease some of the problems of the country's strained economy. "We're in the birth pangs of a new economy and we need lots of things, material resources, to get our economy going," said José Maríe, Jinotega's Agricultural Workers' Association representative. Mario Epelman, General Director of the Ministry of Labor's Division of Occupational Safety and Health, stressed that he supported an increased presence of multinationals as long as "they follow the rules. I would like the plants here to have the same safety and health conditions as they have in the US." But he added, "I know that multinationals go to countries precisely where there are no regulations."

The proposed law has generally been welcomed by foreign businesses already operating in Nicaragua. A commercial attaché at the US Embassy said that multinationals "favor such a law so they'll know what the rules of the game are." Ray Genie, general manager of Electroquímica Pennwalt (40 percent owned by Pennwalt of Philadelphia) agreed: "Any kind of regularization of procedures would be welcomed. It will be a way of knowing exactly what is expected of us."

The prospect of increased foreign investment in Nicaragua has caused some uneasiness. "Some consider it a double-edged sword," said Caldera of the FSLN, with "both advantages and disadvantages." A commercial aide at the US Embassy said that "any law favorable to multinationals would have to go against the goals of the revolution."

One Nicaraguan official told *Multinational Monitor* that the country would be better off without multinationals. Sylvan Howard, tourist development official for Zelaya Province on the Atlantic Coast, pointed to the history of foreign lumber interests in Puerto Cabezas to make his case. "They stayed in Nicaragua for 30 years. And when they left, they left people who were underfed, barefoot, without clothes. Streets were not paved. And they took out millions and millions of dollars but left nothing in return."

Howard would prefer that companies like Hilton and Sheraton stay home in order to maintain the area's "bucolic character and not create a highly urbanized development . . . I really believe that with local people and local resources it will be better for Nicaragua."

The Prospects for Investment

Despite the new code, the prospects for investment in Nicaragua are unclear. "Most businesses would just as soon invest in other countries," a Central American officer for the Commerce Department told the *Monitor*. Nicaragua, he added, "is less appealing than other markets because it doesn't have a healthy private sector." The official doubted that the new investment laws would change the situation. "You don't know until you see how the government implements these changes," he said.

Some observers have stressed that political uncertainties in Nicaragua and throughout Central America may hinder investors from taking advantage of the new law. "As long as a state of emergency prevails, it is difficult to say whether multinationals will invest," said an official with Nicaragua's International Fund for Reconstruction.

But according to the Nicaraguan Embassy, several US businesses have expressed interest in Nicaragua in recent months. Hope Consultants, Inc., a shipbuilding and oil firm based in Louisiana, visited Managua in January. "The American entrepreneurs stated their interest in investing some $20 million," possibly in shipyards, electric power plants or worker training, the embassy reported. In a recent interview with *Latin America Regional Reports,* Hope President Richard

Miles said his company's investments were contingent on the new law. "We shall wait and see what the foreign investment law says before committing ourselves," he said.

But a Nicaraguan Embassy spokesperson stressed the positive implications of Hope Consultants' visit. "If this happens in the situation of the worst propaganda from the Reagan administration and attacks from the contras, that means something," she said, adding, "Any investments would be very welcome."

52. Nicaragua's Agrarian Reform*

By the Central American Historical Institute

"We are going to keep our promise that no Nicaraguan will be left landless," said Nicaraguan Minister of Agriculture Jaime Wheelock at the January 9, 1984, Agrarian Reform ceremony in Nueva Guinea in Central Zelaya. During the ceremony, 816 *campesinos* were given legal title to 45,000 *manzanas* (mz.), (1 mz. = .7 hectares, or 1.7 acres). The granting of title was designed to give the *campesinos* legal security, even though they have occupied this land since Somoza's era.

At the Nueva Guinea ceremony, Wheelock stressed the government's intention to follow up on progress made in restructuring land ownership during 1983. During the year just ended, 347,169 mz. of land were transferred to individual *campesinos* and cooperatives—over two and a half times the amount of land handed over from October 1981 to December 1982. This report will examine the state of the Agrarian Reform process as 1984 begins.

Structure of Land Ownership

Farm Size	1978 Area*	%	1982 Area	%	1983 Area	%
Farms Greater than 500 Mzs.	2,920	41	1,176	16.4	880	12
From 200 to 500 Mzs.	980	14	850	12	730	10
From 50 to 200 Mzs.	2,100	30	2,100	30	2,100	30
From 10 to 50 Mzs.	910	13	910	13	1,000	14
Less than 10 Mzs.	170	2	212	3	280	4
Production Coops	—	—	132	1.8	481	7
People's Property Area (APP)	—	—	1,700	24	1,600	23
Total	7,080	100	7,080	100	7,071	100

*(Area in thousands of manzanas)

As the above table shows, in 1978 those controlling more than 500 mz. owned 41 percent of the current agricultural land. Yet this group represented less than one-half of one percent of Nicaraguan landowners. At the other end of the spectrum, *campesinos* owning less than 10 mz. represented 70 percent of agricultural producers, yet controlled only 2 percent of agricultural land. The vast majority of these small landowners did not earn enough from their land to support their families, and consequently had to work as part-time wage laborers. In addition, nearly a third of

---

*Reprinted from the *Central American Historical Institute Update*, January 13, 1984, Vol. 3, No. 2.

the economically active population in the countryside did not own land, or have stable employment. Thus agricultural reform was designed to meet the needs of these two groups: very small landowners and landless who lacked secure employment.

Two Phases of Land Reform

The first phase of Agrarian Reform began in the fall of 1979 with the expropriation of land belonging to Somoza and his allies. Approximately 1.6 million mz. were included in this phase. Most of this land had belonged to the largest farm category (greater than 500 mz.) and to many of the best farms in the 200–500 mz. range because most of the land expropriated from Somocistas had been used for modern rice farms, coffee plantations, intensive cattle raising, etc.; it was decided not to break up farms into small plots suitable for transferring to *campesinos*. This land became People's Property Area, or APP.

While some of the demands of Nicaraguan *campesinos* could be met by improving conditions of employment that APP inherited (since the majority of rural Nicaraguans do some form of wage labor), the demand for land could only be met in a second phase of the Agrarian Reform. This began in July 1981, when a new Agrarian Reform Law was introduced that allowed for expropriation of abandoned land and of idle and underutilized land belonging to large-scale owners.

Expropriations under the second phase of the reform began in October 1981. By the end of 1983, 518,145 mz. of land had been expropriated. As in the first phase of the reform, the bulk of expropriations affected the largest landowners: the average size of expropriated farms was 890 mz. Nineteen percent of this land was expropriated after having been abandoned. Sixty-three percent was either idle or underutilized, and 18 percent was expropriated because owners were intensively exploiting their tenants.

Land Transferred to Campesinos and Cooperatives Since October 1981

	Land Transferred	Families Benefiting	Manzanas Per Month
Oct. '81-Dec. '82	132,538	7,817	9,467
Dec. '82-Nov. 20, '83	201,954	7,545	18,927
Nov. 20, '83-Dec. '83	145,215	6,710	109,184
Total	479,707	22,072	———

Expropriations and land transfers have caused an important transformation in the pattern of land ownership in Nicaragua. Returning to the first table, note that by the end of 1983, the share of agricultural land belonging to the largest landowners had declined from 41 percent to 12 percent. Most of the land transferred went to the APP and to production cooperatives, though the amount of land controlled by the smallest individual landowners has also increased 65 percent since 1978.

As Table 2 indicates, by the end of 1983, 22,072 families had received land, either individually or in cooperatives. It is believed that under Somoza there were 80,000 rural families who had neither enough land to support themselves nor stable wage employment. Thus a substantial portion of this group has already received land. But these are not the only Nicaraguans who have benefited from the Agrarian Reform. Speaking to the Council of State on November 23, Minister of Agriculture Jaime Wheelock pointed out, "There are also thousands of families who have land that has been provisionally transferred to them, or who are participating in work collectives operating on APP land. Because of our own limitations, we have not yet granted them formal titles, because doing this requires defining an area, doing a series of economic calculations to make sure land being transferred is economically viable, and doing topographical studies. It is rather complicated." The transfer of land has been accelerated; 30 percent of the land given to *campesinos* since October 1981 was granted in the last 41 days of 1983.

Such a rapid transfer of land tests the administrative capacity of the state, as *campesinos* who receive land need different forms of assistance (credit, extension services). On the other hand, if an Agrarian Reform program is to affect the majority of the rural poor, it must not follow the slow rhythm of any state bureaucracy, but rather respond to the social demands of the *campesinos*.

It is interesting to note that while 347,169 mz. of land were transferred to *campesinos* in 1983, only 253,698 mz. were expropriated. The rest of the transferred land came from the APP, the size of which was consequently reduced during the year. A further 200,000–400,000 of current APP land could be transferred to individual *campesinos* and cooperatives in 1984.

This policy reflects two main objectives. First, to transfer APP lands means less reliance on the holdings of large landowners. This will help diminish large landowners' fears and help strengthen national unity. (On November 23, Jaime Wheelock announced that the government would give "certificates of invulnerability" that would guarantee to private producers who are using their land productively that their land would not be expropriated, but it is not yet clear whether these certificates will be given to a significant number of large private landowners.)

Second, the APP land that is being handed over to *campesinos* is generally Pacific Coast cattle-grazing land. Because the Ministry of Agriculture wishes to shift Nicaragua's livestock production to more appropriate lands in central regions, and devote more prime Pacific land to basic grains, the transfer of APP cattle land to *campesinos* meets the goal of bringing this land into basic grain cultivation. It is hoped that livestock production can be expanded on presently unused public lands in central Nicaragua.

Perspectives for the Future

Where is the pattern of land ownership headed in the long run? In his November 23 speech to the Council of State, Jaime Wheelock offered a sketch of Nicaraguan agriculture in 20 to 30 years' time. The APP will represent around 20 percent of agricultural land, and cooperatives 50 percent. As for the sector of large and medium-sized owners: "It will have to be reduced further. But if this sector understands that the Sandinista revolution wishes to guarantee the participation to any national sector that desires to work for a new and more just society, if that sector is efficient, it has a passport to the future. Then we will have 10–20 percent of the land belonging to what we can call medium or large owners." Finally, a fraction of the land will be worked by small, individual owners.

53. The Failed Partnership: Big Growers and the State*

By Joseph Collins (with Francis Moore Lappé and Nick Allen)

When many North Americans imagine "revolutionary Nicaragua," they assume that all the land once belonging to the big plantation owners must now be in the hands of hungry peasants. Not so. Recall that only lands belonging to Somoza and his close associates were confiscated by the government after the fall of the dictatorship.

For the first three months after the victory, the new government thought it had control over 60 percent of Nicaragua's agricultural land. But at a planning session in late October 1979 in Jaime Wheelock's office, a young researcher presented us with startling new estimates which caused an anxious stir in the room. The large and medium-size farmers and ranchers, he reported, controlled over two-thirds of the agricultural land. They accounted for 72 percent of cotton production, 53 percent of coffee, 58 percent of cattle, and 51 percent of sugarcane.

Could private capitalist farmers and ranchers be counted on to maintain and expand urgently needed production? That became the big question for the rest of the afternoon session.

Without public control over the bulk of the export production, the new government realized that the recovery of the economy would hinge in large part on how effectively it could motivate these private growers to revive and eventually step up production. This partnership in the countryside was the heart of the new Nicaragua's plans for a "mixed economy."

Aware of their importance to the economy, the large and medium-size growers organized into producers' associations and drove some hard bargains. Not all the negotiations were formal. It was not unusual for government officials to spend Sunday afternoons in the countryside chatting with, say, some cotton growers to

---

*Reprinted from *What Difference Could a Revolution Make? Food and Farming in the New Nicaragua*. San Francisco, Institute for Food and Development Policy, 1982.

determine just what were their complaints and demands. Moreover, a number of leaders and other officials of the new government came from major land-owning families; they could readily test government proposals on close relatives and family friends.

While the government appealed to patriotic desires to rebuild a better Nicaragua, it was not overly idealistic or naive. In fact, the new government offered the private producers a package of incentives unprecedented even under the Somoza dictatorship:

● Enough credit, at an interest rate below the rate of inflation, to cover all working costs (seeds, fertilizers, fuel, equipment repair and replacement, all wages).

● Guaranteed prices for export crops, calculated to ensure a profit, and renegotiated yearly with the producers' associations in advance of annual planting. The government promised to absorb any drop in international commodity prices but to share with producers the benefits of any unexpected price rises.

● Low-cost government financing for replanting coffee trees infested by coffee blight.

● A seat for the association representing big growers and ranchers (UPANIC) on the Council of State and on various technical commissions.

● Rent decreases, primarily intended to help peasant producers, which also benefited many commercial growers, especially in cotton. In the mid-1970s, 40 percent of cotton growers rented their land from absentee owners, many residing in Miami and California.

● Low taxes on personal income and company profits.

Under this incentive package, the government put up the working capital, guaranteed minimum prices at which any reasonably efficient producer could make a profit, and absorbed any sudden drops in international market prices, while allowing the producers to own (as well as sell and bequeath) the land and equipment. It was tantamount to paying big producers a salary with bonuses tied to performance.

Why such a sweet deal? First, the government didn't want to drive the big producers out since it couldn't take on any more farms and ranches itself. Its hands were full dealing with the Somocista properties. Moreover, the government didn't want the big producers to leave the country because they constituted so much of the nation's scarce technical and administrative experience.

Behind the government overtures to the commercial producers were two other assumptions. The government believed that these incentives would stimulate production, especially of export crops. Through the foreign exchange earned, the government would gain funds it desperately needed for redistributive development as well as social programs. This would be especially true, the reasoning went, since the government had nationalized virtually all export trade and maintained a low rate of exchange, paying producers the official 10 córdobas per dollar, whereas the legal private ("parallel") market gave 25 córdobas to the dollar. In February 1982 this exchange rate was modified in favor of the producers as a further effort to stimulate production: producers could obtain part of the value of their exports effectively in dollars. Second, the Sandinistas believed that national unity was essential in the face of foreign hostility. By not nationalizing private producers and instead building their confidence in the new government, the Sandinistas hoped to avoid a confrontation that might give the US government a rationalization for intervention in Nicaragua.

All this sounds reasonable. But did it work? In the judgment of many, it did not.

At a late night meeting on the eve of the second anniversary, a high official told me, "The private farmers, the big ones and the medium-size ones, have blown an historic opportunity. Once we might have thought we could rely on the private sector at least for a holding action. But now we see most of them are taking us backward economically." In his view, the majority of big producers not only failed to revive production but were systematically draining the rural economy.

Why Did They "Blow It"?

What looked to the Sandinistas like liberal offers may not have seemed so to the big growers, who believed they were losing a great deal. Under Somoza the big growers had unlimited access to cheap labor. Now with lowered land rents, increased employment on the state farms, and substantial government credit going to campesino producers, many poor peasants in the countryside saw themselves freed from the need to seek demeaning and arduous plantation work. "The *patrón* can't humiliate us anymore," is the way I have heard many of them put it. With fewer workers competing for jobs, for the first time the big growers had to negotiate with workers. And under the new order, not only was there no National Guard to prevent agricultural workers from organizing, but the government actually encouraged unions. To the Sandinistas, such worker organizations are the motor force of agrarian change.

"It's unbelievable," an old field hand told me, radiating with satisfaction. The ATC association on a cotton plantation near León had gotten the plantation owner to pay for the workers' medical treatments. Previously, the only medical bills the owner paid were for the horses. On another plantation, when the owner refused to pay the minimum wage, workers organized an ATC local. When the landowner attempted to break up the organization, the workers first struck; then they took over the plantation.

The big growers saw their profits threatened as the government sought to enforce the minimum wage law, mandated improvements in living and working conditions, and directly competed with the owners' price-gouging "company stores" by offering the rural poor basic goods at fixed low prices. Even though all these changes were not effective everywhere overnight, the direction was clear.

Despite these changes, the big growers knew that they could continue to make good profits. After talking with many of them, I'm convinced that their fears for the future were what caused them to dig in their heels against the new government. Knowing that the countryside was alive with the demands of hundreds of thousands of people who had been ruthlessly exploited for generations, it was *la Revolución* that threatened them. And perhaps it was inevitable that at the beginning of a revolution the fears of the rich affect their behavior so that their fears are self-fulfilling. Certainly, as we will see, that seems to be the case in Nicaragua.

Throughout the first year or so, the majority of private agricultural producers appeared undecided about how much they would cooperate with the new government. For one thing, since the Carter administration seemed willing to live with the new order in Managua, many of Nicaragua's agrarian capitalists felt incapable of effectively mobilizing themselves politically and economically against the new government. Still there was a palpable uneasiness and suspicion on every side, each feeding on the other's fears.

After the election of President Reagan, whose party platform called for the overthrow of the Nicaraguan government, the mood in the countryside was expectant. Adding to the tension was a serious incident in late November 1981 which revealed that at least some big growers had moved into direct sabotage of the new government and its agrarian program. Jorge Salazar, president of the Union of Nicaraguan Agricultural Producers (UPANIC), was discovered by police to be carrying concealed arms in his car and was killed in a shoot-out with police. Investigations revealed that Salazar and others, including the president of the Rice-Planters Association, planned to assassinate Sandinista leaders in coordination with an invasion by Somocista elements.

"Death by a Million Cuts"

Visiting Nicaragua at the end of 1980, I found Sandinistas and opponents alike predicting that 1981 would test the partnership between the big growers and the state. I returned to Nicaragua twice during the first half of 1981. I found the ATC, the newly created association of small- and medium-sized farmers and ranchers (UNAG), the pro-Sandinista media, rural workers, and government officials themselves all accusing private producers of "decapitalization." Decapitalization referred to a range of economic sabotage by some large private farmers and ranchers:
- Cutting back on cultivated acres.
- Laying off needed workers and technicians.
- Selling off machinery and livestock, often to buyers in Honduras and Costa Rica.
- Using government production loans fraudulently—converting part of the loan to dollars on the street market, then sending the dollars to foreign bank accounts.
- Over-invoicing for imported machinery, spare parts, fertilizers, pesticides and so on in cooperation with "friendly" corporations in Guatemala or Florida. (The grower or rancher, arguing that the imported item is essential for production, gets dollars from the national bank—at the 10 to 1 rate rather than the 25 to 1 rate on the street market—plus, perhaps a loan. The extra dollars wind up in a Miami bank account.)
- Faking or inflating fees and commissions to foreign firms or individuals, again as a way to siphon dollars out of the country.
- Paying excessive salaries, often in advance, to themselves and their family members.

• Asking for a government loan on the grounds of "saving jobs" once any combination of the above had caused financial losses.

The whole process adds up to "death by a million cuts," a top government economic planning advisor told me in June 1981. "It's not as if there are just four or five of the big guys," he explained. "If there were, you could round up one or two and make an example of them." Knowing that I was a *norteamericano*, he added, "It's like moonshine in Kentucky." There's one big difference though: in Nicaragua the "moonshining" undermines the entire economy.

In his opinion, the Sandinistas had originally underestimated the danger of decapitalization because they had underestimated the number and importance of the medium-size producers. By mid-1981, some ranchers and farms were so decapitalized that, counting in debts, their value was negative.

Specific examples of decapitalization have frequently been pointed out by campesinos and farm workers and their organizations. Of the almost 900 acres of the Hacienda San Pedro in southeastern Nicaragua, approximately 100 grow coffee trees. In July 1981 the ATC charged that a large portion of the trees were ruined or on the verge of ruin because of lack of weeding and control of the coffee blight. The hacienda's 1980-81 coffee harvest dropped to one quarter what it had been the year before. The ATC claimed that by mid-1981, 70 percent of the capitalist farms and ranches in the region had been similarly neglected.

On his 2,800-acre Hacienda Namaslí, near the Honduran border, Alfonso Ramos had 800 acres in coffee trees. In 1980 he got credit from the National Development Bank to cover all projected production expenses. Yet it looked abandoned to a journalist visiting the hacienda in June 1981.

Before the revolution, Ramos employed 200 workers; in 1981, only 27. Left unattended, the coffee trees were hard hit by the coffee blight. When coffee trees are not cared for with weeding, fertilizer, pest control, yields are reduced for years to come. Ramos had also stripped the estate of almost all the machinery, including seven tractors, harvesters, and irrigation pumps—some taken into Honduras. An investigation revealed that he had sold the machinery, converted the money into dollars, and smuggled them out of the country.

Beef production also suffered from economic sabotage. By mid-1981, the government estimated that over 200,000 head of cattle had been rustled across the Honduran border since the start of the revolution. (Exports of beef from Honduras showed a sudden and inexplicable jump of 20 percent.)

In June 1981, the San Martín slaughterhouse laid off its 188 workers and announced it was closing for at least two months. The owners claimed a lack of animals, but the local ATC disputed this excuse. After borrowing money from the National Development Bank, the owners had sent checks totaling over $100,000 to Miami and had withdrawn seven million córdobas from the company accounts to buy dollars in the street, the government charged. The owners, all vociferous critics of the government, included the head of COSEP, the powerful big business chamber of commerce.

Decapitalization hurt sugar production, too. The sugar mill on the San Pedro hacienda mentioned above used to grind 5,000 bundles of cane daily; in 1981 it did not grind any at all. In 1981, the Ministry of Agricultural Development charged that a large number of landowners simply refused either to cultivate or to rent out their lands. Some 30 percent of the normally cultivated land was being left idle, the ministry estimated in July. Driving through the Pacific Coast and Matagalpa and Estelí regions in June and July, I saw fields covered with weeds and pasture grass where the land had obviously been plowed and planted in previous years.

A Bad "Climate"?

A vicious circle of self-fulfilling prophecies was at work. The more landowners decapitalized, the more they were denounced by workers and by the government, and the more insecure all landowners felt (and were). Thus the circle starts again, but this time with more people.

Hitchhiking in Managua in June 1981, I was picked up by a coffee planter in a tinted-windowed Mercedes. He insisted on speaking English and kept calling me "friend." Earlier in the year he had come back to the country from Coconut Grove to "get out what I could while I could," he told me. He was frightened by the worsening "climate," by the mood of more and more workers and campesinos pressuring the government for a harder line (*mano dura*) toward the landowners. The threat of the worsening "climate"—fear of eventual expropriation—is the reason landowners most frequently give for decapitalization.

Yet even Somoza and the National Guard had not provided a secure climate for the wealthy. For years before the Sandinista-led victory over Somoza, those who could often sent their money out of the country. They feared that one day Somoza would fall, despite all the US backing, and they would lose their capital. With the war, of course, the process accelerated. A United Nations commission estimated that $800 million was taken out of the country between 1977 and July 1979. In the last six months of the Somoza dynasty, $315 million disappeared from the country, equivalent to three-quarters of the nation's total export earnings in a good year.

In the new Nicaragua, landowners have found themselves facing two options. One option is to make some córdobas by, say, growing cotton. This option means wading through government paperwork, hassling with increasingly demanding workers, locating spare parts, worrying about the weather and wondering if enough laborers can be hired for the harvest and at what price. The other option is to decapitalize, to sell off assets to get some córdobas which can be exchanged for dollars on the street market. With dollars one can either speculate on their value going up, deposit them outside the country, or go to Miami and buy clothing, appliances, and gadgets for resale in Nicaragua at a nice profit. Of course, an energetic landowner could do both: borrow, produce, and then use the profits to speculate in dollars, perhaps never paying back the government loan. Thus it's hardly an exaggeration when the government calls the big operators who are investing in long-term production "patriotic."

Decapitalization as a Political Weapon

Decapitalization could be understood as simply the big operators looking out for their individual interests. Their actions, however, take on political dimensions whether or not they are directly intended. Production failures that the big landowners themselves help to generate can later be cited as proof that the Sandinista-led government is a failure. Those who criticize the government most loudly for failure to meet production targets are often decapitalizing rather than producing, Sandinista Directorate member Bayardo Arce stated in March 1981.

At least some big landowners actually use decapitalization as deliberate provocation, many believe. If the big landowners can force the government to feel it must take over farms or businesses to keep the economy from collapse, these confiscations can then be cited as proof that the government is "repressive" and "communist." Such "proof" can weaken international support, making it harder for the government to get foreign financial aid. Moreover, some of the dollars drained out of the country by the big landowners probably finance the ex-National Guardsmen training in Florida and Honduras who are responsible for murderous raids on campesinos, teachers, and health workers in the northern border regions.

The Peasants React

Decapitalization of farms and ranches often outrages agricultural workers and campesinos. To them it is far from an abstract concept; they experience its consequences in "flesh and bones," as they say in Spanish. Poor workers, having responded to the government's pleas to restrain their own wage demands in the interests of the nation, then see the extreme selfishness of those infinitely better off than they. In visits to Nicaragua in the first half of 1981, I found widespread anger in the countryside against decapitalizers.

Angry workers on a cotton plantation near Chinandega told me that the *patrón* had taken out a $50,000 loan from the government to import a new tractor from the United States. They led me to a shed where they showed me a beat-up old Ford tractor that the *patrón* in fact bought locally for only a fraction of the loan, probably depositing the rest in a Miami bank account.

In late June 1981, a large group of campesinos from the interior of the country marched into Managua. "We have been forced to farm small plots of marginal land, trying to grow enough food," one of them told the press. "And now we see the gentlemen farmers letting hundreds and hundreds of acres of good land go idle."

The ATC made it clear that if owners were not disposed to plant, its members were. It was not an idle threat. In numerous cases the ATC moved in to complete the coffee harvest when private estate owners fired workers or left trees unpicked.

In the months leading up to the second anniversary, more and more campesinos and rural workers took it upon themselves to implement the government's dictum: no ownership without obligation. Land seizures increased. Often working with the ATC, the largest association of agricultural workers, and UNAG, the union of small producers, they took over the farms and ranches of those unwilling to fulfill the responsibility of ownership.

In June 1981 alone, the San Pedro hacienda, the Rio de Janeiro hacienda, the Namaslí farm, the San Martín slaughterhouse and numerous other properties were taken over by workers and campesinos. In Nueva Segovia, Jinotega and Matagalpa, hundreds of campesinos and workers seized decapitalized farms. The ATC and UNAG leaderships pressured the government to legalize what they considered just seizures—and to do so quickly. "Children's stomachs cannot wait," they argued.

The direct action of campesinos and landless farm workers made it impossible for the public or the government to ignore the issue. Especially in the two months building up to the second anniversary celebrations, union meetings, press conferences, official speeches, and articles and editorials in the two pro-revolution newspapers all denounced decapitalization. On July 8, I watched a demonstration of workers and campesinos from many parts of the country in front of the Government House. They demanded that the government take measures against decapitalization; they suggested confiscation. "Contra la descapitalización—confiscación," the campesinos and workers chanted over and over.

The decapitalization law on the books since March 1980 was absurdly ineffective. The government had to prove in the courts that the owner had decapitalized before the state could intervene, and the courts were inadequate to move quickly. Moreover, the law required legal proof that assets or dollars had been taken out of the country—something rarely possible. The process took so long that by the time the courts decided against the owner, it was literally too late.

"Yes, against decapitalization, confiscation," declared Edgardo García, head of the ATC, at a news conference. "But *timely* confiscation—not when there's nothing left but ruins, debts and a bankrupt farm." As a final absurd touch, the existing law also required the government to pay the owner the value of anything expropriated even if it got only an empty shell; this was tantamount to a financial incentive to decapitalize.

The campesinos and workers were demanding a law of "preventive intervention." Under this law, the farm workers' accusation that a landowner was selling off his machinery would be sufficient not only for an investigation but for an immediate confiscation of the farm by the Ministry of Agricultural Development. If the investigation proved the owner innocent of the charges, the property would be returned to him or her. Decapitalization should include taking money out of a production unit and not necessarily out of the country, the ATC demanded.

Implied in such a law would be a greater role for workers and campesinos. Already in May the ATC had organized 25 workshops to help farm workers detect and deal with decapitalization. The Sandinista newspaper *Barricada* commented, "In the private sector the workers are pressuring more and more to penetrate the 'secrets of production.'" Workers now wanted access to the financial information of the finca or ranch. "The financial data really belong to the people because, after all, they had to be given to the people's bank to get the loans for building production," a coffee estate worker commented. Edgardo García, secretary general of the ATC, insisted that the National Development Bank should immediately respond when the farm's union asked for information about the bank's financing of the farm.

In the government's view, it had given the private sector an "historic opportunity" to enter into a mutually beneficial partnership. While many "patriotic producers" continued to develop their property, the government concluded that, for the most part, the big operators "blew it."

By the eve of the second anniversary in July 1981, workers, peasants, and big owners alike waited tensely to see how the government would change "the rules of the game."

Chapter II:

Building the New Society

Editors' Introduction

This chapter describes what might be called Nicaragua's "New Society."
There is a strong women's movement in Nicaragua. The first reading in this chapter is a history of the Luisa Amanda Espinoza Women's Association (AMNLAE), the principal organization in this movement. It was followed by an interview with Glenda Monterrey, a leader of AMNLAE, and excerpts from a key speech by Tomás Borge, the most popular Nicaraguan leader, on the question of women.

The next reading, "Education for Change," describes Nicaragua's literacy campaign which has reduced the illiteracy rate from 50.3 percent to 12.9 percent in one year. Adult education is discussed in the article that follows, "Pueblo en Marcha."

Part of the philosophy of the new government is that health care is a right for all its citizens. With this orientation, major strides forward have been made in health care delivery since the 1979 revolution, as described in "Developments in Health Care in Nicaragua," a special report from the *New England Journal of Medicine*.

The final reading, "Toward a New Democracy of Culture," by Father Ernesto Cardenal—priest, poet, and Minister of Culture—provides a moving close to this book.

54. From AMPRONAC to AMNLAE*

By the Luisa Amanda Espinoza Women's Association (AMNLAE)

The National Association of Nicaraguan Women "Luisa Amanda Espinoza" was born in September 1977 under the name "AMPRONAC" (Associatión de Mujeres ante la Problemática Nacional). It grew out of the historical need for Nicaraguan women to take full and active part in the revolutionary process of national liberation which the *Frente Sandinista de Liberación Nacional* was furthering.

Our first assembly, held on September 19, 1977, brought together approximately sixty women who denounced the atrocities being committed by the Somoza regime during those long years of martial law and state of siege.

At that time the objectives of the Association were the following:
- Women's participation in studying and seeking a national solution;
- Defense of the social, economic and political rights of Nicaraguan women;
- Defense of human rights in general.

In this way, women began participating in a variety of activities, such as denunciation of disappearances (in an unprecedented assembly which brought more than a thousand people together, the Association denounced the disappearance of hundreds of peasants in the North); churches were occupied and hunger strikes held to demand the release of political prisoners; campaigns were organized against repression, against rising prices, increased taxes, etc. and to inform citizens of their rights.

In January, 1978, AMPRONAC actively participated in the demonstrations and general strike which took place following the killing of journalist and opposition figure Pedro Joaquín Chamorro.

Active in every neighborhood and province, our Association grew stronger every day. Using all means at our disposal, we mobilized women: opposition radio stations gave us broadcast time; we published statements; we published our own monthly bulletin, "Voice of Women," which was circulated nationwide as well as internationally. In this bulletin, the Association published its own analysis of the current situation and provided women with a forum of expression.

AMPRONAC women began deepening their commitment and played a key role in building up the Civil (now Sandinista) Defense Committees. Before the insurrection, the Association undertook to prepare its member organizations so they could participate effectively in the final struggle. It organized first-aid courses and prepared first-aid stations and clandestine clinics in every neighborhood for treating the wounded; it also set up food stocks and established networks for secret information and emergency communication.

---

*Reprinted from *ISIS International Bulletin no. 14.*

In the present national situation, the Nicaraguan woman faces challenges now as before to participate actively in the tasks of national reconstruction and the building of a new society, based on the valuable experience of AMPRONAC and its militant participation in the national liberation struggle.

Thus at this new stage, we felt the need to give our organization a name which reflects its present substance and the combative spirit of the Nicaraguan woman who, now as before, breaks down the traditional barriers which have kept her marginalized, as she stands up to defend and rebuild the liberated homeland. Luisa Amanda Espinoza, a seamstress by trade, was the first woman member of the Frente Sandinista to fall in combat—a symbol of the struggle of the Nicaraguan Women.

Constituting more than 50 percent of the Nicaraguan population, we are called upon to fulfill a key role—like every Nicaraguan—in the restructuring of our country and in building and consolidating a new society free of injustices and exploitation.

From this point of view, the Association's principal goal is to fully integrate women into the economic, social and political life of the country—breaking through the cultural backwardness which has kept them subjugated for centuries.

Thus it is important to provide general educational programs for women through seminars, cultural centers, schools, publications, and also through their extensive participation in the national literacy campaign, "Heroes and Martyrs," which will also help provide basic education for women, especially rural women, who have always been the most marginalized and isolated.

In order to achieve for women a greater share in the productive and economic life of Nicaragua, our Association has another two-fold objective: on the one hand, to encourage professional training programs which will provide women with the necessary background knowledge to take skilled jobs; on the other, to promote day care, child development centers, schools, community kitchens, laundries, and dispensaries, which can alleviate the burden of domestic labor in the household and thus free women to become more fully involved in the political and cultural life of the country.

55. "The FSLN Opened the Door for Us": How Revolution Has Changed the Lives of Women*

By Glenda Monterrey

The following interview with Glenda Monterrey, a leader of the Luisa Amanda Espinoza Women's Association (AMNLAE), was conducted in Managua on September 22, 1981, by Matilde Zimmerman.

Question. The Nicaraguan revolution is famous for the involvement of women fighters—both in the mountains and in the urban insurrections. How have the lives of Nicaraguan women been changed by the revolution?

Answer. We think that the Sandinista National Liberation Front (FSLN) opened the door for us, made it possible for Nicaraguan women to participate, cautiously at first, and then on a massive scale in the years right before the revolution.

We got involved, little by little, especially young women, doing political work in the barrios in the various organizations the FSLN had set up. But I think some of the best work women were able to do was in AMPRONAC, the Association of Women Concerned with National Problems.

It is true that AMPRONAC was not organized around issues pertaining only to women. This was three years ago, and AMPRONAC was organized around the tasks of the moment, which were the practical tasks of the insurrection. These went from learning first aid, in order to take care of our wounded, to taking military training to participate in combat directly.

This happened on a massive scale before the revolution. But today Nicaraguan women have much greater opportunities to get involved.

Why? Before many were afraid to get involved, because of the ferocity of the repression, and also because of the submission and second-class status we had been relegated to.

There have been big changes. We think there are still problems with the degree to which women are incorporated into the work force. This isn't because women don't want to work, or because the government doesn't want us to. The problem is the overall lack of jobs. And it is still sometimes true in our country that when there are two people for only one job, the job is given to the man.

We still have the situation where women do certain types of work, the types that require less physical strength, and generally earn less than male workers. To a

_____

*Reprinted from *Intercontinental Press*, October 26, 1981.

certain extent this is a problem of our industry itself, which is very underdeveloped.

This is beginning to change, because women are getting more organized and participating in a more active way. Women are more organized now than we were a year ago.

Now women workers are members of unions, and are playing new roles in the union movement. But we still have to work on raising the technical skills, the political level, and the class consciousness of women workers so that they assume their rightful role working within the unions to transform society.

Q. In some of the factories I've visited here, I've noticed that the majority of the workers are women. Most of the women workers I've talked to have several children, many are single mothers, and many started to work when they were hardly more than children themselves. Could you talk about some of the special problems of women industrial workers in Nicaragua?

A. It is our opinion that the women of Nicaragua, besides being doubly exploited, are also doubly heroic. Our women get up in the very early hours, take care of all their children's needs—food, clothing, etc. Then they go to work, and they come back in the afternoon to yet more housework, including washing and ironing for themselves, their children, and the whole family.

And these *compañeras*, when they do not also work outside the home, get no recognition for their domestic work.

The fact that they are working hard is not recognized by men, by their families, or even by society. We think that this type of work must gradually be changed into collective work and must be seen as socially valuable by the rest of Nicaraguan society.

Then there are the women who work in the factories or in agriculture. Some people complain that we produce less than male workers. This shows how little they understand the life of a woman, who starts working the minute she gets up, and then comes home from work to the same number of undone jobs. So sometimes in the factory she can't produce as much as a man.

We might be talking about a woman with eight children, or one who has to walk several kilometers to work. These critics don't understand that when a woman is pregnant and works on her feet eight hours a day, she might have to rest sooner than a man.

So, it's true, her productivity might be less. Not always. What happens is that our women want to get ahead so badly, and they want so badly to make enough to feed their children, that they keep up with the pace in the factory. But sometimes at the expense of their health.

Q. I guess AMNLAE's biggest campaign this year has been to recruit women to the Sandinista People's Militias (MPS). I remember one conversation that impressed me a lot, with a man who told me proudly that he had five daughters and every one was a militia member. But it is clear that not all fathers—nor all husbands—feel the same way.

What has been the impact of women joining the militias, on their families and on the women themselves?

A. Organizing women into the militia reserve battalions has not yet been what you would call easy. I gave a speech in Jinotega in which I explained how hard it had been—not so much to organize the women as to win acceptance from the husbands, the families, and in some cases from *compañeros* within the military.

Participation in the militias began on a massive scale in mid-1980. But then it consisted of exercises that were done certain afternoons or a certain day of the week, outside the normal hours of work or school. It was hard work, but women did it, and they found ways to fit it into their schedules.

But the reserve battalions were something else again. They meant going off to the mountains for two or three weeks. They implied a commitment of a different scope—not just in terms of physical training but also of readiness to defend the country at any time, against any type of aggression.

So what happened? There were places where at first people said women were not capable of enduring the physical training. There were others where men refused to let their wives go.

Then there were women who wanted to join the battalions. But who would take care of their children? Then there were those who found someone to watch their children, but then their factory or company said no, this worker is too important, we can't replace her if she goes off for fifteen days or three weeks.

But in practice, we've accomplished great things. For example, we've seen how in León—and this is something we're very proud of—the best battalion in the whole province is the women's battalion.

Women have shown themselves to be capable of being reservists. Capable of the pain—because the physical training is very hard. Capable of the political and military training that's involved. And then capable of returning to their homes or their factories and going on with their work.

There are five women's reserve battalions that have gone out so far, from León, Estelí, Managua, Chinandega, and Carazo. There were also young women who went out in the student reserve battalions. And women who participated in the mixed battalions of men and women reservists.

One thing we have noticed with the women's battalions is that the participants are not necessarily young, not necessarily students, but rather *compañeras* from the barrios, housewives, members of the Sandinista Defense Committees (CDSs).

Q. I'd like to ask you about the role of women in the leadership of the revolution. There are of course many well-known women leaders in the government and the FSLN. But it seems to me that the process elsewhere is somewhat uneven, as might be expected. I was a little surprised to see that the new executive council of the National Union of Nicaraguan Students (UNEN) is all male, since after all, this is the new generation.

A. Our general approach is that if we have women in certain positions, they are not there because they are women but because they earned the responsibility, just like male *compañeros* have to.

But what happens in practice? The truth is that in the governing bodies of the Sandinista Workers Federation (CST) and the Rural Workers Association (ATC) there are almost no women leaders at the national level.

In the youth, there are. I think that half the national leadership of the Sandinista youth are women. And I was surprised too that all those chosen in the latest UNEN election were men. Because our youth has a fighting tradition that goes back many years. And there have always been a lot of women in the ranks of the student movement and before the victory in the Revolutionary Student Front.

What does this mean? Not some big retreat on the part of our youth. But if there has been a decline in the level of participation, then this is something the student comrades should take in hand.

In the CST it is understandable, because we have some catching up to do. We women did not play much of a role in forming or organizing the trade unions. So it wasn't until after the revolution that the real efforts to involve women workers began. And women are responding. But this is not yet reflected much at the national leadership.

So this is why things are uneven. In the Sandinista Defense Committees, on the other hand, there is widespread and leading participation by women. And the majority of the population is organized into the Sandinista Defense Committees.

We just finished a tour of the northern part of the country. And we found that campesina women identify with AMNLAE. They are AMNLAE. The ATC has reached out to them, and they work in the ATC, but the organization they identify with is AMNLAE.

In Estelí we visited a community where women in AMNLAE are part of a cooperative that the ATC has formed. They are also working with the Sandinista children's association and are going to get a child-care center. They just got a health center. And they have formed cultural groups, that children and young people take part in too. It is a model community.

We do not yet have a concrete plan for our work with women workers and peasants. But we're studying the situation, making tours to study the special problems of factory and peasant women, listening to their concerns. And perhaps for 1982, or for the national conference of AMNLAE in November, we will be able to begin to lay out the lines of our work with these sectors.

56. *Women and the Nicaraguan Revolution**

By Tomás Borge

Dear *compañeras,* in the world of today, profound changes are taking place. New offspring of history are being born in the midst of grief, anguish, and heroic

---

*Reprinted from a 1982 pamphlet published by Pathfinder Press, New York.

splendor. Social revolution is the order of the day in Africa, Asia, and Latin America. Central America is being rocked with social earthquakes. Poor people of all latitudes are demanding—each time more vigorously—profound transformations in the old and rotting structures of class exploitation and imperialist domination.

And in Nicaragua, land of volcanoes and wildcats, we are winning national liberation through the Sandinista revolution.

Therefore it's normal, absolutely logical that we now speak of a new revolution—that is, a revolution of women (applause), a revolution that will complete the process of national liberation.

The woman question is nothing more than an aspect of social reality in its totality. The definitive answer to the liberation of women can emerge only with the total resolution of the class contradictions, of the social diseases that originate in a society like ours—politically liberated but with the rope of economic dependence still around our neck.

Nevertheless, we must have patience to deal with the woman question in an independent and concrete manner.

Before the revolutionary triumph, the incorporation of women in productive work was minimal. The great majority of women were condemned to slavery in the home. When women could sell their labor power, in addition to fulfilling their obligations on the job, they had to fulfill their duties in the home to assure the upbringing of their children. All of this in a regime of political oppression and misery imposed by a dependent capitalist society. And subjected, on the other hand, to exploitation by man—the male of the species—who placed on the woman's shoulders the fundamental weight of household chores, thereby endlessly prolonging her working day.

Did this end with the triumph of the Sandinista People's Revolution, we ask ourselves?

The triumph of the Sandinista People's Revolution eliminated terror and opened the way for the process of national liberation, initiating at the same time economic and social transformations that represented a qualitative advance in the conquest of freedom and development.

It can't be said, therefore, that the situation of women in Nicaragua has in no way changed.

Nevertheless, all of us have to honestly admit that we haven't confronted the struggle for women's liberation with the same courage and decisiveness.

Independently of the fact that women, in this stage, continue to bear the main responsibility for reproduction and the care of children, the burden of housework and discrimination still relentlessly weighs down upon them.

From the point of view of daily exertion, women remain fundamentally in the same conditions as in the past.

Of course, behind this objective reality there is an economic basis. Workers' living conditions continue to be difficult and incompatible with the political will of the revolution. For reasons that are well-known to you and because barely three years have passed [since the revolution], it has not been possible to meet legitimate expectations for improvement in workers' general living conditions.

This explains why many times women are still compelled to do work that pays no wages, that is not taken account of anywhere, that is not credited toward social security.

Independently of the fact that women often receive the help of men, the truth is that the customs and level of development of our society impose this superexertion on women. And it is in this sense that women are not only exploited—they're superexploited. They are exploited in their workplaces, if they work. They are exploited by lower wages and exploited in the home. That is, they are triply exploited.

What can be done to eliminate this dramatic plight of women?

There is no other alternative except to change the basic economic structure of society. There is no alternative but to develop an economy that guarantees the satisfaction of the fundamental needs of our people. There is no alternative but to create a productive apparatus whose rationale is not individual profit, but rather satisfaction of the demands of the entire society, the demands of the workers— whose rationale is to reaffirm and emphasize the potential of man and woman to live together socially as human beings.

This process of change, *compañeras*, is complicated, difficult, and will take place over time. But are we going to wait until economic development and social transformation have reached their culmination before we begin to think out the woman question? This would certainly be an inconsistency.

How can we fail to seriously consider the equality of women if we are to be elementally just to their struggle, their sacrifice, and their heroism? How can we not guarantee their participation in social life, in work, and in the political leadership of the country? How can we not guarantee that a woman can be both a mother and a worker, both a mother and a student, both a mother and an artist, both a mother and a political leader, both fulfill all the tasks the revolution demands of her and at the same time fulfill the beautiful work of a self-sacrificing, capable, and loving mother?

A concrete answer to these questions will be possible only to the extent that the individual tasks of women are socialized. It is society that has to provide the necessary daycare centers, laundries, people's restaurants, and other services that will, in effect, free women from household work. This is not easy.

So far, the revolution has only been able to build twenty CDIs [childcare centers]—obviously an insufficient number. The problem is that the cost of construction, equipment, and maintenance is very high. With all the economic difficulties that are holding our country back, it's impossible for us to move forward to the massive creation of these centers. And yet we must do it—not only to enable women to dedicate themselves to productive, social, and cultural tasks, but also to assure that the overall education of our children is as rich as possible.

How can we do it? How can we overcome this contradiction between the possible and the necessary?

We must look for audacious answers, I believe—answers based not so much on purely budgetary considerations but on the initiative, organization, and strength of the masses. Here AMNLAE should be the leading force and catalyst of these initiatives, fundamentally in coordination with the CDSs [Sandinista Defense Committees].

This is possible in a revolutionary society. There is no task that wouldn't be possible for the revolutionary masses and there is no task that wouldn't be possible for Nicaraguan women.

However difficult a task may be, the challenges that are being put forward now can hardly be compared with what Nicaraguan women faced and conquered in the past when they were capable of participating in the trenches with rifles in hand.

On the other hand, the revolution must guarantee equal pay for men and women and at the same time open the doors of production to women's participation in new fields of development—in industry as well as in agriculture.

We have already taken the first steps to guarantee this equal participation. To assure the effectiveness of the principle, "equal pay for equal work," we enacted decrees 573 and 583 for the rural sector. These decrees for the first time established norms governing agricultural labor in coffee and cotton, and provided that everyone above fourteen years of age, man or woman, will be paid directly. Because before the victory, only the head of the household received the wages for the family—the young ones and women were not treated as real workers.

But the important thing is that we watch over the execution of laws the revolution has created to guarantee equality between men and women.

Just as workers gained consciousness of the exploitation they suffered and of their vanguard role in the revolution, women must also gain full consciousness of the discrimination they are still subjected to and of their role in the revolutionary struggle. We said that women were triply exploited, which means that women should be revolutionary in three different dimensions, seeking a single objective— the total liberation of our society.

It's good to remember, however, that economic development by itself will not accomplish the liberation of women, nor will simply the organization of women be sufficient.

We have to struggle against the habits, customs, and prejudices of men and women. We have to embark upon a difficult and prolonged ideological struggle—a struggle that equally benefits men and women.

Men must overcome a multitude of prejudices. We know *compañeros* who are revolutionaries in the street, in their workplaces, in their militia battalions— everywhere—but they're feudal *señores*, feudal lords in the home.

Right now, if we consider the path traveled by AMNLAE from the moment of its founding, it's evident that the self-sacrificing activity of the *compañeras* has achieved quantitative advances, and in some aspects qualitative advances. With respect to the present tasks, and above all regarding the State of Emergency, women's participation has noticeably increased. The work of the Committees of Mothers of Heroes and Martyrs in denouncing the enemy's crimes and plans of aggression against Nicaragua has been outstanding.

However, in the militias, for example, the presence of women varies geographically. In Managua, women are 14 percent of the militia members, but in places like León, their participation is very low. León ranks twelfth in the incorporation of women into the militia, after having been first in the revolutionary struggle in combat against the dictatorship. It's a contradiction that perhaps they will explain to me later.

The participation of women has been important in the People's Health Campaigns. In relation to organizational tasks, we can see a greater stability in leadership cadres, a greater coordination among the various mass organizations, and an advance in the consolidation of the Provincial Executive Committees—and therefore in overseeing the carrying out of tasks in the provinces.

In the field of international relations, it's correct to single out AMNLAE's participation in the Continental Meeting of Women as marking a considerable advance in establishing relations with different political and women's groups worldwide.

It would be an error, however, if we considered these accomplishments satisfactory. The revolution demands that we confront with dedication the deficiencies that limit the development of AMNLAE. The links between the leadership of the association and the ranks are not sufficient. At times general lines of action are put forward without being followed by specific concrete tasks. Adequate forms and mechanisms to assure the active participation of women in the work of the association do not exist.

All this results at times in improvisation and amateurish work habits.

Of course this is not just AMNLAE's problem but a problem of all the mass organizations and forms a part of the process of development of our revolution.

But our revolutionary society has to begin from a fundamental premise—the active, conscious, and permanent participation of each man and woman not only in aspects solely concerned with daily life but also in determining the course of our revolution.

If the masses participate in their workplaces, in their neighborhoods, in their schools, and in their organizations, then this revolution will advance toward a revolutionary society where the dignity of man will be counterposed to the alienation of man.

And we must take into account that analyzing this concrete problem means not only gaining knowledge of one particular aspect, such as legislation, but advancing the process of women's politicization as a whole.

If we don't do this our men and women will not be able to carry the process of liberation to its completion.

Right now AMNLAE should be more a great movement than an organization—a great movement that encourages the participation of women in the various mass organizations, in the CDSs, in the Sandinista Youth, in the ATC [Rural Workers Association], in the CST [Sandinista Workers Federation] —and that at the same time groups women together in their common bond, which is their status as women.

The central task of AMNLAE should be the integration of all women into the revolution, without distinction. It should be a broad and democratic movement that mobilizes women from the various social sectors, so as to provide a channel for their political, social, economic, and cultural demands and to integrate them as a supporting force in the tasks of the Sandinista People's Revolution.

AMNLAE should become a broad propagandistic, educational, and agitational movement that encourages women to play an active role in the economic, political, and social transformations of the country.

The peasant woman, for example, is a peasant and as such has specific demands. But she is also a woman—just like the woman worker, the woman militia member, the woman who is a housewife, the woman student, the professional woman, and so forth.

Being clear on this dual role is key to the development of AMNLAE.

Another immediate task of AMNLAE, we believe, is to deepen the analysis of the status of the Nicaraguan woman, to fight to massively incorporate women in productive work, to reclaim women's right to participate more fully in production, to participate more fully in leading the government, the mass organizations, and the Sandinista National Liberation Front. And to make sure that in scholarship awards, a considerable number are given to women, which in large measure is already happening.

Compañeras: Our National Directorate salutes Nicaraguan women with profound respect and affection. We can assure you we are not going to consider anyone a revolutionary who is not ready to fight the oppression of women. We would not be Sandinistas if in the new society we did not make women an essential pillar of this new society. If we are revolutionaries, even if we are men, we should be with AMNLAE.

From Conchita Alday and Blanca Aráuz to Luisa Amanda Espinoza, women have blazed a path of fire and tenderness that has given life and color to this revolution. Nicaraguan women have not only given the country the fruit of their bellies but also their enthusiasm and courage—selflessly, without limitations.

A revolution with these women is a revolution that will not be defeated by anyone—that will march invincibly into new dawns.

It's important that the imperialists know, that the National Guard murderers know, that the nation's traitors know, that in Nicaragua they will be confronted not only by men but by the women as well. And these women! Women that leave the fragrance of flowers for the fragrance of gunpowder—women who are as fertile in their wombs as they are in revolutionary consciousness.

57. *Education for Change: A Report on the Nicaraguan Literacy Crusade**

By the Council on Interracial Books for Children

The women and men who took up arms against the Somoza regime had as their goal not just the overthrow of a government, but the liberation of a people—and after victory in battle, the next priority was literacy. At the time of Somoza's defeat, half of all Nicaraguans could neither read nor write. In rural areas the illiteracy rate was estimated at 75 to 80 percent, and, for women in many villages, 100 percent.

Plans for a Literacy Crusade, under the direction of Fernando Cardenal, began five weeks after the new government took control. The Literacy Crusade's goal was to bring functional literacy—reading at the third grade level—to 50 percent of the population, or as many as could be reached. The Crusade organizers conducted an extensive examination of literacy programs in other Third World Nations—Cuba, Mozambique, Guinea-Bissau, Cape Verde—and invited the internationally renowned expert Paulo Freire to Managua to consult on methodology.

While method and content were being planned, a village-by-village nationwide census was carried out to determine levels of literacy in each of Nicaragua's 16 provinces. Efforts were also made to ascertain the availability of volunteer teachers.

Influenced by Freire's methodology, the planners hoped to provide one literacy teacher for every four or five *campesinos* (poor country people). Teachers would be assigned to their own province when possible, but tens of thousands of teachers would have to be transported from the cities to the remote areas in the northern mountains and the Atlantic Coast forest regions where available teachers were scarce.

A serious problem was how to mobilize national resources for such a large-scale campaign without interfering with production. During the Revolution, entire sections of Nicaragua's cities had been destroyed by the punitive bombings of the National Guard. Before Somoza fled, he pillaged the national treasury and left massive debts which the new government pledged to honor. Money to pay these debts had to be earned from exports, which meant production of goods had to be increased.

A clever solution was arrived at. Those who volunteered to work in the Literacy Crusade would be divided into two groups. One would consist of young people not yet actively engaged in productive work, who would leave the cities and live with the *campesinos* in the rural areas and mountains for a period of five months. They would give classes in the evenings and by day they would work in the fields, planting

---

*Reprinted from *The Interracial Books for Children Bulletin*, Vol. 12, No. 2, 1981.

crops, harvesting, tending animals and helping to increase the nation's productive capacity. These volunteers would comprise the Popular Literacy Army (EPA), better known as *brigadistas*. The second group would be factory workers, government workers, housewives and professionals who would remain at their regular work in the cities and teach in the urban *barrios* during non-working hours. These were the Popular Literacy Teachers, called "popular alphabetizers (AP)."

The volunteers for the *brigadistas* were young people—high school and college students primarily, although some were as young as twelve. Several reasons account for the youthfulness of the *brigadistas*. For one thing, many had fought in the Revolution and were committed to its goals. (A striking aspect of the Nicaraguan Revolution had been the youth of the liberation fighters—teenagers, or younger.)

In addition, the government made specific efforts to enlist young people in order to raise their consciousness about the realities of the poverty and oppression of the *campesinos* in the rural and mountain areas. (Most of the *brigadistas* were from urban areas, and while illiteracy was high there, it was far, far higher in the country.)

The *brigadistas* were the political descendants of the "Choir of Angels"— children who had formed part of Augusto César Sandino's guerrilla army during the struggle to oust the occupying US Marines in the 1930s. The "Choir" worked to "alphabetize" the *campesinos* in the mountainous provinces of Matagalpa, Jinotega and Nueva Segovia, so that they could read Sandino's literature. In the 1960s this same area became the base for the Sandinista forces—nationalists who derived their names and inspiration from Sandino.

Parental Permission Required

Parental permission was a requisite for minors who wished to join the *brigadistas*. The Crusade organizers found that they faced opposition from some middle-class parents who were not supportive of the Revolution and who, in addition, had traditional parental worries about their children, particularly their daughters. (Working class parents were not, in general, antagonistic.)

Parent hostility was met by widespread discussions about their concerns. Campaign represenatives held weekly meetings in the schools with parents and students. Posters, newspaper articles and TV and radio programs addressed the issues. To allay some of the parents' fears, it was decided to organize single-sex brigades, and young girls would be accompanied by their teachers and live in dormitories, farmhouses, public buildings or schoolrooms. Boys and older girls would live in the homes of the *campesinos*. It is worth noting that children from middle-class homes—who joined the Crusade for a variety of reasons—usually became committed to the goals of the new society Nicaragua is trying to build.

Initial preparations lasted six months. The Literacy Crusade first launched a pilot project in the same northern provinces where the Sandinistas had originally made their base. Undertaken by the 80-member *Patria Libre* brigade, its objective was to test a training design and gain practical experience that would later be transmitted to the other *brigadistas*. The group members also underwent physical training to prepare them for the arduous tasks ahead.

After completing the pilot project, each of the 80 members of the *Patria Libre* conducted workshops and trained 560 more teachers. These, in turn, trained 7,000 teachers. For the final phase, which ended in March 1980, schools and colleges were closed early, releasing thousands of volunteer students for additional training. By the conclusion of the last phase of training, a grand total of 95,000 "alphabetizers" were prepared for the campaign. Of these, 60,000 were the young *brigadistas* who would work and teach in the countryside. The other 35,000 were the "popular alphabetizers," adults for the most part, who remained in the cities to work in the *barrios.*

Groups Support Crusade

The Nicaraguan Revolution had been successful in large part because of the involvement of the people's organizations that had formed in the years preceding 1978. Some of these were the National Union of Teachers, the Sandinista Trade Union Federation, the Organization of Nicaraguan Women, the block- and street-based Sandinista Defense Committee and the Association of Rural Workers. The same groups now provided the Literacy Crusade with massive logistical support, transporting 60,000 *brigadistas* from the cities to the countryside, supplying them with food, medical care, textbooks, etc. They also provided protection; security was a major concern, because remnants of Somoza's National Guard, which had fled into the mountains on the Honduras border, threatened that the *brigadistas* would be killed.

On March 24 of last year, truck convoys by the thousands left the cities of Managua, Estelí, León, Granada and Matagalpa and fanned out to all of Nicaragua's provinces. Because of the terrain, thousands of *brigadistas* had to march by foot. Some traveled by boat, some by helicopter. Each *brigadista* was eventually outfitted with jeans, a gray tunic, a mosquito net, a hammock, a lantern by which to teach at night and a portable blackboard. On *brigadista* arrival day, a special service was held in every church of every denomination to greet the *brigadistas* and to launch the Crusade.

From the end of March until mid-August, the *brigadistas* followed roughly this pattern: by day, work in the fields with the *campesinos* they lived with or chores around the house; by night, two hours of instruction with from five to seven *campesinos* huddled around a gas lamp. On Saturday, there were workshops with other *brigadistas*—usually 30 in number from the same village or a village nearby— to evaluate the week's work, discuss common problems and plan the week ahead. For those *brigadistas* who could not meet together because of distance, all-day Saturday radio programs informed them of news of the campaign and offered advice and encouragement. In the cities, the popular alphabetizers worked at their regular jobs and, in addition, gave two hours of instruction at night; they also had Saturday workshops. Within this general pattern, there were wide variations.

The campaign took its toll: 56 *brigadistas* died during the Crusade. Six were murdered by the National Guard, the rest were killed by accidents and illness. Today, the murdered youth are hailed by Nicaraguans as martyred heroes, and their faces are enshrined on posters and paintings hung everywhere.

The campaign itself was extremely successful. At its end, some 500,000 *campesinos* were no longer illiterate, and the rate of illiteracy was down from a national average of 52 percent to just under 13 percent. Confirming the statistics are the documented exams and the simple sentences that all *campesinos* had to write at the end of the five-month learning period. As important as the literacy they gained, however, was their new awareness of themselves and of their significance to the nation. Prior to the Revolution, *campesinos* had been considered of little or no consequence; but this campaign, a major indication of positive governmental concern, contributed to a new sense of dignity and self-worth.

The influence of the crusade on the *brigadistas* and other "alphabetizers" was also dramatic. They gained a new understanding and respect for the rural poor—and often, as noted, a new commitment to the goals of the Revolution. Participants also learned a variety of skills—life skills as well as teaching skills. All gained a more profound understanding of their nation—and learned that they could play a role in creating a new society.

58. *Pueblo en Marcha: Adult Education in Nicaragua**

By the National Network in Solidarity with the Nicaraguan People

"I learned to read during the Crusade and now I'm studying at level three as well as working as a zone supervisor for Matagalpa and Compasagua. I supervise six Popular Education Collectives (CEPs)," explained Felipe Alvarado, 24, a worker on a government-run cattle ranch, just before the day's adult education class was to start.

Maritza Dormus is 16. She studies second grade in the little town of Muy Muy and in the afternoon teaches 16 family members in their tiny village. "What inspired you to teach a CEP?" I asked. A tremendous smile suddenly brightened her face. "The joy of teaching!" she responded immediately, evidently not needing to give the subject any thought. "Would you like to be a teacher someday?" I asked her. "Oh, yes!" she replied.

People like Felipe and Maritza form the backbone of Nicaragua's Popular Adult Education Program (EPA). They are among 24,000 popular educators who

*Reprinted from: *Nicaragua*, October/November, 1982.

teach 1$5,000 adults in a two-year program designed "to create a nation of not only literate, but critical revolutionaries." 70 percent of the popular educators have not yet finished sixth grade—many, in fact, are only one step ahead of their student neighbors. But they teach each night for two hours and on Saturdays they attend workshops to help them evaluate their work, prepare for the next week, and receive technical and political preparation.

The CEPs grew out of the 1980 National Literacy Crusade, which reduced the illiteracy rate from 52 percent to 12 percent. The Education Ministry realized that the literacy level achieved by the new students was minimal and that they could easily backslide and forget what they had learned. They felt that four to six semesters of additional study were needed before the newly literate would be able to enter technical courses. In 1981 the first two levels of the program were taught and this year third and fourth levels are underway. The program has two long-term goals: to encourage participation in mass organizations through a better understanding of Nicaragua's history and current situation and to develop the technical knowledge needed for production, health, and other national needs.

As in the National Literacy Crusade, the method of teaching is based on Brazilian Educator Paulo Freire's philosophy that adult education in poor countries must be based on consciousness-raising, not only to make it interesting but, most importantly, for it to be true education. An effort is made to help students understand the causes of problems and what *they* can do to solve them. The idea is that the people are and must be the authors of their own development.

Problems to Overcome

The program has had to face many problems—inexperienced teachers; lack of tables, lights, paper and eyeglasses; the isolation of rural communities; and the tiring nature of agrarian work. Because many rural teachers are newly literate and there is an urgency to complete the exercise books and advance to higher levels of literacy, workshops for popular educators tend to focus more on the use of materials than on pedagogy and participation.

Rural areas often lack adequate facilities for CEPs. 70 percent of the collectives in Rivas lack sufficient seating, writing surfaces or blackboards. Three of the seven areas in Estelí are without electricity and many CEPs have not been able to meet because new wicks for Coleman lanterns are not available. Some areas are only reachable by boat and the gasoline supply is often insufficient for supervisors to visit classes and provide materials. It is common for supervisors and popular educators to travel from two to five hours on foot to attend a workshop or meeting.

Special problems exist in agricultural communities. From September to March 1981, 50 percent of the *campesinos* with no land or with small holdings dropped out of the program to migrate north for the harvests. Attempts to hold CEPs in the workcamps proved futile because of physical exhaustion at the end of the day. The floods in late May meant fields had to be cleaned and entire crops replanted in some areas. Relocation of flood victims and reconstruction of homes broke up many

CEPs. In April 1982 increased armed attacks by counterrevolutionaries along the northern border required the mobilization of reserve troops from nearly every community. For these reasons CEPs were postponed for three weeks and the semester extended by a month nationally.

CEPs organized for co-operative farmers and for urban workers have been more successful. In the co-ops, literacy skills are being developed with an eye toward improving production. Information about grain storage was used within the CEPs to significantly improve yield, and construction of grain bins has taken place through the joint effort of CEPs and PROCAMPO, an organization which provides technical assistance.

In many industrial centers all workers are enrolled in CEPs except those awaiting the development of more advanced levels of the program. In the state-run enterprises—and in a few privately owned workplaces—workers spend two hours a day at the CEPs with pay. The advantages of these CEPs extend to the homes of workers as well. "I'm less tired when I get home and since I've already had my class I don't mind taking care of my children while my wife goes," commented one worker.

Counterrevolution Attacks CEPs

The need for critical literacy becomes more important as the counterrevolution escalates its ideological offensive. In isolated rural areas, counterrevolutionaries claiming to be members of evangelical or pentacostal churches denounce the CEPs, militia and health brigades as "unchristian" and a "tool of communist indoctrination." In Wiwilí a CEP worker was murdered by a counterrevolutionary band and in Río Blanco CEP study materials were burned. While most people have remained firm, CEP supervisors believe that enrollment is down in some areas due to fear of the counterrevolution.

A Visit to CEPs in Matagalpa

Despite the problems faced by the program and increased counterrevolutionary activities, CEPs are moving forward. During a visit to several CEPs in a poor neighborhood of Matagalpa, we asked students what they wanted to study when they finished all the levels of basic education. There were answers of typing, carpentry and sewing.

Reyna Mercardo, age 17, is interested in learning how to sew so that she can earn something while she continues studying. Right now she has only seasonal work as a coffee sorter. Ethel Ubeda, age 36 with five children, already sews but says she needs mathematics, especially division, to make patterns for her clients. She got only as far as second grade as a child and is now in level two.

During a level two class in the same neighborhood students were discussing what lessons they liked best. Everyone seemed to appreciate the usefulness of math but the favorite lesson had been about the Atlantic Coast region of Nicaragua, a piece of their own country that for centuries was a world apart.

In another classroom a student was asking about shortages of certain food products, and in another students were learning "New Vocabulary Words," which included "Decapitalization"; "when the owners of a company remove machinery and tools from a factory and take the earnings of the company out of the country instead of using them to improve the business or help the development of the country."

Both the trying and promising aspects of the popular adult education program were summed up in the words of a *campesino* woman in Estelí: "Sometimes I just think, why should I be sitting here struggling with these books when I'm so old? But now that I've started reading, even the newspaper, I feel like I've come to a new country and started all over again."

59. *Developments in Health Care in Nicaragua**

By David C. Halperin and Richard Garfield

David C. Halperin is an M.D. residing in Maine. He has visited Nicaragua on several occasions. Richard Garfield worked in Nicaragua for a year. He is a registered nurse and is currently working on his doctorate at the Columbia School of Public Health.

Nicaragua is much in the news these days because of political turmoil in Central America. Charges and countercharges abound on military and political matters, but little has been reported on developments in health and medicine in Nicaragua. One of us (D.C.H.) spent several weeks in the spring of 1981 in the capital city of Managua and in more remote parts of the country. The other (R.G.) made two visits to Nicaragua in 1980 and worked in the Nicaraguan Ministry of Health as a health-services administrator during the last nine months of 1981. In this report we describe the efforts and changes that have taken place in medicine and public health since the Sandinista revolution.

In July 1979, a coalition of guerilla groups called the Sandinista Front for National Liberation overthrew the Somoza dictatorship after a four-year war that cost 50,000 lives. Before that, in 1972, this country of 2,800,000 had suffered an earthquake that leveled the center of the capital city, killed 20,000 people, and destroyed every acute-care hospital bed. Another 10,000 or more still needed care because of injuries sustained during the earthquake.

*Reprinted from *New England Journal of Medicine,* 307:388–392, 1982.

Health conditions in Nicaragua under the Somoza regime had been abominable, even worse than in most of its Central American neighbors. Thirty-five percent of the urban population and 95 percent of the rural population lacked access to potable water. The Somoza regime paid so little attention to health matters that even such basic data as birth and death certificates were collected for only about 25 percent of the population. The National Social Security Institute, which was designed to provide medical care for working people, covered only 8 percent of the population. Another 20 percent were covered by various state programs for indigents. Several churches ran highly respected hospitals, but for the most part they treated only those who could pay cash. The National Guard had relatively good medical services, including those in most specialties, through a system of hospitals and clinics of its own. The present government estimates that 90 percent of medical services were directed to 10 percent of the population. More than half the doctors and medical beds were located in the capital city.

Malaria, tuberculosis, and parasitism were endemic in much of Nicaragua. One-third of the people contracted malaria at least once in their lives. Measles was a great killer of children. In malnourished children, measles may be accompanied by an overwhelming and often fatal bacterial pneumonia, usually of staphylococcal origin. Studies of malnutrition in recent years have estimated that between 46 and 83 percent of Nicaraguan children were malnourished. These same studies have indicated that a high proportion of these children (25 to 45 percent) had the more severe secondary and tertiary types of malnutrition. Life expectancy at the time of the revolution was 52.9 years. Infant mortality was estimated at between 120 and 140 per thousand (as compared, for example, with Panama's purported rate of 30 per thousand). Among the top 10 causes of death in children were bacterial diarrheas, tetanus, measles, whooping cough, and malaria, all of which can be largely controlled with elementary public-health measures.

In the light of the health problems, some of which are mentioned above, the achievements since July 1979 have been remarkable. About 70 percent of the population, as compared with 28 percent in 1979, now has regular contact with medical care. People have flooded the hospitals and health-care centers in the cities and the newly opened health posts in small towns. There has been a broad educational campaign to communicate the message that all people who live in Nicaragua are now entitled to health care. Health posts, staffed by nursing aides and visited by physicians weekly, have been set up in tiny hamlets. Medical and nursing students accompany migrant agricultural workers who travel to harvest cotton, coffee, and other cash crops. Emergency training and a basic medical kit have been provided to health workers at remote haciendas. Psychiatric day centers have been set up in more central towns, and a traveling dental service reaches areas where such services were never available before.

The most important measures have been public-health programs. Diphtheria-pertussis-tetanus, measles, and bacillus Calmette-Guérin vaccinations have been administered to hundreds of thousands of children. Health campaigns enlisting the general population were mounted in early 1981 to vaccinate children, remove environmental hazards, and eliminate breeding sites of the *Aedes aegypti* mosquito, transmitter of dengue fever. A massive literacy campaign in 1980 was also used for health education. One hundred thousand young people went into the countryside to teach peasants how to read and write. While living and working with the people they were instructing, the "literacy brigades" taught elementary health principles. One in 10 literacy workers received a week's health training. He or she was responsible for distributing preventive medicines and antimalarial agents to other literacy workers. They introduced basic sanitary engineering in many areas.

Despite these efforts, the prevalence of malaria continued to rise. Throughout Central America, malaria control had lost ground because the promiscuous use of insecticides in cotton and rice farming had led to resistance of the Anopheles mosquito vector to conventional means of control. In 1978 approximately 4.4 people per thousand contracted the disease. Control efforts were paralyzed by the war, and the incidence of malaria rose to 7.3 per thousand in 1979. By 1980 it had gone up to 9.4 per thousand. In November 1981, the most recent and largest health campaign mobilized 80,000 trained volunteers to distribute antimalarial drugs to an estimated 75 percent of the country's population, to be taken in a uniform three-day regimen. Regular monthly statistics indicated a 98 percent decline in new cases of malaria in the month after the campaign. Continuing education and epidemiologic vigilance are now in progress in the hope of minimizing malaria transmission. Recent flooding in Nicaragua will put this program to a severe test.

Although vaccination coverage for poliomyelitis was thought to be good, there were still 37 cases in 1981. Because of this 500,000 doses of polio vaccine were distributed in January of 1982. Health institutions were still too few and coverage too incomplete to vaccinate the population well. Thus, volunteers who have been trained through the division of health education in each locality go from door to door on selected days to provide polio vaccine.

Results in the fight against tuberculosis are even harder to measure. A nation-wide treatment protocol has been established. All persons with respiratory illness that lasts longer than 21 days are supposed to undergo x-ray and laboratory studies in search of tuberculosis, particularly in areas where it is endemic, such as mining regions. The rate of dropping out from treatment in 1980 was lowered to 40 percent. In 70 percent of medically attended births, bacillus Calmette-Guérin was given to the newborns. Since only an estimated 40 percent of Nicaraguan births are attended by health professionals, this leaves many infants without coverage. The present goal is to vaccinate 60 percent of all children under five years old through local health centers.

The deadly problem of infant diarrhea is being attacked in an innovative way. Oral-rehydration centers have been set up all over the country, and an educational campaign has been instituted to teach mothers to bring children with diarrhea to such a center. There, balanced electrolyte and glucose solution can be given by mouth to the sick child. Staffed by auxiliary nurses, these centers are usually equipped only to provide primary attention, and they refer gravely ill infants to physician-staffed centers. Although only 170 rehydration centers were initially planned, popular demand and community action have brought the number of centers to 226. About two thirds of the centers, including most of the large and important ones, were reporting encounters with patients by June 1981. In the first 21 months of the program 92,000 children were treated for diarrhea. Eighteen percent had serious diarrhea (5 to 10 percent dehydration), and another 2 percent had grave diarrhea (more than 10 percent dehydration). A total of 2,420 (2.6 percent) needed intravenous therapy, and 17 (0.02 percent) died. Almost two thirds were under the age of one year when they were treated. This program is likely to have a striking effect in reducing infant mortality.

Nicaragua has recently experienced a baby boom of surprising proportions for a country that already had a high fertility rate. The natural rate of population increase was about 3 percent per year during the past decade. In 1980 the rate of increase jumped to an estimated 4.5 percent. Even if the rate has since returned to 3 percent, as some observers believe, the population will double in less than 25 years. The subject of family planning is a difficult one. Most Nicaraguans are Catholic. Indeed, four government ministers, including the foreign minister, are priests. Most contraceptives services are provided through the private International Planned Parenthood affiliate in Nicaragua by contract with the Ministry of Health. A campaign to disseminate birth-control information is being planned according to the format developed for sanitation, vaccination, and nutritional education. Although abortion is not legal, it is not an uncommon practice. Often the abortion is initiated at home, and the patient appears at a hospital for completion of the evacuation. In the first half of 1981, 1,271 incomplete abortions were treated at the Vélez Páez Hospital. During the same period, the hospital recorded 10,217 births and 153 neonatal deaths. The first hospital-initiated therapeutic abortion in Nicaragua was performed in that institution late last year.

Technical and professional health training has been greatly expanded. A second medical school opened in Managua in 1981 to supplement the original one in León. The new school takes advantage of the wealth of clinical material available in the capital. The total class size has been increased from 100 to 500. The number of nursing students has also increased fivefold. Technical-career programs have been set up to train such practitioners as dental assistants, x-ray technicians, and biostatisticians. Postgraduate medical education never really existed in Nicaragua except on a haphazard apprenticeship basis. At present, residency programs are being set up in medicine, surgery, pediatrics, and obstetrics-gynecology. These programs will probably involve two years of hospital work in Nicaragua, followed by an additional one or two years abroad. Dr. Norman Girón, nephrologist and director of the Antonio Lenín Fonseca Hospital, is in charge of the medical residency. He explained that it is impossible even to plan for a full training program in Nicaragua at this point, but that a solid foundation can be given by people available in the country. The most promising residents would then have the opportunity to complete residency training in Cuba, Mexico, the United States, or Europe.

International aid has been of crucial help in health care. Organizations such as the United Nations International Children's Emergency Fund, Oxfam, the World

Health Organization, the Organization of American States, and the European Economic Community have given substantial aid. West Germany has set up an entire small hospital in the north. Aid has come from Sweden, Norway, Austria, Belgium, Italy, and Canada. More than two dozen countries, mostly from the Americas and Western Europe, have sent medical supplies and personnel. More than 400 doctors, nurses, and technicians came in the emergency period after the revolution. Most of the 300 foreign health workers now in Nicaragua are physicians. The majority are Mexican and Cuban, and almost all work in remote rural posts. Broad assistance comes from the World Health Organization and the Pan American Health Organization. Their strategies for the provision of basic health services and their wide experience in implementation are enthusiastically applied. In the first year after the revolution, substantial assistance was given by the United States. Programs for supplemental food distribution, hospital construction, and sanitary engineering were largely supported by the US Agency for International Development. At present, however, only private assistance from the United States continues, in such fields as rehabilitation medicine, family planning, and ophthalmology.

Changes in the fields of curative medicine are occurring more slowly than those in public health. The concept of a unified health system (*Sistema Único de Salud*) was established in 1979, and the structure for regionalization of care throughout the country has been outlined. Effective administration in nine health districts has been established. Other plans remain largely on paper, since the plants, personnel, and funding necessary to implement them are not yet available. A new children's hospital is ready to open in Managua, except for the lack of funds for equipment. There are four main hospitals in Managua and smaller hospitals and health centers scattered around the country. To provide coverage, medical manpower has been spread very thin. In spite of international help, care has been extended so widely that there are shortages everywhere. In Managua this problem has been exacerbated by the referral of many seriously ill patients from remote areas for more sophisticated care. Each hospital in Managua acts as a referral center for a designated part of this country. The Antonio Lenín Fonseca Hospital, for example, with only 300 beds, is the referral hospital for 265,000 people of the northwestern part of the country, as well as the primary hospital for about 160,000 people of Managua. Nicaragua did not suffer a mass exodus of physicians after the revolution, as some had expected. About 300 of the total of about 1,300 doctors are believed to have emigrated.

The average physician, after spending six to eights hours at the hospital or clinic, will return to perhaps four hours of private practice in his or her office or home. A doctor will make more money during this time than during regular salaried service. This supplemental private practice is not discouraged by the government. It provides a source of extra income for physicians, which helps them maintain the standard of living that they are used to, and also provides service with fewer long waits and more pleasant surroundings for those who can afford to pay. The question of professional independence and control is complex. On the one hand, most physicians are expected to work in a hospital or clinic, and their pay for this work is low for upper-middle-class Nicaraguans, though of course extravagant for the average citizen. On the other hand, the professional association of physicians, FESOMENIC, has a seat on the State Council, which is a basically consultative group that represents various major social forces, including business and labor groups. Through its seat on the State Council, the medical association has a direct role in formulating and voting on national legislation. Furthermore, the professional societies are more active now than ever before in advising on health policy, setting standards of care, and promoting in-service education.

Immediately after the revolution, there was a crisis in the availability of pharmaceuticals. The new government was greeted with a staggering debt acquired by its predecessor, and foreign pharmaceutical companies wanted that debt settled before sending any more drugs. The Sandinista government accepted responsibility for the debts in exchange for favorable terms of repayment. Increased numbers of visits by patients have greatly increased the demand for drugs. Nicaragua's private and public pharmaceutical manufacturers have increased production by several hundred percent. Still, drugs remain the largest import item in the health budget. Spot shortages of drugs constantly occur. There is also a problem with x-ray and laboratory equipment. Companies that had been contracted to service this machinery have been unable or unwilling to do so. Cash in advance is required for all repair work. Some parts dealers have stopped investing in new equipment and allowed inventories to dwindle. Thus, when equipment breaks, it may be out of commission for months for lack of a single part. One machine must be cannibalized to fix another. There have been instances of outright fraud with unnecessary or inappropriate repairs. Officials at the Ministry of Health have no interest in going into the equipment-maintenance business, but circumstances are forcing them to do so.

At the time of the revolution, there were 18 beds per thousand population; a minimum of 30 per thousand is recommended by the World Health Organization, and 70 per thousand are available in the United States. These beds were in a total of 42 hospitals, which included several private and church institutions. One private hospital closed last year when its doctors emigrated. In the country as a whole, despite the destruction of the war, there were 15 percent more beds in 1980 than in 1977. These beds were created through hastily equipping wards still under repair from the bombings, putting beds in some small health centers, and adding beds to already crowded rooms and halls in established hospitals. These measures are still insufficient to meet the demand. At times patients are two to a bed, babies two to a crib, and premature infants two or three to an incubator.

As compared with 1977, the last year before the major disruption of the war, Nicaraguan hospital admissions rose by 31 percent in 1980. Since the number of beds rose by only 15 percent, there was clearly an intensification of bed use. The number of surgical interventions rose by 43 percent, and attended deliveries rose by 21 percent. Preliminary data from 1981 indicate a further rise of 25 percent over 1980. The rise in outpatient visits was more dramatic—from 2.5 million in 1977 to 5.0 million in 1980.

Five new hospitals are under construction. These should add 947 more beds by 1983. Four are outside the capital city and will replace or supplement hospitals built as long as 100 years ago. In 1978, the combined budget of the various agencies dealing with health in Nicaragua totaled 202 million córdobas. By 1981, that figure had risen to 1212 million córdobas. In spite of inflation and a great rise in overall government spending, the portion spent for health rose incredibly, from 6 to 17 percent of the national budget.

To put all these developments in health care into a broader context, some other changes should be noted. In 1981 a 10-year program was initiated to develop self-sufficiency in the production and distribution of basic foodstuffs. Thousands of new housing units have been constructed, and 10,000 homes have been provided with sanitation. Twenty-four thousand latrines are being built per year. Funds are being sought to increase latrine production, because at this rate it will take 10 years to meet the demand. The number of students in the country has risen from 500,000 to 800,000. Although increases have occurred at all levels of the educational system, the largest rise has been in higher and adult education. This is a direct result of the literacy campaign of 1980, which reduced the illiteracy rate from 52 percent to 12 percent of the populaton. ("Literacy" for this purpose is defined as reading and writing at a third-grade level.)

In just three years, more has been done in most areas of social welfare than in the 50 years of dictatorship under the Somoza family. Much more remains to be done, and new problems created by the revolution itself demand attention. However, the process is continuing. These changes in housing, nutrition, sanitation, and educa-tion and the developments in health care that we have reported point to a broad and profound change in the nature of Nicaraguan society.

60. Toward a New Democracy of Culture*

By Ernesto Cardenal

Ernesto Cardenal is a priest, famous poet, and minister of culture in Nicaragua. Most North Americans probably remember the picture of the pope shaking his finger at him, reportedly admonishing him for remaining in his governmental position.

The community of Miskitu Indians, a very poor community situated on the banks of the river, had been brought together so that I would speak to them.

---

*Excerpts from the statement of Ernesto Cardenal before UNESCO, Paris, on April 23, 1982, reprinted from *La Democratización de la Cultura*, Colección Popular de Literatura Nicaragüense, No. 2, Ministerio de Cultura, Managua, Nicaragua (1982). Translated by Rebecca Cohn.

While the interpreter was translating my words, I observed in their faces disinterest, indifference and boredom. I told them I was the Minister of Culture who had come to visit them (which I noted also was of no interest to them). Then I began to explain that the Ministry was new and that it had been created by the Revolution for the dances (there I noticed a sudden interest), for the songs, the traditions of the ancestors (and the interest became more obvious), the different languages that we speak, such as their language, which we must preserve and defend, and for the folk arts. This, I had explained, consisted of making beautiful things as well as useful items with the hands. I showed as an example some very primitive drawings that they had carved in some maracas and I showed a *"tuno"* which they had just given to me, a cloth that they make from the bark of a tree, and I explained to them how they could paint on this cloth.

What is the importance of all this? For me its importance is that there I saw how these people were just becoming aware that the Ministry of Culture was especially a Ministry for them, for those who had been exploited for various centuries and now had nothing left but their culture and their language (and that too they were on the verge of losing). But at the same time I, as Minister of Culture, was becoming aware that my Ministry was for them and for all those segregated as they were. And that the Ministry existed especially to oppose cultural ethnocide.

In other countries in America they try to suppress their cultures and their languages. Also they kill them. They hunt them in the plains like deer and send them donations of sugar with arsenic, and clothes with the virus of cholera. But, we have taught them to read in their native language. We believe that they enrich our cultural identity. We want them to progress within their culture, without stagnating, but also without losing it. A language that is lost is an irreparable loss for humanity, a particular view of the world which has been lost.

I founded a small community in Lake Nicaragua in the archipelago of Solentiname, inhabited by poor isolated peasants. There we developed primitive painting and poetry. Their folk arts and crafts were appreciated by other countries and sold in Paris, Switzerland, Germany and New York. Later the community became involved in the struggle of the Sandinista Liberation Front. Consequently Somoza's National Guard destroyed all the community's installations. They destroyed the big library we had with archeological pieces, records, paintings, ceramic and enamel kilns, everything. Because of us, all the peasants in the whole archipelago were repressed. Since the National Guard had prohibited them from painting, many peasant girls went up into the countryside and painted in hiding. If a National Guardsman saw a painting in a hut he broke it with his bayonet.

Why am I telling this? Because I want to show it as an example of the cultural repression in Nicaragua. Literature, theatre and song were suppressed. Books were banned. First it was those books considered more dangerous, and finally it was all books, in that all books were considered subversive. This is why we have a literature which is eminently that of protest, a political song and a popular street theatre which was for agitation, although at times clandestine.

At the triumph of the Revolution some customs workers gave me a "memorandum" which had a long list of prohibited books (among them were my books) which were burned. Tolstoy was prohibited for being a Russian author. *The Rebellion of the Masses* by Ortega and Gasset was prohibited for its title. On the other hand *The Sacred Family* by Marx was allowed to enter because of its title. That they were burned I can verify because once the person who confiscated my books, when I made a trip to the exterior (the United States), assured me solemnly that they weren't "robbing" the books but rather they were burned every Thursday before a Notary Public.

When the Revolution triumphed there was a great thirst for reading among our people. A vendor who before sold books at a great risk in the street now sold his books on the ground in a pavilion in the Ministry of Culture. Book vendors appeared everywhere. A student exclaimed with enthusiasm, "Definitely we now are free, we can read what we want. Before it was difficult."

The Somoza police who prohibited books were frightening. The people closed their doors and didn't even lift their heads when they passed by. Their green uniform and green helmet symbolized terror and death. Now the police, the soldiers of the army and members of the State Security and of the Ministry of the Interior are writing poetry—and very good poetry.

A young woman in an Infantry Batallion wrote this poem:

> It was six in the afternoon on the day of February 17, 1980
> When I fell in love with you, Juan.
> With your camouflage uniform
> and your Galil (machine gun) on the desk
> carrying out your 24 hours of guard post
> I approached you
> and touched your skin, the color of chocolate.

A police officer wrote this poem:

Free as the Birds
> Looking through the window grilles
> that are in front of my room
> I see how the sun comes out
> and its light shines between the leaves of the Guanabana tree,
> On the floor figures are formed
> a zanate poses and sings on the branch of a Jocote tree.
> I think of this bird,
>   in Nicaragua.
> The Salvadorans, the Guatemalans, the Beliceans
>   all of Latinoamerica
> will be free like this bird.

Our armed forces are made up of very young people many of whom are young women. They are the combatants of our liberation struggle. For that reason our police are very different, our soldiers and our state security people are very different from what those of other countries might think.

Before there also was another army of very young men. Somoza's elite army, the sinister EEBI, was made up of boys from a young age trained to assassinate, those who produced the worst terror, the terror of Somoza's army. The trainer would shout:

"What are you?"

And they'd shout back in chorus, "Tigers."

And, "What do tigers eat?"

"Blood."

"Whose blood?"

"The people's."

And the Office of Security? There torture was carried out—that was where they took hooded prisoners. . . . Best we don't talk of that. There exists a great difference between the horror and the smile, between those who tortured and assassinated and those who now write poetry and love.

Before we had a culture of oppression and now we have liberation. We had oppression in every way—also in culture. You can't have the oppression of a people without cultural oppression. Now we have liberation, in culture and in everything.

Last year the government of the United States abruptly denied us a sale of wheat. Our people were going to be without bread. The Ministry of Culture had the idea of a "Corn Fair" with the slogan "Corn, Our Roots," with the objective of promoting all the national dishes made out of corn. The fair was celebrated locally in all parts of the country and culminated in a national contest in the Indian town of Monimbo, legendary for its heroism in the struggle against Somoza. The 250,000 people attending swelled the plaza and streets of Monimbo. Members of the Governing Junta, the Commanders of the Revolution, the Ministers and owners of well-known restaurants of typical food, we were the judges of the best tortillas, tamales (a corn dough wrapped in leaves and eaten with cheese), Indio Viejo ("Old Indian," an indian corn stew with meat and lots of spices and fat), cosas-de-horno ("things from the oven," varied sweet biscuits made from corn), pinol (our national drink, made from corn flour with water), cususa (a strong corn liquor), chicha (wine of the Indians made of fermented corn), and innumerable desserts and delicacies made of corn. From some remote regions of the country dishes were presented that even we ourselves didn't know of and only now were discovering.

We named the fair Xilonem after the Indian God of young corn. According to the myth she sacrificed herself for her people and with her blood they produced a great harvest of corn during a drought year. For us this also was a symbol of all the martyrs of the Revolution who sacrificed themselves for the happiness of their people. The great corn fair served to reaffirm the national and cultural identity of our people.

It also served to help our own people appreciate our own foods as part of our own dishes. And after the triumph of the Revolution, Nicaraguan foods have been appreciated much more along with everything Nicaraguan proceeding from our past—an Indian past, colonial Spanish, and English in our Caribbean coast and over all our "mestizoness."

These topics of which I have spoken serve as an introduction to the theme I'm going to take up here at UNESCO, the democratization of culture in Nicaragua. Why do I come to present some practical but also theoretical things which make up the cultural task in a small country like Nicaragua, which up until now has been very dependent? Because Nicaragua is one of those countries of Latin America, Africa and Asia, recently liberated or on the path of liberation, in which today live more than half of the world's population. Countries where powerful social transformations, encompassing all aspects of life, are taking place. The terrible problems of ignorance, disease, hunger and misery only can be solved by our countries developing their economies in a short historical period and creating new social structures. This is something also eminently cultural, in that our countries are moving forward so rapidly that not only the traditional social structures are changing but also cultural values and cultural necessities. It seems useful that our experience be made known.

The cultural liberation in Nicaragua has been part of the struggle for national liberation. For example, last February in Nicaragua we celebrated the anniversary of the birth of Rubén Darío, our great poet. He was proclaimed a Hero of Cultural Independence and that day was named Cultural Independence Day. The cultural heritage, really anticultural, left by a half-century of dictatorship imposed and maintained by the United States, couldn't have been more catastrophic. When the Revolution triumphed on July 19, 1979 more than half of the Nicaraguan people were illiterate. And for the dominant classes the cultural metropolis was Miami.

Our Revolution is of the present and over all of the future but it is also of the past. In the first place there was a resurrection of the dead (in the conscience of the people). Our history soon was something else. Our patrimony that before couldn't be seen, made itself present. National traditions flourished. All that was national always was unified with the liberation movement, but liberation has been the condition under which it would be converted into common good.

Folk art had been decaying more and more during the long era of Somocismo, and in the end Nicaragua was already a country very poor in folk art. It was thought to be irreversibly lost. The Revolution came to rescue it, and in a very short time in many parts of the country there reappeared the ancient lost popular arts and also new art. It is an expression more of our identity as Nicaraguans to be ourselves. For it struggled against foreign domination and we rescued it with the triumph of the Popular Sandinista Revolution.

The hammock is the crib of the Nicaraguan. It has been woven tirelessly in bright colors in the city of Masaya ever since the war ended. It has been said that it is the best hammock in the world. Hammocks have been given to heads of state. Also there are weavings of *heneken* from Masaya and Comoapa, with bright colors and pre-Colombian and modern designs. In San Juan de Oriente, traditionally a potter's village, they are producing replicas of pre-Colombian ceramics or new creations inspired by ancient art. In Matagalpa and Jinotega they make a very delicate black pottery, blackening the clay with pinewood smoke. Only two families were producing it at the time of the triumph. The Revolution by means of the Ministry of Culture saved this folk craft from extinction. A delicate work of filigree is the white *jícara* (gourd) that only one old woman knew how to make. This millinery folk art we have saved by giving her students, who have learned to carve this intricate lacework of birds, butterflies, and flowers. In Masatepe and Granada ancient wicker furniture has been revived—cool and well-adapted to our tropical climate with its delicate and resistant weaving. An important cultural change is to *not* prefer the furniture of Miami—rather that of Nicaragua. In the northern part of the country there is a mountain of a soft rock with varying streaks of color that the peasant population of the area converts into birds, fish, and the busts of women. We have sent our best sculptor and sculpting professor of Nicaragua to give them orientation and now San Juan de Limay is a sculptor's town. Much of what they produce isn't folk art but rather modern sculpture. In the Atlantic Coast where we have our gold mines, we have revived the golden filigree, a handicraft that had been lost. Also on the Caribbean coast they make new jewelry of tortoise shell, black coral, shark's vertebrae, and pearls. The Miskitu Indians work precious woods turning them into figures that, like their dances, represent their work, fishing, hunting, and farming. The Sumo Indians have returned to making drawings with the inks of their plants, brown, yellow and red, as well as *tuno*, which they make from the bark of a tree.

For all this rich and varied and before unknown folk art, the Ministry of Culture has established different stores and the best samples are exhibited in what we call the Gallery of People's Art in Managua, which before was a branch of the bank.

The needs of the artisan are attended to for cultural, political and economic reasons. To do so, we have found our own way (not the capitalist way), getting rid of intermediaries and giving them state financing. It is a fact that in our countries the penetration of capitalist civilization turns handicrafts into a commodity. They take it out of the marketplace—remove its traditional function and convert it into a product of a boutique. The peasants, deprived of their ceramics, eat off of plastic plates, they stop using *heneken* and the artisan depends on more and more capital for his production. In Nicaragua we are seeking a completely different path.

Culture for us can't be separated from social development. Also one might say that in Nicaragua it is inconceivable to consider economic development without cultural development. In Solentiname a group of peasants met with me once a week bringing their poems. It was a poetry workshop. Also children came. Once a ten-year-old boy brought this short poem:

> I saw a turtle in the lake
> It was swimming
> And I was going by in a sailboat.

It seems that this illustrates quite well the definition of a culture proposed by

UNESCO, that it is all that man adds to nature.

Not long ago in an article in the *Wall Street Journal* it was stated that in the United States works of art and of literature have turned into mere ornaments to be preserved like paper or fiduciary money. The society didn't expect that a Secretary of State had more knowledge of history than the chronology taught in the sixth grade, and the article added, "The United States has made a business of its culture, and its culture into a business." In contrast, in Nicaragua we now have a new concept of culture. The writer Sergio Ramírez, who is a member of the Governing Junta, has said, "If before, culture was a closed circle for a minority, now it is the privilege and right of the masses."

Also we have a new concept of what is intellectual. Colonel Santos López, who fought with Sandino and after was one of the founders of the Sandinista Liberation Front on a jungle river, didn't know how to read. Nevertheless one of the Commanders of our Revolution, Víctor Tirado López, has called him an intellectual. It was considered one of his great virtues that he didn't know how to read. As he himself said, that way he kept a clean mind and sensitive heart to be able to understand all that happened in Nicaragua due to North American intervention. Commander Tirado adds: "That he never went to school to learn his first letters was exactly where his great merit lay." This reminds me of Gramsci, who said that culture is the critic of exploitation.

With our democratization of literacy the peasants didn't only learn their letters, but also about their reality and themselves. As Edmundo, a 16-year-old literacy teacher said, "They learned quickly because we spoke of their reality, that of the exploitation and the Revolution. They weren't just themes in the air."

And for these young literacy teachers it also served as a school of the Revolution. Oscar, another 16-year-old, said, "For me it was the best school, the best workshop, the best study circle because rather than being told how the campesinos lived, we went to see and live in those conditions. We understood that as youth we must try to remedy the errors of past governments. From then I became committed to try to consolidate the Revolution."

They had the experience of doing farmwork. Ligia, a 17-year-old, said, "It was really nice because I didn't know how to plant." Another girl told about how when she returns she wants to study medicine and she hoped that time would go by quickly because the peasants have such a need here. A young woman of 16 says, "After the Crusade many students became imbued with the collective spirit."

Not only those who always were exploited received literacy training but also the ex–National Guard of Somoza who were in jail for the crimes of the dictatorship (50 percent of them were illiterate). For their ignorance they were manipulated into torturing and killing. The Revolution took them out of ignorance. The police in charge of them were their teachers. They didn't use arms while they were teaching literacy. The hand of the Sandinista was placed over the hand of the prisoner in the fraternal gesture of forming the letters. The Revolution taught to read and write those who the dictatorship had taught how to kill. A woman police officer said that she had a very good experience teaching literacy to prisoners in jail in Jinotepe. She had to exercise a lot of patience.

We also had what we call by-products of the Literacy Crusade. Among other things we collected an oral history of the War of National Liberation, and collected flora and fauna, noting typical foods, medicinal herbs, archeological sites, and mineral deposits, and gathered handicrafts, myths, legends, and popular songs.

By means of its art Nicaragua now reveals artistic participation in social transformations. I would like to give as a concrete example certain primitive religious paintings done by the artists of Solentiname. One artist painted a picture of Christ crucified wearing typical Nicaraguan peasant pants and shirt, which later was repeatedly reproduced in Germany. In the interview, she declared, "I painted Christ like one of us, a man, or you could say another guerrilla who came out of the mountains and was taken by the enemy." *The Killing of the Innocents* appears as a massacre of children and youth by Somoza's National Guard in peasant communities. *The Expulsion of the Traders from the Temple* is a Catholic Church of today where Jesus and his peasant disciples get rid of businessmen wearing suits and ties. *The Sermon on the Mount* is Jesus speaking to a group of peasants on Lake Nicaragua. *The Resurrection* is Jesus with the face of Carlos Fonseca Amador, the founder of the Sandinista Liberation Front, rising out of a tomb. Nicaragua is a religious nation. This is part of its popular culture. In this painting the Bible History is the same as the People's History. They are within the history of the Kingdom. Jesus is one of us, a peasant and a guerrilla. The death and resurrection of Jesus are the death and resurrection of the people.

Of course these peasants have had a relationship with theology—the theology of Liberation. During the time of Somoza we studied the Gospel and our commentary was published in the book *The Gospel of Solentiname*. There appears a commentary on the resurrection of the dead by a young peasant, Donald, who died in the liberation struggle. He said, "I don't believe that they will be resurrected in a very material form. Rather they will return in the form of consciousness and the love that the person had. That is the form they will return from their tomb—you could say it's not their bones which will rise and go walking around (everyone laughs) rather it will be a changed society." A commentary was made about the parable of the rich Epulon and the poor Lazarus by Elvis, another youth who also died in the struggle. "The message is also that humanity shouldn't continue like this with two classes, one which has a party every day and the other in the doorway covered with sores."

The Poetry Workshops have been created in the popular neighborhoods and Indian communities of Monimbo and Sutiava and the armed forces. In the workshops, police, soldiers, workers, and peasants learn how to write good poetry. I already spoke about the poetry of our armed forces. In a speech at Harvard, in which I gave the closing words to a Congress on peace and disarmament, I said that our army could give technical assistance to other armies on the theme of poetry. The Venezuelan writer Joaquín Marta Sosa has written about these workshops, "We could say that the Sandinista Revolution for the first time has socialized the means of production of poetry." He adds, "The people have become masters of poetry in Nicaragua not because they read more cheap editions but because they produce it."

I read last week in *Time* magazine that in the United States "poetry books don't usually pile up by cash registers." In Nicaragua the editions of poetry published by the Ministry of Culture quickly run out. Our magazine *Poesía Libre* that we publish on Kraft Paper is sold all over on a popular basis. The first editions we have reprinted because the demand continues.

Because of the lack of foreign exchange and the difficulty of importing many articles, we had a fair we called *"La Piñata"* which has turned into a great national festival for the exposition and sale of Nicaraguan products, handicrafts and small industry. The people attended by the thousands, this great sale of Nicaraguan items: toys, clothes, furniture, books, records, food and ornamental plants. The children came to break a great number of piñatas. Along with the fair was a circus. There was a sale of typical food, music and song.

La Piñata was organized to create a consciousness in the value of our own products. Before, it was believed that only foreign products were any good. La Piñata was not organized to promote a consumer society in the sense of useless consumption and waste. What we do want is good habits of consumption for our people. Our economic-cultural policy has been defined by a person from heroic Monimbo, disabled in the war, who makes toys and who said of the fair, "The question, my friend, is to make better and more durable toys, because a wagon with wheels is something your children can use for years." The great number of sales shows that it was an unprecedented stimulus for handicrafts and cottage industry. Also it was a political response and an alternative to begin to break the dependence on the exterior.

In Nicaragua the bourgeoisie dress from the shops of Miami. The wedding trousseau was bought in Miami (before that in Paris). The Revolution has come to resurrect the popular Nicaraguan clothing, not because of its being picturesque but because of its beauty and its being well adapted to our climate. The *"cotona"* is a white shirt that I wear which has been the traditional shirt of the Nicaraguan peasant. At one time it had practically disappeared while now it is the most popular shirt in Nicaragua. Like the shirt of the peasant it has become a symbol of work, struggle, freedom and of Revolution. The *cotona* was the uniform of the literacy teachers. When thousands of young people came in, triumphant, to Nicaragua they made the commanders of the Revolution put on these *cotonas*. The Commanders who presided over the great public event were not much older than the young people themselves.

We are also beginning to change our relationship with nature. We've eliminated contraband in wild animals and indiscriminate deforestation. We're coming to learn a new harmony with nature.

Our song has had a social use and an aesthetic value. In Nicaragua the means that UNICEF uses to measure the health of a people (number of doctors, paramedics, etc.) now are no longer enough. As during the literacy crusade, the entire population mobilized to carry out a health campaign to eradicate malaria or vaccinate all the children in the country. And through all, the "song" has been present. During the war our great composer Carlos Mejía Godoy used the mazurka to put words teaching how to arm and disarm a Fal, or Galil machine gun. The same happened in popular theatre. Without worrying about the crisis in the concepts of action, time and space which form a big part of contemporary theatre, our peasants, workers, and students bring to the stage their daily life in social and psychological conflicts. In film, Nicaragua began with the war filming on all battle fronts. After, they began presenting all aspects of our new society in the form of documentaries.

Our policy of social communication is to reject all manipulation, to inform rather than "disinform" and to put into practice political discussion. The democracy of information can be seen in the following two programs which I believe only exist in Nicaragua. One is called *Face the People* in which the governing junta weekly goes to a neighborhood in Managua or some other part of the country so that the people can ask them whatever they wish or make any criticism, protest or petition. And this gets transmitted by television all over the country. The other is called *Direct Line* and is where some leader of the Revolution, or minister, or person responsible for a state institution is on a radio program to respond to any question, protest or criticism made by a telephone caller. This is broadcast live throughout the country. The program is not only made with leaders or functionaries but also with other people who have some relevancy. The ambition of every Latin American journalist is to interview the novelist Gabriel García Márquez. Recently García Márquez was in Nicaragua, and over the air, on *Direct Line*, he was interviewed by the people; for two hours he was responding to telephone questions from all over the country. The restructuring of the new society is a political task of the new culture. This also signifies an encounter with our new identity as a free people. For us this is a cultural democracy and democratic culture.

This is the culture that is now being threatened because our Revolution is being threatened. If the *Wall Street Journal* says the United States has made a business of culture and their culture into a business, we could then say that our Revolution is a culture and our culture is a Revolution. President Reagan is taking food away from the children of the United States to squander on Somoza's ex–National Guard. The most dangerous aspect of it for us and for the whole world including the people of the United States is to confuse the interests of Reagan's personal prestige with national security.

Recently a nineteen-year-old Nicaraguan youth, Orlando Tardencilla, caused a defeat in the US State Department when he was taken as a prisoner from a Salvadoran jail to the US to repeat forced lies before journalists. On the contrary he told the truth. He is also a poet and the way he acted before the State Department is a representation of our new culture. From a jail in El Salvador he wrote to his mother, "Now I don't write poetry I write realities." Also he had written these words, which reveal the poet and revolutionary in him, "We were born for all" and also "I feel the song of brotherhood of all peoples so let's join hands as one people."

The greatest advance of our revolution is the brotherhood it has produced, *"compañerismo,"* the introduction in our new daily language of the new word *compañero*—which means fellow companion and before only existed in guerrilla camps.

I believe that the Revolution is a triumph of love. Sandino said, "Our cause will triumph because it is justice and it is love." He also said, "That every man be a brother not a wolf."

Finally in the message I bring from my people I want to say that we want to preserve peace. Our culture is a culture of peace. We made a Revolution with weapons so that we could conquer peace. But they don't want to let us live in peace.

The North American writer Margaret Randall said, with respect to Nicaragua, "The little street vendors, and shoeshine boys are beginning to touch their dreams with their fingers." In a big park that the Revolution made for children (named after a nine-year-old child leader, killed by Somoza's National Guard), 1,500 children were recently congregated in a demonstration. They said, "We want peace so we can have fun."

Not only has the peace of Nicaragua been threatened, but all of Central America and the Caribbean, and ultimately world peace. Now man is the master of his evolution. We can't allow that there be one less planet in our solar system, converted into nothing more than small asteroids. Or let's say a black ball, not blue or pink as the astronauts have seen in outer space, without color as has been seen in the fields and cities of Vietnam and now in certain parts of Central America.

The earth is round. That means that humanity as it continues to populate it more and more must come closer and closer together in union on the surface of this sphere, until humanity forms a new species, one great planetary organism.

I heard a young Nicaraguan literacy teacher speaking of the happiness of future generations. That was what he was interested in. It made me think how humanity is moving more and more quickly (we see it in the youth) towards unity, towards love. Until we are all one. Then although we are dead we will live. Have I ended up talking like a priest? The Nicaraguan Revolution installed a priest as Minister of Culture.

POSTSCRIPT I:

*The Kissinger Commission on Nicaragua**

By Henry Kissinger, *et al.*

In Nicaragua the revolution that overthrew the hated Somoza regime has been captured by self-proclaimed Marxist-Leninists. In July of 1979 the Sandinistas promised the OAS that they would organize "a truly democratic government" and hold free elections, but that promise has not been redeemed. Rather, the government has been brought fully under the control of the Sandinista National Directorate. Only two months after giving their pledge to the OAS and while successfully negotiating loans in Washington, the Sandinistas issued Decree No. 67, which converted their movement into the country's official political party and laid the foundation for the monopoly of political power they now enjoy. The Sandinista Directorate has progressively put in place a Cuban-style regime, complete with mass organizations under its political direction, an internal security system to keep watch on the entire population, and a massive military establishment. This comprehensive police and military establishment not only ensures the monopoly on power within Nicaragua, it also produces an acute sense of insecurity among Nicaragua's neighbors.

From the outset, the Sandinistas have maintained close ties with Cuba and the Soviet Union. There are some 8,000 Cuban advisers now in Nicaragua, including at least 2,000 military advisers, as well as several hundred Soviet, East European, Libyan and PLO advisers. Cuban construction teams have helped build military roads, bases and airfields. According to intelligence sources, an estimated 15,000 tons of Soviet bloc arms and equipment reached the Sandinista army in 1983. This military connection with Cuba, the Soviet Union, and its satellites internationalizes Central America's security problems and adds a menacing new dimension.

Nicaragua's government has made significant gains against illiteracy and disease. But despite significant U.S. aid from 1979 to 1981 (approximately $117 million), its economic performance has been poor, in part because of the disruptions caused by the revolution, in part because of the world recession, and in part because of the mismanagement invariably associated with regimes espousing Marxist-Leninist ideology. National income per capita is less than $1,000, about equal to that of the early 1960s, and Nicaragua is plagued by shortages of food and consumer goods, with the result that extensive rationing has been instituted.

---

*Excerpts from the *Report of the National Bipartisan Commission on Central America*, Office of the President, January 1984.

Under military pressure from Nicaraguan rebels who reportedly receive U.S. support, and under diplomatic pressure from the international community, especially from the Contadora Group, the Sandinistas have recently promised to announce early this year a date and rules for 1985 elections; have offered a partial amnesty to the anti-Sandinista guerrillas; have claimed a relaxation of censorship of *La Prensa*, the only opposition newspaper; have entered into talks with the Roman Catholic hierarchy; and have issued proposals for regional security agreements. In addition, reports from Sandinista sources in Managua have hinted at a permanently reduced Cuban presence and of diminished support to other Marxist-Leninist revolutionary groups in Central America—although we have no confirmation that either has taken place or is likely to take place. Whether any one of these moves reflects a true change of course or merely tactical maneuvers remains to be seen. . . .

The Sandinista military forces are potentially larger than those of all the rest of Central America combined. The government in Managua volunteered to this Commission an intelligence briefing which left no reasonable doubt that Nicaragua is tied into the Cuban, and thereby the Soviet, intelligence network. The Commission encountered no leader in Central America, including democratic and unarmed Costa Rica, who did not express deep foreboding about the impact of a militarized, totalitarian Nicaragua on the peace and security of the region. Several expressed the view that should the Sandinista regime now be consolidated as a totalitarian state, their own freedom, and even their independence, would be jeopardized. In several countries, especially those with democratic traditions, we met leaders who expressed regret and outrage that the revolution against Somoza—which their own governments had supported—had been betrayed by the Sandinistas.

For all of these reasons, the consolidation of a Marxist-Leninist regime in Managua would be seen by its neighbors as constituting a permanent security threat. Because of its secretive nature, the existence of a political order on the Cuban model in Nicaragua would pose major difficulties in negotiating, implementing, and verifying any Sandinista commitment to refrain from supporting insurgency and subversion in other countries. In this sense, the development of an open political system in Nicaragua, with a free press and an active opposition, would provide an important security guarantee for the other countries of the region and would be a key element in any negotiated settlement.

Theoretically, the United States and its friends could abandon any hope of such a settlement and simply try to contain a Nicaragua which continued to receive military supplies on the present scale. In practical terms, however, such a course would present major difficulties. In the absence of a political settlement, there would be little incentive for the Sandinistas to act responsibly, even over a period of time, and much inducement to escalate their efforts to subvert Nicaragua's neighbors. To contain the export of revolution would require a level of vigilance and sustained effort that would be difficult for Nicaragua's neighbors and even for the United States. A fully militarized and equipped Nicaragua, with excellent intelligence and command and control organizations, would weigh heavily on the neighboring countries of the region. This threat would be particularly acute for democratic, unarmed Costa Rica. It would have especially serious implications for vital U.S. interests in the Panama Canal. We would then face the prospect, over time, of the collapse of the other countries of Central America, bringing with it the spectre of Marxist domination of the entire region and thus the danger of a larger war.

The notion that the United States should cope with a Marxist-Leninist Nicaragua, militarily allied to the Soviet Union and Cuba, through long-term containment assumes an analogy between conditions in post-war Europe and the present circumstances of Central America. The experience of the post-war period, however, shows that containment is effective as a long-term strategy only where U.S. military power serves to back up local forces of stable allies fully capable of coping with internal conflict and subversion from without. In such circumstances, the United States can help to assure the deterrence of overt military threats by contributing forces in place, or merely by strategic guarantees.

On the other hand, where internal insecurity is a chronic danger and where local governments are unable to deal with externally supported subversion, a strategy of containment has major disadvantages. It would risk the involvement of U.S. forces as surrogate policemen. Any significant deployment of U.S. forces in Central America would be very costly not just in a domestic political sense but in geo-strategic terms as well. The diversion of funds from the economic, social, medical, and educational development of the region into military containment would exacerbate poverty and encourage internal instability in each of the countries that became heavily militarized.

Furthermore, the dangers facing the other Central American countries might actually grow if each side perceived that the other was tempted to use its increased military power. And the creation of garrison states would almost certainly perpetuate the armies of the region as permanent political elites. The hopes of true democracy would not be enhanced.

Therefore, though the Commission believes that the Sandinista regime will pose a continuing threat to stability in the region, we do not advocate a policy of static containment.

Instead, we recommend, first, an effort to arrange a comprehensive regional settlement. This would elaborate and build upon the 21 objectives of the Contadora Group. (For these, see the annex to this chapter.) Within the framework of basic principles, it would:

• Recognize linkage between democratization and security in the region.

• Relate the incentives of increased development aid and trade concessions to acceptance of mutual security guarantees.

• Engage the United States and other developed nations in the regional peace system.

• Establish an institutional mechanism in the region to implement that system.

The original peace initiatives of Nicaragua have given little cause for optimism that we could move toward these objectives. The latest of the Sandinistas' formal proposals were presented to the United States Government and to the United Nations in October, 1983, as four draft treaties purportedly prepared "within the framework of the Contadora process." The treaties would bind the parties to refrain from sending arms from one country to another in the region, and otherwise to end intervention, "overt or covert," in the internal affairs of other nations of the region. Significantly, these Sandinista proposals would prohibit exercises and maneuvers of the type United States and Honduran forces have carried out, while deferring the question of foreign advisers for later discussion.

More recently, after the U.S. actions in Grenada, Managua has hinted at some accommodations in its external and internal policies. The Commission is not in a position to judge the sincerity and significance of these various signals. But clearly they would require extensive elaboration and more concrete expression before they could give solid grounds for hope.

The Commission believes, however, that whatever the prospects seem to be for productive negotiations, the United States must spare no effort to pursue the diplomatic route. Nicaragua's willingness to enter into a general agreement should be thoroughly tested through negotiations and actions. We must establish whether there is a political alternative to continuing confrontation in the region. Every avenue should be explored to see if the vague signals emanating from Managua in recent weeks can be translated into concrete progress. Our government must demonstrate to the people of the United States and the peoples of the region that the United States earnestly seeks a peaceful settlement.

It is beyond the scope of this Commission's responsibilities to prescribe tactics for the conduct of these negotiations. As a broad generality, we do not believe that it would be wise to dismantle existing incentives and pressures on the Managua regime except in conjunction with demonstrable progress on the negotiating front. With specific reference to the highly controversial question of whether the United States should provide support for the Nicaraguan insurgent forces opposed to the Sandinistas now in authority in Managua, the Commission recognized that an adequate examination of this issue would require treatment of sensitive information not appropriate to a public report. However, the majority of the members of the Commission, in their respective individual judgments, believe that the efforts of the Nicaraguan insurgents represent one of the incentives working in favor of a negotiated settlement and that the future role of the United States in those efforts must therefore be considered in the context of the negotiating process. The Commission has not, however, attempted to come to a collective judgment on whether, and how, the United States should provide support for these insurgent forces.

POSTSCRIPT II:

*Changing Course: Blueprint for Peace in Central America**

By Policy Alternatives for the Caribbean and Central America (PACCA)

A Response to the Report of the National Bipartisan Commission on Central America

> "You come here speaking of Latin America, but this is not important. Nothing important can come from the South. History has never been produced in the South. The axis of history starts in Moscow, goes to Bonn, crosses over to Washington, and then goes to Tokyo. What happens in the South is of no importance."
>
> Henry Kissinger to Gabriel Valdes,
Foreign Minister of Chile, June 1969

The Commission's Recommendations

On January 11, 1984, the National Bipartisan Commission on Central America released its report. The 132-page document, prepared by a twelve-member commission chaired by former Secretary of State Henry Kissinger, charts a policy course to deal with the unrest and instability of the region.

The Kissinger Report acknowledges that the violent upheavals in Central America are rooted in poverty and repression: "Discontents are real, and for much of the population conditions of life are miserable; just as Nicaragua was ripe for revolution, so the conditions that invite revolution are present elsewhere in the region as well." But the Report charges—with an argument built on assertion rather than evidence—that the Soviet Union is the manipulator of indigenous revolution in the region. "The Soviet-Cuban threat is real," the Report emphasizes, because "the conditions which invite revolution . . . have been exploited by hostile forces."[1]

The prescriptions flow directly from this misplaced diagnosis. The Kissinger Commission recommends a $400 million "emergency stabilization program," sub-

Excerpts from Policy Alternatives for the Caribbean and Central America (PACCA), *Changing Course: Blueprint for Peace in Central America and the Caribbean*, 1984, Institute for Policy Studies, Washington, D.C.

stantial increases in military assistance to El Salvador, Honduras, and even Guate-
mala, as well as implicitly condoning a continuation of the "covert" war against
Nicaragua, which the Report euphemistically terms an "incentive" for negotiation.
To attack the root causes of revolution and thwart future Soviet machinations, the
Report proposes an $8 billion five-year aid program with unprecedented US in-
volvement in and responsibility for the economies of Central America.

The Commission's recommendations are alarming in two regards. First, the
military prescriptions would lead to a deepening of US military involvement in a
widening war in Central America. Second, the economic prescriptions would serve
narrow private interests in the United States at a heavy cost to US taxpayers as a
whole. All historical evidence would suggest that the recommended economic aid
program, managed by the current elites in power, would have a negative impact on
the great majority of the people in Central America and would not serve the long-
term interests of US citizens either. Moreover, as the widespread negative response
to the Kissinger Report indicates, adherence to its recommended course will increase political division in the United States. . . .

By not clearly condemning the secret war against Nicaragua, the Commission
lent its voice to the continuation of that war. Aware that more than 10,000 "contras"
financed by the United States are attacking Nicaragua, the Commissioners evidently believe that military pressure either will cause the Nicaraguan government
to change its internal policy in "desirable" directions, or will cause the overthrow
of the Sandinistas. Neither is likely.

As one of the Commissioners, Mayor Henry Cisneros of San Antonio, indicated
in his dissent, the attempt to support domestic opposition by enlisting it in covert
operations backfires. The government has little incentive to negotiate and compromise with domestic political forces that are perceived as acting in concert with a
hostile foreign power in the region, particularly when that power seems committed
to its very overthrow.

The Nicaraguan Revolution faces domestic opposition, but there is nothing to
suggest that a military force operating from Honduras and Costa Rica can overthrow a government that retains wide popular support and national legitimacy. In
more than three years of attacks, the "contras" have been unable to occupy and hold
any Nicaraguan territory. The Sandinista government has armed a large part of its
population and apparently can rely on it to fight forces that are viewed as agents of
the United States committed to restoration of the old order. US tax coffers are
supporting a campaign of terrorism, murder and sabotage. Regrettably, the Kissinger Commission did not identify what vital interests of the United States are served
by these activities which the Administration subsidizes but cannot acknowledge
because they violate our laws, ideals and values.

Ironically, no coherent argument is presented for the assumption that the revolutions represent a threat to US national security. Lacking in evidence and analysis,
the Report's case is reduced to the assertion that there is a "Soviet-Cuban thrust to
make Central America part of their geostrategic challenge" to the United States.[2]
As Senator Daniel Moynihan suggested, this is a "doctrinal position," divorced

from reality.[3] The Nicaraguan government has stated that it will not accept a Soviet base (nor has the Soviet Union indicated any interest in bearing the economic burdens necessary to gain one). Having struggled for national independence, it is inconceivable that post-revolutionary governments would elect to become Soviet bases, particularly since their economies are highly dependent upon Western aid and trade. The Soviets do not need a missile base in Central America and are not likely to risk exploring whether the United States will permit one.

The Report makes much of a domino theory that suggests that revolutions spread like communicable diseases. Ideas and examples do travel. It is hard to understand why the United States should be opposed to the spread of models that work, such as health and literacy programs, no matter who develops them. US influence in the region depends not on quarantining ideas and programs of other countries, but on demonstrating a genuine interest in development and democracy in the region, rather than viewing the countries as so many pawns in a geopolitical chess game. It is noteworthy that the principal "dominoes" of the region for whose sake the security policy is ostensibly pursued—Mexico and Panama—oppose the military course of US policy in Central America. The Commission Report eschews analysis, however, relying on reiteration of a Communist peril: "No nation is immune from terrorism and the threat of armed revolution supported by Moscow and Havana."[4] "Such extreme language," as Senator Edward Kennedy commented, "raises the stakes of the contest to such a level that anything short of total military victory becomes unthinkable. . . . "

1984: A Failure of Policy on All Fronts

In January 1984, President Reagan can point to few successes in the region. The Administration has increased the US commitment to anti-revolutionary forces, and its military and CIA policies offer little hope for improvement.

The CIA's undeclared war against Nicaragua has intensified as its budget requests have gone well beyond the initial $19 million. But its forces have been unable to score battlefield victories or secure significant territory. To be sure, they have inflicted severe damage on port facilities and destroyed oil pipelines and refineries: they also continue to kill Nicaraguan civilians. The US economic campaign has succeeded in cutting off most private bank funds and multilateral financing to Nicaragua. But in defiance of Reagan administration policy, several European allies of the United States maintain aid programs, and in 1983, Sweden doubled its assistance to the Sandinista government. Mexico continues to supply subsidized oil to Nicaragua.[5] In January 1984, another blow was dealt to the Reagan policy when Argentine President Raúl Alfonsín announced that he was officially withdrawing Argentine support for covert actions against Nicaragua. . . .

Flagrant human rights abuses by the security forces remain an embarrassment to the Reagan administration. During late 1983, the death squads became particularly active in attempts to destroy the guerrillas' infrastructure—the thousands of sympathetic civilians who provide food, information, supplies, medical care and other assistance to the combatants. As with the Phoenix program in Vietnam, assassination teams have killed thousands of civilians suspected of sympathy for the left, including teachers, trade unionists and health workers. Also targeted have been political leaders thought to favor talks with FDR/FMLN representatives. The overall civilian death toll is 37,000 for the last four years, most of which is attributed to death squads or uniformed security forces.[6] So troublesome have the killings become to Reagan policy that Vice President George Bush travelled to El Salvador in December of 1983 to warn Salvadoran officials that death squad activity would jeopardize US support.[7]

The one "victory" that President Reagan can claim in the region is the successful October 1983 US invasion of Grenada, sweeping away a revolutionary government which had already been all but liquidated by its own militants. This precipitous invasion, along with the Administration's repeated rebuffs of Nicaraguan peace proposals, diminished the Reagan administration's international prestige. European and Latin American leaders were openly critical of the invasion of Grenada, and some expressed fears that this would embolden the Administration to undertake further military adventures, particularly in Central America.

The historical role played by the United States in Latin America has undercut the ability of the Reagan administration to win support for its policies from Latin Americans. The repeated military interventions throughout the 20th century in Latin America were carried out not by Soviet forces, but by the United States. The specter of the Soviet bogeyman is not a strong selling point for most educated Latin Americans. The historical enemies of freedom and justice in the small countries of Central America have not been communists, much less Soviets, but the ruling aristocracies whose militaries have been trained by the United States and by US forces themselves.

President Reagan has failed to address the deeply held nationalist feelings and ideas of the region and has ignored the social and economic system that has produced the massive unrest. By imposing the ill-fitting East-West framework on Central America, he has squeezed himself into a corner. Since US commitment to defeat revolution has been equated with fighting the Soviets, the very notion of the left winning is viewed as the equivalent to a major Soviet victory. Thus the nation faces a tragic choice of its own making—a self-proclaimed defeat of major proportions or a direct US military intervention in El Salvador or Nicaragua. . . .

An Alternative Policy

Our government is the potent, the omnipresent teacher. For good or for ill, it teaches the whole people by its example. If the government becomes a law-breaker, it breeds contempt for the law; it invites every man to become a law unto himself; it invites anarchy.

US Supreme Court Justice Louis Brandeis

A Program for Peace

Over the past three years, US policy has had the effect of aggravating conflicts in Central America instead of mitigating them. The immediate priority of US policy must be to move back from the brink of the war that now threatens the entire region. The following is a set of concrete steps towards this end.

Nicaragua The Reagan administration bears the primary responsibility for the war against Nicaragua. The *contra* forces operating against Nicaragua from base camps in Honduras and Costa Rica have been armed and trained by the United States. On several occasions, administration spokesmen, including the president himself, have implied that the interests of the United States require the removal of the current government of Nicaragua.

The secret war does not exhaust the Administration's policy of hostility towards Nicaragua. It has been reinforced by a large-scale military build-up in Honduras, including the indefinite deployment of US combat forces under the pretext of military exercises. Finally, the United States has used its considerable leverage in the international financial community to enforce a credit embargo designed to strangle the war-torn Nicaraguan economy.[8]

The war against Nicaragua is both illegal and counterproductive. It exacerbates tensions between Nicaragua and its neighbors, fuels the regional arms race, and thereby increases the danger of regional conflict. It erodes civilian democratic institutions in Honduras, and places greater pressure on Costa Rica's financially strapped democracy. Within Nicaragua, it increases domestic polarization by identifying the internal opposition with the *contras*, and justifies limitations on political freedoms. With their nation under external attack, Nicaragua's leaders are forced to seek military aid. Successful US efforts to deny them access to Western European arms markets leaves Nicaragua with no alternative but to turn to Cuba and the Soviet Union for military support.[9] Instead of encouraging the new government to remain outside the East-West conflict, US policy forces it into that conflict. No country can long remain non-aligned if it is under attack by a superpower.

Although all of these activities represent a clear violation of the UN and OAS charters, the Reagan administration has justified its policy of hostility towards Nicaragua on the grounds that the United States seeks only to prevent Nicaragua from exporting revolution and endangering the security of its neighbors. But if the preservation and strengthening of democratic institutions is understood as an essential element of Costa Rican and Honduran security, then the security of these countries is today more endangered by their role as military staging areas for the war against Nicaragua than by anything Nicaragua itself has done.

Moreover, Nicaragua has offered to negotiate verifiable accords covering all the security concerns of its neighbors. It has made these offers bilaterally, multilaterally through the Contadora process, and has even offered similar negotiations to the United States.[10] As of January 1984, the United States has disparaged and dismissed all Nicaraguan initiatives.

If the real concern of the United States is that Nicaragua live in peace with its neighbors, now is the time for the United States to test the Nicaraguans' sincerity at the bargaining table.

A new policy towards Nicaragua must begin with recognition that the 1979 revolution was an overwhelmingly popular insurrection against a hated dictatorship, and was supported by all sectors of Nicaraguan society. The way in which the domestic revolutionary process has unfolded subsequently, and how it proceeds in the future, is a matter for the Nicaraguan people to decide. This is a fundamental issue of self-determination.

The United States has every right to express its criticism of Nicaragua when internal developments there run contrary to our own values. But we do not have the right to dictate how Nicaraguans organize their own political and economic affairs—especially in view of the long support accorded to the corrupt and brutal Somoza dynasty by the United States.

The United States does, however, have a legitimate interest in how Nicaragua conducts relations with its neighbors. These are issues which can and should be addressed at the negotiating table.

A new policy towards Nicaragua should begin with the following practical steps:

1. Cease support for the paramilitary exile groups attacking Nicaragua from Honduras and Costa Rica, and discourage other nations from providing such support.

2. Cut back the military force the United States has assembled around Nicaragua, including an end to military exercises in Honduras and off the Nicaraguan coast, and the withdrawal of US combat forces currently deployed in Honduras.

3. End the effort to strangle Nicaragua's economy by blocking international credits.

4. Fully support and encourage a negotiated reduction of tension and the normalization of relations between Nicaragua and Costa Rica and Honduras. Such negotiations can take place either bilaterally or under the auspices of the Contadora Group, but should follow the basic outlines of the security proposals made thus far under Contadora's auspices, and should include provisions for adequate verification of compliance. They should also include provisions for a humane resettlement plan for those who were recruited to fight the covert war.

5. Accept Nicaragua's offer to negotiate bilateral security concerns.

Notes

1. *Report of the National Bipartisan Commission on Central America*, January 1984, p. 4.

2. *Ibid.*, p. 12.

3. *New York Times*, January 13, 1984.

4. *Report of the National Bipartisan Commission on Central America*, January 1984, p. 14.

5. Mexico supplies virtually all of Nicaragua's oil imports (which amount to $225 million per year) at a relatively inexpensive rate through a long-term credit arrangement.

6. The Salvadoran armed forces and right-wing death squads killed more than 37,000 Salvadorans between October 1979 and September 1983. Americas Watch, "Human Rights Update on Central America" (Washington, D.C.: Americas Watch, 1983), p. 3.

7. Alvaro Magana, the provisional president of El Salvador, announced that his country would be unable to fully comply with US requests for the exiling of prominent civilian and military death squad figures. *Newsweek*, January 16, 1984, p. 25.

8. For a discussion of the Reagan administration's economic war against Nicaragua, see John Cavanagh and Joy Hackel, "Nicaragua: Making the Economy Scream," *Economic and Political Weekly*, November 5–12, 1983. According to the article's authors, the United States is waging an economic war against Nicaragua that parallels the Nixon administration's economic sanctions against Chile which contributed to the coup which overthrew the democratically elected government of leftist President Salvador Allende.

Nicaraguans estimate the US pressure has deprived them of $354 million in lost trade and loans in 1983, while US pressure internationally has resulted in a loss of $112.5 million in multilateral loans since 1980.

In addition, anti-Sandinista paramilitary forces supported by the United States inflicted damage on Nicaragua's productive apparatus and infrastructure amounting to $130 million in 1982, equal to over 6 percent of the country's gross national product. The authors note the damage on an equivalent scale to the US economy would surpass $92 million, roughly the amount that the US federal government spends yearly on health and education combined.

9. According to the Department of State, between July 1979 and December 1983, Nicaragua received $175 to $200 million in military aid from the Soviet Union, and $50 to $70 million from Cuba, East Germany, Czechoslovakia, Poland, Bulgaria, North Korea and Vietnam. (Telephone interview, US Department of State, January 19, 1984).

10. On October 20, 1983, Nicaraguan Foreign Minister Miguel D'Escoto submitted to the Reagan administration a package of four binding accords under which the Nicaraguan government would pledge to stop the flow of arms traffic across their territory to the Salvadoran guerrillas if the United States would stop supporting anti-Sandinista rebels based in Honduras and Costa Rica. The proposed accords also would permit on-site inspections of Nicaragua and its neighbors and provide for fines and international legal penalties against any country violating the terms of the agreement. See *Washington Post*, October 21, 1983.

SELECTED BIBLIOGRAPHY

Books and Pamphlets about Nicaragua or Central America

Aldaraca, Bridget; Edward Baker; Ileana Rodríguez; and Marc Zimmerman. *Nicaragua in Revolution: The Poets Speak. Studies in Marxism vol. V.* Minneapolis: Anthropology Department, University of Minnesota, 1980.

Barry, Tom; Beth Wood; and Deb Preusch. *Dollars and Dictators: A Guide to Central America.* N.Y.: Grove Press, 1983.

Black, George. *Triumph of the People: The Sandinista Revolution in Nicaragua.* London: Zed Press,1981.

Black, George, and Judy Butler. *Target Nicaragua. NACLA Report on the Americas.* New York: North American Congress on Latin America, 1982.

Booth, John A. *The End and the Beginning: The Nicaraguan Revolution.* Boulder, Colo.: Westview Press, 1981.

Borge, Tomás; Carlos Fonseca; Daniel Ortega, Humberto Ortega; and Jaime Wheelock. *Sandinistas Speak.* New York: Pathfinder Press, 1982.

Burbach, Roger, and Tim Draimin. *Nicaragua's Revolution. NACLA Report on the Americas.* N.Y.:North American Congress on Latin America, 1980.

Butler, Judy, ed. *Central America—Guns of December? NACLA Report on the Americas.* N.Y.: North American Congress on Latin America, 1982.

C.A.H.I. *Chronology of US-Nicaraguan Relations: Policy and Consequences.* (Covers January 1981-January 1983.) Washington, D.C.: Central American Historical Institute, Georgetown University, May, 1983.

Cardenal, Ernesto. *The Gospel of Solentiname*, 4 vols. Maryknoll, N.Y.: Orbis Books, 1976.

Cardenal, Ernesto. *Zero Hour and Other Documentary Poems.* New York: New Directions, 1980.

Collins, Joseph. *What Difference Could a Revolution Make? Food and Farming in the New Nicaragua.* San Francisco: Institute for Food and Development Policy, 1983.

Debray, Regis. *The Revolution on Trial.* London: Penguin, 1978.

De Nogales, Rafael. *The Looting of Nicaragua.* New York: Robert M. McBride & Co., 1928.

Ellman, Richard. *Cocktails at Somozas: A Reporter's Sketchbook of Events in Revolutionary Nicaragua.* Cambridge, Mass.: Applewood Books, 1981.

EPICA Task Force. *Nicaragua: A People's Revolution.* Washington, D.C.: EPICA Task Force, 1980.

Fagen, Richard. *The Nicaraguan Revolution: A Personal Report.* Washington, D.C.: Institute for Policy Studies, 1981.

Hirshon, Sheryl, and Judy Butler. *And Also Teach Them to Read.* Westport, CT: Lawrence Hill & Co., 1983.

Lappé, Frances Moore, and Joseph Collins. *Now We Can Speak: A Journey through the New Nicaragua.* San Francisco: Institute for Food Development Policy, 1983.

Lernoux, Penny. *Cry of the People: United States Involvement in the Rise of Fascism, Torture, and the Persecution of the Catholic Church in Latin America.* New York: Penguin, 1980.

Macaulay, Neill. *The Sandino Affair.* New York: Quadrangle Books, 1967.

Meiselas, Susan. *Nicaragua* (photography). New York: Pantheon Books, 1981.

Millett, Richard. *The Guardians of the Dynasty: A History of the US Created Guardia Nacional de Nicaragua and the Somoza Family.* Maryknoll, N.Y.: Orbis, 1977.

Pearce, Jenny. *Under the Eagle: US Intervention in Central America and the Caribbean.* Boston: South End Press, 1982.

Poelchau, Warner. *White Paper: Whitewash, Interview with Philip Agee on the CIA and El Salvador.* New York: Deep Cover Books, 1981.

Randall, Margaret. *Christians in the Nicaraguan Revolution.* Vancouver: New Star Books, 1983.

Randall, Margaret. *Sandino's Daughters.* Trumansberg, N.Y.: Crossing Press, 1981.

Ryan, John Morris et. al. *Area Handbook for Nicaragua.* Washington, D.C.: US Government Printing Office, 1970.

Selser, Gregorio. *Sandino.* New York: Monthly Review Press, 1981.

Stanford Central America Action Network. *Revolution in Central America.* Boulder, Colo.: Westview Press, 1983.

Swezey, Sean, and Rainer Daxl. *Breaking the Circle of Poison: The IPM Revolution in Nicaragua.* San Francisco: Institute for Food and Development Policy, 1983.

Tijerino, Doris. *Inside the Nicaraguan Revolution.* As told to Margaret Randall. Vancouver, Wash: New Star Books, 1978.

Walker, Thomas W. *Nicaragua: The Land of Sandino.* Boulder, Colo.: Westview Press, 1981.

Walker, Thomas W., ed., *Nicaragua in Revolution.* New York: Praeger, 1982.

Weber, Henri. *Nicaragua: The Sandinist Revolution.* Translated by Patrick Camiller. London: Verso Editions and NLB, 1981.

Weissberg, Arnold. *Nicaragua: An Introduction to the Sandinista Revolution.* New York: Pathfinder Press. 1981.

Wheelock Roman, Jaime. *Nicaragua: The Great Challenge.* An interview with Marta Harnecker. Managua, Nicaragua: Alternative Views, 1984.

Publications with Regular Coverage of Nicaragua

Barricada Internacional (available in English or Spanish). Apartado Postal 576, Managua, Nicaragua. Weekly.

Central America Report. Religious Task Force on Central America, 1747 Connecticut Ave., N.W., Washington, D.C. 20009.

Central America Update, Box 2207 Station P, Toronto, Ontario, M5S 2T2, Canada. Bimonthly.

Christianity and Crisis. 537 W. 121 St., N.Y. Bimonthly.

CounterSpy. P.O. Box 647, Ben Franklin Station, Washington, D.C. 20004. Bimonthly.

Covert Action Information Bulletin. P.O. Box 50272, Washington, D.C. 20004. Bimonthly.

Envío, Instituto Histórico Centroamericano (available in English, Spanish, German, and French). Apartado Postal A-194, Managua, Nicaragua. Monthly.

Food First Action Alert. Institute for Food and Development Policy, 1885 Mission Street, San Francisco, CA. 94103.

Latin American Perspectives. Box 792. Riverside, Calif., 92502. Quarterly.

Latin America Update. Washington Office on Latin America (WOLA). 110 Maryland Ave., N.E., Washington, D.C. 20002. Bimonthly.

Legislative Update. Coalition for a New Foreign and Military Policy, 120 Maryland Ave., N.E., Washington, D.C. 20002. Irregular.

Mesoamerica (English). Apartado 300, San José, Costa Rica. Monthly.

Maryknoll Magazine, Maryknoll, N.Y., 10545. Monthly.

NACLA Report on the Americas. 151 W. 19 St., New York, N.Y. 10011. Bimonthly.

Nicaragua, National Network in Solidarity with the Nicaraguan People, 930 F Street N.W., Room 720, Washington, D.C. 20004. Bimonthly.

Nicaraguan Perspectives. Nicaragua Information Center, P.O. Box 1004, Berkeley, Calif., 94704. Quarterly.

Nicaragua Update. Nicaragua Interfaith Committee for Action, 942 Market St., San Francisco, Calif. 94102. Bimonthly.

Third World (Tercer Mundo) (available in English or Spanish). Apartado 20572-01000, Mexico D.F., Mexico. Monthly.

Update, Central American Historical Institute. Intercultural Center, Georgetown University, Washington, D.C. 20057. Weekly.

Update Central America. Inter-Religious Task Force on El Salvador and Central America, 475 Riverside Dr., Rm. 633, New York, N.Y. 10115. Monthly.

GROVE PRESS BOOKS ON LATIN AMERICA

Barnes, John / EVITA—FIRST LADY: A Biography of Eva Peron / The first major biography of the beautiful and strong-willed leader of the impoverished Argentina of the 1940's. / $4.95 / 17087-3

Barry, Tom, Wood, Beth, and Preusch, Deb / DOLLARS AND DICTATORS: A Guide to Central America / "A thorough and comprehensive study of the effect the ubiquitous corporate presence in the region has had on its politics and on American foreign policy."—*The Progressive* / $6.95 / 62485-8

Borges, Jorge Luis / FICCIONES (ed. and intro. by Anthony Kerrigan) / A collection of short fictional pieces from the man whom *Time* has called "the greatest living writer in the Spanish language today." / $6.95 / 17244-2

Borges, Jorge Luis / A PERSONAL ANTHOLOGY (ed. and frwd. by Anthony Kerrigan) / Borges' personal selections of his work, including "The Circular Ruins," "Death and the Compass," and "A New Refutation of Time." / $6.95 / 17270-1

Fried, Jonathan, et al., eds. / GUATEMALA IN REBELLION: Unfinished History / A sourcebook on the history of Guatemala and its current crisis. / $8.95 / 62455-6

Gettleman, Marvin, et al., eds. / EL SALVADOR: Central America in the New Cold War / A collection of essays, articles, and eye-witness reports on the conflict in El Salvador. "Highly recommended for students, scholars, and policy-makers."—*Library Journal* / $9.95 / 17956-0

Neruda, Pablo / FIVE DECADES: POEMS, 1925-1970 (Bilingual ed. tr. by Ben Belitt) / A collection of more than 200 poems by the Nobel Prize-winning Chilean poet. / $8.95 / 17869-6

Neruda, Pablo / NEW DECADE: POEMS, 1958-1967 (Bilingual ed. tr. by Ben Belitt and Alastair Reid) / $5.95 / 17275-2

Neruda, Pablo / NEW POEMS (1968-1970) (Bilingual ed. tr. and intro. by Ben Belitt) / $8.95 / 17793-2

Neruda, Pablo / SELECTED POEMS (Bilingual ed. tr. by Ben Belitt) / A selection of Neruda's finest work. Intro. by Luis Monguio. / $6.95 / 17243-4

Paz, Octavio / THE LABYRINTH OF SOLITUDE, THE OTHER MEXICO, AND OTHER ESSAYS (New preface by the author. Tr. by Lysander Kemp, Toby Talbot and Rachel Phillips) / A collection of Paz's best-known works and six new essays, one especially written for this volume. / $9.95 / 17992-7

Paz, Octavio / THE OTHER MEXICO: Critique of the Pyramid (tr. by Lysander Kemp) / Paz defined the character and culture of Mexico in what has now become a modern classic of critical interpretation. / $2.45 / 17773-8

Rosset, Peter and Vandermeer, John / THE NICARAGUA READER: Documents of a Revolution Under Fire / A sourcebook of articles on the Nicaraguan revolution and U.S. intervention / $8.95 / 62498-X

Rulfo, Juan / PEDRO PARAMO: A Novel of Mexico (tr. by Lysander Kemp) By the Mexican author whom the *New York Times* says will "rank among the immortals." / $3.95 / 17446-1

Thelwell, Michael / THE HARDER THEY COME / The "masterly achieved novel" (Harold Bloom) by Jamaica's finest novelist. Inspired by the now-classic film by Perry Henzell, starring Jimmy Cliff, it tells the story of a legendary gunman and folk hero who lived in Kingston in the late 1950's. / $7.95 / 17599-9

Books may be ordered directly from Grove Press. Add $1.00 per book postage and handling and send check or money order to: Order Dept., Grove Press, Inc., 196 West Houston Street, New York, N.Y. 10014

Selected Grove Press Paperbacks

E732   ALLEN, DONALD & BUTTERICK, GEORGE F., eds. / The Postmoderns: The New American Poetry Revised 1945-1960 / $9.95

B472   ANONYMOUS / Beatrice / $3.95

B445   ANONYMOUS / The Boudoir / $3.95

B334   ANONYMOUS / My Secret Life / $4.95

B415   ARDEN, JOHN / Plays: One (Sergeant Musgrave's Dance, The Workhouse Donkey, Armstrong's Last Goodnight) / $4.95

B422   AYCKBOURN, ALAN / The Norman Conquests: Table Manners; Living Together; Round and Round the Garden / $3.95

E835   BARASH, DAVID, and LIPTON, JUDITH / Stop Nuclear War! A Handbook / $7.95

B425   BARNES, JOHN / Evita—First Lady: A Biography of Eva Peron / $4.95

E781   BECKETT, SAMUEL / Ill Seen Ill Said / $4.95

E96   BECKETT, SAMUEL / Endgame / $2.95

B78   BECKETT, SAMUEL / Three Novels: Molloy, Malone Dies and The Unnamable / $4.95

E33   BECKETT, SAMUEL / Waiting for Godot / $3.50

B411   BEHAN, BRENDAN / The Complete Plays (The Hostage, The Quare Fellow, Richard's Cork Leg, Three One Act Plays for Radio) / $4.95

E417   BIRCH, CYRIL & KEENE, DONALD, eds. / Anthology of Chinese Literature, Vol. I: From Early Times to the 14th Century / $12.50

E368   BORGES, JORGE LUIS / Ficciones / $6.95

E472   BORGES, JORGE LUIS / A Personal Anthology / $5.95

B312   BRECHT, BERTOLT / The Caucasian Chalk Circle / $2.95

B117   BRECHT, BERTOLT / The Good Woman of Setzuan / $2.95

B120   BRECHT, BERTOLT / Galileo / $2.95

B108   BRECHT, BERTOLT / Mother Courage and Her Children / $2.45

B333   BRECHT, BERTOLT / Threepenny Opera / $2.45

E580   BRETON, ANDRE / Nadja / $3.95

B147   BULGAKOV, MIKHAIL / The Master and Margarita / $4.95

B115   BURROUGHS, WILLIAM S. / Naked Lunch / $3.95

B446   BURROUGHS, WILLIAM S. / The Soft Machine, Nova Express, The Wild Boys / $5.95

E793   COHN, RUBY / New American Dramatists: 1960-1980 / $7.95

E804   COOVER, ROBERT / Spanking the Maid / $4.95

E742   COWARD, NOEL / Three Plays (Private Lives, Hay Fever, Blithe Spirit) / $4.50

B442	CRAFTS, KATHY, & HAUTHER, BRENDA / How To Beat the System: The Student's Guide to Good Grades / $3.95
E869	CROCKETT, JIM, ed. / The Guitar Player Book (Revised and Updated Edition) / $11.95
E190	CUMMINGS, E. E. / 100 Selected Poems / $2.45
E808	DURAS, MARGUERITE / Four Novels: The Square; 10:30 on a Summer Night; The Afternoon of Mr. Andesmas; Moderato Cantabile / $9.95
E380	DURRENMATT, FRIEDRICH / The Physicists / $4.95
B342	FANON, FRANTZ / The Wretched of the Earth / $4.95
E47	FROMM, ERICH / The Forgotten Language / $4.95
B389	GENET, JEAN / Our Lady of the Flowers / $2.45
E760	GERVASI, TOM / Arsenal of Democracy II / $12.95
E792	GETTLEMAN, MARVIN, et. al., eds. / El Salvador: Central America in the New Cold War / $8.95
E830	GIBBS, LOIS MARIE / Love Canal: My Story / $6.95
E704	GINSBERG, ALLEN / Journals: Early Fifties Early Sixties / $6.95
B437	GIRODIAS, MAURICE, ed. / The Olympia Reader / $4.50
E720	GOMBROWICZ, WITOLD / Three Novels: Ferdydurke, Pornografia and Cosmos / $9.95
B448	GOVER, ROBERT / One Hundred Dollar Misunderstanding / $2.95
B376	GREENE, GERALD and CAROLINE / SM: The Last Taboo / $2.95
B152	HARRIS, FRANK / My Life and Loves / $4.95
E769	HARWOOD, RONALD / The Dresser / $5.95
E446	HAVEL, VACLAV / The Memorandum / $5.95
B306	HERNTON, CALVIN / Sex and Racism in America / $2.95
B436	HODIER, ANDRE / Jazz: Its Evolution and Essence / $3.95
B417	INGE, WILLIAM / Four Plays (Come Back, Little Sheba; Picnic; Bus Stop; The Dark at the Top of the Stairs) / $7.95
E259	IONESCO, EUGENE / Rhinoceros & Other Plays / $4.95
E496	JARRY, ALFRED / The Ubu Plays (Ubu Rex, Ubu Cuckolded, Ubu Enchained) / $7.95
E216	KEENE, DONALD, ed. / Anthology of Japanese Literature: Earliest Era to Mid-19th Century / $7.95
E552	KEROUAC, JACK / Mexico City Blues / $4.95
B394	KEROUAC, JACK / Dr. Sax / $3.95
B454	KEROUAC, JACK / The Subterraneans / $3.50
B479	LAWRENCE, D.H. / Lady Chatterley's Lover / $3.50
B262	LESTER, JULIUS / Black Folktales / $3.95
B351	MALCOLM X (Breitman, ed.) / Malcolm X Speaks / $3.95
E741	MALRAUX, ANDRE / Man's Hope / $12.50

E697	MAMET, DAVID / American Buffalo / $3.95
E709	MAMET, DAVID / A Life in the Theatre / $3.95
E712	MAMET, DAVID / Sexual Perversity in Chicago & The Duck Variations / $3.95
E801	MARIANI, PAUL / Crossing Cocytus / $5.95
B325	MILLER, HENRY / Sexus / $4.95
B10	MILLER, HENRY / Tropic of Cancer / $3.95
B59	MILLER, HENRY / Tropic of Capricorn / $3.50
E789	MROZEK, SLAWOMIR / Striptease, Tango, Vatzlav: Three Plays / $12.50
E636	NERUDA, PABLO / Five Decades Poems 1925-1970. Bilingual ed. / $8.95
E364	NERUDA, PABLO / Selected Poems. Bilingual ed. / $6.95
B429	ODETS, CLIFFORD / Six Plays (Waiting for Lefty; Awake and Sing; Golden Boy; Rocket to the Moon; Till the Day I Die; Paradise Lost) / $7.95
E807	OE, KENZABURO / A Personal Matter / $6.95
E687	OE, KENZABURO / Teach Us To Outgrow Our Madness / $4.95
E811	PAZ, OCTAVIO / The Labyrinth of Solitude, The Other Mexico and Other Essays/$9.95
E724	PINTER, HAROLD / Betrayal / $3.95
E315	PINTER, HAROLD / The Birthday Party & The Room / $4.95
E299	PINTER, HAROLD / The Caretaker The Dumb Waiter / $4.95
E411	PINTER, HAROLD / The Homecoming / $4.95
E606	PINTER, HAROLD / Old Times / $3.95
E641	RAHULA, WALPOLA / What The Buddha Taught / $6.95
B438	REAGE, PAULINE / Story of O, Part II: Return to the Chateau / $3.95
B213	RECHY, JOHN / City of Night / $3.95
B171	RECHY, JOHN / Numbers / $2.95
E806	ROBBE-GRILLET, ALAIN / Djinn / $4.95
B133	ROBBE-GRILLET, ALAIN / The Voyeur / $2.95
B207	RULFO, JUAN / Pedro Paramo / $2.45
B138	SADE, MARQUIS DE / The 120 Days of Sodom and Other Writings / $12.50
B313	SELBY, HUBERT / Last Exit to Brooklyn / $2.95
E763	SHAWN, WALLACE, and GREGORY, ANDRE / My Dinner with Andre / $5.95
	SILKO, LESLIE / Storyteller / $9.95
B456	SINGH, KHUSHWANT / Train to Pakistan / $3.25
B618	SNOW, EDGAR / Red Star Over China / $8.95
E785	SRI NISARGADATTA MAHARAJ / Seeds of Consciousness / $9.95

GROVE PRESS, INC., 196 West Houston St., New York, N.Y. 10014

Peter Rosset lives in Nicaragua where he is completing work on a doctoral dissertation on Central American agriculture for the University of Michigan. Professor of Ecology at the University of Michigan, **John Vandermeer** teaches Central American politics and history at the University's Residential College. He has worked in Mexico and Central America for over ten years, conducting research on human ecology in developing countries.